THE EATONS

THE ROYAL HOUSE OF EATON

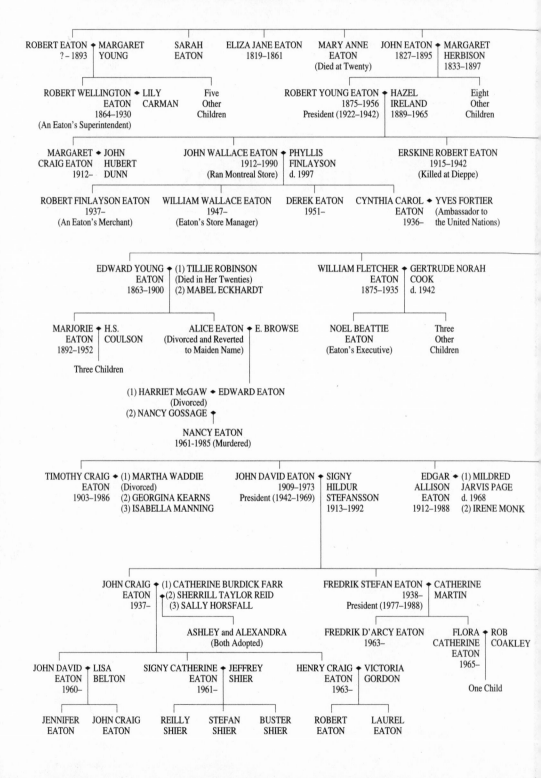

ROBERT EATON ◆ MARGARET
? – 1893 | YOUNG

SARAH
EATON

ELIZA JANE EATON
1819–1861

MARY ANNE
EATON
(Died at Twenty)

JOHN EATON ◆ MARGARET
1827–1895 | HERBISON
1833–1897

ROBERT WELLINGTON ◆ LILY
EATON | CARMAN
1864–1930
(An Eaton's Superintendent)

Five
Other
Children

ROBERT YOUNG EATON ◆ HAZEL
1875–1956 | IRELAND
President (1922–1942) | 1889–1965

Eight
Other
Children

MARGARET ◆ JOHN
CRAIG EATON | HUBERT
1912– | DUNN

JOHN WALLACE EATON ◆ PHYLLIS
1912–1990 | FINLAYSON
(Ran Montreal Store) | d. 1997

ERSKINE ROBERT EATON
1915–1942
(Killed at Dieppe)

ROBERT FINLAYSON EATON
1937–
(An Eaton's Merchant)

WILLIAM WALLACE EATON
1947–
(Eaton's Store Manager)

DEREK EATON
1951–

CYNTHIA CAROL ◆ YVES FORTIER
EATON | (Ambassador to
1936– | the United Nations)

EDWARD YOUNG ◆ (1) TILLIE ROBINSON
EATON | (Died in Her Twenties)
1863–1900 | (2) MABEL ECKHARDT

WILLIAM FLETCHER ◆ GERTRUDE NORAH
EATON | COOK
1875–1935 | d. 1942

MARJORIE ◆ H.S.
EATON | COULSON
1892–1952

Three Children

ALICE EATON ◆ E. BROWSE
(Divorced and Reverted
to Maiden Name)

NOEL BEATTIE
EATON
(Eaton's Executive)

Three
Other
Children

(1) HARRIET McGAW ◆ EDWARD EATON
(Divorced)
(2) NANCY GOSSAGE ◆

NANCY EATON
1961-1985 (Murdered)

TIMOTHY CRAIG ◆ (1) MARTHA WADDIE
EATON | (Divorced)
1903–1986 | (2) GEORGINA KEARNS
| (3) ISABELLA MANNING

JOHN DAVID EATON ◆ SIGNY
1909–1973 | HILDUR
President (1942–1969) | STEFANSSON
| 1913–1992

EDGAR ◆ (1) MILDRED
ALLISON | JARVIS PAGE
EATON | d. 1968
1912–1988 | (2) IRENE MONK

JOHN CRAIG ◆ (1) CATHERINE BURDICK FARR
EATON | ◆(2) SHERRILL TAYLOR REID
1937– | (3) SALLY HORSFALL

FREDRIK STEFAN EATON ◆ CATHERINE
1938– | MARTIN
President (1977–1988)

ASHLEY and ALEXANDRA
(Both Adopted)

FREDRIK D'ARCY EATON
1963–

FLORA ◆ ROB
CATHERINE | COAKLEY
EATON
1965–

One Child

JOHN DAVID ◆ LISA
EATON | BELTON
1960–

SIGNY CATHERINE ◆ JEFFREY
EATON | SHIER
1961–

HENRY CRAIG ◆ VICTORIA
EATON | GORDON
1963–

JENNIFER
EATON

JOHN CRAIG
EATON

REILLY
SHIER

STEFAN
SHIER

BUSTER
SHIER

ROBERT
EATON

LAUREL
EATON

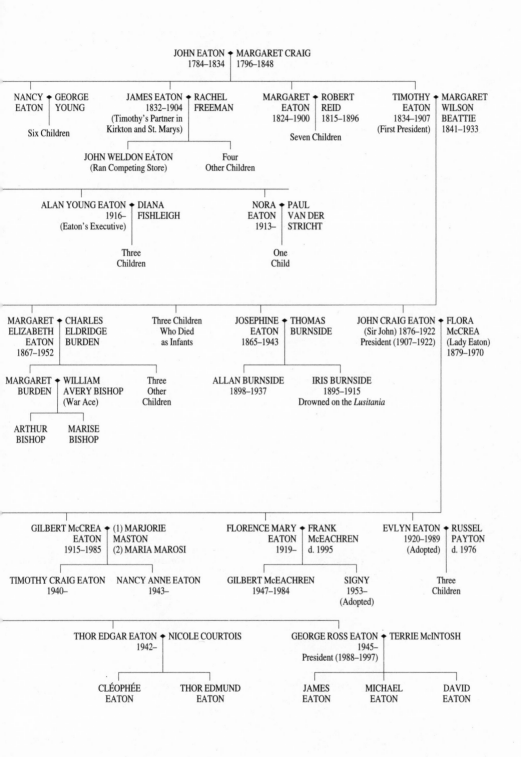

JOHN EATON ◆ MARGARET CRAIG
1784–1834 | 1796–1848

NANCY ◆ GEORGE
EATON | YOUNG

Six Children

JAMES EATON ◆ RACHEL
1832–1904 | FREEMAN
(Timothy's Partner in
Kirkton and St. Marys)

MARGARET ◆ ROBERT
EATON | REID
1824–1900 | 1815–1896

Seven Children

TIMOTHY ◆ MARGARET
EATON | WILSON
1834–1907 | BEATTIE
(First President) | 1841–1933

JOHN WELDON EATON
(Ran Competing Store)

Four
Other Children

ALAN YOUNG EATON ◆ DIANA
1916– | FISHLEIGH
(Eaton's Executive)

Three
Children

NORA ◆ PAUL
EATON | VAN DER
1913– | STRICHT

One
Child

MARGARET ◆ CHARLES
ELIZABETH | ELDRIDGE
EATON | BURDEN
1867–1952

Three Children
Who Died
as Infants

JOSEPHINE ◆ THOMAS
EATON | BURNSIDE
1865–1943

JOHN CRAIG EATON ◆ FLORA
(Sir John) 1876–1922 | McCREA
President (1907–1922) | (Lady Eaton)
| 1879–1970

MARGARET ◆ WILLIAM
BURDEN | AVERY BISHOP
| (War Ace)

Three
Other
Children

ALLAN BURNSIDE
1898–1937

IRIS BURNSIDE
1895–1915
Drowned on the *Lusitania*

ARTHUR
BISHOP

MARISE
BISHOP

GILBERT McCREA ◆ (1) MARJORIE
EATON | MASTON
1915–1985 | (2) MARIA MAROSI

FLORENCE MARY ◆ FRANK
EATON | McEACHREN
1919– | d. 1995

EVLYN EATON ◆ RUSSEL
1920–1989 | PAYTON
(Adopted) | d. 1976

TIMOTHY CRAIG EATON
1940–

NANCY ANNE EATON
1943–

GILBERT McEACHREN
1947–1984

SIGNY
1953–
(Adopted)

Three
Children

THOR EDGAR EATON ◆ NICOLE COURTOIS
1942–

GEORGE ROSS EATON ◆ TERRIE McINTOSH
1945–
President (1988–1997)

CLÉOPHÉE
EATON

THOR EDMUND
EATON

JAMES
EATON

MICHAEL
EATON

DAVID
EATON

THE EATONS

THE RISE AND FALL
OF CANADA'S ROYAL FAMILY

ROD McQUEEN

REVISED EDITION

Published in 1999 by Stoddart Publishing Co. Limited
34 Lesmill Road, Toronto, Canada M3B 2T6
180 Varick Street, 9th Floor, New York, New York 10014

Distributed in Canada by:
General Distribution Services Ltd.
30 Lesmill Road, Toronto, Ontario M3B 2T6
Tel. (416) 445-3333   Fax (416) 445-5967
Email customer.service@ccmailgw.genpub.com

Distributed in the United States by:
General Distribution Services Inc.
85 River Rock Drive, Suite 202, Buffalo, New York 14207
Toll-free Tel.1-800-805-1083   Toll-free Fax 1-800-481-6207
Email gdsinc@genpub.com

First published in hardcover in 1998 by Stoddart Publishing Co. Limited

03 02 01 00 99 1 2 3 4 5

Cataloguing in Publication Data

McQueen, Rod, 1944–
The Eatons: the rise and fall of Canada's royal family

Rev. ed.
ISBN 0-7737-6078-4

1. Eaton family. 2. T. Eaton Co. I. Title.

HF5465.C34E34 1999   381'.141'092271   C99-931517-X

Cover Design: Angel Guerra
Text Design: Andrew Smith
Page Composition: Joseph Gisini/Andrew Smith Graphics Inc.

Printed and bound in Canada

We acknowledge for their financial support of our publishing program the Canada Council, the Ontario Arts Council, and the Government of Canada through the Book Publishing Industry Development Program (BPIDP).

CONTENTS

PREFACE
TO THE PAPERBACK EDITION

⟵

THE REACTION BY CANADIANS TO THE HARDCOVER
edition of this book, published in 1998, was both enthusiastic and emotional.
Open-line radio shows on which I appeared quickly turned into group ther-
apy sessions. Every caller had recollections about Eaton's that resonated. Perhaps it was Toyland and the Christmas windows, working in one of the stores,
or meeting a member of Canada's Royal Family. Bookstore signings took on
the trappings of television's *Antiques Roadshow*. One woman brought along a
shirt box stuffed with Christmas cards sent by the First Family. The treasured
collection began in 1919 and continued well into the 1960s. Another woman
carried in a lovely nineteenth-century watercolour painting by Hilda Eaton
and was crestfallen to learn that the artist was not part of the famous family.

The national outpouring underscored one of the book's main themes:
Canadians cared more about Eaton's than did the family itself. That keening
concern has persisted as Eaton's tried to restore its former glory but instead
spiralled ever lower in an increasingly competitive marketplace. This new edition details the final days of the Empire.

This is, in every sense, an unauthorized look at a family dynasty and a
family business.

I interviewed George Eaton for *The Financial Post* the day after he made
the historic announcement on February 27, 1997, that T. Eaton Co. Ltd. had
received court protection under an arcane piece of federal legislation called
the Companies' Creditors Arrangement Act.

Such is the power of the Eatons that some of my attempts to interview
friends and associates were stalled when the intended interviewee begged off
by saying he or she would have to check with the family first.

If they asked George for permission, there was often no interview. His
elder brother, Fred, was far more amenable. Fred agreed to an on-the-record

interview in March 1998, which lasted almost four hours. Many other members of the family were also helpful, including Florence McEachren, sister to John David, father of the four brothers, and the only member of that generation who is still alive. Forthcoming, too, were all three young men of the fifth generation: John David, Henry, and Fred, Jr. So was Kitty Eaton, John Craig's first wife, as well as Alan Eaton, son of R.Y. Eaton, president from 1922 to 1942, Alan's wife Diana, and R.Y.'s grandson, Robert. Flora Agnew, a great-niece of Lady Eaton, also supplied vivid recollections.

Despite the Eaton family's persistent official opposition, I conducted more than two hundred interviews, although some people with particularly close connections talked to me only after I agreed not to name them as a source. I have honoured those commitments and want to thank those individuals. You know who you are.

I carried out extensive archival research in the Eaton Collection at the Archives of Ontario and was also the happy recipient of a constant flow of rich and relevant newspaper accounts, particularly covering the period 1890–1925, from Toronto historian Mike Filey.

My thanks also to my agent, Linda McKnight, and her colleague, Bruce Westwood, of Westwood Creative Artists, for their savvy. Every writer needs a good editor and I had one of the best in Anne Holloway. Stoddart managing editor Don Bastian offered cheerful support; copy editor Maryan Gibson made countless constructive comments.

The final manuscript benefitted greatly from the unerring eye of Angela Ferrante, a true friend.

My deepest debt, as always, is to Sandy, my mate and muse. Without her, no words would ever have come.

ROD McQUEEN
Toronto
September 1999

INTRODUCTION

—

FRED EATON PLANTS HIMSELF IN FRONT OF
the podium, adjusts his tortoiseshell glasses, and makes a futile attempt to
chase back into place a stray strand of sandy-brown hair that has fallen across
his forehead. As master of ceremonies he looks every inch the aristocratic merchant in his dark blue suit, blue-striped shirt with white collar and cuffs, and
polka-dotted navy tie. A gold signet ring winks from the pinky of his left hand.

There are some familiar faces among the two hundred people seated
under the marquee with him this May 1997 morning. There are old pals, like
boyhood chum Douglas Bassett. There are old pols, like former prime minister Brian Mulroney. There's even erstwhile royalty, in the person of Sarah Fer-
guson, Duchess of York.

· All are assembled to honour Hungarian-born Peter Munk, who has made
and lost several fortunes in Canada, Egypt, Fiji, and Australia. At sixty-nine
years old, he is atop the heap once more at Barrick Gold Corp. The reason
for the ceremony is Munk's $6 million bequest to The Toronto Hospital (for-
merly Toronto General Hospital) for a cardiac centre bearing his name.

Fred, who was chief executive officer of T. Eaton Co. Ltd. from 1977 to
1991, is chair, hospital board of trustees, just one of the many roles into which
he was born. As the fourth generation to run the department store business,
Fred also inherited from his father, John David, the position of trustee at this
institution where entire wings have honoured the family name since 1910
when Fred's grandfather, who later became Sir John, gave $365,000 to build
and equip the hospital's Timothy Eaton surgical wing, an amount equal to
Munk's $6 million in today's dollars.

But Fred has barely begun to introduce the platform guests when his words
are interrupted by the wail of a siren fired up by a gaggle of placard-carrying
protesters from the Canadian Union of Public Employees. Unhappy about

1

health-care cutbacks, they are milling around on the sidewalk beyond the marquee, out of sight of the platform party, but watched closely by police with horse vans held in reserve.

Fred is able to add four more words before there is loud chanting: "Health care is not for sale." He leans closer to the microphone, but even so, many of his words are drowned out by the hubbub.

Poor Fred Eaton. Even in this honorific role as chair and longtime benefactor, the masses shout him down and show him no respect. Fewer than three months have passed since the Eatons took the ignominious step of publicly seeking court protection for their department-store business, and look who's getting all the accolades — Munk, a man who cuckolded Fred's older brother, John Craig.

John Craig and his first wife, Kitty, were divorced in 1971 after she and Munk had a torrid affair. She left John Craig for Munk, but Munk married his current wife, Melanie, instead. Even Kitty saw the irony in the new social pecking order when she visited The Toronto Hospital in the fall of 1997. "I saw one sign pointing to Munk, another pointing to Eaton, and I thought, which way do I go?"

Now, for the first time this century, an Eaton is an also-ran at The Toronto Hospital. Those attendees not focused on the flavour-of-the-moment Munk are craning to see Fergie, currently shilling her tell-all book as she attempts to turn herself into a brand name.

Fred Eaton could tell her a thing or two about how hard that is. On this day, both of them face their publics, rudely dethroned.

In Ireland generations were reared on potatoes and the shorter catechism. In Canada it was cornflakes and the Eaton's catalogue.

In a land that reluctantly seeks myths, among a people remarkably short of icons, the Eatons were revered. Every so often the family would sally forth, fit a gold key into a front door, and declare a new store officially open. Crowds cheered, the family waved, anthems were sung. To the Eatons, the entire world must always have smelled of fresh paint.

The rich are certainly different from the rest of us, but the Eatons are a wealthy clan unlike any other in Canada. Their name was emblazoned on buildings right across the country, the only family to have such national prominence.

The total number of Canadians who have worked at Eaton's, or have a family member who did, must rank right up there with the number who've toiled for the federal government and the armed forces combined. Add the shopping public, and Eaton's has touched the life of every Canadian in a way unequalled by any other institution.

It was in 1869 that founder Timothy launched his name into the galaxy of retailing giants that includes John Wannamaker, Adam Gimbel and Rowland Macy in the United States, Charles Harrod in the United Kingdom, and Aristide Boucicault in France. The generations of employees who followed referred to themselves proudly as Eatonians, a designation that smacked of olde England, school ties, and conferred privilege. Pay packets for salesclerks might have been paltry, but garden parties and Christmas galas were held at Eaton Hall, a family castle where awestruck Eatonians were made to feel as if they were in the presence of royalty.

For much of the first half of this century, the Royal House of Eaton flourished. Timothy's son, Sir John, who died in 1922, single-handedly drove growth beyond Toronto to Moncton, Winnipeg, and elsewhere in the Canadian West. His cousin, R.Y., who was president for the next twenty years, increased the number of locations tenfold. John David, son of Sir John, assumed the throne in 1942 and took the company to both coasts.

The business was always private, the family almost furtive. The famous surname, luxurious lifestyle, and ruddy good looks created a cachet enjoyed by no other Canadian family. Whenever the outside world caught a fleeting glimpse of an Eaton, their billionaire lifestyle was beyond belief. After all, the Eatons could command whatever they desired simply by turning on a golden faucet of funds; they enjoyed cut-stone mansions in Forest Hill, weekend farm retreats in Caledon, hideaway holiday islands in Georgian Bay, gated compounds in Florida, and fishing camps in the northern woods, all with hot and cold running servants.

The Eatons who ran the empire into the ground — John Craig, Fred, Thor, and George — are still widely referred to as "the boys" even though they range in age from sixty-two to fifty-four. They possess every toy and trapping imaginable from gleaming Rolls-Royce automobiles to seagoing yachts. John Craig wears the uniform of honorary colonel in the 400 Squadron of the Air Force Reserve. Fred served as Canadian High Commissioner to the Court of St. James's. Thor owns a string of thoroughbred horses. George was the first Canadian to race Formula One cars full-time.

The empire was inextricably linked with the building of the country.

There was a time when Eaton's provided ordinary folks with a chance to dream. The catalogue, published from 1884 to 1976, was a book of hope and bounty. Window-shopping or browsing the stores offered entertainment for those who couldn't afford a ticket to the latest touring Broadway show. The Eaton's-sponsored Santa Claus Parade delighted generations of children. The family was renowned for its philanthropic good works.

Many illustrious Canadians worked at Eaton's in Toronto before they became famous in other fields. When broadcaster Gordon Sinclair joined Eaton's general office around 1920, his pay doubled from the $25 a month he'd received at the Bank of Nova Scotia. He was pleasantly surprised the first time he was off sick for a day and his pay was not docked for being absent. Actor William Hutt was an usher at Eaton Auditorium. Singer Lois Marshall worked in mail order. Author Peter C. Newman spent a Christmas season as an assistant to magician John Giordmaine in Toyland. Comedian John Candy kept co-workers laughing in the hardware department at Eaton's College Street. Singer Tommy Hunter worked in paints. Billy Butlin, who went on to create holiday camps for the masses in Britain, served in the London, England, office.

For decades, descriptions of the Eatons in the media were unremittingly adulatory. "There is hardly a name in Canada, with the possible exception of the Prime Minister, so well known to the people at large as that of Mr. Timothy Eaton," said the *Globe* on September 9, 1905, sixteen months before his death.

"Canada with her vast territory, great mountains, sweeping prairies, wide rivers, and incalculable natural resources is also not without immensities in her social institutions," declared the *Illustrated London News* in its February 18, 1911, issue. "The T. Eaton Co. of Toronto can claim their stores are the greatest in the British Empire."

"Eaton's operates the greatest department-store chain and mail-order business in the British Commonwealth," agreed the *Saturday Evening Post* in 1952.[1] In 1960 the *New York Times* described John David Eaton, third-generation president, as the "undisputed merchant king of Canada and possibly its wealthiest citizen . . . a man whose surname is a household word from sea to sea."[2]

Canadians felt such a kinship with Eaton's that they claimed ownership of the retailing empire for themselves. In 1977 when the Toronto Eaton Centre opened, a *Toronto Star* writer reminded the family just who was boss: "Those four nice young chaps may think they own Eaton's. But anyone who's been in these parts any length of time knows it really belongs to us and you tamper with it at risk."[3]

Canada's most famous literary character, Anne of Green Gables, knew all about Eaton's. In Lucy Maud Montgomery's *Anne's House of Dreams*, icon met icon: " 'Well, you certainly have a lovely day for your wedding, Anne,' said Diana, as she slipped a voluminous apron over her silken array. 'You couldn't have had a finer one if you'd ordered it from Eaton's.' " [4]

A 1980 National Film Board animated short by Roch Carrier called *The Sweater* tells of a ten-year-old boy in Ste. Justine, Quebec, who became disconsolate after "Monsieur Eaton" sent him a Toronto Maple Leafs sweater instead of the Montreal Canadiens version that was ordered from the catalogue.

As an infant, Winnipeg poet George Morrissette was placed in an orphanage, then later adopted. In his blank-verse poem, *Finding Mom at Eaton's*, Morrissette wrote how, in 1970 at thirty-two, he finally learned the name of his birth mother. He tracked her down by telephone and she agreed to meet him. The rendezvous location she picked: Timothy Eaton's statue in the Winnipeg store.

> Timothy in Bronze
> was sternly watching
> me wait for my mother [5]

The reunion was a success.

The first statue of Timothy was erected in the Toronto Queen Street store on December 8, 1919, to celebrate Eaton's fiftieth anniversary. A gift from the employees, Timothy in bronze is seated and wears a double-breasted Edwardian coat and wing collar; he holds a pen and scroll of paper. His demeanour is dour and unforgiving. Passersby have worn the toe of the left shoe shiny by rubbing it, hoping to obtain some of Timothy's good fortune.

"I grew up on a farm in the 1940s and the arrival of the new catalogue was a great event," says author Peter C. Newman. "When my parents went shopping, we went to Eaton's. You wouldn't think of going anywhere else. You knew if anything went wrong you could take it back. Fifty years later, when Minister of National Defence Doug Young was asked about some policy and whether he could guarantee results, he said, 'I'm not Eaton's.' "

—

But behind the brick facades and glossy flyers, there has for decades been an inexorable downward slide at the department stores and within the family dynasty itself. In 1930 Eaton's held a commanding 58 per cent of all department-store sales. In 1999 Eaton's market share had become less than 10 per cent.

Business leaders may be divided into three groups: entrepreneurs who start their own companies; hired guns who manage corporations for others; and members of the "lucky sperm club," those who, like the fourth-generation Eaton boys, inherited their status from their fathers before them. Such ancestry is both a strength and a weakness. No matter how much money there is or what financial results flow in a given year, these winners of the gene-pool lottery never know if their achievements are the result of their own work and knowhow or simply because they have been handed the reins.

Their blundering means that the Eatons no longer rank as one of Canada's billionaire dynasties. In 1992 *Forbes* estimated their net worth as US $1.2 billion (about C $1.6 billion). Today they're worth only one-third as much. Canada's other billionaires have continued to prosper: Ken Thomson (travel and publishing); Galen Weston (bakeries and grocery stores); Charles and Edgar Bronfman (entertainment and spirits); and the sons of K. C. Irving — James, Arthur, and John, also known as Gassy, Oily, and Greasy (timber, refineries, service stations, media); Jimmy Pattison (packaging, food); and Izzy Asper (television, real estate). Of those, Eaton's is the only family business to make it to the fifth generation, but the silver spoon has become a tad tarnished.

Eaton's fatal flaws did not suddenly combust in the few months preceding the embarrassing announcement of February 1997. Nor could those flaws be fixed: in 1999, the Canadian icon was bankrupt.

The luck of the Irish had run out.

CHAPTER ONE

TIMOTHY: THE GOVERNOR

In MARCH 1834 A CHILD WAS BORN TO MARGARET Craig Eaton at Clogher, two miles north of the market town of Ballymena in the Northern Ireland county of Antrim. Her husband, John, had died two months earlier, taken swiftly by an epidemic. His posthumous son was called Timothy; he had five sisters and three brothers; the oldest, Robert, was eighteen.

The family was prosperous and lived in a two-storey stucco building on forty acres, twice the size of the average farm in the region. In the far distance rose Mount Slemish, said to be the place where St. Patrick, the patron saint of Ireland, herded sheep in the fifth century.

Timothy was no scholar. His mother once visited his school in Ballymena to complain he wasn't being taught grammar. "Very well, madam," the teacher replied. "Have him learn it and I shall hear him say it." [1]

In 1847 Timothy left school and was apprenticed to William Smith, owner of a store selling grain, hardware, and liquor in Portglenone, nine miles away. Margaret paid a £100 bond guaranteeing he would stay five years. Smith was a hard taskmaster. Although Smith lived near the Eaton home the arrangement did not include transportation. Timothy worked from before sunrise until after sundown, often sleeping under the counter because there was too little time to walk home and back. Timothy quickly learned how to measure the quality of crops, cloth, produce, and people. His duties included serving a tot of liquor to farmers going to market at four in the morning, an experience that made him a lifelong teetotaller.

In 1848 his mother died at fifty-two, thereby forcing further self-reliance on a lad who knew little else. His apprenticeship completed, Canada beckoned. Brother Robert was living in the Ottawa Valley. A sister, Margaret, had married a former neighbour, Robert Reid, who had a farm near Georgetown, twenty miles west of Toronto. Sisters Sarah and Nancy had joined her.

So in 1854, at the age of twenty, Timothy decided to follow the thousands who had fled Ireland's potato blights and famine. His employer returned the £100 bond, gave him the suit of clothes it was customary to bestow, and a bonus — a silver pocket watch. Nothing is known of Timothy's first year in Canada although he likely joined his brother, Robert. He then moved to Georgetown, where he lived with Margaret and became a junior clerk in a general store in nearby Glen Williams.

As the Grand Trunk Railway opened up southwestern Ontario, Robert established a dry-goods store in St. Marys. In 1856 Timothy and another brother, James, settled in Kirkton, ten miles from St. Marys, and started the J. and T. Eaton General Store in a log building on the banks of Fish Creek. For added revenue and increased customer traffic, Timothy became acting postmaster.

He taught Sunday school at the Presbyterian church but turned Methodist after becoming caught up in the fervour of an exuberant outdoor prayer meeting. Even after the conversion his views remained coloured by caution. "Let hope predominate," he wrote, "but do not be visionary." [2] In 1860 brothers James and Timothy moved to St. Marys to sell dry goods, boots, farm tools, and kitchenware.

The following year Timothy met Margaret Wilson Beattie, then twenty. Born in Toronto of similar Ulster ancestry, she had moved with her family to nearby Eastwood. "Something warned me that this young man was likely to prove dangerous," Margaret later joked, "and when he approached I always crossed the road to avoid meeting him." [3]

Even at a young age, Timothy was an imposing figure. Broad of shoulder, he had piercing eyes and spoke with a lilting North-of-Ireland accent. Margaret was a dark-haired, vivacious beauty who could be both demure and daunting. Her quick wit and lighter touch were a tonic for Timothy's sober nature. They were married a year after they met. During the next five years she bore him three children, a son, Edward Young, and two daughters, Josephine Smith and Margaret Beattie.

By 1868 an inventory showed stock on hand worth $11,000, but success brought sibling rivalry. The brothers quarrelled and their partnership dissolved. James decided to stay in St. Marys; Timothy, with the encouragement of Margaret, moved to Toronto where he was among his own. Of Toronto's fifty thousand inhabitants, 40 per cent were Irish, the Orange Lodge all-powerful. [4] "The Toronto of '69 was no Promised Land," wrote Augustus Bridle of the *Toronto Daily Star*. "It was a small college city of banks and warehouses and mid-Victorian Tories who wore furbelows, took snuff, read long novels and danced Sir Roger de Coverley. Only a man with the moral courage of John Knox could have chosen it as a field for bargain days and page advertisements." [5]

Timothy rented a three-storey frame house at 12 Gloucester Street and bought a dry-goods and haberdashery business at 178 Yonge Street (at Queen Street) for $6,500 cash from fellow Methodist James Jennings. During a turkey dinner at Jennings's home to celebrate, Jennings began to talk shop. Timothy cut him off, saying: "I never talk business while eating. It affects digestion. Let's talk about church." [6]

The industrial revolution was causing change everywhere. Mass production meant mass distribution. In Paris in 1852 Aristide Boucicault opened Bon Marché, the first department store with plainly marked prices, no haggling, one price for all, and goods returned if not satisfactory. The advertisement Timothy ran in the *Globe* to announce the opening of T. Eaton & Co. on December 8, 1869, declared a similarly innovative approach: "We propose to sell our goods for CASH ONLY — In selling goods, to have only one price."

"Timothy Eaton was not the first merchant to try to apply any of these policies; many others had experimented with variations on all of them, particularly a cash system," wrote historian Michael Bliss in *Northern Enterprise: Five Centuries of Canadian Business*. "Eaton was the first in Toronto to make the new methods work as a general storekeeping strategy." [7]

Timothy's operations would become a department store, but not Canada's first. That honour went to Henry Morgan, who opened his Montreal outlet in 1845, and began the "departmental" system in 1878. Robert Simpson followed Timothy by three years. The Hudson's Bay Co., which had operated since 1670, didn't have its first department store until an outlet was opened in Winnipeg in 1881. Woodward's wouldn't start in Vancouver until 1892.

The first Eaton's store had four employees (two men, a woman, and a boy) and measured twenty-four feet across by sixty feet deep. Fancy dress goods were available starting at ten cents. Buttons, gloves, and underwear were popular. Most shoppers would spend a dollar or less.

Things were soon going well enough that Timothy hired a floorwalker to welcome shoppers and make sure a clerk was immediately available. Windows were "dressed" and signs lured passersby. One notice trumpeted four hundred yards of cotton for five cents. Shoppers expecting a bolt of fabric might have been a bit disappointed, once they were inside, to learn that Timothy was touting only a spool of cotton thread. Timothy also sought patrons through the monthly distribution of forty thousand handbills. Eaton's best-known slogan first appeared on notices distributed to working-class houses on payday in the spring of 1870: "Goods satisfactory or money refunded."

In order to grow, Timothy became ruthless with wholesalers by making regular forays to Britain to purchase items direct from the manufacturer. "Eaton and men like him would sell whatever they wanted to whomever they chose at whatever price they could get," wrote Bliss. "They would buy wherever they could, do their own wholesaling, and do their own manufacturing if it paid or if it was necessary to protect their freedom. The fact that the growth of his business meant the destruction of any number of small merchants' livelihoods did not trouble him." [8]

Sales at Eaton's rose from $24,000 in 1870 to $55,000 in 1874, and hit $155,000 in 1880 when the number of employees reached fifty, most female. By then, the store had expanded to include carpets, millinery, jewellery, and laces. In 1883 Eaton's moved to 190-196 Yonge Street, where Timothy had purchased a row of shops that gave him a fifty-two-foot frontage. There were twenty-five thousand square feet of selling space, tall plate-glass show windows, and an interior atrium that allowed natural light to fall throughout the store's three floors. Robert Simpson wanted Eaton's old site, so Timothy paid the rent until the lease expired the following year just to frustrate his competitor.

When a minister, Reverend John Potts, was shown how much space Timothy had taken, his eyes filled with tears. "I am so sorry, Mr. Eaton," said Potts. "You are ruined. What will you do with this great barn of a place?"

"Fill it with goods and sell them," replied Timothy. [9]

Timothy's progress was not halted by personal tragedies. Three of the Eatons' children died in infancy (Edward, William, Josephine, and Margaret all survived). By the time the fifth and youngest surviving child, John Craig, was born in 1876, the Eatons lived on fashionable Orde Street near the provincial legislature. In 1880 Timothy's eldest son, seventeen-year-old Edward, started as a parcel boy. By the time he was twenty he was in charge of city-wide delivery, and by 1888, a partner. Edward designed the store's delivery wagons with their ivory-colored wheels, dark blue body and red cage, pulled by dapple-greys.

Timothy and Edward proved to be innovative in many areas. In 1884 the first store telephone was installed. So was a system of overhead pneumatic tubes that carried cash from the counter to a central office where correct change was made and returned via the same device. By 1886 the premises at 190 Yonge were deemed too small, and a Queen Street section was added that more than doubled the selling space.

Timothy wrote his own ads. After others took over, he continued to send suggestions. "A good name is better to be chosen than riches," he'd say. "Tell your story to the public — what you have and what you propose to sell. Promise them not only bargains but that every article will be found just what it is guaranteed to be. Use no deception in the smallest degree — nothing you cannot defend before God and Man." [10]

Eaton's first passenger elevator, Fenson's Patent Hydraulic Elevator, was installed in 1886. The model was known as a "plunger," because it didn't stop on the way down until it reached the main floor. Shoppers were supposed to take the elevator up, then walk down the stairs, thereby spying other purchase possibilities. On the first day of operation, customers were in awe but few dared to ride. To gain public confidence, Timothy ordered wax dummies be used as "passengers."

Employees were full of ideas, too. Back from a buying trip in Europe, Timothy was surprised to see women thronging to the second floor where some $5 and $6 coats had been designated "old lines" for sale at $2 and $3. "The very thing," declared Timothy. "Just the idea I wanted." [11] And so was launched Friday Bargain Day.

Timothy was equally responsive when it came to easing the long work weeks. Shopping hours throughout Toronto were from 8 a.m. to 10 p.m. on weekdays, 6 p.m. on Saturday. Timothy led the way to earlier closing: 8 p.m. in 1877, then 6 p.m. in 1880. His advertisements encouraged customers to support his effort, as if it were a moral obligation: "Ladies, take up the agitation . . . Liberate your fellow-beings!" [12] Later that decade he introduced 2 p.m. Saturday closings during July and August.

For Timothy, paternalism was a powerful tool. During one particularly severe winter, Timothy wrote a cheque for $3000 on his own account and told the store's employment office to spread the money among workers who were ill. "When it's all gone," he instructed, "let me know." [13] If someone's story touched him personally, Timothy gave that person cash from his own pocket. His secretary ensured there was always $100 in small bills in his golden oak rolltop desk for dispensing to worthy supplicants.

On the first Saturday half holiday, Timothy and Margaret held an employee picnic in High Park in Toronto's west end. Each Christmas, there was a staff party at the Eaton home. As numbers grew, the party was held at the store. In return, Timothy expected total fealty and was so set against Labour Day that he would fire anyone who so much as peeked out a window as the workers' parade passed the store.

His growing wealth and paternalistic benevolence did not change Toronto society's view of Timothy as being in "trade." He was seen to be several steps below a manufacturer, with nowhere near the cachet of a broker or banker. The trades, after all, used the side door. In an attempt to acquire a higher social standing, Timothy took to calling himself the Governor, the same honorific title used since 1670 by the nonexecutive chairman of the Hudson's Bay Co. board.

Timothy believed that determination and a Christian character were all a man needed. If asked about his success, Timothy would supply a copy of the Book of Proverbs. "If almost Starved depend upon yourself and not upon others," he wrote in his notebook. But he was no naive psalm-singer. "Beware of men who praise you to your face," he wrote. "They are ever to be suspected." [14]

Of all Timothy's accomplishments few achieved the lustre and longevity of Eaton's catalogue. His wasn't the first such publication in North America — Montgomery Ward's began in 1872 — but Eaton's catalogue became the gold standard in Canada. Success was almost an accident. The first edition, published in 1884, was called *The Wishing Book*. Measuring six by nine inches, the catalogue contained thirty-two pink pages of goods and was given away in September at the Industrial Exhibition, later known as the Canadian National Exhibition.

People took the publication home and began sending in orders. Eaton's seemed almost surprised. "It was necessary for one woman to devote her entire time to the filling of the orders, with the aid of a small boy to do the parceling," said a company report. [15] The timing was perfect. Since Timothy opened his first store, the number of post offices in Canada had increased by more than five thousand. The completion of the CPR in 1885 meant that mail orders for the entire country could be shipped from Toronto.

Canadians quickly felt connected to the family. One customer ordering sheet music asked that "Mrs. Eaton, or one of her family, will try it over on the melodeon." [16] If the Eatons liked the music, said the customer, she would, too. Another woman sent a basket of plums for Mrs. Eaton, so pleased was she with her purchases. A priest requested twelve catalogues for the reading instruction of parish children. Children wrote asking Eaton's to send them a baby brother or sister.

The 1888 catalogue praised Timothy's success and attempted a chatty style. "You've seen us grow from a little store to a big one. You've been right with us all that time. If we have been crooked and mean, you know all about it; so we needn't make any confessions. If we've been upright and generous, you know all about that, too."

From farm tools to fashion, wedding rings to prefabricated houses, Eaton's catalogue carried everything, even home remedies like Hallmore's Expectorant, Kickapoo Indian Oil, Warner's Safe Diabetic Cure, Dr. Williams's Pink Pills for Pale People, and Humphrey's Homeopathic Specifics. The latter was said to benefit both man and beast by curing everything from piles to hog cholera, flushes to belly staggers.

By 1896 the "Farmer's Bible" ran to four hundred pages twice a year. In large type on the catalogue's cover Eaton's declared itself "CANADA'S GREATEST STORE." Starting in 1899, the catalogue invited francophone shoppers to contact Eaton's in French, assuring them they would receive a reply in the same language. (The first all-French catalogue was not issued until 1927.)

There was a hand-powered washing machine for $3.75; a hamper of food including such items as figs, prunes, currants, ketchup, raspberries, pepper, vanilla, coconut, mixed peel, tea and coffee for $15; or a year's supply of food for a man going on the Klondike gold rush (including, among other items, five hundred pounds of flour, two hundred pounds of bacon, and a pound of pepper), all for $68.69.

In 1903 the mail-order department moved to its own redbrick building on Albert Street next to the main store. In 1909 two more buildings were added on nearby Louisa Street. "If difficulties arise," said a catalogue message, "try to write us a good-natured letter, but if you cannot, then write to us anyway."

Smaller merchants were feeling the pressure. "Dad looked at the Eaton's catalogue and he said it would be the death of him. It had everything in it," said a storekeeper's child quoted in Barry Broadfoot's oral history, *The Pioneer Years 1895-1914*. Because country stores often doubled as post offices, they had little choice but to distribute Eaton's catalogues. Once catalogue buyers had selected wanted items, they'd return. "[H]e'd see them going down to the back to the wicket and he knew darn well that they were buying postal orders in his own store to send off to Winnipeg." [17] Eaton's showed little sympathy. "No need to patronize a merchant tailor at any time," declared the 1896 catalogue. "The way we sell watches and jewellery is just right for you, but pretty tough on the jewellers."

In the United States, outrage was more avidly demonstrated. Piles of catalogues from Sears, Roebuck and Montgomery Ward were publicly burned by storekeepers. Eaton's suffered no such indignity. Timothy maintained smooth relations with postmasters by inviting them to his annual Christmas parties.

On one occasion the catalogue even helped to halt fraud. In 1903 Reverend Isaac Barr led two thousand settlers from England to the Canadian West. Being an Anglican clergyman did not stop him from overcharging the colonists for food, seed, and implements. Eaton's saw such newcomers as prospective customers, and distributed catalogues in their tent city. The settlers quickly discovered that there was a cheaper source of supplies. Barr fled and the settlers composed a song that censured him and praised their saviour:

> We've got Barr on the run finally
> Though he's turned his collar round can't you see?
> With the help of Eaton's book
> We know that we've been took,
> But we'll tar old Father Barr thoroughly. [18]

⟶

For all Timothy's innovation in the store, nothing was more important than the dynasty he was creating. During the busy Christmas season of 1882, a six-year-old boy occupied a prime spot in the middle of Eaton's. For a week the curly-haired lad demonstrated tops, plucking them one at a time from a box, then spinning them on a plate. With every purchase at twenty-five cents, he'd call out a thank-you, dig out another top, and set that one a-spinning in order to captivate the next customer who had a lad like him at home.

Although he was christened John Craig, the young salesclerk was known to all as Master Jack. By the time he was eight, Timothy's youngest son was such a Saturday regular that Timothy was moved to comment: "Now I know who will succeed me in this business." [19]

Jack instinctively knew when peril demanded prudence. At sixteen, against his mother's orders, he and a friend went rabbit-hunting. Since they would be shooting near the city, Jack insisted that they remove half the charge from each cartridge. The forethought was wise. As they climbed a fence, his companion's shotgun discharged and Jack was hit in the ankle. A full load would have been devastating. As it was, doctors wanted to amputate his foot.

Timothy refused to let them. As Jack lay abed, Timothy held his boy's foot all that night, saying, "No, no, no." Recuperation took a year. The boy was not left with a limp, although he did set his feet down "rather solidly," wrote Gregory Clark in 1959. "We old fellows well remember how Jack Eaton walked." [20]

Timothy sent Jack to Upper Canada College, where he was memorable for his family wealth. "The future Sir John sat near me on one of the long oak benches which filled the old Prayer Hall," recalled a schoolmate. "He was one of the first boys to own a Waterbury watch, and it always made me jealous when he took it from his pocket, and dangling it from the end of a bright nickel chain, started to wind it." [21]

In 1896 Timothy dispatched Jack, then nineteen, on a buying trip to Kyoto, Peking, Hong Kong, Singapore, Colombo, and through the Suez Canal to London. It was on this mission that Jack proved his retailing mettle. He saw material at $4 a yard that he liked, but the local Eaton's representative told Jack his selection would never sell. Jack persisted and the fabric flew out of the Toronto store as fast as it could be shipped.

Timothy pushed Edward to be decisive as well. When Timothy was vacationing in Muskoka, Edward was supposed to be in charge, but he had problems making up his mind. Edward once sent a telegram to his father asking for his views about a European buying trip. There was no reply. Edward sent a second telegram, then a third. Timothy finally dispatched a two-word response telling him to follow his own counsel. It said: "See Edward." [22]

Timothy wasn't just a seller of merchandise, he was becoming a conspicuous consumer, too. In the 1890s the Eaton family moved to a large, newly built Victorian mansion at 182 Lowther Avenue, a dwelling almost as grand as Government House on King Street. There were conservatories filled with palm trees, reception rooms hung with *pointe de Venise* lace curtains, as well as French gilt chairs and ornament-filled glass display cases at every turn.

The Eatons were known — even to each other — as Mother and Father. "I could never find another woman like Mother," Timothy would say, "and anyway I hadn't time." As Sunday dinner began, with butler and maids at their beck and call, Mother would declare: "Eat hearty and give the house a good name." Father's favourite dish was cold mashed potatoes mixed with buttermilk.

Rather than force it on others, he'd have a bowl of the concoction for dessert. [23]

Beginning in the 1880s, Timothy and Margaret spent summer vacations at Windermere House, on Lake Rosseau in Muskoka. In 1894 eldest son Edward bought property directly across the bay; Timothy purchased four and a half acres from him in 1896 and built Ravenscrag, later adding six guest cottages.

In 1894 Timothy bought the *Wapenao*, a forty-one-foot steam yacht built in Kingston, Ontario, to travel the twenty-six miles to Ravenscrag from the train station at Muskoka Wharf. In 1898 he had a larger steam yacht built by Polson Iron Works of Toronto. Measuring fifty-four feet long but less than nine feet wide, the *Wanda* was meant for speed. In 1905, after a faster yacht appeared on the lake, she was traded in for the *Wanda II*. At ninety-four feet long and twelve feet across, the new vessel looked like a pencil sitting in the water. (In 1914, *Wanda II* was destroyed in a daylight boathouse fire. Margaret took delivery of the *Wanda III* in 1915. The new vessel cost $34,574, and was the same size as the *Wanda II*, but even faster — she could do the equivalent of twenty-four miles an hour. In 1930 the boat was sold for use as a yacht for guests at Bigwin Inn until 1949, then went through several owners. In 1993 the *Wanda III* was acquired by the Muskoka Steamship and Historical Society, which spent three years and $600,000 restoring her for group charters out of Gravenhurst.)

In addition to the house in town and the summer home in Muskoka, Timothy acquired three rural properties during the 1890s. A one-hundred-acre farm in Georgetown was meant to keep son Edward busy when he wasn't occupied at the store. Timothy went to even greater lengths to save his son William from an indolent life. Timothy purchased land in 1894 near Darlingford, Manitoba, built a house on the property, and sent Bill west with two hired hands. With his red hair and ears that stuck out, Bill always looked like something of a rascal. He had quit school in his teens, started at Eaton's as a parcel boy, and never seemed to advance. "Once a parcel boy, always a parcel boy," he'd say. [24] After Bill's marriage in 1897 to Gertrude Norah Cook, the couple lived on the farm for a while but soon returned to Toronto, where Bill continued to work at the store.

In 1892 Timothy bought a two-hundred-acre dairy farm in Islington, west of Toronto, to supply cream for the store's summer soda fountain. The following winter, someone had the bright idea that the cream could be used for oyster stew. At ten cents a bowl, with crackers, Eaton's was soon selling five hundred bowls daily. Pie and tea were added; the twenty-five-cent lunch was born.

As Toronto grew, so did Eaton's. By 1890 the city's population was approaching two hundred thousand. Eaton's annual sales were almost $1 million; the number of employees had reached 750. While new departments were being added all the time, playing cards, liquor, and tobacco remained unavailable. Shot, cartridges, and guns were stocked, but not dynamite.

Each department was run as a separate entity by a manager who ordered goods, arranged displays, and supervised staff. The same philosophy spread to service areas such as electrical, carpentry, and delivery. Such decentralization meant fiefdoms run by petty potentates and created a corporate culture that made the business as difficult to govern as the sprawling country itself.

In an attempt to impose order, The T. Eaton Co., Limited was officially incorporated in 1891 with Timothy as president. Of the 5000 shares available, 2485 were divided thus: Timothy held 2310; Edward, as vice-president, 145; Mrs. Eaton and the two daughters, Josephine and Margaret, 10 each. Some of the remaining shares were held by senior employees, but Timothy was careful to maintain control.

He was equally careful about planning succession. While he admired son Jack's salesmanship, Timothy's first choice to take over the business was his eldest son, Edward. But Edward, a diabetic, died on October 3, 1900, at thirty-seven. Bill, the next son in line, lacked business talent. The era would never have allowed either of the daughters, Josephine or Margaret, to run the company; and neither of their husbands was interested.

That left but one choice: the youngest son, John Craig, then twenty-four. Just as well the far-sighted Timothy had an heir and a spare. But did John Craig have what it took? His meteoric rise to vice-president had given even Jack pause and he asked his father:

"Father, what do I have to do as vice-president?"

"Can you say 'Yes' and 'No'?"

"Yes, I can do that."

"Can you decide which one to say at the right time?"

"Well, that might be different."

"But it's all you have to do." [25]

Timothy had created a corporate structure, however, that did not rely on Jack or any other individual because senior managers were able to participate as shareholders. Timothy knew full well that even the savviest son needs help.

For Timothy no field was too large to plow. The family dynasty he established would inherit what today would be called a vertically intergrated business with "just in time" operations. He embarked on manufacturing operations in 1889 when he happened upon a male employee making window blinds because sufficient stock was unavailable. "Your time is too valuable to be spent at a sewing machine," declared the Governor. "Get two machines. Put a girl at each of them. A girl can sew better than you can."[26]

Timothy also convinced mills to sell him raw material to make men's and women's underwear. By 1893 he'd built a four-storey factory at the corner of James and Albert Streets for the manufacture of women's coats, capes, skirts, and dresses. A millinery workroom was located next to the watchmakers, who would toss mainsprings over the partitions for use in supporting ostrich plumes on hats. By the turn of the century, Eaton's employed seven hundred factory workers producing 4500 garments daily. House-brand goods for the catalogue and the stores was another way to cut out the wholesaler and reduce transportation costs. "Eaton's for the masses, Simpson's for the classes," the saying went.

New products offered for sale included furniture, ready-to-wear clothing, toiletries, patent medicines, jewellery, patterns, and sporting goods. Restaurants and bus services to and from the train stations meant that shoppers from out of town could stay within Eaton's walls all day and not lack for anything. Buying offices were opened in London in 1893 and Paris in 1898.

In the Gilded Age of the 1890s money was easy to make and — with no income tax — even easier to keep. "The ten prosperous years in Canada before 1890 had done wonders for the aggressive," wrote longtime Simpson's owner C. L. Burton in 1952.[27] "Most wholesalers amassed fortunes. One hundred thousand dollars was perhaps as much then as a million is today, and there were plenty with a hundred thousand or more. They could drive a carriage and pair, have a coachman, sometimes a footman. They wore frock coats and silk hats, and had their ladies appear in apparel of equivalent or corresponding character."

Timothy's silk top hat was a mood indicator. Everyone knew that how it was perched on his head governed how one should respond to him. Pulled low on his forehead meant, Watch out! Sitting back meant, Say good morning.

Timothy fought hard to protect his turf, even against his own kind. In 1895 John Weldon Eaton, eldest son of Timothy's brother James, opened a four-storey department store two blocks from Timothy's emporium. Advertising coyly referred to it as the "little Eaton."[28] Timothy's response to his kinsmen's venture was derisive. "Those people who're always beginning at the top are sure to reach the bottom sooner or later," declared one ad. The upstart didn't last. A week after the store's second anniversary in May 1897, the enterprise was destroyed by fire. John Eaton moved to New York, tried to establish an advertising agency, and died in 1900 at thirty-two.

In the interests of his booming retail operation, Timothy cultivated strong ties to the community. After Wilfrid Laurier became prime minister of Canada in 1896, Laurier set out to consolidate his position. The morning *Globe* was Liberal and supported him, but not unconditionally, so Laurier sought a friendly evening newspaper in Toronto. Likeliest candidate was the *Toronto Evening Star*. The paper, launched in 1892, had no politics at the time and was foundering after a succession of four owners.

Timothy had not previously been identified as a Liberal, but in 1899 he went in with a group of Laurier Liberals to pay $75,000 for the *Evening Star* and installed Joseph E. Atkinson as editor and manager. Other investors included: Senator George Cox; biscuit king William Christie; Postmaster General Sir William Mulock; CPR contractor Plunkett Magann; Salada Tea Co. founder Peter Larkin; Toronto lawyer E. T. Malone; Walter Massey, president of farm-implement company Massey-Harris; and Lyman Jones, who'd been president of A. Harris, Son and Co. before the merger with Massey Manufacturing in 1890.

When Atkinson called on Timothy to sell him advertising space, Timothy produced a copy of the Philadelphia *North American*. The back-page ad had a bold red headline that said: "Wannamaker's Daily Store News."

"Can you do that?" the retailer asked.

"No other paper in North America can or does carry a red line," Atkinson replied.

"You do it, then come and see me again." [29]

By Easter Atkinson had the necessary press equipment, and on June 6, 1900, an Eaton's ad ran for the first time on the back page. At the top, in forty-eight-point type, was the headline: "Eaton's Daily Store News." *In red.*

Within eight years, the *Star* overtook the *Telegram* in circulation and never looked back. Except for a brief period in the 1920s, the Eaton's ad occupied the back page for decades.

Atkinson said later that Timothy taught him an important business lesson. Atkinson was visiting Ravenscrag when a slip of paper arrived for Timothy. The retailer read it, then put the paper in his pocket.

"Have you any idea what was on that paper, Atkinson?"

"No, sir."

"That's what the boys took in at the store on Saturday. Do you know what the *Star* took in yesterday?"

"No, I don't," the editor confessed.

"Then you should," Timothy retorted.

For Timothy, there was no magic behind success, just hard work. Proceeding through the store, he once called out to a hapless clerk: "Mr. M., what do you know about mens wear?"

"Mr. Eaton, I don't know a thing," came the reply.

"Good!" said Timothy. "You'll learn." [30]

It was "dogged as does it," he'd say. He concluded one meeting with the admonition: "Go to the ant, thou sluggard, consider her ways and be wise." [31] His philosophy of getting ahead was "Grow or go." He'd put people in difficult roles just to see how well they'd do, but there was a downside, too: some employees were allowed to stay on long after their juice was gone. "Many an esteemed employee held on during his lifetime for years after growth had stopped," said nephew R.Y. Eaton, who joined the business in 1897. [32]

Timothy would come up with ideas overnight and give orders to the first person he encountered, whether or not that individual was responsible. He was not above using senior managers to do his dirty work. According to one contemporary account in *Dry Goods Review*, they saw "themselves the power behind the throne" and were "there for no other purpose than to veil and cloak the hand that held the whip."

Staff literally quaked in their boots, by far preferring to deal with Jack. Even the official company history published twelve years after Timothy's death referred to him as an "autocrat." In every man's strength, however, resides his weakness. Employees could be reduced to tears by his scolding, then later feel the Governor's consoling hand on their shoulders trying to win back their loyalty. He rebuked one employee for going to the expense of sending a telegram when a letter would do, then the next day presented him, along with three others, with Packard automobiles. [33]

Church was an integral part of Timothy's week, and every Sunday he'd place a five-dollar bill on the collection plate. One Sunday the torn half of a ten-dollar bill showed up. Those in charge knew exactly who the donor was. As they expected, the other half arrived the following Sunday.

His charitable donations grew, but Timothy was very specific about how his largesse was to be used. A $25 donation to the Salvation Army was to be directed toward something permanent, like shelter, rather than stopgap help, like soup.

Beyond such bequests, Timothy was not above burnishing his own legend. Copy in the 1894 catalogue about the store's beginnings is a fine example of revisionist history. "Nobody sold for cash in those days. We had to. We hadn't money or credit enough to do anything else." He also loved to offer advice. "Never argue with a man when he is angry," he once told Jack. "An angry man always knows he is right and you can't convince him otherwise. Meet him next day — the man will then listen to reason." [34] There were also specific rules concerning deportment. One guideline required female clerks to keep at least one foot on the floor at all times "even when reaching for high packages." [35]

As the nineteenth century came to an end, store space in Toronto reached ten acres; sales exceeded $5 million a year. On New Year's Eve 1898 Timothy held a dinner for the entire staff — 2475 people — all seated at tables throughout the store. There were forty cooks and 250 waiters. Fifty thousand pieces of silverware were used for oyster patties, roast turkey, tongue, potato croquettes, plum pudding, ice cream, cakes, fruit, nuts and raisins, bonbons and coffee. A Reverend Dr. Briggs was heard to remark that the occasion was the biggest "Eatin' Company" he'd ever clapped eyes on. Miss Jessie Alexander recited a poem called "Bargain Day" that she'd written for the occasion. Timothy delivered a speech, carefully referring to his "fellow associates," saying that the word "employees" would be "done away with." [36]

Timothy was returning from his Islington farm one day in 1899 when his high-spirited team of horses became skittish and shied. He hung on to the reins and was dragged from the buggy, injuring his shoulder and breaking his hip. [37] Timothy tried to restore full use of his legs by exercising on a stationary bicycle, but he never walked again without the help of crutches. At sixty-four, his body did not mend like it once would have. An elevator was installed at the house. He'd be driven to the store, would hobble in on crutches, then be pushed to his office in a wheeled chair. On days when he did not leave home, a store employee would arrive at 7 a.m. to read him the papers, make telephone calls, and do other errands.

Timothy was forced to turn the business over to Jack. For a time Jack relied heavily on senior managers, but as his confidence grew, many of them were found wanting. "One after another have been given the reins of management only to find themselves eventually dropped," said the July 1904 issue of *Dry Goods Review*. "The persistent growth of the business carries some of them to heights they never dreamed of, and it isn't to be wondered at that heads got turned and egotism became rampant, with comparatively little to fall back on when the end came . . . one only has to study the developments of the last year or two to see how easily and quickly the best of them are 'thrown.'"

Still, Timothy had reason to worry about Jack. Timothy disliked parties and did not touch spirits; Jack loved whisky, cigars, and night life. Because he lived at home, he'd often sleep at the office rather than disturb his parents by coming in late after carousing. Once when Timothy was called to the store because of a predawn fire, he arrived only to discover Jack already in charge. "Commendable, very commendable," said Timothy. "You've really taken hold, I see." [38]

Drinking, however, was becoming a problem for Jack, and the family wanted a place where he could dry out. They chose Rotherham House, a twenty-bed hospital on Isabella Street, a place the Toronto establishment favoured for its care, discretion, and fine china. Prior to Jack's being admitted, the owner of the hospital, Dr. Holford Walker, told the staff: "Routine life in a hospital is going to be trying for a young man. You must do what you can in your free time to make things pleasant and agreeable for him." [39]

Among the staff was a woman with the same small-town sensibilities and practical nature as Timothy's wife, Margaret. Flora McCrea was born, one of eight children, in Omemee, Ontario, east of Toronto, in 1879. Her father, John, was a cabinet-maker of Irish descent. In 1900, Flora moved to Toronto to train as a nurse at Toronto General Hospital. After three probationary months Flora was told by the superintendent, one Miss Snively, "I don't think you are fitted to be a nurse. You are much too slow." [40]

Slow perhaps, but persistent. Flora was accepted that afternoon at Rotherham House. She learned massage, how to sterilize instruments and prepare dressings. Flora's failure at Toronto General turned out to be fortuitous.

To a girl who'd grown up with four brothers, the instruction given by Dr. Walker meant nothing but fun. The youngest nurse was soon being given flowers and candy by the youngest patient.

Jack was smitten by Flora's shining blond hair, light complexion, and bright blue eyes. As for what drew the young lion to her, Flora was modest. "Certainly I was most unsophisticated, with a rather puritanical outlook, and, being a country girl, I suspected that he liked me because I had the manners of one unaccustomed to the social advantages of those born and bred to them

— those girls who made their bow to society by a coming-out ball or début. I never did come out; like Topsy, I 'just growed.'" [41]

So did their mutual love. For Timothy, Flora was a godsend. She was invited to dinner, received parental approval, and was informed by her employer that a marriage proposal was in the offing. As befitted a polite young gentleman in 1901, Jack made the pilgrimage to Omemee to ask Flora's father for her hand. John McCrea readily consented. Flora was twenty; Jack was twenty-four. She quit her training and moved back to Omemee to prepare for the wedding.

On a May morning in 1901 the Eatons, accompanied by friends and relatives, arrived by special train. Omemee had never seen anything quite so grand. It was as if Flora had been plucked from their midst to become a princess. So numerous were the participants that the cry went out to nearby towns for more conveyances. Said the Bobcaygeon *Independent*: "All the rubber-tired carriages from Lindsay and all the rubber-necked people from Omemee were at Miss Flora McCrea's wedding."

Her drop-shoulder dress was white chiffon over white taffeta, with shirring on the bodice and long sleeves. The short train was touched with fine Alençon lace. Jack gave her a pearl-and-diamond circle brooch. From her inlaws, she received a pendant watch of gold-and-black enamel with a fleur-de-lis in diamonds and pearls.

The couple honeymooned for a month at Ravenscrag; Jack helped overhaul the *Wanda* for summer service. In June they returned to Toronto, where Timothy lavished on them a fully furnished three-storey home on Walmer Road.

Flora might not have brought money to the marriage, but she had strength of character. Jack, who had been raised and coddled by servants, quickly learned that Flora expected him to pick up after himself and polish his own shoes. "Jack was strong-willed, and so was I; both of us quickly recognized this fact and set ourselves to learn to give and take," she later wrote. "Now, after my many years of living and observing, I firmly believe that a woman needs to know intuitively when it is wise to be immovable, and when it is better to yield to her husband's decision. The 'fifty-fifty' arrangement, which sounds so fair, is not enough; sometimes it requires the whole hundred per cent. The result, a continuing, happy marriage, is well worth the effort, even though at the time it is anything but easy to give up one's own conviction of being completely in the right." [42]

Their life was idyllic. There were family picnics in High Park and walks along the Humber River, full-dress evening balls, concerts in the glass house at Allan Gardens, and Race Week at Woodbine. The house was open to everyone from neighbours to visiting potentates, such as the Crown Prince and Princess Rupprecht of Bavaria.

All the whims and trappings of the upper class were theirs. There were only half a dozen Winton automobiles in Toronto, but Jack's two-seater phaeton carried Ontario licence number one. Even their driving accidents were genteel. Once, with Flora at the controls, her electric runabout suddenly ran amok and crashed through the closed ornamental gate of Miss Veales's School for Young Ladies. The wild ride ended with the vehicle resting atop the fallen wrought iron gate.

Timothy continued to make major pronouncements even though Jack was taking charge. For two decades Eaton's had been closing on weekdays at six. In a speech to employees in a packed Massey Hall on January 2, 1904, Timothy declared a five o'clock closing. For all his apparent beneficence, he had a practical explanation. "People can buy just as much before five o'clock." [43]

But Timothy also knew how to let go. Jack suggested that Eaton's expand to Winnipeg. At first, Timothy worried that operations fifteen hundred miles away would be impossible to oversee, but the city beckoned. The "Gateway to the Golden West," as Winnipeg was called, was a thriving commercial centre with a population of seventy-five thousand and more millionaires than Toronto. The Hudson's Bay Company had a store in Winnipeg, but Jack argued there was room for a competitor. Timothy relented and by 1904, Eaton's had bought up a city block on Portage Avenue near Main Street. The original plan called for six storeys, but Timothy fretted that such a structure would be too large, so Jack agreed to build five.

The family journeyed to Winnipeg on a private railway car for the official opening on Saturday, July 15, 1905. After a lunch for local dignitaries, the Eatons gathered near the elevators at two-thirty in the afternoon while staff stood in black-and-white uniformed readiness. A white-bearded Timothy was wheeled through the store bearing on his knee his grandson and namesake, Timothy Craig, Jack and Flora's firstborn, who had just turned two that May. They pressed a button that sounded a bell, and the doors were flung open. First across the threshold was a young man. Timothy presented him with a five-dollar bill. The boy spent the rest of the day following the old man throughout the store, agog at both the sights and his good fortune. In all, twenty-five thousand people roamed the store that day.

At eight o'clock Monday morning the doors opened for business; family members were high-profile participants. Flora, Edward's widow, Mabel, and Jack's sister, Margaret, worked in ladies' handkerchiefs and the ribbon circle, and acted as cashiers. Timothy's wife, Margaret, was a floorwalker. Each was paid, by official company cheque, an honorarium of fifty cents.

Most local retail prices were set so that pennies weren't needed. But Jack had decided that Winnipeg prices would be the same as in Toronto, for example, twenty-eight cents or $1.39. To accommodate making change, he had $500 worth of coppers shipped west. Expecting customer reluctance, he placed charity boxes at every cash register for donations by those who refused the change. Eaton's also sold newspapers at a discount price of two cents, not the usual nickel. Within a few months donations dwindled; pennies went instead into pocket or purse. Resistance was over; Eaton's had won the revolution.

The Winnipeg store was an immediate success. Eaton's fed six thousand diners a day in the cafeteria and restaurants, which included the Grill Room with its oak panelling, beamed ceiling, iron chandeliers, Minton china, and string quartet at lunch. The cafeteria was enlarged within a month. Staff of seven hundred, including 250 transferred from Toronto, grew to 1250 within a week. Sales in the first year exceeded $2.5 million. Over the next fifteen years, three more storeys were added, a powerhouse was built, and two mail-order buildings erected, one eight storeys, the other nine. The empire's western battlements grew to cover twenty-one acres, and by 1919 employment reached eight thousand.

With Jack well ensconced and able to run the business, Timothy and Margaret began to enjoy their wealth and station. In December 1905 Timothy took delivery of a 1906 Packard landaulette, the only one in Canada. Made in Detroit, the car was thirteen feet long and had a forty-horsepower engine. The exterior was black, the interior green, and there was a roof that could be removed in fine weather. He liked the Packard so much he ordered another, a limousine brougham, and in 1906 the couple toured the British Isles by automobile.

For smoother passage to his Islington farm Timothy paid for a three-mile stretch of macadam road. The first version of the motorway was not to his liking; he had the work torn up and redone. He also acquired other means of travel. In 1904 Timothy and Margaret were bound for Atlantic City by train. A reservation mix-up meant that their drawing room was already occupied when they arrived at Toronto's Union Station. The man graciously withdrew, but Timothy decided that such a kerfuffle should never happen again. He ordered a private railway car from Barney & Smith Car Co., of Dayton, Ohio.

The *Eatonia* was delivered in 1905. There were two large bedrooms, a bathroom with shower, an observation lounge, and a dining room that could seat ten. Two stewards were always in attendance.

Jack inherited his father's taste for luxury and feasted even more heartily. Colonel John Bayne Maclean, founder of the MacLean Publishing Co., introduced Jack to the Rolls-Royce.[44] Maclean had earlier met Charles Rolls in England and urged him to visit North America. By 1904 Rolls had joined Henry Royce to produce their first automobile. Rolls visited New York in 1906 and sold three vehicles. In December Rolls journeyed to Toronto bringing a six-cylinder thirty-horsepower demonstrator. After a round of lunches and dinners, Rolls made a fourth sale — to Jack, who became Canada's first Rolls-Royce owner.

In his final years Timothy grew philosophical. Once, when asked how big the business might become, he replied: "I have already been mistaken in my estimate three times, so I don't intend to foretell its growth again. All depends on the integrity of those who are to follow after me."[45]

He was little interested in the arts and rarely attended the theatre, but he encouraged Margaret's involvement. She formed a drama club with other women whom she would regale with memorized passages from Dickens and Shakespeare. She was always ready with an appropriate couplet or epithet. In her garden she might present a visitor with a rose and say: "To you it is a rose/To me it is my heart."[46] If anyone said, "I can't," Margaret would respond, "There's no 'Can't' in the 'Try' Company."[47]

Margaret became a patron to Emma Scott Raff, a young widow who taught at University of Toronto's Victoria College. Raff had opened an elocution studio called the School of Expression, which grew to include literature, voice, and physical education. In 1906 Timothy donated money to build the Margaret Eaton School of Literature and Expression.[48] The Greek Revival structure, which included a theatre, was on North Street (now Bay Street), just south of Bloor Street in Toronto. Exterior inscriptions in Greek proclaimed the school's mission: "Beauty and Fitness."[49]

With Raff as principal, studies for women included drama, physical education, as well as spoken and written expression. Graduates taught at girls' schools and colleges, or worked in social services, physical education, and dramatic art. Timothy attended the official opening on January 7, 1907. It would be his last public event.

Later that month Jack telephoned Flora and urged her to come for afternoon tea with Timothy in his office. The visit over, Timothy was bundled off home. That night he contracted a high fever and chest cold. Two days later his lungs filled with fluid. The family gathered at his bedside. "Take good care of mother," Timothy said. "Always be good to mother. She's grand."[50] Despite the fact that Timothy was on his death bed, inexplicably Margaret and Jack decided to travel to Ottawa where a group from the Margaret Eaton School was presenting a play. Only Flora was at Timothy's side when he died of pneumonia on January 31, 1907.

Eaton's stores and factories were shut, with all blinds closed and curtains drawn, for four days. Three hundred floral tributes filled Timothy's Lowther Avenue home. More than 2500 mourners filed by the copper-lined casket with a plate bearing the simple inscription: "Died. Timothy Eaton, January 31st, 1907, in his 73rd year." Several thousand more stood in the rain the next day, clogging the streets for blocks around, for the afternoon service. Said the pastor: "Timothy Eaton's success was as great in his own line as that of the Fathers of Confederation."

A procession of 230 carriages accompanied his remains to Mount Pleasant Cemetery and his final resting place, the Eaton mausoleum, erected twenty years earlier. Designed by architects W. R. Mead and Sproatt & Rolph, the mausoleum was meant to resemble a Roman temple, and was fashioned after the Maison Carrée, in Nîmes, France.[51]

One editorial writer called Timothy "the genius that modernized and revolutionized the retail commerce of Canada."[52] "A greater merchant than Timothy Eaton never lived in any age or in any country," said the *Telegram*.[53] Declared the *Toronto Daily Star*: "The position taken by Mr. Eaton in shortening the hours of work was an immense boon to all who are employed in the retail trade of Toronto."[54]

Timothy left an estate worth $5.3 million and an empire that would weave itself into the very fabric of the land and the vital fibre of its people. Immortality may be an impossible goal, but his achievements were more than most men dream, let alone do.

CHAPTER TWO

SIR JOHN: THE MERCHANT PRINCE

—

Upon the death of his father, Jack moved swiftly to take unquestioned control. Jack was handsome, stood five foot nine inches, and weighed about 160 pounds. A fashion plate, he favoured fawn-coloured coats. He had direct, blue eyes and a ready smile. His chestnut hair had a natural wave and was tinged with gold, as if he had money in his mane. By fiat of the new president any shares owned by senior managers were converted into bonds. The monetary value stayed the same but the new paper carried no votes. Officers of the company reverted to being hired hands, able to counsel but never control. The family business had become fully private again. Feudalism prevailed.

But so did fun. Jack instinctively knew that retailing was as much about entertainment as anything else. Timothy may have launched the ship, but Jack set out to ensure that everyone aboard had a good time. Christmas 1903, the same year Jack's first child, Timothy Craig, was born, was the first when an entire floor was devoted to Toyland. In 1905 Eaton's held the first Santa Claus Parades in Toronto and Winnipeg. Santa travelled from Toronto's Union Station to the store sitting on a packing case that was perched on a horse-drawn wagon decorated with bunting.

Jack seized upon the parade as a major marketing event and became a happy participant. In 1911 he rode in his car at the head of the procession, a custom he continued throughout his life. On one occasion, it was rumoured, the chubby man in the Santa suit was the president himself. In 1913 four live reindeer pulled Santa's sleigh. They'd been transported by government steamer from Labrador to Quebec City, then brought the rest of the way by train. In 1919 Santa arrived by airplane. An Eaton's-sponsored film of the event played to packed houses in local theatres. By then, Eaton's Santa was receiving fifteen thousand letters from children.

The store's display windows were another way to reach the masses, who were eager to dream. Robert Edwin Peary's successful expedition to the North Pole in 1909 was featured in miniature. Jack himself dearly wished to go on a similar adventure. Among his most prized possessions was a postcard from British explorer Sir Ernest Shackleton, which read: "To Jack from Shack — wish you were here." [1] Jack pledged $100,000 for a Shackleton expedition to the Beaufort Sea and planned to accompany the great man so he could bask in the honour and bravery. His donation was contingent upon a contribution by the federal government, but no funds were forthcoming and the trip was shelved.

Jack may not have been able to travel with Shack, but his trips abroad were extravaganzas of planning and execution. One Atlantic crossing in 1907 on the *Lusitania* from New York involved a party of eleven that included Jack and Flora, several friends, their young son Timothy, and his nurse.

Minding tickets, exchanging currency, checking accounts, and transferring the dozens of pieces of baggage was a full-time job, so company secretary J.J. Vaughan came along. The Eatons stayed in the ship's Royal Suite, which had three double bedrooms, all with baths, as well as a sitting room, sun room, and dining room. Bowls of orchids and roses graced every surface. The party visited London, Paris, Zurich, and made a pilgrimage to the Governor's birthplace, Ballymena, and Portglenone, where Timothy had apprenticed as a lad. Jack paid for restoration of family headstones in the local cemetery.

Jack further honoured his heritage by continuing Timothy's shorter-hours movement. In 1908 Christmas Day was a Friday, so the store closed Thursday night and did not open until the following Monday. New Year's Day was also a Friday, so the store was closed the next day, again reopening on Monday. Thankful employees arranged a celebration at the Armoury to honour their beneficent patron.

By 1910 Toronto operations had become a helter-skelter of walkways and tunnels linking each new building as it was erected. There were 11,700 employees, including five thousand women, with half of the total working in the factories producing whitewear, harnesses, embroidery, and hosiery.

Timothy had opened buying offices in London and Paris; before the First World War Jack added Manchester for cottons, New York for ready-to-wear,

Belfast for linen, Leicester for knits and laces, Berlin and Zurich for clocks and watches, Yokohama for silks, and Kobe for porcelain.

The Eaton Research Bureau, established in 1916, tested everything from strength of knitted fabrics through purity of drugs to dependability of corsets. The bureau also monitored Eaton's ads for veracity. What some might call Alaska sable, Eaton's would label as skunk.

Jack became one of the city's most generous philanthropists. Pork baron Sir Joseph Flavelle called on him in 1909, looking to raise funds for Toronto General Hospital. Before his death, Timothy had pledged $50,000. Flavelle wanted Jack to increase that amount to $250,000. Flavelle later wrote: "When I went in and laid before him some photographs showing the wards of the surgical side, he said: 'Do you know what you are showing me? You are showing me the wards of the surgical wing of the hospital that will be erected in memory of my father.'

"Having said this he passed to other matters as though it were a mere incident. You may be sure that it did not seem a mere incident to me, and that I was not very sure whether I was head up or feet up, as I had prepared myself for a long struggle, and found that I had no part to play at all except to listen to his statement." Jack donated $365,000. [2]

Margaret wanted additional memorials and so, in 1909, the idea of a church was born. Jack donated land on St. Clair Avenue for an English Gothic edifice with a one-hundred-foot tower and twenty-one-bell carillon. Jack gave the completed church to the congregation in 1914, debt-free, and made no stipulation about the name. Not surprisingly, the congregation decided to call it Timothy Eaton Memorial Church. Because the church attracted not just members of the Eaton family but many senior store employees as well it soon became known as "St. Timothy and all Eatons."

Jack could buy anything, great or small. He once spotted a woman selling shoelaces on the street near the store. "Hello, mother, what do you want for these?" "They're five cents a pair, sir." He gave her a ten-dollar bill and said: "Now run along home. We can't have competition established next door." [3]

Nor could he continue to live on Walmer Road. In 1909 Jack bought eleven acres on the brow of the hill east of Casa Loma, the folly of Sir Henry Pellatt. The vendor was fellow Dominion Bank director, Albert Austin, who lived north of Casa Loma in a house called Spadina. On January 22, 1909, Jack arrived in Austin's downtown office to close the deal carrying a black valise containing the $100,000 purchase price — all in banknotes secured with elastic bands — in order to limit the number of people who would know what he'd paid. A cheque clearing through the Dominion Bank would have been far less discreet.

Architects were retained and work was begun on Ardwold — Irish for "high green hill." Such was the community's interest in the massive project that in 1910 Jack was made a Six Nations chief at a ceremony during the Canadian National Exhibition. His native name was Onusonowan, meaning "Big House."

Much of the construction on the crest of the escarpment was carried out while his wife and family were abroad, so Jack was able to pick them up at Union Station upon their return in 1911 and take them directly to their new, fully furnished home. Eldest son Timothy immediately set out to explore every nook and cranny. John David, then two years old, was miserable. The toddler, who had just been carted all over Europe, sat on the bottom step of the grand staircase and wailed: "I don't like this hotel. I want to go home." [4]

The yellow-brick and stone-trimmed Georgian mansion was indeed large enough to be a grand hotel. There were fifty rooms, fourteen bathrooms, and an underground vaulted swimming pool reached through a tunnel in the basement. On the east end of the main floor were the dining room, sun porch, and a music room with a Steinway grand piano. On the west, a pan-elled library, billiard room, and lounge lined with Circassian walnut.

The focal point was a two-storey Great Hall with an aeolian mechanical pipe organ that Jack operated nightly after dinner using a motor mechanism that drove perforated paper music rolls. He would adjust the volume and cre-ate various combinations with the stops as he played operas, symphonies, band pieces, and overtures. At Christmas a forty-foot spruce tree was bedecked with lit candles that were changed daily.

On the second floor was the master suite with two bathrooms, a dressing room, and sitting room; also four other bedrooms, as well as an elevator to the third floor. This level contained three more bedrooms, three baths, a sewing and linen room, and a nursery suite with kitchen. There was a small hospital with two bedrooms for patients, an operating room, a white-tiled room for sterilizing equipment, and another room designated for physicians' scrubbing. Surgery could be conducted, but the main reason for the hospital was to isolate family members with contagious diseases, while keeping them close at hand for care.

A formal Italian-style garden offered commanding views of the city and Lake Ontario. On a clear day the mists rising above Niagara Falls fifty miles away were visible. "Not only have you a splendid view," one of the architects told Jack, "but just imagine being able to look out at the three hundred thousand people who work for you!" Although construction costs are not known, ten years later Ardwold was valued for estate purposes at $300,000. With Spadina and Casa

Loma to the immediate west, and piano manufacturer Samuel Nordheimer's Glenedyth to the east, Jack was amid Toronto's wealthiest citizens.

A constant flow of guests to Ardwold gave further credence to young John David's description of the house as a hotel. Travelling entertainers ranged from Parisian flautist René Le Roy to the pride of Glasgow, vaudevillian Sir Harry Lauder. Jack was said to be something of an entertainer himself. "He has a gift of mimicry and dialect that might be the envy of many a legitimate stage comedian," wrote Augustus Bridle in the 1919 book celebrating the company's jubilee year. "He can tell a droll story, impersonating a Chinaman, a negro, an Englishman, a Scotchman or an Irishman, an Italian, a Jew or even [a minstrel show] end man as easily as he can write his cheque for a large sum to help the community." [5]

Such performances were usually private. Public appearances were carefully orchestrated, such as the time he bought a Packard, then posed at the wheel for pictures. Under a headline "Finest Automobile in Canada," the description read: "[S]peed from three to 55 miles an hour . . . seven people can be accommodated . . . engine has enough power to run up a steep incline at the rate of 25 miles an hour . . . canopy and side curtains . . . and the car costs as much as a fair-sized house . . . $7,500." [6]

Among the assets he'd inherited from his father was an 11.7 per cent interest in the *Toronto Daily Star*. Despite that connection, Jack felt no compunction to give media interviews. "In fact," said the *Financial Post*, "the company has always discouraged, with evident success, the appearance in the local daily press of any news concerning its affairs not regarded as of constructive value." [7]

He did, however, try to influence both public opinion and editorial policy. The government of Wilfrid Laurier sought trade reciprocity with the United States and, supported by the *Star*, had come to an agreement with the United States. Many Canadian business leaders, Jack among them, were opposed. Free trade would mean an end to their protected markets. Jack was one of eighteen prominent Toronto Liberals who signed a manifesto denouncing the agreement. In the election of 1911 Canadians rejected free trade, choosing the Conservatives under Robert Borden.

There was an equally bitter battle within Eaton's itself. In 1910 union printer Jimmy Simpson, who later became mayor of Toronto, said: "We want to lick

Eaton good and we are going to lick him good. These monuments, hospitals and buildings are donated by the oppressors of the people and paid for with sweat money." [8]

For all its sunny methods, paternalism had a dark side and labour relations suffered. Eaton's had kept wages low by having prospective employees reveal rent payments and other living costs so that their pay could be geared to their needs and no more. Printing was Eaton's only unionized operation and relations were often tense. In 1912 there was confrontation in the factories over job loss due to automation. When management asked male tailors to work overtime, they refused and were locked out. Cloak makers walked out in protest.

On February 16, 1912, Jimmy Simpson spoke to one thousand Eaton's workers in the Labour Temple. "If organized labour wish to have their demands for a fair wage in any way considered by the company, it is up to them to start now," he said. [9] Simpson also complained about police ejecting factory workers from the meeting at Jack's request. The standoff continued into March with two thousand locked-out garment and cloak makers — accompanied by several van loads of strikers' children — spending one Saturday circling what was referred to on page one of the *Toronto Sunday World* as "the Big Store."

Negotiations continued, but management wanted agitators punished and refused to rehire everyone. The union insisted any settlement must include a return to work by all strikers, as well as recognition of the International Ladies Garment Workers Union.

In May Jack agreed to a deal, but demanded there be no public celebration. Strikers celebrated anyway. Jack changed his offer; he would reinstate strikers with no concessions — but only if they apologized. Four months later the strike collapsed. The workers returned, with nothing to show for their efforts.

By contrast, Jack's obvious wealth was causing resentment among his employees. In 1912 he took delivery of three new Rolls-Royce automobiles. Two were open touring models: the blue one was called Bluebird, and a goldfinch-yellow car became Yellowbird. The third was Ladybird, a double limousine. Other Eaton-family Rolls-Royce buyers included cousin Robert Wellington (son of Robert, Timothy's eldest brother, and a store superintendent), Mabel, the widow of his brother, Edward, and the T. Eaton Co. itself. Of the fifty Rolls-Royce automobiles sold in Canada prior to the First World War, the Eatons owned at least seven of them. [10]

For Jack, mechanical contraptions of any sort were nothing but toys for his own amusement. As he more and more became the portly portrait of the thoughtless tycoon, he acted as though rules were for the plebes. He'd regularly race Lucy Tinning, one of Toronto's first female drivers, on the Avenue Road hill. If a police officer spotted them, "he'd wave us over and yell at us but John would say, 'Come on, I'll buy you a drink,'" recalled Tinning in an interview years later. "And off they'd go off for that drink and we never got any tickets." [11]

On one occasion, as he travelled to Omemee by train, Jack stepped off his private car in Peterborough and convinced the platform superintendent to let him ride with the engineer. Once ensconced between coal bin and fire box, Jack bullied the engineer into turning over the throttle. Jack took the train out of the Peterborough yards, across a bridge, up a grade, and right into Omemee station.

Along with the best in conveyances there were summer homes and ships. In 1906 Jack and Flora paid $2,500 for a log cabin and four acres in Muskoka. The cabin stood on a rocky point with a stand of white pine at the northern end of Lake Rosseau. In 1912 they added forty acres, giving them thirty-five hundred feet of shoreline, and named the property Kawandag, Ojibway for "meeting place of the pines." Construction was started in 1914 on a two-storey mansion with a front portico and four white pillars. The design became a landmark on the lake.

In 1910 Jack bought a ninety-four-foot steel schooner in Italy, christened the *Tekla*, for outings on Lake Ontario. It could sleep five and required a crew of ten to operate the yards of canvas that billowed above the decks. The *Tekla* was the first yacht at the Royal Canadian Yacht Club to be equipped with a wireless so that Jack could communicate with the store.

He also bought a steel steam yacht weighing 237 gross tons, with a length of 172 feet overall, built at the Crescent Shipyards in Elizabeth, New Jersey. The vessel was slightly longer than the *Corsair*, the 165-foot oceangoing steam yacht owned by John Pierpoint Morgan, the American banker who at one point owned 70 per cent of the steel industry and one-third of all United States railroads. The *Florence* had a white hull, two masts, featured a mahogany-panelled dining saloon, slept eight, and had a crew of eighteen. In 1913 Jack brought the *Florence*, easily capable of an Atlantic crossing, to Toronto harbour and a tumultuous welcome at the Royal Canadian Yacht Club. There, the ship flew his private flag, a blue swallowtail with gold border and monogram.

Although he was just thirty-seven, Jack Eaton was at the peak of his powers. He was impetuously generous and could dramatically change a life with his Midas touch. "He loves a good boat and a good car, but he would like everyone to own them, too. Failing that, he shares his with many," a friend once said. [12] A steward on the *Florence* had a young niece named Violet Murray, and when Jack heard her sing he announced he would pay for private lessons. And thus was launched a career. "I'm sure he assumed I would be an opera singer, but I was much more attracted to the dazzle and excitement of the music hall," Murray said in an interview in 1979.

The family's first long voyage on the *Florence* to Quebec City in 1913 was a fateful one. Third son Edgar, born the previous year, suffered convulsions aboard ship and became paralysed on one side. Contaminated milk was believed to be the cause. The events of that night marked Edgar forever. An eye required painful treatment, convalescence took months, and he dragged his right foot for several years. Upon their return to Toronto, Flora left that ship with her little boy and never set foot on the vessel again.

─

The darkening clouds in Europe soon became the First World War and Jack seized those far-off events to make a series of moves that were both bold and benevolent. In 1914, Jack donated the armour-plated *Florence* — stripped of its elegant panelling and furnishings but retaining its private wireless station — to the government of Canada. A year later the *Florence* was sunk off the coast of Trinidad, the victim of enemy action.

The ship wasn't his only contribution to the war effort. Weapons, particularly the deadly new machine gun, were in short supply. Canadian Minister of Militia and Defence Sir Sam Hughes decided Canada should have a machine-gun brigade and approached Jack for financial help. He contributed $100,000 and the outfit took his name: the Eaton Machine Gun Battery. The backing meant not only paying for quick-firing Vickers-Maxim guns mounted on fourteen armoured vehicles, but also receiving uniforms for himself and his boys.

Eaton's staff flooded into the service. A married man who volunteered remained on full pay; a single man received half pay. Before any employee embarked, a photograph was taken and hung in the store. Soldiers abroad could draw on their Eaton's wages through their savings accounts (paying 10 per cent interest) in the Eaton's office in London or Paris. Prisoners of war received regular packages organized by the Zurich office.

Ardwold became the focus of fund-raisers and troop entertainment. Flora was in charge of a door-to-door canvas in the city's west end. Eaton's employees collectively contributed $600,000 to the war effort. Profits from factory contracts for war materiel were turned back to the government.

Jack's cousin Tom, a department head, was killed in action in Flanders in 1917. The war even took the life of an Eaton who should have been far from the conflict. The marriage of Timothy's elder daughter, Josephine, to English businessman Tom Burnside had failed — Tom had refused to move to Canada, despite the offer of a job at Eaton's, and Josephine disliked living in England. The two agreed to separate before the war and she returned to Canada.

Their daughter, Iris, then twenty, was to split her time between her parents, so in 1915 Josephine and Iris booked passage to England on the *Lusitania*. Mother and daughter were in their stateroom when a torpedo from a German U-boat struck the vessel off the coast of Ireland and the *Lusitania* began to sink. They scrambled to the deck, but the ship was listing so badly that many lifeboats were not accessible. A further explosion threw them into the sea and young Iris drowned. Other survivors pulled Josephine onto an overturned lifeboat. She was so covered with oil and soot they thought she must have been a member of the crew — until they spied her jewellery. Eight chilling hours later she was rescued. Three Eaton's buyers, also aboard the *Lusitania*, died. (George Graham, a Winnipeg-based buyer, went down on the *Titanic* in 1912.)

The war also brought romance to the house of Eaton. William Avery "Billy" Bishop, the first Canadian airman to win the Victoria Cross, returned home on leave in 1917 with a friend, Henry Burden. Both were already renowned aces. (By war's end, Burden would shoot down twenty-one enemy aircraft, Bishop seventy-two.) Bishop immediately fell in love with Henry's sister, Margaret, a granddaughter of Timothy's. A wedding soon followed at Timothy Eaton Memorial Church. Eight-year-old John David, wearing a tricorn hat, was a train-bearer.

For his war efforts Jack's name was included as a Knight Bachelor on the 1915 honours list of King George V. The ceremony was conducted that fall at Rideau Hall in Ottawa by the Duke of Connaught, Governor General of Canada. Lady Eaton wore a dress with a pink sequined train; she carried a matching fan with mother-of-pearl ribbing. The procedure was as ancient as it was memorable. Jack knelt, was touched on both shoulders by a sword, and told, "Arise, Sir Knight."

Jack also pressed into service his private rail car. The *Eatonia* rail car purchased for Timothy had been destroyed by fire, so in 1916, Jack ordered *Eatonia II* from Pullman Co. of Chicago. The car was seventy-eight feet long, had four staterooms panelled in Cuban mahogany, an observation area, a dining room with seating for ten on leather chairs, full kitchen, and servants' quarters. Over the next six years, *Eatonia II* made 168 trips and logged 170,000 miles. (In 1930 the car was sold to Canadian National Railways and was used for royal tours in 1939 and 1951, as well as for trips by federal cabinet ministers in the 1950s and other VIP services. In 1972 Eaton's repurchased and restored the car, then donated it to Calgary's Heritage Park.)

One of those runs was in response to the explosion following the collision of two ships in Halifax harbour in 1917 that killed more than sixteen hundred and injured nine thousand. Sir John filled the *Eatonia II* and another rail car with medical supplies, blankets, and food, then headed for Halifax with the store pharmacist and two nurses from Ardwold. He established a depot with a staff of seventeen to give away clothing and building materials. One man appeared at four in the morning saying that he had just dug his wife and four children out of the ruins of their house. All were dead. "I never saw Sir John cry before," said H. S. Thornton, a member of the Eaton team in Halifax. "He was almost dead with exhaustion himself, but he spent an hour outfitting that poor, sad man." [13]

Those who accompanied Sir John were later awarded silver pins engraved E.W.S. (Eaton's Welfare Service) to honour their efforts just as if they had gone into battle beside their king. The commemorative jewellery gave Lady Eaton the idea to expand the concept. Four hundred staffers were appointed Eaton's Welfare Secretaries to assist the 12,000 female employees. In Lady Eaton's view, many of the women needed help with greedy landlords, tyrannical parents, unwanted pregnancies, and urban stress. "If they had someone they knew in whom they could confide, most of their problems could be overcome or avoided," she said. [14]

The hectic pace maintained by Sir John was too much for Lady Eaton. Under doctor's orders, in 1917 she fled to the wilds of New Brunswick and spent most of the summer canoeing on the Miramichi River with a friend, Anne Pringle. Accompanied by two guides and a cook, they wore flannel shirts, hunting breeches, and high boots. They caught trout, fought off mosquitoes, and slept in tents. When Jack joined them for some fishing during the final ten days, his wife was almost unrecognizable. Lady Eaton wrote in her diary: "Jack hardly knew me, I was so hot and red, and greasy with fly dope." [15]

On November 11, 1918, word of the war's end was flashed around the world and reached Toronto at 2:55 a.m. "Eaton's big 'wildcat' siren awakened the whole city," reported the *Globe*. "Toronto citizens rubbed their eyes and could not believe their senses. The newspaper offices were swamped with telephone calls."

The war had not interrupted Eaton's growth. Sales were $22 million in 1907, $53 million in 1914, and $141 million in 1920. Of that, $60 million was from the mail-order division with its new six-storey building, which opened in Moncton in 1919.

The success of the Winnipeg store had demonstrated that Eaton's could profitably run operations outside Toronto. In addition to Moncton, in 1916 a warehouse was built in Saskatoon for such heavy goods as furniture, farm implements, and stoves. In 1917 a similar structure was erected in Regina. On a visit to inspect construction, Jack stopped the tour, pointed west, and proclaimed, "There's our future market." [16] He spoke while standing on a cement floor that was not yet dry. The footprints he left behind were framed and remained as a reminder of the family's presence right into the second half of the century.

Other aspects of the business were also expanding. In March 1919 Eaton's bought the Guelph Stove Co., then spent $100,000 to extend and improve the facilities. The company, incorporated in 1902, had previously been selling most of the stoves it produced to Eaton's.

The catalogue had grown to 588 pages and contained almost nine thousand illustrations. Fiddles started at $3.95, a wood stove was $46.50. Plans and materials for a complete three-bedroom house cost $999.77. For Christmas there were bobsleds for boys and Eaton's Beauty dolls for girls. The German-made dolls with bisque china heads, moveable limbs, lifelike curly hair, and eyes that opened and closed were every girl's dream. The first doll in 1901 cost $1, and the two-foot tall version was $3.50. For twenty-five cents, younger sister could have the White Doll or Sunbeam Coon. By 1942 the last year the dolls were available, the price had increased from $1 to $1.29, but could run to $12 for the deluxe model. [17]

The catalogue and the company behind it had become so inextricably linked with the country that, when a town was founded in 1917 by the Canadian Northern Railway, about 140 miles southwest of Saskatoon, the locals called it Eaton. In 1921, to end postal confusion with nearby Eston, the name was changed to Eatonia. Photos of the Eatonia railway station and main street were featured on the cover of the 1955 spring/summer catalogue.

As Jack expanded the stores, he added employee facilities until they became the most extensive of any corporation in Canada. Beginning in 1911, Jack established house-league teams in baseball, lacrosse, cricket, hockey, and football. The hockey team from Toronto travelled to Winnipeg for games and gained such prominence that horses in the Toronto stables were named after the players. On occasion Jack himself would show up in his suit and bowler hat to start proceedings.

While the culture was paternalistic, there was newfound financial independence and freedom, particularly for women who previously had few career choices beyond nurse, teacher, or domestic. Eaton's provided women with jobs and an opportunity to meet new people, participate in organized events, rent their own accommodation, and escape the confines of small towns and protective parents. Female employees also had their own downtown Toronto club rooms with a pool, gymnasium, and library, as well as rooms dedicated to sewing, singing, and dancing.

A summer camp for men was established in 1917 in Toronto's east end, complete with tents for sleeping, a swimming tank, and sports programs. Employees could spend their summer vacations at Work-a-day camp, as it was called, or simply stay the night. Cost was modest — just enough to cover meals. There was a fishing lodge for managers near Parry Sound. In Winnipeg, there was a company hospital on the seventh floor staffed by nurses, a doctor, dentist, and a chiropractor.

In 1919 a quarter-century club was founded by seventy-six men, each with twenty-five years' service. Starting in 1923, members received six weeks' vacation with pay. That was also the first year that inductees received a commemorative gift: for men, a gold watch and chain; for women, a wristwatch.

Sir John had single-handedly created a self-contained parallel society, a kingdom for the chosen. An employee could work, holiday, join a club, be nursed back to health, find a mate, and be guaranteed friends in retirement — all within the embracing arms of the Eaton's "family."

Family festivities became more and more elaborate. A newspaper ad appeared on December 31, 1918, announcing a year-long celebration called the Golden Jubilee to be held throughout 1919. The announcement, signed by Sir John, also trumpeted the changes Eaton's had wrought. "Fifty years ago the custom was no fixed prices, no return of purchases and redress in case of error. Sometimes one was even pestered to buy. Shopping was no child's play. It was a match of wits, so it was usually done by the head of the house. In contrast today even a child may do the purchasing either in person, by Mail Order or Telephone, without any thoughts of being imposed upon."

Sir John announced that the Saturday one o'clock closing hours previously in vogue from May through September would be extended throughout the rest of the year. The five-and-a-half-day week had arrived. In July and

August, the store would close all day Saturday. Employees, including piece-workers, would receive the same money as before.

Sir John launched Jubilee proceedings at eight-thirty on Thursday morning, January 2, 1919, when he arrived, wearing a silk hat and a white rose boutonniere, at the door of the Toronto store and met his mother. Flags flew from every window. Bunting abounded. He handed Margaret a solid-gold key. She opened the door, stepped inside the vestibule, and pulled a bell cord that sounded a gong. The fire and floor bells rang for ten seconds, then the doors were opened to the waiting public. The key used for the opening was placed in a miniature gold replica of Timothy's first store. Tin versions, complete with slots for use as savings banks, were given away by the thousands to schoolchildren.

Employees lined up in adoring rows along the main aisle to applaud as the matriarch passed among them, accompanied by the other members of the royal family: Sir John and Lady Eaton and three of their four sons — Timothy, Edgar, and John David. Margaret was presented with a bouquet of sweetheart roses, violets, and mignonettes by Margaret Smith, at fourteen one of the store's youngest employees. A three-hundred-member employee choir, accompanied by an orchestra, sang the doxology:

> *Praise God from whom all blessings flow*
> *Praise him all creatures here below*
> *Praise him above ye heavenly host*
> *Praise Father, Son, and Holy Ghost*

They could just as well have been singing, "Praise John from whom all blessings flow," such was the reverence with which the Eatons were viewed by the rank and file.

The regal procession continued up, floor by cheering floor, to the seventh and uppermost level, then flowed back down again, nodding regally and exchanging greetings all the way. "God Save the King" was sung, as was "O Canada." There were more presentations and, the final flurry, three cheers for Sir John.

The only speaker at lunch that day was Lady Eaton who said of her husband: "From his father he inherits vision and the ability to seize the opportune moment to do a courageous thing, in a business sense, for the betterment of workers. From his mother, he inherits kindness, consideration for the comfort of others and generosity." [18]

Eaton's now employed twenty-two thousand. The buildings covered sixty acres in Toronto alone. One telephone in 1885 had become 120 central lines. The Shopping Service, begun in 1911, not only took orders, but personnel now made gift suggestions. Delivery depots were placed throughout the city; goods were transported on a twice-daily route by a system that included 200 wagons and 310 horses, all greys and bays, working half days, as well as sixty-six trucks. In Winnipeg in 1923 there were 123 horses. Delivery men wore uniforms of blue Irish tweed with a cap of the same colour; they were trained to bring goods to the side door. If chores were requested by customers, drivers were told to undertake them cheerfully.

When mothers shopped, they could drop off their children at Frolic Park, near Toyland. Under a matron's supervision, the youngsters enjoyed merry-go-rounds, teeter-totters, and sand piles. Mothers could rest assured their offspring enjoyed fresh air, for healthy breezes were said to blow in from Lake Ontario.

As part of the Golden Jubilee celebrations, managers held an elaborate seven-course dinner to honour Sir John; there were speeches, entertainers, and a singalong accompanied by an orchestra. Tunes ran the gamut from the patriotic "Never Let the Old Flag Fall" to the maudlin "Mother Machree."

On June 24, 1919, ten thousand employees assembled at the Armoury in homage to Sir John. A choir sang and the band of the 110th Regiment played. A composing-room foreman from the printing department made a laudatory speech, presented bound volumes containing the signatures of twelve thousand employees, and announced their gift. Employees had collected $20,000 toward extending the X-ray wing and endowing a cot in Sir John's name at the Hospital for Sick Children in Toronto.

"We all love children; God bless them all," he said in his brief reply. "I need not say more. I hope that the all-day Saturday holiday will be enjoyed by one and all." [19] The Eaton children were showered with even greater largesse. When fifth child and first girl Florence Mary was born on November 15, 1919, Sir John bought Victory Bonds in her name worth $1 million.

On December 8, 1919, ten thousand employees gathered at eight in the morning in the Queen Street store, which was decorated with wreaths of golden laurels tied with blue ribbon. "O Canada" was sung by the Eaton Choral Society, formed earlier that Jubilee year. Vice-president Harry McGee unveiled a gift from employees to Margaret, the bronze statue of Timothy, created by Ivor Lewis, an artist and actor who worked in the advertising department. The throng cheered. Margaret openly wept.

In his speech McGee referred to Margaret as "the mother of us all" and the staff as "your boys and girls." Sir John replied in kind: "That it is your thought for my mother's happiness makes it valuable indeed, that it is the beautiful result of the work of one of our own boys makes it more precious, that it is a lasting tribute to my father's memory makes it priceless.

"I cannot express what I feel, but speaking for mother, want you to know you have the grateful thanks of us all, my mother — our mother." [20] Each employee was presented with a copy of *Golden Jubilee*, a 289-page book detailing the history of the store and its founding father.

Coincident with the Golden Jubilee celebrations, Eaton's honoured its employees recently returned from war. On Saturday night, December 20, the 1300 Toronto employees who had fought overseas were feted at a dinner given in the furniture building. In all, there were 741 casualties, including 238 who were killed in action or later died of wounds. Eaton's paid $2.2 million in wages to 3327 soldiers.

"I cannot say how glad I am that you are safe home again," said Sir John. "You have left behind you consecrated ground in foreign countries, and for the fallen my sense of personal loss is great. You have mentioned what I have done for you, but all that was slight in comparison with what you over there were doing for us." [21]

Each man received a rectangular gold medal bearing the Eaton coat of arms and the motto "Vincit Omnia Veritas" (Truth Conquers All). The reverse bore the inscription "Presented by Sir John Eaton, as a mark of appreciation of service in the great war, 1914-18." Mayor T. L. Church said in his speech: "I wish we had more Sir Johns in the city of Toronto. Sir John is one of nature's noblemen." In his reply on behalf of the men, Sergeant-Major E. Dounard paraphrased Rudyard Kipling's "Appreciation of Lord Roberts' treatment of the soldiers":

> This ain't no bloomin' ode.
> But you've eased the soldier's load,
> And for benefits bestowed —
> Bless ye — Sir John. [22]

As the joyous sounds of the Jubilee faded, rumours began to circulate that Eaton's was for sale. Throughout 1920, stories continually cropped up that a large American retailer had acquired Eaton's or was negotiating to do so. Gossip also claimed that downward pressure on prices might cause Eaton's to close its doors between Christmas and New Year's, dismiss staff, reduce prices, and rehire employees at prewar wages.

Company denials were issued, but the whispers persisted. Finally Sir John himself weighed in at a year-end dinner on December 6, 1920, in the Grill Room given by the department managers for the directors. In his reply to a toast Sir John said: "There is not enough money in the whole world to buy my father's name." [23] His welcome reassurance was greeted by a burst of cheering.

Foreign buyers or not, Eaton's was attracting international attention. "Are we not right, then, in holding that this is a business unique in character as well as exceptional in magnitude?" wrote S. H. Ditchett, editor of *Dry Goods Economist*, in a book published in New York in 1923 entitled *Eaton's of Canada: A Unique Institution of Extraordinary Magnitude.* "And will not a depiction of the monument this concern has reared and of the ways in which its erection was accomplished be of real value to every merchant, near or far, who is anxious to know what others have done so that he may thereby check up on the ideals, principles and policies to which his own business owes its progress and success?" [24]

The book gave detailed floor-by-floor descriptions of the Eaton's stores in Winnipeg and Toronto, including photographs of sumptuous window displays. "An observer experienced in the departmental field is also struck by the fact that no matter how early the hour the store is busy. It is an almost unanimous complaint with department store owners throughout the United States that the public cannot be brought into the store during the first part of the forenoon.

"At the Eaton store the conditions are entirely different. No sooner has the store opened — at 8:30 — than the aisles and counters begin to be occupied by customers. Not infrequently there will be one or two hundred people waiting for the doors to be opened.

"As the day goes on, the crowds of purchasers increase and long before noon congestion has set in. This continues right up to the closing hour — 5 p.m. — and is in evidence on all of the five floors and basement devoted to selling. Numerous are the elevators and despite their reinforcement with escalators, they are continually thronged with those who wish to go from one floor to another." [25]

For all his business acumen, Sir John was happiest away from the office, even if he was simply playing a prank with his mother. One favourite routine involved

Sir John holding out his hat and urging his mother to do a "high kick." Once she'd accomplished the stunt, he'd raise his hat a few inches, then a few inches more. She always managed to make her foot reach the target.

Sir John also included her in more adventuresome pursuits. Home from service overseas, war aces Billy Bishop and Henry Burden launched an air service. Among the first passengers was Margaret, who was always game for just about anything.

One day in 1919 Sir John showed up at Ravenscrag and asked: "Mother, will you fly with me?"

Her reply was immediate. "Of course I will. I have wanted to fly all my life."

And so Billy Bishop flew the two of them high over the Muskoka lakes. When she landed, Margaret said: "From heights I discovered unknown lakes hidden in the woods, and realized for the first time what a bird's eye view meant."

"Mother," said Sir John, "I was never so proud of you as at this moment — seventy-eight and a good sport." [26]

As his fortune grew and his fame spread, Sir John's circle of acquaintances expanded to include every luminary of the day, from boxer Georges Carpentier through industrialist Henry Ford to naturalist John Burroughs. But of all the great names in their life, none had a greater impact, particularly on Lady Eaton, than Edward Johnson.

Born in Guelph, Ontario, in 1878, Johnson studied singing in New York, Paris, and Florence, and made his operatic debut in Padua, Italy, in 1912. In 1919 the tenor joined the Chicago opera and in 1922 began thirteen seasons with New York's Metropolitan Opera, then continued as general manager until he retired in 1950.

Johnson met the Eatons when he first returned from Europe in 1919 on his way to Chicago. After that, "Edoardo Di Giovanni," as he called himself, spelling the name in his own way, would stay with the Eatons and once spent a summer rehearsing at Kawandag. The handsome Johnson, who gave singing lessons to many young women, encouraged Lady Eaton's singing, although she lacked the soaring talent of his other students.

Flattered by Johnson's interest, Lady Eaton agreed to perform at a fund-raising concert. A contralto, she took lessons for several months and rehearsed diligently. For the event before a full-dress audience at Toronto's Massey Hall in 1920, Lady Eaton wore a gown of blue-and-silver brocade. Sir John gave his wife a platinum bracelet with the first bar of her opening number, "Bois Épais," in black enamel and diamonds. She planned to wear a diamond tiara of maple leaves specially made for the occasion, but at the last minute, the piece didn't quite fit, so Lady Eaton donned another tiara already in her collection. The reception was polite and the benefit concert for the blind raised $6000.

The graciousness of Sir John's society profile did not carry over into business. The *Star*'s Joseph Atkinson was not on the same good terms with the son that he'd been with the father. First there was the bitter battle over reciprocity in 1911, with the two men holding opposing views. In 1912 the paper sided with the striking cloak makers. Sir John took Atkinson to task, pointing out that Timothy had helped finance his start. Atkinson reminded Sir John that his job was running a store, not a newspaper, and offered to buy out his holdings.

Finally, in 1920 Sir John agreed to sell and on June 8, 1921, cancelled the back-page ad "Eaton's Daily Store News." The purported reason was an increase in advertising rates; more likely it was meant as punishment. Simpson's wanted to take the vacated space, but Atkinson refused. Instead he created a two-section paper and placed Simpson's on the back page of the first section. The other back page he devoted to pictures, pending Eaton's return. And return Eaton's eventually did — on June 28, 1922, on inside pages first, then eighteen months later on the back page.

In January 1922 Sir John travelled to Montreal for a board meeting of the Canadian Pacific Railway. While there, he contracted the flu, and by the time he'd returned home pneumonia had set in. For the next seven weeks, Sir John lay abed in the hospital suite at Ardwold. Treatment couldn't have been more complete, the medical community more attentive. After all, he had donated $500,000 in 1919 to endow a chair in the department of medicine at the University of Toronto; the surgical wing of the Toronto General Hospital was named after his father.[27] But local physicians could do nothing, nor could the specialists called in from Johns Hopkins Hospital in Baltimore, Maryland.

For a time his condition improved, but four weeks into the recovery, a general infection set in. In mid-March eldest son Timothy was summoned home from boarding school in England. As Sir John's life ebbed away, he was watched constantly by a changing guard that included his wife, mother, valet, nurses, and his brother Bill (known as Colonel William, after his war effort), who had moved in from his Oakville home, Ballymena, to stay at Ardwold for the duration.

There was a final rally. Optimism returned and the daily bulletins detailing Sir John's condition were discontinued. Then, just as suddenly, there was a turn for the worse. On Thursday, March 30, 1922, at 9:40 p.m., Sir John Craig Eaton died. He was forty-six. Lamented his mother Margaret: "He was so needed by so many and lived such a useful, unselfish life, while here I am, of no use to anyone. Why couldn't it have been me?" [28]

The Eaton's stores, factories, warehouses, and foreign buying offices were closed until after the interment the following Tuesday. Men attending the service wore morning coats, dark gloves, and black Christies or silk hats. The mayor ordered all city flags flown at half mast. The University of Toronto cancelled classes. Tens of thousands gathered outside Timothy Eaton Memorial Church during the service. A further twenty-five thousand lined the roadway as Sir John's body was borne to the family mausoleum in Mount Pleasant Cemetery.

At his death Sir John's net worth was $13,980,623. [29] In addition, he had given away an estimated $4 million during his lifetime to various causes, from the Navy League to the Royal Ontario Museum. Among his holdings were stocks valued at $4,973,837; his 9888 Eaton common shares accounted for the bulk of that amount. Real estate amounted to $3,329,155. Cash and bonds accounted for a further $4,548,565; mortgages, $52,087. There was only one small life insurance policy of $1000 in the T. Eaton Life Assurance Co., the company established in 1920 to sell policies to employees.

According to the terms of the will, Lady Eaton was given a life interest in Ardwold (Kawandag was already in her name), household furniture and effects, and an annual income of $100,000, an amount that could be increased by the trustees. Additional funds for the support and education of the children were at the discretion of the trustees: Lady Eaton, cousin R.Y., and three Eaton's directors. His mother and sisters Josephine and Margaret were each to receive $25,000 a year; his brother, Colonel William, $15,000. Members of staff at Ardwold shared $69,000. [30]

There was public praise at every turn. "A merchant prince, he was a prince among men," declared the *Montreal Star*. The obituary quoted an unnamed friend who had said some years earlier: "Jack Eaton is the one rich man in Toronto who knows how to spend his money. Whether he is erecting a twelve-storey factory, filling his garage with new automobiles, building a new home on the Hill or giving a quarter-million for the Hospital, it is all done on the same broad-gauged, unlimited scale. He understands the economy of expenditure."

Added the anonymous friend: "If the old way of making money was by

saving money, Jack Eaton had long since discarded it. Money wisely and lav-
ishly spent was the principle on which he worked. And of course he had the
money to spend; not having been compelled to make most of it by his own
individual effort. . . ."

Concluded the obituary: "Sir John Eaton worked while he worked and
played while he played. He enjoyed business and he rollicked in sport. He recognized his humblest acquaintances and he was ever ready to swap a story or
perpetrate a joke. His life was constant action, and for weeks at a time he
almost lived in his private car. He had few theories, and was not strong on
abstract ideas. He was a man of action throughout." [31]

The Embro, Ontario, *Courier* published a poem by Edith Catherine Slater
that was typical of the worshipful outpouring at his death:

> Thy kingly kindness will thy tomb
> Keep haloed in our eyes
> Till heaven ushers in the morn
> Thou'll from Mount Pleasant rise. [32]

Lady Eaton was plunged into months of despair. "I felt like a stone," she
later wrote. "It was an ordeal even to see my closest friends. I wished I could
have rushed away into the woods and hidden like a suffering animal." [33]

But the death of Sir John in 1922 had an impact far beyond the very real
loss of a husband and father, or the untimely departure of a company president. His demise was a seismic event for Eaton's. There would be peaks and
valleys in the decades ahead, but the inexorable decline and fall of the Eaton
empire and the royal family itself had begun.

Shirtsleeves to shirtsleeves in three generations, goes the old saw. The
Eatons might manage to hang on to their money, but leadership and vision
were another matter. There would be no merchant princes of Sir John's
stature among his offspring or among the generations to come.

CHAPTER THREE

R.Y.: THE
INTERREGNUM

—

SIR JOHN'S LAST WILL AND TESTAMENT NAMED
no specific successor. Instead, all of his shares in the T. Eaton Co. were to go
to the son considered most fit by the estate's trustees. If none of the four boys
was deemed worthy, his only daughter Florence, or her husband, could be
designated as president. Once a selection had been made, the other four siblings were each to receive legacies of $2 million. The will also stipulated that
the next president could not be named until attaining the age of twenty-
seven, thereby allowing the trustees time to gauge the business potential of all
the respective possibilities. Timothy, the eldest, would not be twenty-seven
until 1930, Gilbert, the youngest son, 1942, and Florence, 1946. As a result,
Cousin Bob stepped into the breach.

Robert Young Eaton did not hold any shares in Eaton's. He was a "worker
Eaton" not an "owner Eaton" and his sudden arrival in the role of president
signalled the beginning not just of an interregnum but also of a tense time.
While Cousin Bob would build the company through the 1920s and see it
through the Great Depression until Sir John's heirs could resume running
things, there would be fierce rivalry between the two factions.

The death of Sir John as a relatively young man meant that succession was
not as smooth as it had been when Timothy had died in 1907, but at least
there was a place to turn. In fact, it was as if the hand of the Governor himself had reached beyond the grave. When Timothy visited his native County
Antrim in 1897, he met his nephew, R.Y., as he was known. At the time, the

tall and muscular twenty-two-year old was living on the farm of his late father, Timothy's brother John. R.Y. was a schoolteacher but his dream was to enter the civil service.

Timothy spotted another quality. "My boy," he said, "it's not the civil service that will ever satisfy you. You should be in commercial business." [1] R.Y. heard the call. That same year he joined Eaton's London office as a shipping clerk and studied in the evenings for his bachelor of arts degree from the University of London. He was transferred to Paris in 1899, emigrated to Toronto in 1902, and became secretary of the company in 1904. In 1907 he was named a director and first vice-president. He quickly became imbued with the corporate culture. "Before a man can become a valued Eaton employee," R.Y. would say in his Irish lilt, "he's got to get the Eaton spirit into his blood." [2]

Where Sir John was a bon vivant who needed to be liked, R.Y. seemed not to care a fig for anyone's opinion. He stood six foot five, weighed 230 pounds, had large ears, a prominent nose, and a bald pate. Like Timothy and Sir John, R.Y. fell in love with a small-town girl. Hazel Margaret Ireland had come to Toronto in 1906 from Carberry, Manitoba, to study piano at the Toronto Conservatory of Music. When she met R.Y., she was bedazzled by his status and power. Once, after it began raining, he stopped at Eaton's to pick up a raincoat. Although the clerk made a note of the item for billing to his account, all Hazel saw was R.Y.'s ability to commandeer whatever he wanted.

After Hazel graduated from the Conservatory, she returned to Carberry, taught piano, and was a church organist and choir leader. R.Y.'s courtship included a visit to meet her father, who owned two lumber mills and was the town's first mayor.

On December 13, 1911, R.Y. and Hazel were married in Carberry; the schools closed for the day as if by royal decree. "Nothing so important had occurred there since the celebration of Queen Victoria's Diamond Jubilee or the return of the community's two Boer War heroes. Never, except for political purposes, had a plush private car been sidetracked in Carberry's railway yards," a resident later wrote. "The bride's sister and brother, Edith and Erskine, were among our childhood playmates and we rated an extra scoop of pink ice cream — right out of the freezer in the kitchen — as the band played 'Local Gal Makes Good.'" [3]

Revered in Carberry, R.Y. was feared in the stores. "He was a very cold character," remembers David Kinnear, another Irish immigrant who joined

Eaton's in 1928. Kinnear was posted to Hamilton, Ontario, eighteen months later, and R.Y. visited shortly thereafter. "I put my hand out to shake his hand and he walked right past it."

"He became his own perambulating suggestion box as he made his frequent rounds," wrote Mary-Etta Macpherson in *Shopkeepers to a Nation*. "He liked to stand for a while in Mattress or China, watching the triumphant final act of merchandising; he seemed unaware of his conspicuousness, but every clerk knew this towering mountain of a man with the unsmiling face and the balding dome, and anybody passing close by would hear the tuneless, toneless whistle which was his fixed habit, whether alone or in conversation. After such inspection visits the managers could expect a little hand-written note suggesting improvements in displays or the conduct of personnel." [4]

At the death of her husband, Lady Eaton believed it was her sovereign right to assume the throne and rule the empire. She had been appointed to the board in 1921, and the directors were willing to let her continue in that role following the death of her consort, but they were not about to be ordered around by a female president.

When the crown went to R.Y., a man she considered no more than a pretender, the battle lines were drawn. Her disdain for him and his family was poorly concealed. "She had to fight off the competition from 'R.Y. Bob' as I call him — the cousins — and he was very much into trying to get it away from her," recalls her daughter, Florence McEachren, during an interview beside the swimming pool in her Toronto home. "She managed to keep him at bay. She was guarding it for her late husband. She was very much duty-bound."

There was talk that Edward Johnson and Lady Eaton might marry — he'd been a widower since 1919 — but the relationship never developed that far. Lady Eaton worried that remarriage might complicate the process of her family retaking control at the store. Moreover, she would have had to give up her title, a step she was loath to take. Many among the Toronto establishment still looked down their collective noses at Lady Eaton because she was "trade." As her ladyship, she possessed a royal imprimatur given to few others.

The two branches of the family — "owner Eatons" and "worker Eatons" — were never on easy terms again following Sir John's death. When Lady Eaton asked for a ship so she could sail on the Mediterranean, R.Y. turned her down, arguing that all the money should stay in the business to pay for growth. In the years to come, when Lady Eaton's line returned to power, R.Y.'s own sons in the business would feel thwarted at every turn. Vengeance might take time, but it would be sweet.

⟶

In the 1920s Canadians were becoming avid consumers. Shopping went beyond necessities to include crystal, linen, and other finery. A survey of farmers in southern Ontario found that while only 30 per cent claimed to be doing well economically, 63 per cent had automobiles, 41 per cent owned an organ or piano, and all bought packaged breakfast cereal. In Manitoba a similar study of three hundred farms found that half had no running water and three-quarters no electricity, but 80 per cent had an automobile and 84 per cent a piano, organ, or gramophone. [5]

R.Y. rode the swift current of that demand into Eaton's boldest expansion ever. In 1922, when he assumed power, there were twenty-three Eaton's stores, factories, and buying offices. When R.Y. retired in 1942, the number of locations had increased almost tenfold to 210. Lady Eaton may have disliked him, but R.Y.'s abilities were undeniable.

The Eaton's board of directors met every Tuesday; on Mondays Lady Eaton lay abed. She found such repose salutary and said the day off nicely divided her duties as a director from her role as a mother. She tried to visit every store in the country annually. Inspections always began on the top floor, then moved down through every department, rest room, and lunch room as she chatted to employees along the way.

On one of her first official visits as a vice-president and director, Lady Eaton toured the Winnipeg mail-order buildings with the general manager, Herbert Madison Tucker. The inspection complete, Lady Eaton realized the tour had not been a success and complained to Tucker how little had been accomplished. "Neither one of us smiled," she said. Replied he: "But I don't smile readily."

"You'll have to learn, and we're both going to do better this afternoon," she told him. That walkabout had a different air, and Lady Eaton pronounced their reception more positive as a result. [6]

Following each such walkabout, Lady Eaton prepared written reports containing specific recommendations for her fellow directors. Among the changes she urged were better restaurant facilities in Toronto. She had supped in the dining rooms of department stores in London, England, and admired the Chippendale furniture, Oriental rugs, and brocade curtains. By contrast, the Toronto dining facilities were dowdy. There was a five-hundred-seat cafeteria, a managers' lunch room that held 450, plus the Quick Lunch

Room in the basement. Only the Grill Room could be regarded as even approaching what might be considered well appointed. When the directors refused her request, she said, "I have one favour to ask. I want you to close down the restaurant we now have, for I am ashamed of it." [7]

Later that same day R.Y. called on Lady Eaton at Ardwold to let her know that he had changed his mind. She could oversee the creation of a new restaurant. Lady Eaton immediately engaged Violet Ryley, who had supervised staff and dinners at the Eatons' Walmer Road house before becoming chief dietitian for Canadian military hospitals during the First World War. The result was the Georgian Room, which opened on the ninth floor of the Queen Street store in 1924. Designed by French architect René Cera, it was the city's first fine restaurant. Despite their lack of early support, the directors became enthusiastic and were given their own corner table. An orchestra played at lunch and during afternoon tea. The walls were mirrored, the chandeliers twinkled. Silver was always polished and Lady Eaton regularly inspected the waitresses' nails and hairbands.

Among the veteran waitresses was Sarah, who in the past had prepared lunch for Timothy in his office and was treated as an Eaton-family friend. When Lady Eaton's son Gilbert was later working in Winnipeg and had come to Toronto for a visit that included lunch in the Georgian Room, it was Sarah who served him. "Well, Mr. Gilbert!" she said. "I don't know whether to shake your hand or tie your napkin around your neck!" Replied Gilbert, "I'd like you to do both, Sarah." [8]

Lady Eaton often cited the Georgian Room as a high-profile example of her involvement in operations. When asked in 1929 if she was interested in the stores, she launched into a lecture. "Mercy! I follow everything about the business. That's my job. I'm a director. And let me tell you this: the Georgian Room is my contribution — all mine. That room is the child of my imagination. Me in the business! Why, I spent all day yesterday at the store!

"I know I'm only a woman," she continued, "but did you ever think how useful a woman could be in a business like that? A woman hasn't her nose on the grindstone like a man does. Her instinct is just as good as their business principle. Then, a woman knows the attitude of the buying public. And I travel a great deal and see other stores — that helps." [9]

Lady Eaton's abiding interest in the business seemed deeper than her concern for her own offspring, with whom she spent little time. Sir John had been raised with a plan in place for his future. Such far-sightedness did not seem to exist for the next generation. All Sir John's progeny were simply shuffled out of sight. Timothy, born in 1903, had attended St. Andrew's College, lived in California with a tutor, then went to Brown Public School, University of Toronto Schools, and Appleby College. He was just completing arrangements to enter Cambridge when his father died in 1922.

Timothy carried on with those plans, and within a year of Sir John's death, the next two boys in line, John David and Edgar, were also dispatched to English boarding schools. "After all, it's all British — and my boys are British," Lady Eaton explained. "Here in Canada they'd be expected to live up to a ready-made reputation instead of making their own. And my boys are all big for their years — and perhaps too much would have been expected of them." [10]

Timothy became enamoured of rural life in England and rode with the West Kent Hounds. By the time he was twenty-five in 1928, he was joint master of the Newmarket and Thurlow Hunt, sixty miles north of London, a role he filled for the next three years. Later, from 1933 to 1937, he was joint master of the Toronto and North York Hunt. He worked briefly in the Eaton's engineering department in Winnipeg. "I was put through the mill for several years in Toronto and Winnipeg as just an ordinary employee," said Timothy. "After a certain time, I was allowed to drift away." [11] How different he was from his namesake and grandfather.

John David, born in 1909, followed a similar educational path: Upper Canada College, Trinity College School in Port Hope, then Stowe in Buckinghamshire where the emphasis was on sports and building character. After Stowe, he studied languages at Corpus Christi College, Cambridge. The third son, Edgar, born in 1912, also attended UCC, a prep school at Winkfield Row, Bracknell, then Stowe. In 1934, he began working for the Montreal Eaton's in auto accessories. Gilbert, the youngest, attended Crescent School in Toronto and was shipped off to Wellington House in Kent, followed by Château Boulains, an English school near Fontainebleau, then Collège Municipale in Cannes.

Before going away to school, Gilbert spent most of his early years at home. Both he and his younger sister, Florence, were what was then described as "delicate," and doctors recommended winters in warmer climes. Lady Eaton, herself prone to nervous disorders, seized upon the suggestion and in 1924 rented a villa in Cannes. One of the family's Rolls-Royce automobiles, Bluebird, shipped to London in 1919, was available for her use. Also on hand were a chauffeur and a footman.

While in Cannes, Lady Eaton adopted a four-year-old English girl, Evlyn, who was six months younger than Florence. Evlyn was meant to be a companion for Florence, but the idea backfired badly. Florence came to realize that her mother's rationale was "not a good reason to adopt anyone. It's cruel. She really didn't like her."

Evlyn was everything Florence was not: dark, irreverent, and lively. The two were dressed alike but not treated alike. When they visited the couturiers in Paris to be outfitted, the chief *vendeuse* was instructed: "Ignore the dark one." (Lady Eaton was such a prized client at Givenchy that as late as 1961 Elizabeth Dingman of the *Toronto Daily Star* wrote that when the chief *vendeuse* had learned Dingman was from Canada, she reverently showed the writer a photo autographed decades earlier by Lady Eaton.)

Relations between the girls were uneasy. "It wasn't a terribly happy situation," recalls her daughter Florence. "I got along [with Evlyn] all right. We fought, of course. We had our private language. I really don't think anyone could understand us. We developed our own language between English, French, and Italian. It was a protection against the adults." (The sour experience did not dissuade Florence from adoption, however. Her son, Gilbert, was born in 1947, and after several miscarriages, she and her husband, Frank McEachren, adopted a daughter, Signy. Signy now has three children and is divorced. Gilbert died of cancer in 1984. He and his wife had no children.)

As she began spending more time abroad, Lady Eaton's direct involvement with the stores became limited to the few months each year she spent in Canada. As a result, R.Y. was, for the most part, free to run the business as he chose. By every account, he was not an easy man. While touring the Moncton store, all scrubbed for his visit, he commented to the manager: "The store is so tidy and clean. Don't you ever do any business here?" [12]

On another occasion he became embroiled in a controversy with another manager, one of his own clan. An employee had made a mistake and R.Y. wanted him fired; the manager thought the employee deserved a second chance. After a heated debate, the manager said: "Cousin Bob, why do you have to be so hard to get along with?"

"When you own a business yourself," he replied, "it is easy to be lenient, to grant largesse and to be popular with everyone. When you have been given the responsibility of running a business *in trust* for someone else, it is a different matter." [13]

To hide his fears of inferiority, R.Y. adopted a brusque manner that often frightened others. When one particular suggestion was not carried out as quickly as he believed it should have been, he upbraided the employee, saying: "The gestation period of an elephant is eleven months. You seem to be taking almost that long to act."

At times his directives were so cryptic they were misunderstood. He once called Jack Brockie, head of public relations, and blurted without explanation: "What's the matter with 137? Fix it." Brockie had no idea what R.Y. was talking about, but said he would get on to the situation immediately. He finally concluded that R.Y. must have been referring to one of the delivery wagons. When Brockie phoned delivery and repeated R.Y.'s question, he got a speedy apology and an admission that, yes, 137 had inadvertently been dispatched that morning without its usual overnight wash.

On another occasion R.Y. suggested Eaton's broadcast a choir that was singing in the Georgian Room. Staff dutifully arranged for a local radio station to carry the show only to have him complain: "I didn't hear the singers." He'd meant for the concert to be carried over the store's public-address system. The choral group returned for an encore performance, this time piped throughout the store.

R.Y. was painfully shy and an awkward conversationalist. He lamented, referring to his daughter-in-law Diana: "She's got the gift of the gab and I never had it." He'd spend hours each day putting his thoughts on paper and sending out lengthy letters and memos, rather than dealing directly with people. One such missive was sent to the advertising writer who had drafted an outline for a booklet. Wrote R.Y.: "Cannot imagination run riot as one thinks of Madam Canada sitting snugly by her fireside, while in far Japan, the Eaton Buyers, Toronto & Winnipeg men, are reaching out-of-the-way places for silks, kimonos and crockery that she may be able to see these products in her own store . . . Madam Toronto may in an afternoon walk through her favourite shopping place, see & compare the products of every country of the old world and the new, welcome to ask questions, to be shown gladly but no importunity to buy . . . And to do it in a way that no one is obliged to keep anything that he does not want to keep?" [14]

R.Y. would labour mightily over a memo, then read the entire contents aloud to senior executives. He would also pen brief, pithy epithets that were meant to buck up staff and encourage hard work. "If you keep your shop," he wrote on January 15, 1935, "it will keep you." "The World Contributes, We Distribute," he declared in a memo dated November 10, 1934. [15]

R.Y. even communicated with his family in writing, sending letters to his children — long after they became adults — on an almost daily basis. The only one who rebelled was Alan. At seventeen he informed his father that he would no longer reply. If his father had something to say, he should speak directly. R.Y. agreed; everyone else continued to receive letters.

At times R.Y. functioned as the de facto head of both branches of the family, some of whom were wastrels. Sir John's brother, Colonel William Fletcher Eaton, ran the Eaton's factory in Oshawa that produced ladies' ready-to-wear items, then in 1916 headed the knitting mill in Hamilton. He relied almost totally on Sir John's generosity for the wherewithal of daily life and for the upkeep of Ballymena, his estate in Oakville, where he kept horses.

During the 1920s the Colonel made annual forays to England, purportedly on behalf of the Eaton Knitting Co. Half his expenses were paid by Eaton's; he was personally responsible for the rest. His extravagant reputation was such that every year Percy Portlock, an antiques and wine connoisseur who supervised European offices from London, would be reminded by memo that the Colonel's return transportation was prepaid and he was carrying ample funds. Portlock, first engaged as an office boy in 1905, was warned not to pay for anything and certainly not to let the visitor charge any items to Eaton's London office account.

Sir John's will specified that any debts owed by family members were to be forgiven. And R.Y. had to see that this provision was carried out. In William's case the total was $650,000. William argued that everything hadn't gone into his own pockets. He claimed that a large proportion of the money had been spent on Sir John's behalf when he, William, served as Commissioner of the Boy Scouts of Canada doling out bequests. During the war he'd been on the staff of the assistant director of recruiting for Canada, travelling to raise troops. Even so, the tens of thousands a year that flowed to him from Sir John was a substantial sum in an era when a new car cost $2000. Despite the largesse, by 1926 the Colonel was in financial trouble. Sir John's and the Colonel's sister, Josephine Burnside, decided she wanted to help, so R.Y. was called in to meet with Timothy's widow, Margaret, and Lady Eaton to arrange forgiveness of a $200,000 mortgage held by the three women on the Colonel's house. William died in 1935 at fifty-nine. His wife, Gertrude, died in 1942, after spending the last dozen years of her life at Ballymena as an invalid.

Josephine handled her money in a more astute manner. Her Clarendon Avenue mansion, Burnside, built in 1930 on two acres, had a gazebo, porte-cochère entrance, and a system with two dozen bells to call the help. The garden contained forty different trees and shrubs, as well as a birdbath with the inscription "When the birds are here, are the angels?" [16] When she died in 1943, her estate was valued at $962,869. At that time Josephine had been living on Dunvegan Avenue, having donated Burnside to the Canadian Mothercraft

Society in return for a token payment. The society used the mansion for twenty-one years to teach infant care, then sold the house, with its sixteen bedrooms and eight baths, for $350,000 to the Canadian Imperial Bank of Commerce for use as a staff training centre. All else was disposed of at auction: paintings, china, furniture, even nightdresses that had never been worn.

—

While R.Y. worked, the owner Eatons played. Lady Eaton's annual schedule took on a predictable rhythm during the 1920s: a fall store tour, winters in Europe and summers at Kawandag with its oak interiors and two cut-stone fireplaces. Rooms were named after the decor, like the Butterfly Room, or the view, like the Sunrise and Sunset rooms. Flowers from the garden filled turquoise terra cotta vases throughout the house. Breakfast was outside on the patio under a pergola. Honey was served in containers shaped like bees, the milk pitchers featured cats. Picnics were extravaganzas prepared by staff and carried to the designated site. Corn roasts featured individual servings of butter, wrapped in cheesecloth, which were then kept on ice until the very moment they were needed on the hot cobs.

There were horses for riding on wooded trails, a golf course that grew to six holes, swimming in the lake, cricket on a cinder pitch, or tennis taught by a pro on clay courts. The two-storey boathouse built in 1925 had ten rooms and four slips for boats that included the thirty-foot cabin cruiser *Dolly Durkin* and the seventy-five-foot *Kawandag*, a solid-mahogany gasoline-powered yacht built in 1922 at the Ditchburn boatworks in nearby Gravenhurst. When Lady Eaton wanted to withdraw from the hurly-burly, she retreated to the property's two-room log cabin with its two fireplaces.

An engineer and his family lived on the property year round, grounds maintenance required a crew of fifteen, while the gardener had half a dozen assistants. Lady Eaton's brother, Arthur, worked at Eaton's for a time, then retired to live at Kawandag. He joined the Bracebridge Rotary Club and had the welcome, if unusual, habit of paying his annual membership fees several times each year. (In 1945 Lady Eaton sold Kawandag, which was then run as a lodge until the 1960s. For two years it was Fort Kawandag, a theme park featuring mock battles between British redcoats and native Canadians. At thirty cents apiece, children were provided with Daisy smoke rifles and cardboard garrison hats so they could help defend the fort. In 1967 Rosseau Lake College opened on the property, a co-ed residential private school with one hundred students. On January 30, 1973, the mansion was destroyed by fire.)

After the first two winters in Cannes, Lady Eaton and her court moved to Fiesole, just north of Florence, Italy. They stayed at Villa Natalia, originally built for Queen Elizabeth of Romania who, fifty years earlier, wrote novels using the pen name Carmen Sylva. Lady Eaton's staff was sizable. In addition to several local Italian servants, there was the Ardwold butler, his wife, the chauffeur (who would eventually teach all the children how to drive), a tutor, even a dentist brought from Toronto.

For long vacations, the boys would travel to Italy from boarding school in England; sometimes they would all meet in Switzerland for skiing. Although the girls saw more of Lady Eaton than did their brothers, most of their upbringing was carried out by a nurse. At fourteen Florence and Evlyn were sent to Moira House, an English boarding school in Eastbourne. In 1937 they attended Villa Malatesta, a finishing school in Florence where they studied everything from fencing to the art of polite conversation. They were assured that most people from England used a sponge in their baths, so a guaranteed conversation starter was said to be: "Do you suck your sponge?" The girls yearned for home. On one occasion, as Lady Eaton departed on her own to set sail for Canada, Florence wailed: "Oh, Mother, please bring a bit of grass from home — I want to eat it." [17]

Times together were packed with pomp and meant to be educational. The boys would travel in Canada with their mother, her maid, their tutor, and a French governess. Whenever the group visited a location where there was an Eaton store, they were met by the local manager, who would see to all their needs.

One such excursion took them through the Canadian West to Vancouver, then by steamer north to Juneau and into Yukon. Another was a motor tour to the Maritimes. In Sydney, Nova Scotia, Lady Eaton, accompanied by Timothy and John David, descended nine hundred feet into a coal mine. Wrote an interviewer in 1930: "To hear Lady Eaton tell of donning oil-skins, getting up on one of the small mine-cars behind the electric locomotive, and riding three miles under the sea to the coal face, was as good as reading a 'best seller.' Now and then Timothy added his contribution to the story, which had the virtue of being fact, not fiction." [18]

R.Y.'s family enjoyed an equally privileged life. During the 1920s R.Y.'s five children (Margaret, Jack, Erskine, Alan, and Nora) spent two years living in the south of France with their mother, a nanny, and a governess. R.Y. had worked in Paris but never learned French; he did not want his children to be similarly unilingual. Hazel seized the opportunity to study piano in Paris. R.Y. would travel by ocean liner to visit.

When the family returned home from one such sojourn in the fall of 1923, R.Y., freshly minted as president of Eaton's the previous year, had decided that they would move from Forest Hill to Rosedale. He'd bought One Highland Avenue from Mrs. Harry Ryrie, widow of the high-fashion jeweller. R.Y. named it Killyree, after his birthplace.

The huge mansion sprawled nearly twenty thousand square feet on four acres of land. Six hundred guests could attend a Christmas reception. For more intimate dinners the favoured predinner drink was an old-fashioned. The butler made the concoctions in the kitchen starting with a cube of sugar in the bottom of each glass. He then added a splash of bitters and let the two get used to each other's presence. Next came the rye and fruit; by the time the drinks were served, the sugar would have fully dissolved and the constituent parts have smoothly blended.

Dinner was served by the butler and two maids, then guests retired to the two-storey music room that R.Y. had added to the original dwelling. The eighty-by-forty-foot room could easily seat 150 guests for recitals on the grand piano or pipe organ and often included many of the important personages of the day. Among the regulars was George Drew, who in 1936 married Fiorenza, daughter of opera tenor Edward Johnson, and was premier of Ontario from 1943 to 1948, then leader of the federal Progressive Conservative Party until 1956.

Following Sunday-morning services at Timothy Eaton Memorial Church was a roast-beef dinner for family and a few close friends. If one of the offspring had invited a date to lunch, R.Y. peppered the guest with questions. He was only satisfied if the visitor had all the facts at hand to buttress any statement. On Christmas day one year R.Y. received a phone call from a customer complaining that his food order from Eaton's had not arrived. Within the hour R.Y. was at the customer's door with the items.

In addition to the Toronto mansion, R.Y. also had a ten-room summer place called Glen Ireton. The fifteen-acre property on Lake Ontario half an hour west of Toronto in Port Credit had a sixty-foot pool, all-weather tennis court, brick-and-stucco dining-room building, as well as servants' quarters, dock, boathouse, and a garage for eight cars. An employee from delivery was transferred to Glen Ireton in the summer to look after the horses. If a child's bedroom needed a decorative border, the store's best painter was dispatched.

By the mid-1930s Port Credit was no longer fashionable, so he sold that home and bought another summer place, which he called Ryestone, on Georgian Bay near Go Home Bay.

While both the owner and worker Eatons lived in opulence, R.Y. looked at life differently. Unlike the children of the owner Eatons, who seemed to be simply set adrift, R.Y.'s offspring were raised to excel. "You had to be a champion to even say you could do anything in that family," says daughter-in-law Diana, a fashion commentator who married Alan in 1951. "R.Y. hadn't had the chance as a child but he thought, 'I've got the chance, I've got this money, my kids are going to make it,' and they had to be winners."

They learned to play tennis and piano and to ride horses. R.Y. believed that if you knew how to manage a horse, you'd be able to manage people. The horses were stabled at the family's Oriole Farm in North Toronto (later sold to the Eglinton Hunt Club), and the boys regularly entered jumping events in Canada, the United States, and the United Kingdom. A trainer named Paddy once rode the course during a competition in which R.Y.'s offspring were entered. R.Y. fired him for his insolence; Paddy's job was to instruct Eatons, not indulge himself. The daughters were raised in a manner appropriate for young women of privilege. In 1932 Hazel and daughters Margaret and Nora were presented at Buckingham Palace.

In 1931 Erskine, then eighteen, and Jack, nineteen, were part of a four-member Canadian team entered in the Royal Olympia horse show in London. The two, along with Don Hunter of Toronto and Marshall Cleland of Hamilton, wore the uniforms of the Governor General's Body Guards. Erskine finished second in an open jumping class out of sixty-four entries. They went on to the Dublin horse show, where Jack came fourth in a field of thirty-seven. Erskine entered two events, despite having been injured in England. Alan Eaton, then fifteen, took a fourth in one of the civilian jumps.

"The sons of prominent families have a tough time, after all, in the field of sport," wrote Gregory Clark of their exploits in the *Star Weekly*. "In other fields of endeavour, their lives are handicapped by the necessity of living up to the traditions of success of their forebears. How splendid then for these four young horsemen, after twenty-two years of Canada's absence from the high places of the sport of kings and warriors, to submit themselves to the military rigours, the hard training, the day-in, day-out cold routine of preparing to meet, in the supreme test, the picked masters of an ancient art from all the leading military nations of the earth. And how fine of them to bring home coveted honours for which governments of the world spend hard money." [19]

R.Y. may not have been an owner, but he certainly shared Timothy's and Sir John's mania for building the company. In March 1925 R.Y.'s expansion program began in earnest when he acquired Goodwin's Ltd., a department store on Montreal's Ste-Catherine Street. Once the purchase was completed, R.Y. invoked the Victorian views he'd been taught by Timothy. He killed a program known as the Homelovers' Club that allowed shoppers to defer payments. He preferred cash, despite the fact that credit was becoming increasingly popular — more than 20 per cent of all retail sales in Canada were made using instalment plans.

Over the next eighteen months the old store was pulled down, replaced by a six-storey structure of white Manitoba marble that, by 1930, had grown to nine storeys in the block bounded by Ste-Catherine, Victoria, Burnside, and University. The display windows were framed in bronze, with friezes and cornices above; the floors were finished in travertine; the basement had a groceteria. "A sturdy and handsome brother of the pretentious Eaton stores in Toronto and Winnipeg," declared the *Montreal Star.* [20]

Also included was an art deco restaurant on the ninth floor that could seat 550. Architect Jacques Carlu was a professor of design at the Massachusetts Institute of Technology and director of the American Summer School of Fine Arts in Fontainebleau, France. The restaurant had raised platforms at either end for fashion shows and a public-address system concealed behind metal grille work. There were marble columns, clerestory windows, and an opaque skylight, all meant to evoke the dining salons Carlu had designed for the luxury French liner, *Île de France.*

In 1926 R.Y. built a warehouse in Montreal, a factory in Saint John, New Brunswick, and a store in Regina. During the next three years, Eaton's added stores in Hamilton, Saskatoon, Calgary, and Edmonton. In 1928 alone, R.Y. opened three new Eaton's locations, a fifteen-store Teco chain, fifty-four mail-order outlets, forty-three groceterias, and a buying office. He also paid $4.5 million for Canadian Department Stores Ltd., a twenty-one store group formed two years earlier by struggling independents. The new association hadn't helped; CDS was bankrupt. Except for one location in downtown Montreal, all the stores were in Ontario and continued to operate under the separate banner. [21]

One spur to the expansion was the strong economy, but there was another propelling need. Growth in the mail-order business had stalled. After peaking at $60 million a year in 1920, sales began to fall. Canadians were becoming more mobile, and even rural shoppers no longer relied on the catalogue for all their needs. Farm families could drive to town to shop where the choice of gramophone record titles might go beyond the catalogue's offerings: "The Little Ford Rambled Right Along," "Si's Been Drinking Cider," and "Bounce Me, John, I've Rubber Heels On."

Eaton's opened more warehouses for catalogue goods and more mail-order outlets in an attempt to speed up delivery as a way of competing with local merchants. But such expansion was expensive and seemed to do little to meet the changes in the marketplace.

As the empire grew, R.Y. also tried to emulate his predecessors' patriarchal ways. In 1923 he acquired 225 acres near Stouffville, thirty-five miles north of Toronto, and built a summer camp. Called Shadow Lake, it was used by female employees for the next three decades. There was a nine-hole golf course, two tennis courts, horseback riding, boating, and swimming in a twenty-acre lake. Campers slept in five bungalows; milk, cream, eggs, and vegetables came from the camp farm. Attire was middy and bloomers; fee for a week was $5.

The Eaton Operatic Society (first formed in 1919 as Eaton's Choral Society) performed Gilbert and Sullivan for the general public. Moncton had a Girls' Club, and Vancouver held an annual picnic. There was also a dental clinic and two hospitals for Toronto employees, one for the Queen Street store, the other for the factories, where shoppers who felt indisposed could also turn for treatment.

In Winnipeg, men bought their own arena for curling and employee facilities on the outskirts of the city included two baseball diamonds, two football fields, a cricket pitch, cinder running track, six tennis courts, and sand piles for the children. Twice a day in the Winnipeg mail-order building, employees halted work and spent fifteen minutes doing calisthenics to music in their own gym.

Such building on the past was encouraged; fresh thinking was frowned on. Each of the ten men who were directors with R.Y. during the 1920s had begun at the bottom, usually at age fifteen working for $5 a week, then battled their way up. Department heads were no different. Sweat and detailed inside knowledge were the only criteria for the top. R.Y.'s senior managers, J.J. Vaughan and Harry McGee, were both long-term employees. Vaughan had joined Eaton's in 1903 and quickly gained Sir John's confidence. He was elected a director in 1917, secretary-treasurer in 1918, and a vice-president in 1933.

McGee, who'd started in 1883 at $6 a week, had become a vice-president with duties that included construction, engineering, and carpentry. In 1928, on the occasion of his forty-fifth anniversary with the firm, R.Y. gave him a Rolls-Royce. Employees sang a song to McGee they had written to the tune of "When You and I Were Young, Maggie":

> I walked by the carpets today, Harry,
> And thought all the salesmen were slow,
> For there I remembered the way, Harry,
> You yanked up the stocks from below. [22]

R.Y. tried to instil his own highbrow interests in the average consumer. In 1926 he opened the Fine Art Galleries on the fifth floor of the Toronto home furnishings building. The first exhibit had fifteen paintings, including a Sir Joshua Reynolds from the collection of Viscount Leverhulme. Not content with visiting exhibits, R.Y. travelled to London in 1928 and acquired a painting by famous Dutch artist Rembrandt van Rijn. *Portrait of a Woman with a Handkerchief* cost Eaton's $150,000. The painting was displayed in stores in Winnipeg, Saskatoon, Montreal, Calgary, and Toronto.

Private pleasures were one thing, but public life was painful for R.Y. At receptions he relied on Hazel to whisper names in his ear as they met guests he'd been introduced to on earlier occasions. There was the requisite box at the Royal Winter Fair, seats for the Toronto Symphony, and membership on the board of governors of the Toronto Conservatory of Music. R.Y. had a particular interest in the Art Gallery of Toronto (renamed the Art Gallery of Ontario in 1966) and was president from 1922 to 1940.

At home R.Y. had to be in total control. His Georgian Bay property, Ryestone, was on Townsend Island six miles from Honey Harbour. (Former Ontario premier Bill Davis and other members of his family have occupied the southern half of the island since 1928.) The main chalet had four bedrooms and seven bathrooms. There was also a four-bedroom guest house, as well as a cottage for Henri, who looked after the property.

All visitors, even family members, followed the regimented schedule R.Y. posted daily; it covered meals, fishing outings, tennis matches, and canasta games. Visitors at Ryestone included Edward Johnson, who seemed readily able to transfer his fealty from the owner Eatons to the worker Eatons. Johnson would arrive by boat and break into song as soon as he set foot on the dock. As he walked up to the house, the tenor would continue singing as a joyful way of announcing his presence. Family members and guests would gather, as cottagers often do, to have a drink and watch the sunset. As the fiery disc first touched the horizon, Johnson would strike a note, hold it until the final shard disappeared from view, then swing into another song.

Across the country the growing number of stores meant increased sales, but by 1929 profitability was lagging. Costs had risen substantially. Eaton's sales in Toronto were twice the level of Simpson's, but operating profit was only one-third higher than it had been at the beginning of the decade.

The financial difficulties caused rumours of family quarrelling. Stories also resurfaced about new owners coming in from outside. A Toronto friend of Timothy's cabled him in England to say he'd heard a report of feuding in the family. A syndicate was said to be buying control. Timothy contacted John David at Cambridge; he in turn consulted Lady Eaton in Florence. She responded by issuing a public statement: "Lady Eaton replies rumours of internal disagreement most malicious, untrue and absolutely without foundation. You may tell your syndicate there is no sale of my stock. You could as easily purchase the Bank of England." [23]

For proof of Eaton's potent rank and powerful standing, in 1929 no one needed to look further than the massive edifice under construction in Toronto. In 1910 Jack had begun assembling land at Yonge and College, but kept his acquisitions so secret that the Toronto newspapers called it the "mystery block." In 1912 the *Toronto World* revealed Eaton's as the owners, based on architectural drawings seen at customs on their way to Toronto from New York. After spending an estimated $3 million on land, Eaton's was said to be planning a $2-million ten-storey structure. The war intervened and all plans were put on hold.

In the early 1920s Eaton's encouraged Simpson's to join in a northward relocation of both retailers by offering the competitor the eastern portion of Eaton's holdings. Simpson's declined and in 1923 began expanding its own Queen Street store west to Bay Street. The $6 million addition, including the Arcadian Court restaurant, was completed in 1928. That July Eaton's announced a thirty-storey building rising 670 feet at College Street. The plan was for all of Eaton's operations at Queen Street — stores, factories, and offices — to move the six blocks north and leave Simpson's stranded.

Despite the fact that R.Y. was in charge, the owner branch of the family was always on hand to receive the glory. In September 1929 Lady Eaton, accompanied by her two daughters, inspected the construction site. Amid the din of steam shovels, cement mixers, and shouting workmen, she seized the opportunity to remind the journalists who'd assembled that this project had been her husband's idea nearly twenty years before.

As for R.Y., he got but a condescending nod. "If he has any fault, it is that he is exceedingly modest. He doesn't like to let his right hand know what his left is doing. Sometimes I think it wise to let the public know just what we are doing." [24]

She expected her offspring to join the business. "There is ample room for all of them, even the girls." She had already spotted a possible heir apparent. "It is not yet decided on whom the mantle of Sir John Eaton will fall but I believe my second boy John David has the personality, ability and temperament to undertake the task." [25]

In an interview given at Ardwold later that month she continued her campaign on John David's behalf: "He has a flair for business. He has what you might call the buying and selling instinct — some people seem born for it." [26]

At ten o'clock sharp Thursday morning, October 30, 1930, a limousine deposited John David and Lady Eaton at the newly completed College Street store. Police on horseback controlled the crowds surging to see the dapper young man with his silk hat, morning coat, and spats.

This was more than just a symbolic family participation in the grand opening of the country's largest home-furnishings building. At twenty-one John David had given up his university studies to join the business. His presence charged the occasion with a meaning not unlike the investiture of the Prince of Wales. It would be another twelve years before the crown was officially passed to John David, but the title of heir apparent was now officially conferred. Barely eight years into his twenty-year regency, R.Y. had become passé.

As cameras recorded the arrival of the young prince before a crowd estimated at ten thousand, John David was greeted by George Fenton, Eaton's longest-serving doorman. John David then fitted a golden key into the lock — the same key used by his older brother, Timothy, to open the Winnipeg store in 1905. Inside, John David threw a switch, which sounded gongs, and the store was officially declared open. Thousands of eager shoppers poured in, filling the aisles and storming three banks of marble-faced elevators.

"Surely, too, it was one of the most representative gatherings Toronto has ever witnessed!" gushed a report in the *Eaton News*. "Didn't we see a precious little black pickaninny about three years old, battered sailor cap cocked over one ear, stockings hanging down-o, while he dragged on the skirt of his mammy? And weren't there 'ristocratic ladies and knighted gentlemen just as thrilled about it all as our own enthusiastic office boy?" [27]

But the College Street store was nothing like the thirty-six-storey edifice originally announced. The planned five million square feet of retail space had shrunk to slightly more than six hundred thousand. Among the invited guests was Sir Joseph Flavelle, who asked Eaton's vice-president Charles Boothe: "Charlie, why didn't you finish this building and move the business up to College Street?" Replied Boothe: "Sir Joseph, we didn't have the resources." [28] Boothe's lament went to the heart of the family's problem: there was always money for personal pleasure, but business ventures could often be starved for cash. Harry McGee, vice-president of construction, bravely predicted that the building would eventually be some six times larger, but such expansion was impossible.

"Astoundingly, these grand plans were not accompanied by any well-conceived building programme," wrote Cynthia Jane Wright in her doctoral thesis on retailing at Eaton's from 1920 to 1950. "Eaton's had little idea how to proceed after the first stage of the building was completed in 1930. For example, while a tower was projected, the plans for it contained no provision for elevators or staircases." [29] That lack of foresight became Eaton's perennial problem. Refusal by the family to leave money in the business for capital expenditure and a continuing lack of vision were serious failings that would haunt the business in the decades to come.

What was erected stood as a poignant reminder of the excesses of the Roaring Twenties in the depth of the Great Depression. The building signalled both the peak of Eaton's and the beginning of the end. The exterior of the seven-storey building was done in ivory Tyndall limestone from a quarry east of Winnipeg. The cladding soon gave the store its derogatory descriptive "The White Elephant." There was also brown granite from Gananoque, Ontario, and black granite from Mount Johnson, Quebec. The brown-veined marble used for the pillars and colonnade came from Europe. Fittings were of burl walnut and ebonized birch. Period display rooms were filled with fine furniture that few could afford. On the fifth floor was a reproduction of Marie Antoinette's boudoir at Versailles, along with representations of rooms from Hampton Court and the days of King Charles I. An entire room had been removed from an English manor, Haddon Hall, transported to College Street, and reassembled in meticulous detail. In a fine-art gallery on the second floor

were temporary exhibits, as well as items from the growing permanent collection, including R.Y.'s Rembrandt and a replica of Rodin's *The Thinker.*

Architect Jacques Carlu was again hired to design the restaurant. The
Round Room was decorated in banana yellow, black, silver, and beige. Under
a domed ceiling were murals by his wife, Natasha, and a central fountain of
glass with underwater lighting.

The seventh-floor Eaton Auditorium, with a concert stage and seating for
1275, opened on March 26, 1931. Also designed by Carlu, the auditorium followed the same colour scheme as the restaurant. Walls were covered in pale
gold fabricord, chairs were swathed in black upholstery, and diffused lighting
glowed between bands of ebonized wood.

The organ, built by world-renowned Casavant Frères of St. Hyacinthe, Quebec, had 5804 pipes set as a semicircular backdrop on stage, four keyboards,
and ninety stops, and was equipped for harp and chime effects. R.Y.'s direc-
tive to the auditorium manager about the tony clientele the new musical
venue was hoping to attract was unapologetic in its snobbery: "The audiences
that come are to wear formal evening dress." [30]

Since Timothy's time, Eaton's customers had tended to be working- or mid-
dle-class Canadians. The 1920s had seen a decline in goods produced at home
and a resulting increase in the number of purchased items. Fine furniture was
the heart of Eaton's College Street, a selection of goods that was not only meant
to convey that newfound consumerism to the carriage trade, but also to serve as
the arbiter of good taste. A group of interior decorators was assembled, led by
Herbert Irvine, who travelled the world foraging for furniture and fabrics.

Eaton's sponsored a contest to design the Ideal Ontario Home, a two-
storey residence that was fully reproduced in the store. The winning entry
had four bedrooms, three bathrooms, servants' quarters, and a billiard room
and cost $30,000. Eaton's had gone so far upscale that much of what was dis-
played was well beyond the reach of all but a few customers.

Still, the structure captivated Torontonians. "Standing, the other night, some
twelve miles north of the corner of College and Yonge Streets, the unexpected
advent of a beam of dazzling light flashed from the western horizon to the eastern, illuminating as it had never been illuminated before, the beautiful landscape
of North York," wrote a columnist in the November 1930 issue of *Construction.*

" 'That,' said the friend who was beside us, 'is the beacon upon the roof of
Eaton's new store.' Judged by all standards, what better method of advertising
could a commercial institution 'hit upon' than the use of this colossal shaft of
light which, flashing at a few moments' interval throughout the night and to

all points of the compass, reminds hundreds of thousands of spectators of the existence and prestige of the T. Eaton Company Limited?" [31]

The Great Depression ended any hope for prestige. World trade collapsed and few countries were hit harder than Canada. Between 1929 and 1933 Canada's gross national product fell 42 per cent. Unemployment rose to 30 per cent. The western provinces were bankrupt.

Canadians had little money to spend on anything but basics. The average sale in the Toronto store in 1924 was $1.18; by 1933 it was ninety-one cents. In Winnipeg the average sale in 1929 was $1.01; by 1933, sixty-four cents. Montreal fell from $1.64 in 1929 to $1.07 in 1933. The typical mail order dropped from $1.93 in 1924 to $1.26 in 1933. Profits in Montreal collapsed from more than $1 million a year in 1929 to just over $100,000 four years later. The Queen Street store lost $2 million in two years. At Canadian Department Stores only three of the twenty-one outlets were profitable. The College Street store was a consistent money loser.

The Eaton family floated blissfully above the financial catastrophe. In the nine years ending 1933 the T. Eaton Co. paid dividends averaging $525,555 annually, with Sir John's estate receiving 89 per cent of that payout. In 1929 there was a one-time dividend of $940,000 to the family, a last draining of the goblet from the riotous twenties.

In 1929 all real estate, stores, and warehouses were gathered together and "sold" by the family to a new company, T. Eaton Realty Co. "In the process, the assets were appreciated $16,000,000 and the estate came out with $12,000,000 in stock of the realty company," reported the June 1934 issue of *Dry Goods and Stylewear Review*. The timing couldn't have been better. Values of those real estate assets, in some cases held in family hands for decades, had reached their peak and would not see such heights again for twenty-five years. Lady Eaton's message to the country was sanguine. "If worry would clean up present world conditions," she said in 1932, "it would have been accomplished in 1929." [32]

Even in death the Eatons seem to transcend the struggles of mere mortals. In March 1933 Timothy's widow, Margaret, lay ill with pneumonia at Raymar, her Tudor-style home in Oakville, west of Toronto. [33] Doctors judged her condition too grave for her to return to her Lowther Avenue house in Toronto.

There was nothing left to do but keep her comfortable and ease her breathing with oxygen. As Margaret's life ebbed away, the gods seemed to be ordering events. Joe Fisher was the first janitor at the Margaret Eaton School of Literature and Expression. Because the building was done in Greek Revival style and had a Greek motto, Margaret had always called him Hermes, as if Fisher were the messenger for the gods. But Hermes had another role in mythology; he conducted souls to the next world.

On Thursday, March 16, 1933, school principal Emma Scott Nasmith was at home worriedly awaiting news of Margaret's condition. The telephone rang and a trembling voice announced: "Mrs. Nasmith, Grandfather died last night — Joe Fisher. You remember — Hermes." [34]

With the path properly prepared by her Hermes, Margaret Eaton died two days later, at ninety-one. Declared an editorial in the *Toronto Star*: "Somehow, like Queen Victoria, she came to represent in concrete example certain simplicities and loyalties that the people not only admired but loved." [35]

Over the door at Raymar were these lines by Van Dyke:

> The lintel low enough to keep out pomp and pride.
> The threshold high enough to turn deceit aside,
> The door-bands strong enough from robbers to defend,
> This door will open at a touch to every friend. [36]

In the eye of the depression's storm, governments pleaded with Eaton's to maintain employment levels. Instead, Eaton's wielded a double-edged sword, eliminating jobs for many and reducing wages for the rest. Sixty years of mutual loyalty were suddenly unravelled. Employment at Eaton's fell from 30,764 in 1929 to 25,736 in 1933. Wages were slashed by 10 per cent to 22 per cent, depending on the department. Employee discounts on purchases were halved, falling from 10 per cent to 5 per cent. The Saturday half holiday was cancelled, except during the summer. If a single female married a non-Eaton's employee, she was expected to quit. Her husband would provide, went the thinking. If two Eaton's employees were wed, again, the wife was forced to resign. Many was the wedding kept secret to preserve both pay packets.

Just before Christmas 1930, R.Y. thanked customers and staff, claiming that Eaton's had delivered more parcels that year than ever before. The following year, his message was equally upbeat: "Our aisles filled with busy buying crowds was in these days a cheering sight for all." [37]

At times, R.Y. appeared oblivious. "I'd sooner dance than eat," he once said. At Round Room parties he'd take a twirl around the floor with an employee. The Eaton Auditorium featured appearances by Nelson Eddy, Lily Pons, mezzo soprano Risë Stevens, and comedienne Gracie Fields.

For ordinary Canadians, tickets for such performances were out of reach. In Winnipeg farmers would bring their eggs to the Eaton's grading station and be given vouchers that could be redeemed in the store. Eaton's had its own creamery in the Alexander Avenue warehouse where they made Sun Glow butter, as well as buttermilk that sold for three cents a glass at the store's third-floor standup bar.

Rather than interior design gee-gaws there was instead a blood tonic made by the Eaton's drug factory, called Beef, Iron & Wine. The standing joke was that the concoction consisted of 90 per cent cheap Portuguese sherry, an Oxo cube, and a rusty nail. Once the sherry barrels were empty, they were packed with mincemeat for weeks of aging. "When the barrels were opened, the bakers could get high from the aroma," recalls Alan Finnbogason, who joined the Winnipeg store in the 1930s at seventeen and stayed forty-seven years, rising to operating manager. "No wonder everyone in Winnipeg thought that Eaton's mincemeat pies were the best."

But the glorious past of Eaton's would never be savoured again. "The great departmentals would . . . survive the Depression years," wrote David Monod in *Store Wars*. "But they would emerge chastened — less eager to cut prices, less anxious to bare-fist it with their competitors. They were now more willing to behave like yesterday's heroes: giants that moved a little more slowly, saw a little less clearly, and were having trouble keeping up with the wild enthusiasms of their younger rivals." [38]

Eaton's heyday was at an end. Timothy had begun the voyage, Sir John had guided the vessel in the second generation. Cousin Bob had enjoyed at his back the warm trade winds of the 1920s when a steady hand on the tiller was sufficient to keep the empire moving. In the decades that followed, Eaton's would glide along with all sails set. To all outward appearances she seemed seaworthy enough, but below decks the dry rot had begun.

CHAPTER FOUR

LADY EATON: THE DOWAGER QUEEN

⸻

Timothy may have been the visionary founder and Sir John the gadabout heir, but neither captured public attention for as long as Sir John's widow, Lady Eaton. For much of the twentieth century she was the perennial First Lady for an adoring public. More than any other member of the House of Eaton, it was she who formed and framed the nation's perception of Canada's royal family.

Where R.Y. was taciturn, Flora McCrea Eaton was outspoken. Where he was furtive, she flounced. While the business was private, she was most definitely a public — even theatrical — persona. She joined picket lines, wrote letters to the editor, injected herself into politics, and revelled in organizing great events. For a small-town girl, she swiftly learned how to live in grand style.

When Lady Eaton returned to Canada from her annual Mediterranean sojourn, she'd want the world to know that the court was back. She'd invite a journalist to Ardwold for tea, then try to outdo her own outrageous remarks of previous years. Her most audacious and controversial comments were about Italy and that country's Fascist dictator Benito Mussolini prior to the Second World War.

"Italy is the brightest and happiest of lands. Mussolini has done much for the country and no more do the beggars in the streets and around the cathedrals annoy everyone," she said in 1927. "The streets are clean as if they had been newly swept and all the cities look better. I have never seen such happy people as in Italy today."

She praised Il Duce, saying that as long as he remained in charge, Italy would be able to withstand any storm. "Mussolini is not really in good health, he suffers intense pain and the only relief he gets is in distracting his thoughts by playing the violin." [1]

"I think it is so fine that despite the rigid economy Italy has been under, Mussolini realized the value of music and backed the opera there while in England Mr. Churchill refused the opera support," she reported in 1929. "Such a difference from ten years ago. The people are happy and prosperous and the country spells progress." [2]

In 1930 she told of hearing Mussolini speak in Florence. "Just after Mussolini had made that speech, my little girl and I left the most crowded part of the Cascine. As he drove by we cheered, bowed and clapped our hands in our British way. Mussolini turned, bowed in return, and then gave us a full salute, and as he did so he smiled in a way that illuminated his whole countenance. He has a wonderful smile and is far from being the grim ogre depicted by the cartoonists." [3]

Her son, Gilbert, became similarly enamoured of Germany in the mid-1930s. He published several glowing pieces in *Canadian Comment,* including one describing his visit to the Nazi school at Feldafing in the Bavarian Alps. Gilbert swallowed the official line that this was not a military school even though the 220 young men had each been issued four different military uniforms and most of them planned careers as soldiers.

"The class I visited consisted of boys about 12 years of age," wrote Gilbert. "They were discussing the Jewish problem. It was interesting to note that they did not speak vindictively of the Jews, they merely said that most of the Jews in Germany were of an undesirable type which entered the country, having no national feelings for it, to profit at the expense of the German citizens, and were therefore undesirable." [4]

After the Second World began, Lady Eaton's tune changed. In 1941, for example, she went on a tirade against those Canadians who were slow to buy war bonds. "During the years from 1935 to 1937 I spent three or four months each year in Germany. Nothing that has been done so far in Canada can equal the warlike show that I saw daily no matter what part of Germany I happened to be in. Today I saw the first tanks that I have seen in Canada. In 1936 I saw them rolling through the streets of Munich in just such a military show. I was in Austria between 1933 and 1935 and was in Vienna when Hitler was elected. There were many in those days who thought perhaps Hitler would be the solution for their troubles in Austria. I never could see this, and said so whenever it was mentioned." [5]

Such public statements were not the only way Lady Eaton sought attention.

In 1933 she was invited to be presented at court to George V and Queen Mary. Being selected was a signal honour; much preparation was required. A floor-length gown was ordered and fitted, the art of curtseying closely studied, and there was a round of tea parties to attend.

On the designated day Buckingham Palace was a scurry of white-wigged servants in buckled shoes. The long queue of guests had to pass by a footman with a wand whose role was to spread out a lady's train in the approved manner. Each loyal subject was announced, then genuflected to their enthroned Royal Majesties. During the two-hour ceremony, some eight hundred people were thus presented.

When she was next in Toronto, nothing would do but for Lady Eaton to don the very dress she'd worn at court so the members of the Eaton Girls' Club could gape at the splendour. It was pink, shading to rose at the hem, with a similarly shaded and beaded train. She carried a pink ostrich fan and wore a diamond tiara.

That was not her only encounter with the royals. There were garden parties, attendance at the 1937 coronation of George VI in Westminster Abbey, and a one-hour audience with Queen Mary at Marlborough House.

For all her gadding about, Lady Eaton claimed to dislike high society. "I believe I'm a sociable being, as far as that goes — but I never had any particular flair for 'society' life. I'm afraid I wouldn't be called what is a social success. The kind of life I lead prevents it. I really couldn't give up my time to that sort of thing." [6]

Lady Eaton's poor protests were lost amid the problems of the depression as Eaton's tried to distract Canadians from their economic ills. The company sponsored a seven-week series of one-hour radio concerts featuring Handel, Bizet, Tchaikovsky, and Gilbert and Sullivan. Eaton's also launched the Good Deed Club in Hamilton in 1933, and the idea soon spread to Winnipeg, Edmonton, Calgary, and Vancouver. The Saturday-morning radio show featured public school children talking about how they'd been helpful to each other. The youngster who'd done the best "good deed of the week" was awarded a certificate and a fifteen-jewel watch.

In an effort to spur spending, Eaton's ran what today would be called advocacy ads, trumpeting the macro-economic benefits of consumerism. A full-page ad that ran January 3, 1933 included a column of sale items (boys' shirts at sixty-nine cents and girls' sweaters for $1.69) plus a lesson in economics. "If people refrain from buying, a shrinkage in employment occurs. . . . Less spending means less work to do and more unemployment. Unemployment is universally regarded as the bane of today. Unemployment is simply consumption falling away below capacity for production."

In Ontario alone, claimed the ad, 278 municipalities had benefitted during the previous year from Eaton's purchases of goods. Figures cited ranged from $22 million in Toronto to $141,000 in Carleton Place. "We are ready to buy more and more according to public demand." [7]

But Eaton's had serious problems beyond its image that no public-relations campaign could fix. Like most politicians, Prime Minister R. B. Bennett was not above shifting blame for bad times. So when Trade and Commerce Minister Henry Herbert Stevens decided to take on the top-hat crowd, Bennett did not dissuade him. Stevens, who was first elected to parliament in 1911 as the Conservative member for Vancouver City and had been defeated by Bennett for the party's leadership in 1927, had his own agenda. Although he was a former businessman, he despised the wealthy and admired leftwing radicals. He decided he would enhance his reputation with a populist campaign.

In January 1934 Stevens denounced "unfair or unethical trading practices" that had "developed like a canker" and threatened to "destroy the system" itself. [8] His charges were all-encompassing: manufacturers forced people to work in sweatshops while making huge profits; pork producers paid farmers prices that were too low; a bakery combine kept prices too high. The worst villains, according to Stevens, were the department stores. "They used their mass buying power to blackmail manufacturers into selling to them at unrealistically low prices; small merchants, unable to obtain their merchandise on the same terms, were forced out of business. In the frantic scramble for survival, small manufacturers and retailers cut wages and imposed sweatshop conditions on their workers." Stevens's audience cheered the message, and supportive letters poured in at the rate of one hundred a day. Bennett appointed Stevens as chairman of a parliamentary committee to investigate the spread between what the producer received and the consumer paid.

Eaton's had only itself to blame for drawing his fire. A newspaper ad earlier that month had trumpeted a special purchase of Scottish madras suitable for curtains. Scottish weavers usually charge a fixed price, declared the ad, and a buyer might "as well attempt to move the rock beneath Edinburgh Castle as seek to change the price." [9]

Eaton's had, however, obtained 232,000 yards of madras at seven cents a yard, rather than the normal eight and one-quarter cents. Landed in Canada, the cost was ten and three-quarters cents, and the retail price was sixteen cents a yard, a markup of nearly 50 per cent. Stevens said the ad was "boastful" and further accused Eaton's of ordering one thousand dresses at $5.95 apiece, then, after they'd arrived, refusing delivery unless the dresses were reduced to $3.75.

Stevens called dozens of witnesses before his committee that met sixty times during the next six months. He took particular pleasure in making odious comparisons such as the difference between the $25,000 annual income of Imperial Tobacco president Gray Miller and the United Cigar store clerk who earned $25 a week.

When the chasm between wealth and want was measured, Eaton's stood revealed among the worst offenders. Annie Wells, an Eaton's factory seamstress, testified that she was paid nine and one-half cents to make a dress that sold in the store for $1.59. The top forty Eaton's executives were paid $2.2 million, or an average of $55,000 each in 1929. Even after reducing their compensation during the depression, in 1933 their average annual income was still $34,000. In addition, the top forty and others shared $1.6 million in annual bonuses; in 1933 that total had been reduced, but was still $923,767.

The attitude towards employee pensions was parsimonious. An employee at sixty-five with twenty-five years of service received a monthly stipend of $5 plus 10 per cent of weekly salary. Directors fared far better. A $3.3 million retirement fund established in 1924 paid out pensions to a dozen directors that averaged $27,000 a year for ten years.

Stevens was hailed as a champion of the little guy against fat-cat capitalists profiting on the backs of workers. Big was bad and Eaton's, with operations in 170 Canadian cities, had become an easy target. There were 13 large department stores, 5 mail-order distribution centres, 32 smaller department stores, 57 groceterias, 3 creameries, 112 mail-order offices, 7 factories, and 9 buying offices.

In Toronto alone the stores served thirty-eight million customers annually. In Winnipeg Eaton's dominated with 90 per cent of the department-store market share. Nationally Eaton's accounted for 58 per cent of all department-store sales, more than twice as much as Hudson's Bay Co. and Simpson's combined.

The committee uncovered such predatory practices by Eaton's as bringing furniture in from the United States, showing the items to Canadian manufacturers, then demanding they produce similar pieces. Eaton's would play one maker off against the other until one of them agreed to supply items — even at a loss — in order to retain Eaton's business and keep a plant open during the tough times.

Eaton's fought back by pointing out that total sales in 1929 were $225 million, but had fallen to $133 million in 1933, a level similar to a decade earlier. The chain said losses were $2.5 million in 1931 and $2 million in 1932, and claimed that they had been able to eke out a meagre profit of only $878,000 in 1933. As for gross margins, Eaton's said that even in 1932, when margins of 26.3 per cent were the highest among the three years scrutinized, they were still less than the markups enjoyed by 317 American retailers for the same period.

Measured another way, however, the markups were actually much higher. Eaton's was organized in such a manner that each department functioned as an individual entity. The manager was responsible for buying, advertising, transportation, and hiring. In return he was paid a salary plus an annual bonus based on profitability. But each department was also charged with a portion of central costs such as rent or interest on money borrowed. In addition, other levies attributable to operating costs such as maintenance or delivery of goods were also charged back to each department using a technique called "loading," or charging more than actual expenditures.

The result was an apparent higher cost of goods on top of which profit margins were added to yield the selling price. Not surprisingly the result was that Eaton's retail prices were generally much higher than those of most other stores. The parliamentary committee concluded that Eaton's margins were 47.9 per cent — higher than those of any other retailer except Montreal's Dupuis Frères.

In August, in what was supposed to be a private speech, Stevens embelished his findings and claimed that Simpson's and Eaton's had been found guilty of various improprieties. C. L. Burton of Simpson's sent a telegram to Prime Minister Bennett saying that Stevens's statements were in accord neither with sworn testimony nor with the facts. He declared that publication would be a "contumacious libel." Burton's speedy intervention meant that few Canadian newspapers published the content of the speech.

Under pressure from industrialists, Bennett turned against Stevens, who resigned from the commission and the cabinet. The final report was watered down, criticizing Eaton's only for such misjudgments as expanding too quickly. Some laws affecting loss leaders were changed and there were a few modifications to the combines code, but little else came of the probe. Nor did

Stevens achieve much personally. He was eventually barred from the Conservative caucus, formed the Reconstructionist Party, and won 8.7 per cent of the popular vote in the 1935 general election, but was the only member of his party elected. As for Bennett, he was swept out of office that year by the Liberals under Mackenzie King.

Despite the ineffectual conclusion, Stevens's public scrutiny had a profound and lasting impact on Eaton's. "They'd been forging ahead, had 60 per cent of the department-store business and everything was rosy," recalls R.Y.'s son Alan. "The Stevens thing was tough. They hadn't been under attack for many years and they were under attack. They lost their confidence."

R.Y. was certainly aware of the vulnerabilities. In a memo dated October 3, 1933, R.Y. noted that Simpson's had launched Saturday-night shopping in Hamilton the previous December. He was not going to follow suit, but he did urge advertising that would "electrify." On June 25, 1934, he wrote again about Simpson's, referring to it as R. S. Co. "We can continue as we have been doing during the last five years, when we permitted R. S. Co. to increase their proportion of our sales from 47 per cent to 67 per cent. If so, then five years hence R. S. sales will be 107 per cent of ours."

"Forty years ago Eaton values were proverbial," he lamented in another ten-page memo. "They must again be proverbial if we are to keep far in the lead. Unless this growth materializes, this business is going to sink to second place and from second place it would run grave risk of going to pieces. It is not a matter of choice. It is a case of do this, or else head straight for eventual disappearance of the business, or selling out at a sacrifice price in a manner that would disgrace a name which now stands high in the retail world."

"It will take nerve and high courage, enterprise and hard work," R.Y. concluded. "Or what else is there to do?"

The company that had once been so innovative now seemed stuck. The few changes brought about were modest. For example, paper bags were introduced, thus ending the labour-intensive process of wrapping every parcel with paper and string. Yet, for the most part, unresponsive merchandising methods continued. R.Y. refused to match the credit plans of competitors. For him, as for Timothy, cash was king. In 1931 Eaton's began to offer delayed payments in Halifax but it took until 1936 before the practice spread to other stores and until 1939 to reach all locations. The type of credit available, however, was limited to one month only.

"Even after the Second World War, Eaton's credit arrangements lagged far behind those of major retailers in both the United States and Canada," stated Cynthia Jane Wright in her doctoral thesis. "While Eaton's was aware that consumers were returning to instalment buying after the difficult years of the depression and war, store management was undecided whether it even wanted credit business." [10] Revolving credit, where only a portion of the balance had to be paid off each month, was not instituted until 1958.

Modernization also came slowly to the delivery system. Simpson's moved from horses to motorized vehicles in 1928. In 1930 Eaton's stable was the largest ever, four hundred horses in all. In Toronto, the final sixty animals were auctioned off in 1937. In Winnipeg, horses were used for another decade.

Eaton's catalogues seemed equally out of step and insensitive to the diversity of the market. "An 'Eskimo doll' is a run-of-the-mill doll in, of all things, a clown suit with pom-poms and ruff at the neck," wrote Fredelle Bruser Maynard of the 1928 catalogue in her book *Raisins and Almonds*. "A leading fashion colour is 'Nigger Brown.' A featured toy, 'Hey, Hey,' is a comic-vaudeville representation of a Negro in cheap bright tin. The figure holds a squawking chicken. Wind it up, and the darkie shuffles along with his stolen bird, while a small dog, yapping furiously, attaches itself to the seat of his trousers. Another toy — 'very amusing, sure to please' — features two dancing Negroes on a shanty-shaped box from whose windows peer little golliwog children." [11]

Eaton's had once led the pack in the way they treated employees, but labour relations were going the way of innovation. Simpson's paid better than Eaton's. The minimum wage at the time was $12.50 a week. Two-thirds of the female staff at Eaton's were right on the line, making less than $13 a week. The proportion of female employees at Simpson's paid only $12.50 a week was closer to 50 per cent.

According to the *Telegram*, marchers in the 1934 Toronto Labour Day parade "dipped their flags in sorrow as they passed Eaton's." R.Y. demanded a retraction; the newspaper refused. R.Y. declared he would never again speak to a journalist; anything he had to say would be announced directly to the public through advertisements. The edict was all-encompassing; no one at Eaton's was to speak to the media.

Eaton's had now declared war on three fronts: Ottawa, labour, and journalists. A corporate culture based on fear had been created. The private company had become paranoid and began turning in on itself. The result was paralysis. Even the ethnic makeup of employees failed to reflect reality. Just as Timothy had favoured immigrants from northern Ireland, Eaton's under R.Y. had a decidedly Orange hue. According to company lore, an Asian gentleman once applied for a job at Eaton's saying: "Me Ballymena man."

An internal study during the 1930s of the eleven thousand Eaton's employees in Toronto found that 94 per cent were either Canadian or British-born. More than 80 per cent of employees were members of the Anglican, Presbyterian, or United churches. In contrast, only 61 per cent of Toronto residents belonged to those three faiths. Non-British, non-Protestant, non-Canadian employees who did find work were more likely to be out of sight in a factory than on the sales floor. [12]

Catholics represented 14.3 per cent of the Toronto population, but only 7.6 per cent of Eaton's workforce. For Jews, a job at Eaton's was even less likely. There were only twenty Jews among the 8500 clerks in Toronto. [13] Peggy Laskin, wife of Bora Laskin, who was chief justice of Canada from 1973-84, could not get a job as a beautician at Eaton's during the 1930s "because, as it was delicately explained to her, Eaton's did not hire Jews." [14]

Service to minority customers could be poor, abrupt, and offensive. Gabrielle Roy, born in 1909 of Franco-Manitoban origin, devotes the first chapter of her autobiography, *Enchantment and Sorrow*, to the treatment she and her mother received after "crossing the border" from St-Boniface for the "harrowing expedition" of shopping at Eaton's in Winnipeg. "[I]f Maman was having one of her good days, if her confidence was up and her tongue felt nimble, she'd take the offensive and demand one of our compatriots to wait on us." More likely, Maman would feel beaten before she began. "[A]t such times she found it simpler and less taxing to 'bring out' her English, as she used to say." [15] "We came home from our expeditions dog-tired and, in truth, almost always depressed." [16]

In 1939, when Roy settled in Montreal, treatment was little different. "I was dumbfounded and began to feel there was no cure for the misfortune of being French Canadian." [17]

Lady Eaton liked to believe that Eaton's former glory would be restored once her son and designated heir, John David, was enthroned. To demonstrate John David's retailing talent, she'd tell how she visited him at school in England when he was seventeen and found him with a new gramophone. When asked how he'd acquired it, John David replied: "Oh, I sold my old one for thirty shillings and added some of my Christmas money." [18]

In later years John David would joke about how his student days had been cut short in 1930 so he could return to Canada and enter the business. "Some people say I left university because I wanted to go to work. But there are others who maintain it was because I wanted to get out of work," he told interviewer Wilfred List for *Liberty* magazine.

Toronto Daily Star feature writer R. E. Knowles, who freely admitted to hero worship when it came to the Eaton family, encountered John David in 1930 working in menswear. "If I have ever seen real modesty — and in the teeth of much provocation to the contrary — it is to be found in this winsome stripling who only two short weeks ago buckled on the armor and began the long battle of what he has chosen as his life career," wrote Knowles. "He is tall, just tall enough, broad of shoulders, well-knit of frame, husky and athletic looking — and with a boyish ruddiness of complexion that bespeaks vigor and overflowing health." But he was also "rather difficult to talk to — quite lovably so — as if he didn't know what it was all about."

As for working in the store, John David could only say: "Well, it's a way of the family." He didn't feel he was attracting special attention. "Nobody looks at me, why would they? Nobody even knows I'm there. I'm just there because I'm there." [19] That reluctant sense of duty to the family's heritage would mark John David all his days.

After four months of working in Toronto, John David moved in February 1931 to the Winnipeg store, where his duties ranged from driving a delivery truck to carrying out comparisons with competitors. "We bought grapefruit from every retail outlet in Winnipeg, bags and bags of the stuff. Then we carted the grapefruit to the research department, weighed and squeezed each fruit, and finally had to drink grapefruit juice all afternoon." [20]

Off hours, John David was a sight to behold in his Auburn roadster and raccoon coat, hatless even when Winnipeg's temperatures plunged to forty below. He was introduced to Signy Hildur Stefansson (the Icelandic name was Anglicized to Stephenson), a receptionist in a dentist's office, and began to court her, soon asking for her hand in marriage. She was petite and had silvery-blonde hair. Her father, Fredrik, arrived in Canada at age seven with his parents. He became a printer and part-owner of a publishing firm that produced *Lögberg*, a newspaper in the Icelandic language, the tongue the family spoke at home.

Signy's mother, Anna, was the daughter of immigrants who settled on the shores of Lake Winnipeg. Her grandfather, a member of the Icelandic parliament, was part of the first wave of immigrants who arrived in 1875 and grew to number fifteen thousand in Manitoba by the time of the First World War.

They were proud of their heritage, even referring to themselves as Vikings. Others used a more derogatory term: goolies.

Signy grew up on Victor Street in cultured surroundings. Her father played the clarinet in the Winnipeg Symphony. Edwin, eldest of the six children, farmed near Morden, Manitoba, and would travel to St. Paul, Minnesota, for the opera. Brother Harald's interest in such pursuits took a different path. As the ne'er-do-well of the family he plunged into the reckless glamour of the Cotton Club in Harlem during the 1930s. He later lived in Montreal, was in charge of the book department at Eaton's, and became an alcoholic. Signy took a particular interest in her baby brother, Thor, and watched over him well into his adult life when he became an aeronautical engineer.

Lady Eaton's power was through her control over the family, so she moved swiftly to bring Signy into her orbit. Lady Eaton oversaw an afternoon introductory reception at Ardwold where the two thousand guests were piped up the drive by members of the Irish Regiment. Men in white flannels and ladies in organdy and chiffon slowly made their way to the south terrace where Signy, then a tender twenty, shook each hand. Under a marquee there were long tables bearing food and bouquets of pink peonies. Beyond was the rose garden, ivy-covered pergolas, and the city vista.

Lady Eaton also made all the arrangements for the obligatory trip to London, where Signy was presented at Court to King George and Queen Mary. The wedding to John David, twenty-four at the time, was held August 9, 1933, at Kawandag, Lady Eaton's summer home, where the Union Jack and the flag of Iceland flew. Decor at the five o'clock ceremony followed a nautical motif with white sailcloth carpet on the aisle and guests seated on rows of blue Italian chairs cordoned off by ropes and anchors. Signy's Paris gown was white chiffon over silver lamé topped off by a silver-winged Viking headdress. A youthful choir — children of the staff who worked on the estate — filled the air with songs.

As attendees gathered under the dowager queen's watchful eye, no ordinary introductions to this sizeable clan would do. Henry Burden, the groom's first cousin, entertained everyone by tacking a roll of shelf paper to a handy birch tree and, with a crayon, spent an hour drawing a detailed family genealogy.

Lady Eaton was the sort of mother a son such as John David would want to please, so he had returned to Toronto that February to supervise the men's shop in the same College Street store he had officially opened three years earlier. In 1934 he was made a director of the company, then moved through a variety of roles, including business development, manufacturing, and merchandising before being named a vice-president in 1937. A suitable dwelling was required for the future king and his new queen. John David hired two architects, Eric Haldenby and Alvan "Shy" Mathers, to create a Bauhaus-style family home at 120 Dunvegan Road in the Toronto enclave of Forest Hill.

In 1935 Lady Eaton married off another of her sons, Timothy, to Martha Waddie, the widow of a Hamilton industrialist. Timothy Eaton Memorial Church was decorated with blue irises and golden-hued roses, the colours of the North York Hunt, where he was master and his betrothed was a member. The ceremony was held in January, but Ardwold looked liked spring. Lady Eaton filled the mansion with yellow forsythia and blue iris for the wedding breakfast. She outshone the bride in her Maggy Rouff Romney gown of burgundy taffeta, matching velvet cape with collar, deep border and muff of Russian sable. For their honeymoon the newlyweds skied in Switzerland and hunted in England, then took up residence in Toronto.

Despite her proclamations of being a social misfit, Lady Eaton presided over just about every grand occasion and worthy cause in the city. She was president of the United Welfare Chest, vice-president of the Canadian Red Cross, and life member of the Women's Hospital Aid Association. She was named a Dame of Grace of the St. John Ambulance, was joint master of the Toronto and North York Hunt, and worked with both the Canadian National Institute for the Blind and the Canadian National Committee for Mental Hygiene.

In most cases organizations benefitted from their association with Lady Eaton. In 1937, for example, she continued the donation to the Faculty of Medicine at the University of Toronto, paid at the rate of $25,000 a year. Other times she would donate funds only when certain conditions were met. At Timothy Eaton Memorial, for example, she was on the board of trustees and was a member of the Session (the bodies that oversaw financial and spiritual matters), the only woman to serve on both in her lifetime. She chose and ordered the vestments, sang in the choir, and on occasion performed as a soloist at services.

During her visits to Britain with Sir John, Lady Eaton had become enamoured of the pomp and ceremony of the Church of England. After his death, her interest in ritual grew. Vestments for clergy, symbolic of the seasons in the Christian year, were adopted following consultation between Lady Eaton and the dean of Westminster Abbey. The kneeling benches with pads produced by the Royal Needleworkers at St. Paul's in London only fed the controversy about the direction she was single-handedly taking all adherents.

In 1929 she asked that a processional and recessional be added to services at Eaton Memorial. There was little interest; such liturgical pageantry was not welcome among members of the congregation that had since 1925 been part of the United Church of Canada. Lady Eaton adopted a new approach. She proposed, in memory of Sir John, a sixty-two-foot extension to the nave. The front of the church, including the choir loft, was to be modified and a forty-five-foot chancel created so the communion table and altar could be more centrally located against the front wall. Parishioners eventually gave in, and construction was completed in 1938. The new floor plan was closer to the Church of England than the Methodist tradition.

At the chancel dedication service in December 1938, there was one final skirmish. Just before the ceremony began, W. C. Kettlewell, secretary to the board of trustees, spied candelabra sitting on the altar. He was apoplectic and complained to the senior minister, Reverend D. A. MacLennan, that this practice was "too Popish." Kettlewell removed the offending candelabra himself. When Lady Eaton arrived a few minutes later, she restored the candelabra to the altar. Checkmate. Protests by parishioners, no matter what their official standing, meant nothing to her. Lady Eaton always got her way. [21]

With none of her sons living at home, in 1936 Lady Eaton decided to move from Ardwold. (Edgar was in Montreal and wouldn't return to Toronto until 1942 when he joined T. Eaton Life Assurance Co. He married Mildred Jarvis Page of Baie d'Urfé, Quebec, in 1944. Gilbert had spent two years in the Berlin office before being posted to Winnipeg in 1938. In 1939 he married Marjorie Maston of Wilmington, Delaware. The couple had met while she was studying in Lausanne and he was visiting Lady Eaton, who was staying at a nearby hotel.) It was as if she'd set out to expunge her past. She ordered many household items sold at auction. Sir John's pride, his aeolian organ, was purchased by a church. Other buyers trucked off the flooring, panelling, and library bookcases. Bronze and silver chandeliers went, too; so did the eavestroughing with its owls cast in bronze.

Lady Eaton had come to dislike Ardwold so intensely that she ordered the mansion demolished. Normal wrecking methods were insufficient for the thick walls; they had to be blasted to smithereens with dynamite. Such a destructive approach can only be described as desecration, or at best, wildly eccentric. A home that resonated with history and beauty was reduced to rubble. After only twenty-five years Ardwold vanished, and the eleven-acre site was divided into building lots. [22]

Before his death Sir John began buying what would become a 750-acre tract of land that included woods, pastures, and a forty-five-acre lake (later named Lake Jonda) in King Township, twenty-five miles north of Toronto. In 1937 Lady Eaton ordered construction to begin on that site of a massive country house in the style of a sixteenth-century Norman chateau. Built with Credit Valley stone and red roof tiles, the turreted Eaton Hall had thirty-five rooms. Lady Eaton claimed she had good reason to replace Ardwold with another dwelling almost as large. "John David seemed to feel it was too big but a small house would be little use to me as a family centre and surely with John Craig [born that May] as a beginning there is an interesting future to be looked forward to," Lady Eaton wrote to Eaton's executive O.D. Vaughan in a letter dated September 29, 1937. [23]

Most of the living area faced southwest for the views. The main floor featured a great hall, which connected to two wings. One wing had a library and music room with organ and harp, the other a dining room, kitchen, and pantry. A suspended circular staircase, with paintings of Timothy and Margaret on the walls, led to the second floor, where Lady Eaton's bedroom was at one end. At the other end were a small dining room, kitchen, and four guest bedrooms. Staff quarters were on the third floor.

Decor was eclectic. Knotty pine was used throughout the house, but the thirty-five-by-twenty-five-foot music room had ormolu-trimmed walnut furniture in the style of Louis XVI with upholstery by Gobelin. On display was a scale model of her father's carpentry shop in Omemee, a reminder from whence she had come.

Some of the stone benches and bronze figures from Ardwold were carted to King. Lawn replaced meadow, spring bulbs were added to the naturally blooming woodland flowers. Across the lake was a recreational area for Eaton's employees.

"Flora's Folly" some in the family called the edifice. "People were quite impressed with it, but Eaton Hall was never my bag at all," says daughter Florence. "I found that I had signed a paper that she could do this because, evidently, all the offspring had to sign and say this was fine, she could go ahead, but I didn't know what was going on. I was fifteen or something. I came home [from Europe] to find this thing."

In 1938 Lady Eaton presented Florence and Evlyn at the court of King George and Queen Elizabeth. That same year Lady Eaton presided over their debutante party, a dance with a circus theme, at Eaton Auditorium that went on until three in the morning. Florence met her future husband that night. Frank McEachren arrived late, but it was love at first sight. He was the grandson of Sir Joseph Flavelle, had just recently attained junior officer rank in the 48th Highlanders, and looked splendid in his scarlet kilt.

Lady Eaton went all out for the wedding in 1940. The bride wore ivory slipper satin; the couple used Ladybird, the 1912 Rolls-Royce limousine that had become Lady Eaton's favourite, in the procession to Eaton Hall for the reception that followed. It was lined with satin and driven by Lady Eaton's chauffeur, Larkin. (At the 1980 wedding of Florence's daughter, Signy, Ladybird conveyed the bride to the church but not to the reception for fear that the historic vehicle might expire on the second leg. Ladybird is now displayed at the Canadian Automotive Museum in Oshawa, Ontario.)

Lady Eaton continued to handle adopted daughter Evlyn differently. Evlyn had fallen in love with a man in Europe, but Lady Eaton wouldn't allow the marriage. Instead, on June 12, 1943, at Timothy Eaton Memorial Church, Evlyn married Captain Russel Payton of Ottawa. The reception was held at 120 Dunvegan, not Eaton Hall. Ignore the dark one.

In the years leading up to the Second World War, both Eaton's and Lady Eaton herself typified the British attachment felt by much of Canada. In 1937, when George VI was crowned, Eaton's commissioned a reproduction of the coronation chair, complete with a duplicate Stone of Scone. The life-size copy was made in England, shipped to Canada, and displayed in several stores. So realistic was the chair that in 1951 it was flown to London for display at the British Industries Fair held at Earls Court.

The family was treated like royalty on a tour of the colonies. In 1938 Timothy was named a Six Nations chief, wore a headdress of eagle feathers, and inherited the same name, "Big House," as had been bestowed in 1910 on his father, Sir John. They lived like royalty, too. During the war R.Y. owned seven cars just so he could put four of them up on blocks and have plenty of gasoline ration coupons for the other three kept in active service. His favourite was a Rolls-Royce, which he drove so fast that he once offered to prepay speeding fines so he could travel at whatever pace he pleased on the way to and from his summer home. The police did not approve his scheme.

John David had learned to fly while working in Winnipeg and in 1939 acquired a twin-engine Beechcraft capable of carrying six passengers and a two-man crew at 195 miles an hour. When war broke out, John David followed his father Sir John's earlier example and turned over his Beechcraft, one of only five like it in the country, to the government for use as a trainer. He also donated *Chimon*, his sixty-five-foot schooner. He bought the *Shamrock*, a forty-foot steamboat, fuelled by burning wood. No wartime gas rationing would stop him from getting out on the water.

During the war Lady Eaton's castle in King Township, Eaton Hall, served as a safe haven for seven children and two women from England. In 1944 she turned the house over to the Royal Canadian Navy as a convalescent home for seventy-five servicemen.

She was also active on the barricades. In 1916 the federal government had converted a grimy factory on Toronto's Christie Street into a hospital for soldiers wounded in the First World War. Meant originally as a temporary measure, there were plans in 1943 to add a wing for those wounded in the Second World War. Lady Eaton was appalled at the continuing use of a building she felt was well below par. "This idea of adding a wing to Christie Street Hospital (God forgive the insult) at $500,000 of our taxes, and suggesting it is for the care of wounded soldiers is too awful to think about," she wrote in a letter published in the *Globe and Mail*. "Why must Government officials always wait till the hour of necessity arises before they act? I suggest that the Minister of Pensions put it on a personal basis and that he go and spend a week there. Wounded soldiers are prisoners of their disabilities, and should have proper surroundings of the best we can give them." [24]

On September 9, 1944, she joined other women carrying placards on the sidewalk outside the hospital. Hers read: "Get our wounded out of Christie St." The protest worked. The addition did not proceed and Christie Street was eventually replaced by a new veterans' facility on Bayview Avenue, Sunnybrook Hospital.

Lady Eaton's power remained so strong through the 1930s and early 1940s that R.Y. had warned his sons not to join Eaton's. He knew, once he stepped down as president and the owner Eatons resumed power, that the "worker Eatons" would be allowed to rise only so far in the organization. All three sons joined the business anyway. John Wallace, known as Jack, was born in 1912, studied at Royal Military College and Cambridge, then started in the meat department in 1934 and later went into women's wear. Whereas Jack was what they call in the business a "people person," his brother Alan preferred numbers. Alan graduated from the University of Toronto in 1937, won a scholarship to attend Cambridge, where he obtained a Master's degree in law in 1939, then received an MBA from Harvard in 1941.

A third son, Erskine, called "Irksome" by his friends at University of Toronto Schools, was the family daredevil. The family's English nurse had a habit of saying "Oh really," which sounded to her young charges like "Oh rawlly," so they formed the Rawlly Club to entertain their parents. The first display featured Erskine on a toboggan flying off the roof of their Highland Avenue home into the backyard below, then continuing full tilt down the steep slope into the wooded ravine beyond. The club was disbanded immediately by parental decree.

With the arrival of the Second World War the worker Eatons embraced events. Jack enlisted with the Governor General's Horse Guards in 1940, served overseas with the 8th New Brunswick Hussars, and became Lieutenant-Colonel in the First Canadian Corps in Italy. On his return Jack became an assistant superintendent, was transferred to Montreal in 1947 because he spoke French, and was named assistant general manager of the Montreal store in 1949. He married Phyllis Finlayson, daughter of the Honourable William Finlayson, Ontario minister of lands and forests.

Alan joined Eaton's in 1941 and became head of Eaton's Wartime Regulations Office. He served with the Royal Canadian Artillery from 1943 to 1945 as a lieutenant, then spent eighteen months with the Wartime Prices and Trade Board before rejoining Eaton's in 1947 as assistant general manager at Eaton's College Street.

Erskine left his job in the stock-audit department of the Montreal Eaton's to join Les Fusiliers Mont-Royal. A dashing six-foot-two playboy, he was named as a co-respondent in a British divorce action. He made captain and served as an intelligence officer with the Fifth Brigade. On August 19, 1942, shortly after stepping off the landing craft at Dieppe, Erskine was killed, one among the nine hundred Canadians who died in the disastrous raid across the English Channel. He was twenty-seven.

Jack's twin, Margaret, volunteered with the Canadian Red Cross in 1939, was appointed national adjutant of the uniformed Red Cross in 1941, and later that year enlisted in the Canadian Women's Army Corps (CWAC). She served as a staff officer in Toronto and Montreal, went overseas attached to the Auxiliary Territorial Corps, and in 1944 was named a full colonel and director-general of CWAC. She married John Hubert Dunn, a Harley Street doctor, and lived in London.

Her younger sister, Nora, married a Belgian, Paul van der Stricht, who was a spy with the OSS during the war and later lived in Greenwich, Connecticut.

Unlike the worker Eatons, none of the owner Eatons went overseas, although Florence at least tried to enlist. In those days a husband's permission was required and Frank refused. "That," says Florence, "was a bone of contention. His mother put him up to it. No daughter of mine will ever go through what I went through. [I say] give me my chance; I'll see if I can do it." Florence was a volunteer truck driver in Toronto for the Canadian Red Cross while Frank was away at war.

━

In 1942, the time came when R.Y. could no longer protect his sons. There were forty-five roses on R.Y.'s desk as he celebrated his forty-fifth anniversary with the firm and stepped aside. Sir John's youngest son, Gilbert, was twenty-seven. Trustees could now choose a successor as had been contemplated in Sir John's will.

Also retiring was J.J. Vaughan, R.Y.'s right-hand man, who was given a painting from the Eaton collection, *Portrait of Michael Le Blon*, by Flemish master Anthony Van Dyck, valued at $50,000. For R.Y., there was an even more generous sendoff. He was presented with Rembrandt's *Woman with a Handkerchief*, which he'd purchased for the company at auction in 1928. By 1942 it was valued at $200,000.

The painting hung at Killyree until 1956, the year R.Y. took ill at his Georgian Bay home and died at the age of eighty-one. It was lent to the Art Gallery of Toronto and donated permanently following the death in 1965 of Hazel, R.Y.'s widow. For a time the painting continued to be an object of desire. Thieves broke into the gallery in September 1959, cut the *Woman with a Handkerchief* and five other paintings from their frames, rolled them up, and carried them away. Everything was recovered three weeks later.

But was R.Y.'s bequest really by Rembrandt? Was it worth the $300,000 the gallery claimed at the time of the robbery? At the beginning of this century there were thought to be in existence about one thousand paintings by Rembrandt. In 1968 a group of Dutch art experts, known as the Rembrandt Research Project, began a study of all known works and has determined that perhaps less than four hundred should still be attributed to the old master.

Many of the group's conclusions have been controversial. In some cases, museums have refused to accept the findings. From the time the Eaton Rembrandt was first displayed at the gallery, however, every expert declared that it was not by Rembrandt. (J.J. Vaughan's Van Dyck has fared better. The work was donated to the gallery in 1965, and its authenticity has never been questioned.)

In 1972 the Rembrandt Research Project took detailed photographs and X-rays, then announced that the work was not by the Dutch master. The gallery accepted the finding and in 1974 changed the attribution to "school of Rembrandt." In 1985 the Rembrandt Research Project changed its mind and decided that the painting was the work of Carel Fabritius, a gifted pupil of Rembrandt's who died at thirty-two in a gunpowder explosion that devastated Delft in 1654. That finding caused a ripple of pleasure among gallery staff. Better a first-rate Fabritius than a second-rate Rembrandt.

On that basis, the painting was lent to a 1991-1992 exhibition entitled "Rembrandt: The Master and his Workshop" held in Berlin, Amsterdam, and London. Every scholar who saw the painting on tour disputed the Fabritius attribution. Today the gallery label reads "follower of Rembrandt," indicating that the painting was by an unknown student of Rembrandt.

The ever-changing attribution paralleled the sinking fortunes of Eaton's. Nothing was as it appeared to be. During R.Y.'s time, profit had become a dirty word at Eaton's, something that provoked embarrassing public scrutiny. More than three decades after the Stevens inquiry, in the family-approved book *The Store that Timothy Built* published in 1969, author William Stephenson wrote that Eaton's profits were "sinful and must never be allowed to become the sole criterion of success. Never again must there be even the flimsiest excuse for an investigation."

R.Y. himself never got over the attack; others in senior ranks seemed equally haunted. "So powerfully did this odd business philosophy infect the Eaton psyche that even as late as the Nineteen-Fifties the manager of one large store would be severely reprimanded for making too much money and be ordered to stop it at once," wrote Stephenson. "In some departments managers were never allowed to know how much profit they made after deductions for space, personnel and other factors were taken into account; only the sales and expense officers knew the true story, and such men were carefully chosen for their abilities to keep their mouths shut." [25]

At sixty-two, Lady Eaton was finally about to see her prince crowned. Without a profit motive, however, the very core of the free-market system, no business could expect to flourish for long.

CHAPTER FIVE

JOHN DAVID: THE RELUCTANT RULER

In A BOARDROOM CEREMONY ON DECEMBER 9, 1942, John David Eaton, second son of Sir John and grandson of Timothy, was designated president of the T. Eaton Co. Ltd. His acceptance speech was modest and self-deprecating. "It has fallen to my lot to follow in the presidency of the company three very remarkable and outstanding men," he said. "I can only tell you that I shall endeavour with all my earnestness to perform my responsibilities in a manner worthy of the fine example set and the good traditions established by those who have presided before me." [1]

A *Toronto Daily Star* reporter who caught up with John David the same day had his own view of those traditions. "We pointed out to him that to be the son of a good man is hard enough, but to be also the grandson of a good man adds more than double the burden on the best of men."

Replied John David quietly: "I don't expect it to be anything but difficult." [2]

As the fourth Eaton to head the firm, John David, thirty-three, was the first to succeed a living president. While the directors claimed that they closely scrutinized all members of that generation and selected the best, in fact, it was no contest. "The best one in that family was Florence Mary," says cousin Alan, R.Y.'s son. A female president, however, was not an acceptable option in that era. "The others were all pretty hopeless. Timothy liked playing with trains, Edgar was always sick, and Gilbert was a lightweight. John David was the best of a bad lot."

"After working for a short time in the store, I was allowed to drift away,"

Timothy, the eldest, said in 1974. "Looking back, I think I would have been happiest in engineering." [3]

Florence agreed with the choice. "My name was in there, I knew that, but I'm awfully glad it didn't come to fruition," says Florence. "Everyone picked John. There was no contest at all, which was fine by the rest of us. The others didn't have the talent. You need a certain talent; look what's happening now," she says, referring to the 1997 financial crisis.

"Timothy should have been allowed to be a mechanic or a farmer," says Florence. "He was very good with animals and vehicles. Edgar was a very simple soul, kindly and gentle. He wasn't a go-go person at all. Gilbert was Mama's Prince Charming. He travelled around Europe with her for quite a long time and looked after her. He got into the indolent life."

Timothy served as a director of the Eaton Life Assurance Co. and had a master key for the stores. If he were going with friends to Maple Leaf Gardens, he would park in the Eaton's College Street lot, then prowl through the store on the way. An enthusiastic model railroader, he filled the second floor of his house with his trains and had railway tracks on his land near St. Andrew's College north of Toronto. He'd clamp a pipe in his mouth, put on an engineer's hat, then set rolling the one-sixth-scale model steam locomotive while sounding the engine's bell and grinning with delight.

Timothy wanted a control tower to supervise proceedings, just like at a real railyard, so Eaton's carpenter Laurie Davis built him one. The creation was trucked to his property, but when Timothy's wife clapped eyes on the monstrosity, she ordered the structure be sent away before it was even unloaded. When he wasn't near his trains, Timothy liked to pretend he was still aboard. A bell mounted on the trunk of his Rolls-Royce could be operated from the backseat. "When streetcars ding at me," he'd say, "I ding back."

Timothy moved to Royal Tunbridge Wells, south of London, England, in the early 1970s. There he indulged his passion for Winston Churchill by listening daily to his recorded speeches. Married three times, he was divorced twice. He loved children, but had none from his three unions, so he'd visit two nearby orphanages in Kent where he was known as "Uncle Tim."

He seemed cowed by his heritage. A near life-size portrait of his father, Sir John, hung in the dining room. Beside it was a portrait of himself in hunting scarlet. "My father's portrait is exactly six inches higher than my own," he once said. "It was important to me that he was above my head."

An alcoholic, Timothy passed his last fifteen years in poor health and required constant medical attention. Even in death at eighty-three in 1986, family tradition took precedence over his own preference. He had wanted to be buried at Ballymena in Northern Ireland. Instead, he was entombed in the family crypt in Toronto.

Edgar, the third son, had a sunny disposition but delicate health. After his schooling, he spent a year in France to improve his facility with the language, then worked in the Montreal store from 1934 to 1946. After that his only association with the business was an occasional visit to the Queen Street store notions department, where he'd peek around the pillars at the female clerks selling cosmetics.

Edgar established a business selling cold and asthma pills, then became associated with David Fingard, an American and self-described co-inventor of a home remedy for the common cold. With Edgar as president, Wood-Fingard-Eaton Co. Ltd. sold Inhal-it, a $7.95 electric cup that produced medicated vapours. Edgar was clearly trading on his name more than any medical miracle. A letter sent to doctors over Edgar's signature claimed that Inhal-it had cured members of his family. His brother, John David, heard about this assertion and demanded a correction. Edgar wrote again to the doctors saying that the cures had occurred in his immediate household, not among his more famous retailing family.

A full-page ad in the October 26, 1949, issue of the *Toronto Daily Star* announced Inhal-it as the "greatest discovery in two decades of medical research." Another full-page ad in the *Globe and Mail* of November 27, 1950, claimed that the product was "the only medication of its type, to our knowledge, allowed to use the word CURED in advertising in the treatment of colds, hay fever, asthma, catarrh, sinusitis, bronchitis and other respiratory diseases."

In fact, the Ontario Securities Commission (OSC) had already warned Fingard not to use the word "cured" in advertising and threatened criminal proceedings. The company offered 500,000 shares at $1 a share to the public through a Toronto brokerage firm, D. J. Scanlon & Co. Ltd. Edgar and his wife Mildred were listed as executives and owners of a 10 per cent interest. [4] The offering, and its medical claims, attracted further scrutiny by the Department of National Health and the OSC. The firm collapsed shortly after and Edgar then became a manufacturer's agent with modest success. In 1966 he had his last moment in the public eye when he was fined $200 for doing one hundred miles an hour on Toronto's Don Valley Parkway.

Edgar's first wife, Mildred, died in 1968. In 1977, on his sixty-fifth birthday, he married Irene Monk, a fifty-nine-year-old divorcée and retired legal secretary from London, Ontario. They lived on his estate near Campbellville, west of Toronto. He died in 1988 in Waterloo, Ontario, at seventy-six.

Youngest son Gilbert was in the very early stages of his career when the presidential choice was made in 1942. He'd been in Winnipeg since 1938 and was eventually named a director on several Eaton's company boards, but had little impact. He and his first wife, Marjorie, had a troubled marriage and both became alcoholics. He retired in 1963, lived for a time in the Caribbean, then moved to Miami, where he died in 1985, leaving his widow, Maria Marosi.

With John David safely ensconced as president, Lady Eaton was able to cease worrying about the "worker Eatons." The interregnum was ended, the rightful family restored. Three weeks later she retired as a director after serving twenty-one years.

At five foot ten John David was the runt of the family. He had a large head with a square-cut face dominated by heavy-lidded eyes. "He looks not unlike a well-groomed older version of Orson Welles in size and stature," said a contemporary account in *Saturday Night*.[5] His shy smile seemed to suggest a reluctant presence — as if he were not of this world and dwelt somewhere in a dimension of his own creation.

John David did some modest shuffling among the courtiers. Secretary-treasurer J.J. Vaughan was replaced with J.J.'s younger brother, Orval Douglas Vaughan. O.D. had joined Eaton's in 1920 in home furnishings, was made head of the department in 1925, and was elected a director in 1937. Just as his brother, John James, was always referred to as J.J., so Orval was O.D. to all, including his wife, Nora. She was a commerce-and-finance graduate from the University of Toronto, headed Eaton's home-shopping service, and became the store's first female buyer. Nora resigned when they were married in 1927.

The Eaton's that John David inherited was a vast empire stretching across seven provinces, with fifty-two stores, 189 catalogue offices, and thirty-two thousand employees. The image required no burnishing; everything came with a permanent sheen. "The story of Eaton's is a cavalcade from old to modern times," declared an editorial in the December 14, 1944, edition of the *Globe and Mail*. "The business which started in a remodelled house of three storeys and an attic has become a Canadian institution."

John David tried to establish himself as someone with thoughtful views on the economic landscape, but his statements tended to be more predictable than prescient. "More people flowing into Canada means more mouths to feed, more houses to build, more tools to make, more trains to operate, more clothing, more cars, more everything," he said in one interview. "As we increase in population we are going ahead, we are not sliding back. As a farmer sells more of his products, he puts money into the pockets of men who make shoes, saws, buttons, a million other things. The twentieth century has been said to belong to Canada. We should realize that more than half that century still lies before us." [6]

Everything was handed to him because of his name, not because of what he'd done himself. In 1944 John David joined the board of the Dominion Bank, the family seat occupied by his father and grandfather before him. In one of his last official acts as mayor of Toronto, Fred Conboy presented John David with a testimonial in a three-foot-high gilt frame. The wording acknowledged "the tremendous influence your company has had in promoting the steady and progressive development of the City of Toronto since the early days of the Confederation of Canada." [7]

When Germany surrendered and the Second World War ended, Eaton's celebrated along with the rest of the country. Tuesday, May 8, 1945, was declared a public holiday, and Eaton's remained closed for two days. Downtown office workers jammed the streets; jubilant drivers sounded automobile horns. John David drove his two eldest sons, John Craig and Fred, to the Queen Street store to help unfurl the flags in celebration. John Craig was almost eight; Fred would turn seven the following month. It was their first visit to the source of the family's power and fortune.

Viewed from the outside, Eaton's looked much as it had before the war. But like a great oak with a slowly rotting core, Eaton's was at risk of being felled by the winds of economic change. Two key decisions taken during the war weakened the firm for the next thirty years. First, all profits from wartime contracts were returned to the government. The same practice had been followed by Eaton's during the First World War, but the plants were newer then. By the end of the Second World War the factories were so decrepit they would never recover. Eaton's had no capital available to invest in modernization. Second, in response to wartime wage-and-price controls, Eaton's had created unnecessary levels of management as a way of circumventing the rules. Those top-heavy executive ranks, not pared back until the 1970s, hobbled the decision-making process and proved to be a continuing drain on monetary resources.

John David held a welcome-home party at Eaton Hall for 1700 employees returning from war service. They were a thankful troop; they had survived. Moreover, if their military pay had been lower than their Eaton's salary, the company made up the difference during the war. They listened to speeches, dined under marquees beside the lake, and were received by Lady Eaton herself, bearing a bouquet of roses.

Sir John gave First World War veterans a gold medal; John David presented gold signet rings to the nearly 5700 Eatonians who served in the Second World War. Each ring bore the design of the General Service lapel badge issued to all Canadians on discharge and had the individual's name engraved on the inside.

Across the country a series of similar ceremonies celebrated God, country, and family. For those 263 Eatonians who had died in the war, next of kin were invited in their stead. Each event featured a choir that sang hymns, and the Eatons were out in force: R.Y., John David, Gilbert, and Lady Eaton. "If I can only make you understand the sympathetic feeling which goes from this Eaton family — both the Big Family and the small one — I shall have succeeded in my privilege in addressing you tonight," Lady Eaton told the gathering in Montreal in September 1946.

"I cannot tell you how proud we all are of the part you played in the theatres of war. You offered all you had. There are those who paid the supreme sacrifice. Them we shall hold in our hearts always. Their motto could have been 'Freely ye have received, freely give.' They gave me inspiration and courage and on their behalf I can only say thank you a thousand times for your generous approval and gratitude." [8]

In Germany prewar commerce resumed as if nothing had happened. Eaton's representative in Berlin, Nicholas von Struve, had hidden all the company's books when war commenced. He fought for the Nazis, then laid down arms, recovered the records, and resumed his former role as an Eaton's buyer.

In Canada a widespread fear existed that the wartime growth would cease and the country would simply revert to how it had been during the depression. Instead, the economy boomed. Demobbed members of the service married, bought houses, and began having families.

John David oversaw some innovative moves. To reach the emerging youth market, Eaton's heavily promoted two programs for high school students: Junior Fashion Council, begun in 1940 for young women (the name changed later in the decade to Junior Council); and Junior Executive, begun in 1942 for young men. Eaton's chose one male and one female, age sixteen to eighteen, from every local high school. They met Saturday mornings to offer style and fashion advice, heard speakers, then worked on the store floor. Dances with orchestras capped off a busy day. Members wore blue blazers with gray flannel pants or skirts. The idea was to do market research, create leaders, attract high school customers, and discover merchandising talent.

A two-part series published in *Maclean's* in 1947 featured a portrait of John David by Karsh. The story included a passage claiming that some mail-order customers believed that he was personally involved in every sale. "But the truth of the matter is that Mr. Eaton doesn't fill all those orders himself," declared the writer. "In the underwear chapter the men still stand around in the blabriggins examining golf clubs and rifles with easy detachment. The shapely ladies in ankle-length combinations, who in another generation filled the place in small boys' literature now occupied by pin-up girls, display the same circumspect voluptuousness complete with gussets." [9]

After six years of settling into his role, in 1948 John David made his boldest move when he paid $15 million for David Spencer Ltd. of British Columbia. Eaton's had been eyeing Spencer's, a string of department stores, since the 1920s. Fellow founders David Spencer and Timothy were both immigrants, Methodists, and sold on a cash-only basis. Spencer, a lay preacher from Wales, bought a dry-goods shop in Victoria in 1873, four years after Timothy opened Eaton's in Toronto.

Spencer's was the province's largest department-store chain, with three thousand employees and eight stores located in Victoria, Vancouver, New Westminster, Nanaimo, Courtenay, Chilliwack, Mission, and Duncan. Chris Spencer, then eighty, had approached Eaton's, saying: "Our founder said if you ever sell, we'd like to sell to Eaton's." Recalls David Kinnear, who was part of the team sent from Toronto to run the acquisitions: "They'd lost their zest for life." The deal closed on September 18, 1948, but the sale was kept secret until November 30, when Spencer and John David jointly made the announcement from the mezzanine in the Hastings Street store.

Their words were reassuring, but there was little regard for Spencer's history. Overnight, Spencer's merchandise tickets were replaced by Eaton's; new uniforms for elevator operators and signs for store exteriors soon followed. Sunday window-shopping was no more; curtains were drawn in keeping with the Eaton's tradition. Spencer's cigarette counters — which had sold tobacco grown in the Fraser Valley — were torn out.

Spencer's employees were bitter about the pre-Christmas swoop. They called the fifty managers sent from Toronto "the wise men from the east." Eaton's had already blackened its reputation locally by reneging on a promise made the previous March when John David had flown in on his private DC-3 to announce that he'd paid $1.85 million for the Hotel Vancouver and intended to build a new ten-storey department store in its place.

Construction was to begin immediately and buildings were razed. Then Eaton's changed its mind, saying only that it would build "eventually." The site, at Granville, Georgia, and Howe Streets, served as a parking lot for the next two decades.

Eaton's also erred in stocking the former Spencer's stores. During the more than two months that passed between signing and announcing, Spencer's allowed inventory levels to fall precipitously. Although Eaton's shipped goods from the East and kept them at the ready on rail sidings to be placed on shelves after the announcement, there weren't sufficient in-store items to satisfy Christmas demand.

The urgent call went out to other Eaton's outlets to send whatever goods they didn't need. Most stores seized the opportunity to unload out-of-style articles they'd been unable to sell. The British Columbia stores were deluged with dreck, and thus was created an image the eastern arriviste was unable to shake. For the next twenty-five years, measured by market share, Eaton's ran a poor third behind Woodward's and The Bay.

Although the Spencer's purchase was handled badly on just about every front, John David always regarded the acquisition as his finest hour. He wanted the chain to be national, no matter what the cost. Financial success and local acceptance were irrelevant. With Newfoundland's entry into Confederation in 1949, Eaton's opened in Gander, then Corner Brook in 1953. In 1955 a $1-million store in Charlottetown meant that Eaton's had sixty stores and was positioned in every province at last.

Despite the expansion, the underlying culture remained conservative and unchanged. Female employees who met the public were to wear black, blue, or brown from September 15 to April 15. Reported *Coronet* in 1949: "Recently there was considerable comment when word went round that *grey* was now officially acceptable in some departments." [10]

There was one modest concession to changing morality: Eaton's began to sell that instrument of the devil, playing cards. Also creeping in quietly were cigarette machines, papers and tubes, ashtrays, and lighters, but no cigarettes. Rum-and-toffee candies were also available, nonalcoholic of course, but the suggestive name meant they could not be advertised.

R.Y. chafed on the sidelines, watching the organization become flabby. Mediocrity was not only permitted, it was almost celebrated. No one was ever dismissed, even with cause. "They've forgotten the word 'fire,'" R.Y. complained to son Alan. A store manager might be hopeless, but if he was a hunting pal of John David's he was untouchable.

January stocktaking was the one time during the year that John David played a hands-on role. Every department took inventory, then compared what had been counted to goods received minus actual sales. John David would arrive in Montreal, for example, ensconce himself in one of the executive offices, and have the forty merchandise managers line up at the door. When individually summoned, each would show John David their numbers, specifically the variance due to theft, loss, or poor paperwork.

Some years, a variance of 1 per cent might be allowed. If a department showed a 1½ per cent variance, the manager might get away with it — but not 2 per cent. "You knew what your standard was, but very often you didn't meet it. If you were not in good shape, you did it again and again," says Ed Walls, who joined Eaton's in 1945 and worked in Montreal, Hamilton, and Toronto.

In the early years of his reign, before John David's health began to fail, those sessions were his main control mechanism over the organization. Each January he'd visit two of the four main centres, Vancouver, Winnipeg, Toronto, and Montreal. "It was a great ceremony. It scared the hell out of us. It made us do our job properly all year," says Walls.

His other appearances across the country were not always the morale boosters they were meant to be. Once, in Winnipeg, John David rose to deliver a speech to some loyal Eatonians, then sat down again without a word escaping his lips. Shy? Uncomfortable? Incapable? Inebriated? All of the above? Who knew?

His main contact with Toronto employees came each Christmas when John David met everyone from the assistant-manager level and higher who had earned a bonus. Each recipient would be called to his office to receive a handshake and a slip of paper announcing the amount of the bonus. "It was the only time of the year you'd ever hear of him, speak to him, see him, know him," says Bob Butler, who later became president. "The fact that he knew your name was always a surprise."

For the most part, however, John David was a passive president. "[He] was clever enough to have very good people around him," says Walls. "He pretty much did what he was told to do."

Only eight and a half years separated John David and Signy's youngest son from the oldest. John Craig was the first, born May 30, 1937. Fredrik Stefan followed on June 26, 1938, then Thor Edgar on August 22, 1942, and George Ross on November 12, 1945.

Three elements are key to understanding "the boys" as they are still called: birth order, money, and Upper Canada College. In his bestselling book *Born to Rebel*, Frank Sulloway argues that birth order is crucial to personality development. Firstborns tend to adopt their parents' perspective on life, thus preserving the status quo. Later-borns are more rebellious and pursue a range of interests as they try to achieve their own niche within the family, thereby attracting parental interest and approval.

"The family does not provide a monolithic experience that automatically immerses its offspring in a single environmental bath," writes Sulloway. "Families do share interests and social values. But siblings differ even in their interests and values, and these differences are caused, in substantial part, by differences in niches within the family." [11]

Firstborns use their position and size to maintain and defend their special status. As a young man, John Craig would beat his chest at family gatherings and cry, "I'm the king, I'm the king," a reminder to everyone that he was the eldest, the one who traditionally assumed the throne and ruled the empire.

Second-borns are more likely to try harder because they have to play catch-up. Fred joined Eaton's in September 1962 as assistant to the merchandise manager on the outer reaches of the empire in Victoria, B.C. He whizzed about with Nicky, his young blond wife, in a black Corvette. Fred told a Victoria colleague, John Williams, who had joined Eaton's in 1959, "I want to be the boss."

"Why do you say that?" asked Williams.

"Second son of a second son," replied Fred, indicating that he knew he had to work harder in order to succeed.

Once Williams met John Craig, he knew Fred was a more likely leader. "John wasn't as serious as Fred. Fred had good people skills. I don't know if he had fire in the belly, but he certainly had a yearning, the desire to be president. He was interested in what had to be done."

As third in line, Thor was not the aggressive firstborn, the ambitious second-born, or the rebellious last-born. His personality was dominated by a shyness caused from being lost in the shuffle. "Thor's very deceptive. His image isn't as good as who he is," says longtime friend Phil Lind. "Because he hasn't staked out any territory, he's the undefined Eaton. Actually, he's quite ubiquitous and knows quite a bit about a lot of things."

Last-borns like George will try to achieve cooperation, but when that doesn't work they'll use their status as "the baby" to get their own way. "He liked danger," says George's friend, novelist Susan Swan. "He was a hippie. He wore long hair and beads. I don't think he had any intention of working for the family firm. They were the conservative ones. George was part of that sixties rebellion."

George smoked marijuana. One of his favourite expressions was "Peace." If things were going badly, he'd say "ooga-booga." If they got worse, it was "ca-ca." As a teenager he had a few run-ins with the police. In 1969 he was clocked at one hundred miles an hour, forty over the speed limit, on Highway 401 east of Toronto and was fined $100.

The second thing that marked the boys was their inherited money; the impact of that was not all to the good. The 1932 kidnap and murder of American aviator Charles Lindbergh's two-year-old son made many a wealthy parent fearful. John David and Signy hired a former Toronto policeman, Alec Dean, as live-in security at 120 Dunvegan to make sure the boys travelled to and from school safely.

John Craig was once asked if he had any problems as a result of being wealthy. "It's like being born on third base," he replied. George's response was similar. "Are you kidding? I'm what everybody in the world would like to be — a rich kid. The word 'need' simply has never existed for me." [12]

Wealth did not, however, include pocket money. "Most of the time they borrowed money, a dollar for the movies," recalls Duff Scott, a friend from prep school days. "They didn't carry much money on them." But people wanted to be with the Eatons, so they put up with the family's foibles and helped financed their lifestyle.

The third formative influence was Upper Canada College (UCC). All of them attended for varying lengths of time and with differing degrees of success. John Craig made it through grade thirteen. Fred passed grade twelve but missed his senior matriculation in two tries, first at UCC, then at Thornton Hall, a cram school. Neither Thor nor George liked UCC. Thor left for Forest Hill Collegiate, then St. Andrew's College. George, who suffered from dyslexia, also went to Forest Hill and finished up at another cram school, Cantab Coaching College.

Opened in 1829, UCC was synonymous in Canada with blue-blood breeding. Yet, by all accounts, it was a brutal environment. Until the 1970s, canings were commonplace; the place reeked of urine and formaldehyde. Some masters seemed almost perverted, more interested in meting out lashes than making leaders. Many of the boys had been discarded by their families and dumped into the school.

According to Conrad Black, pal of the Eatons and fellow student for eight years, UCC had the "pervasive air of the Waspy, snotty, parochial play-pen for Rosedale and Forest Hill, where the likes of Vincent Massey had appeared every few years to bore a new generation of school-leavers, an inordinate number of them on their way to Bay Street to live somnolently ever after from the avails of the old school tie." [13]

Boy Staunton, the protagonist in Robertson Davies's *Fifth Business*, was, according to his creator, himself a UCC grad, "a type which was very well represented in that school — the rich privileged person who had it made, who was clever and not a bad person, but unaware of much about life." [14]

John Craig attended UCC from 1945 to 1957, was associate editor of the school paper, *Current Times*, and played on the school hockey team. He was a winger, and while he wasn't the team's top scorer, he was a good skater who used his shoulders to deke opponents. In his final two years the team twice won the Little Big Four championship playing Ridley, Trinity College School, and St. Andrew's.

John Craig was, in modern parlance, a party animal. The house on Dunvegan was only a block from the school, so it was a favourite hangout. Among the drawing cards were two movie projectors. A first-run film could be run without an interruption to change reels.

In 1994 former UCC student James FitzGerald published *Old Boys: The Powerful Legacy of Upper Canada College*. Many of the seventy-one old boys he quoted recalled capricious cruelty by the masters and an environment that promoted bullying. No Canadian prime minister has ever attended UCC. By contrast, Eton, upon which UCC liked to pattern itself, has produced nineteen British PMs.

A classmate of John Craig's, Tom Godwin, who became a cardiologist, recalled visiting Vancouver in the early 1990s. He read in a local newspaper that a group from Eaton's was also visiting the city, looking to acquire an entire city block. His reaction? "Guess who's the head of the negotiating team? John Eaton, I thought, Holy shit! He was a nice guy, but he didn't have the brains." [15]

John Craig claimed that he enjoyed his time at UCC and has wonderful memories of all his masters. His recollections were strikingly different from those of the majority of his fellow old boys quoted in FitzGerald's book.

"I always believe: If it ain't broke, don't fix it. Upper Canada ain't broke in more ways than one," John Craig told FitzGerald. "Upper Canada is sailing along. Sure, you tighten a bolt here and there. She ain't young and beautiful anymore. But she's got a couple of new buildings and she's looking pretty damn good. She can go a few more miles." [16] As for caning, he carried no lasting scars. "Corporal punishment existed in those days, but I don't think it hurt anybody. It hurt at the time, I can verify that. I remember being caned. It hurt, but you survived. I loved UCC. . . . But you have to work at it. It isn't handed to you on a plate." [17]

The Eatons didn't have it handed to them on a plate? "The Conachers were jocks, so for five generations the Conachers will be jocks," said Andrew Ignatieff, a community worker whose great-grandfather built the boarding school. "The Eatons are dumb but will go into trade, so it doesn't matter." [18]

The fourth influence on the boys, and perhaps the most powerful of all, was John White Hughes Bassett. For the Eaton boys, whose own father was little more than an absentee landlord, the ebullient Bassett became a surrogate father.

About the only thing John David had in common with Bassett was Northern Ireland. The Eatons were from County Antrim, the Bassetts from Tyrone. The two fathers couldn't have been more different about child-rearing. Bassett spent time with his sons and instilled in them a competitive spirit. On the tennis courts, he gave no quarter. The quarrels were loud and punctuated by profanities. Eldest son Johnny F. once punched his father in the nose after a match.

John David gave the family name and fortune to his sons, but little else. The only punishment the boys ever received was Signy's disappointment. John David spent so much time alone or away that Signy became the rock on which the family was built. "Signy had wonderful taste and great interest in the arts," says lawyer Eddie Goodman. "I give Signy the credit for what the boys have learned about helping institutions."

"Both of [my parents] believed very strongly in giving back to the community," says Fred. "My mother was always interested in intellectual pursuits. She loved music, the arts, the art gallery, dance and ballet. I certainly learned about music because of her."

"She tried to keep the boys normal," says Diana, wife of cousin Alan. "But people fawn all over them and make them feel different. It's sort of like Prince Charles; they're isolated in their own world." Fred insists they were also taught that "work is an honourable thing and is to be admired at whatever level. You're no better because you're leading the troops than the person at the bottom who is doing the fighting."

John Bassett was six years younger than John David and had grown up in a family where the major politicians, businessmen, and aristocracy of the day were friends of his father, who was Ottawa correspondent for the Montreal *Gazette* and later president and owner of the *Sherbrooke Daily Record.*

In 1938 Bassett married Moira Bradley, the daughter of a Sherbrooke dentist. They had three sons, John, Douglas, and David. Big John, as the father came to be known, fought in the Second World War with the Seaforth Highlanders, then ran unsuccessfully for the Progressive Conservative Party in Sherbrooke in the 1945 federal election. For three years prior to the war he'd worked for the *Globe and Mail,* but he'd had enough of the reporter's life, so he bought the *Record* from his father.

In 1948 Bassett returned to Toronto as advertising director, then general manager, at the *Telegram.* When owner George McCullagh died in 1952, Bassett entered the ownership bidding war and beat out two other hopefuls, both of them rascals in their own right. One was Jack Kent Cooke, who later left Canada for Washington, D.C., and became owner of the National Football League Redskins and the Los Angeles *Daily News.* The other was William Loeb, ultraconservative publisher of the *Manchester Union Leader,* scourge of any politician campaigning in the New Hampshire primaries. (Bassett knew Cooke but had never heard of Loeb. When he asked around, someone told him: "I'm a careful man with my money, but if I ordered a carload of sonsabitches, and I got the car with only Loeb in it, I'd figure the order was filled.")

But Bassett had no money of his own, just the moxie to make the move. For the necessary funds he turned to John David, who guaranteed a bank loan for the full purchase price of $4,250,000 and thus became the paper's owner. The personalities of the two men were completely opposite. Bassett was the extrovert who enjoyed being in the public eye. John David was the introvert who shrank from the social obligations imposed by his position. Together they made a whole. Just as Eaton money completed the picture for Bassett, Big John was the man John David wished he were.

After the deal closed, Bassett was invited around to 120 Dunvegan. Seated with John David was his lawyer, a gentleman with the imposing name of Gordon Dorward deSalaberry Wotherspoon. Wotherspoon had been with the Toronto law firm of Osler, Hoskin & Harcourt since 1939, and was a longtime Eaton family counsellor. He was called Swatty, an odd nickname rendered even odder by the fact that it was also applied to his brother, his children, and his nephews.

Wotherspoon had devised a plan to ensure that Bassett stayed around to mind the newspaper for John David. "Mr. Eaton wants to give you 30 per cent of the *Telegram,*" said Wotherspoon.

"I can't take that," replied Bassett. "My agreement is to run it; that's a gift I can't take."

"If Mrs. Helen Reid asked you to go down to New York and become publisher of the *Herald-Tribune,* what would you do?"

"I'd go," Bassett shot back.

"Well, what would Mr. Eaton do with the *Telegram?*"

"He'd get somebody else to run it or he'd sell it."

"That isn't the idea," said Wotherspoon. "He got involved because of your friendship. What would you do if you owned 30 per cent of the *Telegram?*"

"I wouldn't go to New York," said Bassett.

"Well, you've got 30 per cent."

Eager to avoid his sons' having to pay stiff succession taxes on his death, Bassett quickly came up with a plan for his 30-percent share of the *Tely.* Turning to the hitherto silent John David, he said, "I've got three sons, you've got four. Why don't we set up a trust and give all of our *Telegram* common shares to the boys, 10 per cent for each of mine and 17½ per cent for each of yours. It couldn't be a better time. The common shares aren't worth a dime. We paid $4.25 million and we borrowed every cent of it."

John David finally bestirred himself. "If that's what you want to do, that's fine."

The trust was called Telegram Corporation Ltd., and Bassett announced that he'd also donate his ownership in the *Sherbrooke Daily Record* to it.

Bassett's salary as publisher was $30,000 a year, but the *Tely* also paid all his expenses, including house, cars, and entertainment. "John Bassett was not an accumulator of wealth," said lawyer Eddie Goodman in his 1988 memoirs. "He never tired of saying that he did not want to die a millionaire as long as he could live like a millionaire, which he did." [19]

A favourite haunt for Bassett was the long-since-demolished Berkley Hotel, at Simcoe and Front Streets, with its band and chorus line. When Moira was at their summer home in the Eastern Townships, he'd spend many an evening at the Berkley. John David had a roving eye, too, but around Toronto he guarded his reputation. Because he was careful to have his fun out of town, Signy did not protest. Divorce in those days was unusual, a status-destroying step taken only by a few rash souls. Most wives soldiered on, suffering in silence.

In Montreal John David was a different man. He would stay at the Mount Royal Hotel where he maintained a permanent suite. Checking on the store wasn't the only reason for his visits. Beginning in the 1950s, there was another attraction, a mistress, whom he kept for a number of years.

The elegant French-Canadian brunette, then in her early forties, operated a hotel north of Montreal near Ste. Agathe in the Laurentians. While the two were never seen together in public, key managers selling fashion and furs in the Eaton's store knew full well the identity of this big spender and how to handle her purchases in the store. "She would do it on an account, then the fudging of the accounts would be done upstairs in the executive office," says Ed Walls, who managed the departments where she made her selections. "They were all paid for."

Signy had every reason to seek solace elsewhere, not just because of John David's peccadilloes but also because he was not an easy man to live with. "[John David] was a kind man but he was up and down emotionally like a yo-yo," John Craig's first wife, Kitty, said in 1979. "And like many people who drink too much he would turn on you. He was a very scary person that way."

Big John Bassett became a source of strength and a fountain of fun for Signy. "Bassett was around the Eatons' Dunvegan Road home a great deal. I always knew he was coming because Signy would get very cheery — little girlish I called it. We usually gathered in the library. Old J.D. would sit there reading, Signy and John [Bassett] would talk over on the couch and I would watch TV with one or two of my kids. Moira Bassett would occasionally come along but nobody paid much attention to her," said Kitty. [20]

As the special bond grew between Big John and Signy, so did the gossip. "There was chatter about Bassett's relationship with [John David's] wife," recalls banker Allen Lambert. "It was sufficiently unique to cause people to wonder if there was more than appeared on the surface. I never saw anything."

"John Bassett *thought* he had a very special relationship with her," says Florence, Signy's sister-in-law. "I think maybe she was flattered at all the attention. I think it also wore off. I didn't like to see him anywhere near her, I must say. I don't know how close it actually became. He was just smarming at her, really, and she could have fallen for it. It's very flattering to have someone that seems to be so entranced of you. But he also tried to make me think the same thing — and I ain't Signy."

Still, the talk became so widespread and scurrilous that some members of Toronto society still believe to this day that one of the Eaton boys was sired by Big John Bassett. "None of us looks like him," says Fred, the only one of the boys who was prepared to be interviewed on family matters. "If you ever saw a bunch of people who looked like they were brothers, it's the four of us. I mean, there's no question about that. I think it's a figment of somebody's imagination and I don't believe it."

"I loved Signy as a person. We weren't lovers," said Bassett a few months before he died in April 1998. "People would be envious of the Eatons, and, I suppose, envious of me, some. I was very visible in Toronto. I never had an affair with her. It wasn't that kind of a relationship. I loved the both of them.

"I suppose people did say I had an affair with Signy because if John was away and she was alone, I'd take her out to dinner or take her to the theatre, that sort of thing. Never thought a thing about it, neither did she, neither did John. It wasn't that kind of a situation. I had other girls, in those days," Bassett said with a chortle, "one or two, but not her."

Despite John David's deep need for Big John's friendship, there were limits to John David's forbearance. Bassett once joined John David in Windsor, Ontario, for a lake cruise. The group was sitting on the top deck, eating lobster and drinking champagne. Bassett made a toast and then exuberantly tossed his glass overboard.

The others laughed, but not John David. "That's enough," he snapped. "You don't get a glass, a plate or a fork to eat with for the rest of the trip." Bassett flushed crimson with embarrassment and fled below. John David was as good as his word; Bassett had to make do with his fingers. [21]

In 1962 Bassett ran for Parliament in the downtown Toronto riding of Spadina and lost to Perry Ryan, a Liberal. After the ritual visits to his own committee room and his opponent's headquarters, Bassett drove to 120 Dunvegan. John David heard his car pull up, came outside, and was so relieved his friend wasn't headed for Ottawa that he hugged Bassett and said: "I know you feel badly and I know I shouldn't say it, but I'm so glad."

During the 1963 federal election, Bassett abandoned the Tory party. He disagreed with Prime Minister John Diefenbaker's position against U.S. nuclear weapons on Canadian soil. In a front-page editorial the *Tely* did the unthinkable. The forever-blue newspaper urged readers to elect a Liberal majority.

Over dinner shortly after Signy asked him how he was going to vote. Bassett said he couldn't bring himself to vote for the Liberal Ryan, who was running for re-election, so he was just going to stay home. An irate Signy told him: "You can't take such a high and mighty ground writing editorials telling people what they should do and skulk home on election day." [22] Bassett hung his head, held his nose, and voted for Ryan.

By then, Bassett was in the process of leaving his first wife in favour of Isabel Crawford, a *Tely* reporter and former high school teacher who'd been named Miss Byline 1965. Aware of the scandal a divorce would cause, Bassett advised John David and Signy in advance, then added: "If this embarrasses you or the family, I'll resign as publisher."

Asked John David: "Well, what will you do?"

Bassett said he might go to London and work for one of Roy Thomson's newspapers. "They were both horrified," recalled Bassett. "They said, 'Stay here, you don't have to resign.'"

John David and Signy supported Big John socially during the brouhaha that developed about the divorce. John David was equally supportive about the newspaper and never interfered in the running of the *Telegram*. "He never made a suggestion. He was a totally hands-off owner," said Bassett. "He was the kind of owner that a manager would think he'd died and gone to heaven."

Maybe John David never asked for favours at what he sometimes referred to as the *Daily Bugle* because he didn't need to. In 1955, for example, when John David joined the Eaton's Quarter Century Club as member number 8496, the company issued a lengthy press release extolling its president's virtues. After a newsy start to the report of the nonevent, the *Telegram* published the corporate handout verbatim.

John David's connection to broadcasting was also made through Bassett. Bassett won a television licence from the Board of Broadcast Governors (now the Canadian Radio-television and Telecommunications Commission) and CFTO-TV was launched in January 1961. The new corporate entity, Baton Broadcasting Inc., was added to the newspaper holdings of the four Eaton sons and three Bassett sons in Telegram Corp — a remarkably generous move, considering that John David had no financial stake in Baton. (The corporate name, Baton, had a mysterious origin. For whatever reason, Bassett told two stories with equal insistence over the years. The first was that the name had been created by combining letters from the two family surnames. The second explanation was that Bay and Wellington streets in downtown Toronto had supplied the root letters.)

As close as they were in Toronto, John David and Big John Bassett were not regular travelling companions, but the two sons of the soil once visited Northern Ireland together. They then made their way through Europe, and ended their journey in the south of France, where John David had rented a villa at Cap d'Antibes for a family holiday.

To celebrate Signy's July 1 birthday, John David took everyone to Au Bon Auberge, a three-star restaurant nearby. John David decided to order some champagne. Everyone waited expectantly while he perused the wine list at great length. Finally he looked up, and the sommelier leaned closer to hear the selection. John David waved the wine list at him and deadpanned with feigned derision: "Domestic." There were hoots of laughter all round.

John David could afford to be droll. Eaton's had forty-five thousand employees, sixty thousand at Christmas. They worked in 14 main stores, 42 branch stores, 6 foreign buying offices, 4 mail-order warehouses, 4 factories, and 299 order offices.

But a foreign invader had arrived, and the kingdom would never be the same again.

CHAPTER SIX

THE FIRM THAT TIME FORGOT

I N 1952 GENERAL E. R. WOOD, CHAIRMAN OF
Sears, Roebuck & Co., of Chicago, approached Edgar Burton, then president
of Simpson's, proposing joint ownership of the two companies' catalogue and
mail-order businesses. Burton saw the potential synergy and accepted. Retailing in Canada changed forever.

Eaton's was not prepared for the interloper, its own strength sapped by a
bitter five-year battle with the Retail, Wholesale and Department Store Union.
The union movement had been gaining strength in both the U.S. and
Canada. The Canadian Congress of Labour was formed in 1940, and by 1947
there were nearly one million union members in Canada. There had been
one failed attempt in 1943 to organize Simpson's.

Organizers designated Eaton's as a prime target. The Toronto operations
had grown huge, with sixteen thousand employees spread over more than a
dozen locations. In September 1947 Eaton's seemed like fertile ground for Local
1000 of the Retail, Wholesale and Department Store Union. Women started at
$20 a week, married men were paid $32 at a time when the Toronto Welfare
Council estimated the weekly needs of a family of five to be $44.45. [1] By the end
of 1948, fifteen hundred employees had signed union membership cards.

Eaton's tried to slow the union's progress that fall by announcing "The New
Deal for Employees," a contributory pension plan. Employees would put 5 per
cent of their earnings into the fund and Eaton's would match the amount. John
David donated $50 million of the company's money to launch the scheme.

Despite the welcome step, the number of Eatonians who signed cards grew to five thousand in 1949, and on October 18, 1950, an application for certification was filed with the Ontario Labour Relations Board on behalf of 6629 signed members. Protests by Eaton's meant seven months of hearings before the vote was finally set for December 1951.

Some employees, who called themselves "Loyal Eatonians," launched a weekly paper extolling the virtues of the family firm. Eaton's published its own anti-union leaflets. On one occasion in the time running up to the vote, Lady Eaton appeared outside the College Street store before 8:30 a.m. offering encouragement to oppose the certification. The following morning, she showed up at the doors of the Queen Street store.

When the December vote was held, the union was rejected by 49.2 per cent, with 40.5 per cent voting for the union. (The remainder consisted of spoiled ballots and those who did not vote.) In September 1953, with the union threat gone, the Saturday half day off was cancelled and the six-day week was back. Weekday store hours were also extended by thirty minutes to 5:30 p.m.

The new retailing threat from the United States would not be so easily beaten. Employee loyalty alone would not attract shoppers to Eaton's. Other U.S. giants had previously arrived on the Canadian retailing scene — Woolworth in 1912 and Kresge in 1928 — but neither of those five-and-dimes had much impact on Eaton's. Sears was different. It understood the mentality of the new suburban consumer and had built its first suburban outlet in Aurora, Illinois, in 1928. In 1946 Eaton's had opened a store in a mall in Deep River, Ontario, but showed no interest in pursuing the approach as a general strategy. When Canada's first major shopping centre opened at Park Royal North in Vancouver in 1950, Woodward's was a tenant. A Woodward's official distinctly remembers the dismissive comment made at the official opening by a senior Eaton's executive: "It'll never work." [2]

The landmark deal that closed January 8, 1953, was a precursor of how business would be done in the future. Simpson's put its mail-order division into a new company that became known as Simpsons-Sears Limited. Sears contributed $20 million. Along with that investment came some of the Sears lines, such as Coldspot refrigerators and Craftsman tools.

Simpson's retained its five stores in Toronto, Montreal, London, Regina, and Halifax. New Simpsons-Sears stores — based on the Sears model — could be built anywhere as long as they were at least twenty-five miles from an existing Simpson's store. Simpson's was restricted to the urban centres where its stores were already located. (The arrangement was altered in 1972 to allow either to go anywhere if the other agreed.)

The first Simpsons-Sears opened in Hamilton in 1954. Six more quickly followed using a stylish and efficient design that contrasted with most Eaton's stores, which had not been altered or updated in decades. Eaton's was even slow to respond to changes in Toronto's infrastructure. The Toronto subway opened in 1954, and initially Eaton's refused to allow direct access into the store. It was only when Simpson's embraced the idea that Eaton's reluctantly followed.

Simpsons-Sears also declared all-out war on Eaton's mail-order business. In the first catalogue after the merger, Simpsons-Sears announced that any home appliance priced at $200 or more could be purchased for a $10 down payment. Eaton's stuck with its 10 per cent minimum. Prices at Simpsons-Sears on appliances and furniture did not include shipping costs. Eaton's continued to show prices with freight included. As a result Simpsons-Sears prices looked lower and Eaton's was stuck paying costs — to whatever heights they might rise.

That first Simpsons-Sears catalogue was larger than Eaton's, 556 pages to 552. For the next edition Eaton's went to 676 pages, but Sears swelled to 708. Eaton's tried an appeal to patriotism by contrasting the "foreign" origins of its competitor with Eaton's made-in-Canada roots. The cover of the winter 1955 Simpsons-Sears catalogue featured a woman's coat and hat outfit. The cover of the Eaton's winter 1955 issue was all type. Under the heading "What's in a Name?" Eaton's extolled the virtues of "85 years under the management of the Eaton family . . . a distinctly Canadian name."

At the bottom a new corporate name appeared: "Eaton's of Canada." (The designation lasted a decade, then was abandoned and just plain Eaton's returned.) Inside, there were maps of Canada; Union Jacks flew beside British-made goods. Even the budgies were said to be "from Canadian talking strains." The patriotic marketing plan was soon scuppered by an embarrassing blunder. That Christmas, a featured Eaton's of Canada toy truck was found to be carrying another designation: "Made in Japan."

In 1955 Simpson's began Friday-night shopping, then soon added Thursday nights. It wasn't until Christmas 1956 that Eaton's followed suit. "The change has been made with the greatest reluctance," declared John David in a statement. At the same time he said that if it were possible "for by-laws to be enacted across the country prohibiting night openings of stores, we would give such a proposition our full support." Even then, Eaton's longer hours were just at Christmas. Not until 1959 were weeknight openings year-round.

Eaton's was also facing rising competition from discount outlets, but Lady Eaton was opposed to Eaton's price-conscious shoppers. "What's all this about bargain centres?" she said to John David. "Are we going to start a place like Honest Ned's?"

Replied her son: "You should know, Mother, that anything they can do we can do better." [3] Despite his offhand reply, a direct response by Eaton's to discount outlets wouldn't come for another fifteen years.

In 1956 Eaton's opened a three-level 135,000-square-foot store in the Oshawa Shopping Centre in Oshawa, where General Motors was expanding. By then, there were sixty-four shopping centres in Canada, yet this was Eaton's first major mall venture. By 1960 Eaton's was beginning to fall so far behind the competition that its share of department-store sales had dropped to 39 per cent, down eleven percentage points from a decade earlier.

The organization that had once prided itself on being first with just about every innovation — the first deposit accounts in 1904, the first shopping service in 1911, the first wedding bureau in the mid-1930s, the first electric lights, escalators, telephones, fashion shows — was now rarely out in front except in arrogance. "Whenever it was necessary to discuss a mutual problem — store hours, for example — their approach was very aristocratic," wrote James Bryant in his 1977 book *Department Store Disease*. "They stated *their* plans, and other stores were expected to follow meekly behind." Increasingly competitors paid no attention and pressed ahead. By contrast, Eaton's management was stagnant. In 1962 Eaton's conducted a survey and found that the average manager was fifty-five, had a high school education, and wore the gold watch attesting to membership in the Quarter Century Club.

Despite Eaton's slippage, senior executives lived like kings. J.J. Vaughan, for instance, owned a mansion on Bayview Avenue that, after his death in 1963, became part of Sunnybrook Medical Centre. His brother, O.D., who was John David's right-hand man, lived on Beaumont Road, a cul-de-sac overlooking the Rosedale ravine in Toronto. The mansion could easily hold a reception for 150 people and contained sculptures by Brancusi, Giacometti, and Hepworth, as well as drawings by Picasso and Braque. O.D. Vaughn's wife, Nora, was outfitted by the best couturiers, including Balenciaga and Schiaparelli. O.D. also had a farm near Georgetown and a summer home on Georgian Bay.

O.D. retired in 1961 and died in 1976. When Nora died in 1993, the house fetched $4 million. Her bequests included $300,000 to the Canadian National Institute for the Blind and $1 million to each of the University of Toronto and the Ontario College of Art. Nora's designer wardrobe, which had filled two rooms in the house, went to the Royal Ontario Museum.

But the brothers Vaughan weren't the only millionaires created by

Eaton's. Whether they were in Toronto, Montreal, or Winnipeg, most senior managers lived in the finest houses. In fact, houses that today are occupied by corporate presidents who earn millions in salaries, bonuses, and stock options were often owned, in the past, by Eaton's merchants. Irish-born John McKee, who started at Eaton's in 1907 and became a director in 1937, lived at 125 Dunvegan; David Kinnear, who joined in 1928 and stayed until 1992, lived at 31 Forest Hill Road. Rosedale's Chestnut Park Road was also popular with directors: Charles Boothe lived at 73, and Chester Leishman was next door at 77.

Montreal manager Fred Walls had a country home in the Laurentians and a downtown pied-à-terre on Sherbrooke Street West. Winnipeg bigwigs usually lived on Wellington Crescent. Sam Wilson, who was assistant to the general manager in Winnipeg in 1917 and was made a director in 1920, built himself a lodge on two islands near Manitou east of Winnipeg that later became Birch Island Resort.

The chagrin caused by the 1930s price-spreads committee had, apparently, not reduced executive compensation. In fact, the brief rays of sunlight on the inner workings of Eaton's had the opposite effect. Concern that excessive profiteering might cause renewed political allegations caused bloated salaries and hefty bonuses right through the 1940s, 1950s, and 1960s, rather than see the money go to the bottom line as profits.

"The company was very conservative in its attempt to make a profit, and the company's senior management would tend to be critical of any area where the profits exceeded one or two percent," says Greg Purchase, who joined Eaton's in 1954 and later rose to chief operating officer. "This desire to be conservative in the amount of money that the company made meant that the company would tend to overcompensate its middle and senior management." [4]

There were also opportunities for executives to invest quietly in land next door to a planned store location or make easy money in the stock market using information, not widely available, gleaned from suppliers or bankers. Payments and gifts from suppliers were commonplace. Management mediocrity was not only practised, it was rewarded in what had become a culture of contentment.

John David and Lady Eaton could dicker about discount outlets all they liked; both of them were wrong for the company, each in their own unhelpful way. Lady Eaton was resolutely traditional; John David didn't have sufficient strength of character to stand up either to her or his managers. Because no one had a vision for the future, little was achieved.

Lady Eaton continued to make public pronouncements on just about every topic. Letters to the editor, always signed Flora McCrea Eaton, were splenetic. In 1950 she complained how overhanging signs on Toronto's Yonge Street made it "the ugliest main street in the world." A 1961 missive castigated a reviewer over a piano recital they had both attended; a 1962 letter defended Saskatchewan doctors in their protest against medicare.

Speeches were another occasion to sound off. She denounced the commercialization of Mother's Day in a 1948 address to the Men's Bible Class at Rogers Memorial Presbyterian Church. "For weeks before the appointed day, you can find pages of advertising telling you what to buy mother on her day, but not a word about the love and honour that the originator [of the idea] had intended we should show mothers." [5]

In 1957 she told the Canadian Women's Club of Winnipeg about her recent trip to the Middle East. "Lady Eaton noted the reaction in Jerusalem to the partition of Palestine," said the report in the *Winnipeg Free Press*. "Hitler made martyrs of the Jews and from that moment it couldn't work, she said. The Jewish people weren't satisfied to stay in the land that was given to them but tried to take more, Lady Eaton said. They have interfered with the rights of the Arabs and Arab forays have resulted." [6]

Dr. Sidney Kobrinsky of Winnipeg wrote a letter to the editor, calling the comments "shocking and disgraceful," and asked if Lady Eaton needed to be reminded of the six million Jews who died in the Holocaust. Kobrinsky demanded an apology because, he said, her views "have an all too familiar ring." [7]

Lady Eaton revelled in being the centre of attention. She preened when all eyes were on her, whether she was giving an interview, officiating at an event, or delivering a speech. She'd arrive decked out in draped dresses, a hat with ostrich plumes, and mink mittens for the arthritis in her hands. On her birthdays she expected appropriate homage. In 1959, when she turned eighty, she quoted founder Timothy in turn quoting his own mother: "If you're as good as you're old, you're all right." In the next breath Lady Eaton pretended she was not as old as she really was. Although she'd been born in 1879, she told the assemblage she was born sometime during the decade that followed.

She also seized on such occasions to offer advice to professional women. "Now that women have entered the high places of business, they can no longer expect the concessions they received as demure ladies sewing a fine seam," she said at one celebration. [8] "They should never forget they are women," she said on another natal day. "They should remain feminine, not try to compete with men, and so avoid becoming neither man nor woman, genderless." [9]

Her views on a woman's place in society hadn't advanced much since 1927 when she said she did not favour the vote for women. "I do not see that women have gained much by the vote — it has merely complicated the problem because the vote is not restricted to intelligent women. I think the vote is rather a nuisance myself for it is something which I have to do now. I have four sons and if I am the right kind of mother I should have some influence on their vote — so that means four instead of just one." [10]

After the war Lady Eaton had returned to Eaton Hall and continued her public life. In 1948 she was installed as executive chairman of the United Emergency Fund for Britain and in that role travelled to England to confer with Lady Mountbatten. With Lady Eaton's involvement, the group was able to raise $700,000 — although there were questions about the organizer, Herbert Daly. Some reports suggested that much of the money collected went to pay his salary and office and travel costs, rather than to food parcels for Britain.

The persona of the grande dame leading good works on behalf of war-battered Britain suited Lady Eaton's sensibilities. "I'm a traditionalist of the first water. I still say the British 'Empire' — it's still the Dominion of Canada to me — and the Royal Mail is still Royal," she told the Eaton Business Girls' Council in 1952.[11] In 1953 she led a family group to the coronation of Queen Elizabeth. She also received royal guests in Canada. Princess Alice, Countess of Athlone, wife of the governor general from 1940 to 1946 and great aunt of the Queen, visited at Eaton Hall for a week in 1959.

Large receptions that had been cancelled by the war were resumed. Senior Eaton's staff with their spouses, a group numbering in the hundreds, attended the annual Christmas parties at the home in King. Delivery drivers were conscripted to park the cars, a valet service few attendees were accorded on any other occasion. Trees near the house were decorated with lights. A creche held the place of honour near the front door. Queen Mary's personal Christmas card was displayed on a mantel. Swags of cedar hung in the hunt ballroom where a buffet table ran the length of the room.

The family Christmas celebration at Eaton Hall was a major production, the one time during the year when all the members of the Royal household gathered under Lady Eaton's roof. Lady Eaton, wearing three strands of pearls and a pin with three maple leaves in diamonds on a red dress with rustling green petticoats, presided. In a ritual begun while Lady Eaton and Sir

John lived at Ardwold, communion service was conducted by the incumbent pastor of Timothy Eaton Memorial. David Ouchterlony, the organist at Eaton Memorial for more than three decades — "Dr. O." as he was known to the church regulars — played the organ.

An afternoon reception on the lower level featured oysters, caviar, and Rhine wine. Johnny Giordmaine would entertain with tricks. Just five feet tall, Johnny, known as the "Merry Magician," looked like an elf and functioned as the unofficial court jester to the family. Born in Malta, he'd started out selling novelty items in a Yonge Street store and worked at Eaton's from 1930 to 1960. He appeared on the *Ed Sullivan Show* in January 1957, where, among other televised stunts, he produced from his vest pocket an eight-foot pole topped by a flag. Giordmaine's signature joke was prompted by someone asking, "What time is it?" whereupon he would pull out an oversize pocket watch, produce a cookie from its false lid, and reply, "Time for lunch!"

Bob Hollingsworth, Lady Eaton's groomsman for forty-nine years, played Santa and handed out gifts to all the children. Lady Eaton would seek out ideas for each child in advance. If a little girl wanted skates, she not only got them, but the entire ensemble: stockings, skirt, sweater, hat, and muff. After the gifts were opened, everyone moved to the main-floor dining room. There, the seating followed a plan meticulously worked out by Lady Eaton to intersperse adults and children. Children were declared VIPs for the day, and one of them would be selected to serve as master of ceremonies during the dinner of roast turkey and carrot pudding.

While the Christmas meal was as predictable as it was grand, visitors during the rest of the year were often surprised by the fare. Lady Eaton followed every health fad with enthusiasm and happily ingested numerous cures for diseases she didn't have.

Among Lady Eaton's books were numerous weight-loss plans, including *Tomorrow We Diet*, written by Nina Wilcox in 1922, and the popular Hay diet from *Health Via Food*, written by William Howard Hay in 1929. If Lady Eaton were adhering to a particular regimen, as she often did, guests were forced to follow suit. One she tried featured a breakfast that consisted of alternate sips of orange juice and milk.

After one such siege, the guests who had suffered through several days of near-fasting were saying their goodbyes and preparing to depart. Lady Eaton asked her great-niece, also named Flora, if she'd had a good time. "No," replied the little girl, speaking freely as only a child can. "I've been hungry and I've been thirsty, too."

Sometimes Lady Eaton carried her concern about health and appearance to extremes. As a young woman, she had been amply endowed. She didn't like her buxom appearance, so, after all her children were born, she set out to have her breasts surgically reduced. The procedure was more like butchery. She was left with horrific scars and had to wear padded brassieres.

Hunting-class horses were bred on the farm, and even before she began riding to hounds herself, Lady Eaton would entertain the members of the Toronto and North York Hunt at breakfasts. She would don the appropriate gear, mount a horse, greet the guests, then remain behind as they rode off. For a time Lady Eaton used Simpson's catering because Eaton's did not have such a service. The secret was revealed one day as the guests rode up the long, tree-lined drive and spotted two Simpson's trucks. Among those on horseback that morning was Simpson's president Allan Burton (brother of Edgar, the former president), who took some ribbing from his companions about the lengths he would go to advertise. The drivers had become lost on the way north, arrived late, and so had not been able to make their usual discreet delivery, then disappear before the guests arrived. Lady Eaton cancelled the contract.

———

While Lady Eaton was showing off, John David hid in the shadows. He didn't like to fly commercially, so Eaton's had four aircraft, including a $1 million four-engine Lockheed JetStar delivered in March 1962. Eaton's was the first Canadian corporation to own a JetStar, capable of travelling at six hundred miles an hour.

But for all his inherited wealth and expensive toys, John David had acquired little finesse. He couldn't even seem to give money away with style. When asked why he supported the Ontario Crippled Children's Centre, John David said: "It's a real tear-jerker. So we raised the money, built the hospital — and now, well, we have to run the thing. I suppose it's a case of 'there but for the grace of God' sort of thing." [12]

His wife Signy was just the opposite; she loved to see and be seen and could carry off public appearances with élan. In 1959 the government of Iceland named her a Knight of the Order of the Falcon, the highest civilian honour that country bestows. In 1967 she gave a speech in Icelandic in Gimli, Manitoba, and served as Fjallkonen (maid of the mountain), a mythical creature who, according to legend, descends from the mountains to preside over the annual festival. In 1961, when York University was founded, she was appointed to the board of governors and served for ten years.

Signy was forever slim and favoured tailored clothing — suits and sheath dresses — in colours such as beige, gray, or black. The hems of her formal outfits tended to be short, and her evening wear often set the style for the season. In 1952 she was cited as one of the best-dressed women in Toronto; in 1962 the *Telegram* named her to the Fashion Hall of Fame.

Signy's moneyed profile also made her a target. In November 1967 thieves broke into the house on Dunvegan and stripped paintings from the walls. Interrupted, they abandoned some items, but fled with works by Thelma Van Alystyne, Marc Chagall, Georges Rouault, Jean-Paul Riopelle, and Roloff Beny. They were never recovered. The loss was estimated at $250,000. In June 1968, while a dinner dance on Queen's Plate weekend was in progress, a cat burglar took cash, jewellery, and loose precious stones valued at $1.4 million from Signy's second-floor strongbox. The booty, including a twenty-carat diamond worth $150,000, was later recovered.

Fashion meant little to John David. He wore bespoke suits from a London tailor, but always managed to look rumpled. Nor was he concerned about colour coordination; wearing brown shoes with a blue suit caused him no qualms. John David's feet were huge, size twelve, and one of the manufacturers had created a special last for him. Every season the maker produced a complete range of styles in John David's size, from bluchers to brogues, which were kept on a separate shelf in the Queen Street shoe department. Harry Gapp from Parry Sound was John David's only fitter. Gapp was a ringer, an employee who was not hired for his capacity as a salesman, but because he was a top hockey player and could contribute mightily to the Eaton's team.

When word was dispatched that the boss needed new footwear, Gapp would assemble that season's selections. John David did not like to sit in the men's shoe department, because he found the area too enclosed. Moreover, he might be cheek by jowl with actual customers and have to converse with them. So the tycoon would have Gapp fit him among the toddlers in children's shoes, where there were more chairs, more space, and less likelihood of chitchat.

It was Signy who filled their Toronto home with art. Beside a fireplace stood a three-foot-tall pottery jar that was two thousand years old and had been brought up from the sands in an Aegean harbour. She also owned several ancient Chinese pieces and some eighteenth-century Italian painted chairs, but her most significant treasures were by twentieth-century painters such as Utrillo, Picasso, Chagall, and Dufy, as well as sculpture by Henry

Moore. In 1967 she was among three collectors who donated forty contemporary prints by Canadian artists to the permanent collection of New York City's Museum of Modern Art on the occasion of Canada's centennial. (The other donors were Samuel Zacks, president of the Art Gallery of Toronto, and Mrs. Samuel Bronfman.) After being shown at the MOMA, the exhibition travelled extensively in the United States.

One event that underscored the different personalities of John David and Signy occurred when piano prodigy Glenn Gould was invited to play at 120 Dunvegan for a group of their society friends. As he walked along a hall that Saturday afternoon, Gould passed a darkened room where John David was sitting alone, drinking, and watching football on television.

Much of the time, however, privacy was almost impossible for John David. There always seemed to be something going on at the house — for the Children's Aid Society, the Toronto Symphony, the Opera, or the National Ballet. John David arrived home one night, found the place strangely quiet, and wryly remarked: "It's nice to come to my own front door and not have to pay to get in." [13] Nor did he show any interest when Signy became so enraptured with Eastern spiritual pursuits that she invited Swami Vishnu from Toronto's Sivananda Centre to stay at their Georgian Bay home.

Even when he was an investor, he always wanted to be a silent partner. It was John David's habit to invest in the person with the idea, rather than the idea itself. He'd bet on the jockey, not the horse. Few deals were as public as his ownership of the *Telegram* and his connection to Bassett. More typical was the time he backed Tommy Holmes, who had been a boxer, became a bodyguard to Ontario Premier Mitch Hepburn, and later became Ontario sales manager for Labatt's. In the 1950s, when Holmes wanted to start his own nightclub business, he turned to John David for $30,000 to start Club 12 on Adelaide Street East in Toronto. "John David gave it to him just like that," recalls lawyer Eddie Goodman. "He liked Tommy and wanted to help him. He'd back people regardless of their upbringing. He didn't just like to have friends in so-called society."

By 1969, after twenty-seven years as president, John David was worth an estimated $400 million. Most of the money he spent on himself was to escape the social whirl. He bought a twelve-acre island in Georgian Bay from the Ontario Department of Lands and Forests and built a main house, as well as sleeping cottages that could easily accommodate twenty people — more for the traditional July first celebration of Signy's birthday. Someone suggested he should have flower beds. "To hell with it," he exploded. "The reason I come up here is to get away from it all." [14] There was, however, a tennis court, a man-made beach, and a bar that dispensed fountain Coke. The family also had a farm on the mainland where they grew a few vegetables. "I can't tell you," Signy once sighed, "how much each pea costs."

No amount of money seemed to be able to buy good health, and John David suffered from several chronic problems. "He was a proud man," says banker Allen Lambert. "He bore his ailments without much complaint. He just wanted to be alone, by himself." For years he had a tic that caused his head to shake from side to side. Everyone assumed he had Parkinson's disease, but he developed no other symptoms. He also suffered from arthritis in both hips, necessitating a constant intake of painkillers. Every year the couple would invite friends to spend New Year's Eve at their home in Caledon; on one occasion the pain was so bad that John David spent the evening lying flat on his back on the floor in a desperate search for relief.

A life of smoking, heavy alcohol consumption, and overeating contributed to his decline. In 1956 he visited the Vancouver Eaton's with David Kinnear, then general manager for British Columbia. In the first-aid department they decided to weigh themselves. "He was grossly overweight, I was well overweight," Kinnear recalls. "So I said, 'We've got to do something about this.' He went on a diet and went down from 230 to about 180. He looked great and then he blew up again."

Dewar's was John David's preferred drink. "We had to be careful with him when we had a party," says Kinnear. "There was a waiter that we had, and when he got somebody that really liked a big scotch, he poured them a big scotch. And we had to tell him, 'You don't do that.' You can only take so much, eh?"

Once, at Kinnear's house in Vancouver, John David drank so heavily that he passed out, and his pal, Charlie Van Norman, had to help the boss back to his hotel. As it happened, John Craig was with his father that evening. Recalls Kinnear: "He was disgusted."

Asked John Craig: "Does he always do this?"

Replied Kinnear: "Never before."

The events of the evening seemed to have had no lasting impact. "He was around, kicking, the next day," says Kinnear.

Was he an alcoholic? "He certainly drank," confirms his son Fred, "but I don't know what an alcoholic is. I've heard it described as someone who has a drink every day, and I figure if that's what an alcoholic is, I'm a bad alcoholic. But if you get technical about it, I guess he was. To me, it's a matter of functioning in society, which he was capable of doing. I've met people who, by lunchtime, it was all over, and he certainly wasn't in that class."

After a time it became hard to tell whether the booze was a cause of John David's health problems or an escape from the life he lived. "I think a lot of us have assisted the health problems with alcohol," says his sister Florence, soon to be eighty. "Bodily parts disintegrate." For her, drinking is almost a part of the Eatons' genetic heritage, like the pleasure that family members feel behind the wheel of a car. "We've all got gasoline in our veins," she says. "And alcohol."

The two faces of the Eaton family were the flamboyant mother and the unfathomable son. Whatever John David thought remained unsaid. Whatever Lady Eaton believed, she blurted. After the 1962 Cuban missile crisis, when President John Kennedy stared down Nikita Khrushchev, she said of the Soviet leader: "Why doesn't some person tell him where to get off at? He thinks he's got the world terrified."

As the Cold War tensions grew, Lady Eaton believed she was personally prepared. In addition to Eaton Hall, she had a Toronto city home at 2 Old Forest Hill Road. Features included Italian marble fireplaces, a hand-carved walnut staircase, and a third floor tricked up to look like a northlands cabin with log-and-mortar walls, a stone fireplace, and British Columbia fir floors. At a time when everyone was talking about building underground bunkers in case of nuclear attack, Lady Eaton was convinced that the room would serve as a safe haven, even though it was well above ground.

For daytime public occasions Lady Eaton's attire usually included a brooch that featured two keys. One had been used to open the Calgary store in 1929, the other the Eaton Electronics Laboratory, built in 1950 with $200,000 donated to McGill University by Eaton's. She felt the brooch, which symbolized her twin interests in business and philanthropy, made a good conversation piece.

Lady Eaton served on committees of the Art Gallery of Toronto and the Royal Ontario Museum. In 1963 she was also the benefactor of $20,000 to purchase a rare violin for Stratford violinist Otto Armin, who had started his musical career with a $5 model from the Eaton's catalogue. After she heard Sonya Sydell, an eleven-year-old pianist, play at an afternoon tea, Lady Eaton gave her a baby grand. Sydell, whose first piano had been rescued from a junkpile by her father, went on to become a concert pianist.

One of her longest-running acts as a patron of the arts began in 1954 when actor Douglas Campbell was speaking to the University Women's Club. The Stratford Festival had been inaugurated the previous year, and Campbell was talking about extending the company's audience.

"How much money would you need to establish a touring company in Canada?" asked someone from the audience.

"Fifty to sixty thousand dollars," said Campbell.

"That shouldn't be too difficult," replied the voice. It was Lady Eaton.

Her interest went far beyond being a financial angel. She'd show up in jodhpurs at the actors' rehearsal camp in Haliburton, Ontario, or fly to Halifax to make sure everyone was properly fed on opening night.

She understood actresses and actors: her own life was all about being centre stage. "I think she is a lady who always enjoys the theatrical — just as an actor enjoys a situation in which he can be resplendent," said Campbell in 1960. "She enjoys situations, like a lot of people do — but she does it well and with a sense of humour. And there's a practical woman under this grand lady. She's no fool." [15]

Honours flowed from her largesse. She collected an honorary doctor of laws degree in 1964 from Waterloo Lutheran University to go with LL.D. degrees from McGill University and the University of Western Ontario in 1950 and the University of Toronto in 1941, as well as an honorary degree of doctor of civil law from Bishop's College in 1952.

As generous as she could be with strangers, her beneficence to close relatives was quirky. On the one hand, for years Lady Eaton helped look after her sister, Anna, who was an accomplished pianist, nature-lover, and student of bird life. As an adult, Anna became crippled by arthritis. In October 1952 she went on a motoring holiday in southern Ontario with a friend. In Port Elgin she was left sitting alone for a few minutes in the friend's parked car. The vehicle began slowly rolling backward down an incline onto a dock, hung in midair at the edge for a few seconds, then plunged into Lake Huron. Helpless, Anna drowned in nineteen feet of water.

On the other hand, Lady Eaton's attitude toward her adopted daughter, Evlyn, was decidedly different. In 1955 Evlyn received two letters in one week. One informed her that Lady Eaton had agreed that she could now be told the identity of her birth mother; the other was from a solicitor in England saying that her birth mother had died and left a small bequest.

Evlyn boarded a plane for London the same day and within twelve hours was reunited with members of her birth family. (A brother who had also been adopted did not respond to the solicitor's letter.) A sister and another

THE FIRM THAT TIME FORGOT

brother, who was a minister, later visited Canada, where they met Lady Eaton and some other members of the family.

Evlyn attained a reputation as a gifted amateur painter — her work was exhibited in New York galleries — but the 1976 death of her husband, Russel, severely altered her circumstances. He died without a will and Evlyn was left with nothing. She became so afflicted by arthritis that she could neither paint nor play the piano, which she also loved. Embittered, she could find little positive to say about the Eatons during a 1978 interview. "Because my mother was so social, John David and the others went the other way; they had log cabins and were alone a lot, not seeing anyone," she said. "They didn't like the social life. Because of their background, there wasn't really any home. There isn't one of them that's socially inclined; they prefer modesty and privacy. It killed them if they ever had to get up and say something." [16] Only Signy stayed in touch and supplied Evlyn with a house until her death in 1989.

Travel was Lady Eaton's other passion, but companions went along at their peril. "When you travelled with her, there was a price. She was generous but there was always a string attached. You were at her beck and call," says her great-niece Flora Agnew, who accompanied Lady Eaton in 1952 to England, Ireland, and the opening ceremonies of the Olympics in Helsinki. On such occasions, Lady Eaton was received as if she were an official representative of Canada. The head of Finland's hydroelectric system had visited Canada a few years earlier and had been waiting ever since for the opportunity to return the hospitality. He gave Lady Eaton a country-wide tour of facilities. Included was a flight to the Arctic Circle for lunch at a site so remote that the plane had to first make a low pass to shoo the reindeer off the runway before landing.

In 1961, at eighty-two, she spent five months in Egypt, Ethiopia, and Madagascar. The following year she visited the Canadian Arctic. The voyage was first discussed with Sir John some fifty years earlier, but had been postponed because of the First World War. This time she did go, despite having to walk with a crutch and wear a brace on an ankle she'd recently broken. "I have always wanted to see what's just around the corner," said the inveterate traveller. "My grandson says I'll live to be 150 years old but I know time is running out." [17]

The Department of Northern Affairs organized the itinerary. Lady Eaton travelled 5350 miles in ten days on a chartered DC-3 piloted by Frank Pickles, whom Lady Eaton jokingly called "Captain Dill." She visited Great Whale River, Fort Chimo, Frobisher Bay, Hall Beach, Cambridge Bay, Baker Lake, and Churchill. In some locations, the house belonging to the local Northern

Affairs official was turned over to her. At other stops the RCMP officer would move out for the night.

Her attire included a heavy wool riding shirt, sweater, jacket, parka, jodhpurs, and a bright red beret. On the plane, she wrapped herself in a lavender stole. Some of the routes were rough. After bumping around Broughton Island, Lady Eaton commented: "I don't think I've ever been on so newborn a road." [18] She visited DEW Line installations, RCMP outposts, armed-forces barracks, and Inuit villages, where she was known as "Lady Eaton of Eaton's catalogue." She revelled in having her picture taken in front of every Hudson's Bay outpost she spied.

Once, while travelling to New York, Lady Eaton was aided by an airport official and decided to reward him. A friend was joining her a few days later, so Lady Eaton phoned to ask her friend to bring some liquor for the official and a negligée for his wife. The friend wrapped the new lingerie around a bottle, then used an old nightgown of her own to cradle some more bottles for use at the hotel. Of course, the inevitable happened and the wrong parcel was left at the airport. Lady Eaton would tell the story with tears of mirth in her eyes and exclaim: "I've always wondered what they thought of Canadians." [19]

Lady Eaton regarded regal treatment as her due. "She may have had an inflated idea of her own importance, but so many people kowtowed to her for so long," says her great-niece Flora Agnew. Wherever she went, accommodation was deluxe. In London it was the Dorchester, in Paris the Plaza Athenée. There was always an Eaton's car and a driver at her disposal. Lunch would be eaten in a restaurant, but in the evening she always dined in her hotel suite, the meal wheeled in on a silver trolley with never a thought for cost. "She just spent what she spent and somebody paid," says Agnew. "She had no money of her own. She just had the jewels."

So many jewels that she couldn't take them all with her on her travels. In March 1949, while she was holidaying in the south, thieves backed a truck up to the house in King and made off with jewellery worth $100,000, six oriental rugs, chairs, and a washing machine. Two months later the jewellery was found in a Gladstone bag stashed under a cottage at nearby Wasaga Beach.

In 1955 she fell and injured both knees, but still journeyed to Vienna for several performances at the newly reopened Opera House. In 1957 she visited the old homestead in Ballymena with her seventeen-year-old grandson, Timothy, Gilbert's only son. Another year there was an extended four-month trip to Athens for Easter, then Istanbul, Beirut, Jerusalem, Damascus, Mecca, and Rome.

With the passage of time Lady Eaton mellowed on one score — the well-known temperance views of Timothy. She and a friend toured the American Southwest and Vancouver, then decided to go to Whitehorse to meet Martha Black, a Chicago-born woman who had moved north at the time of the Klondike gold rush. In 1935 Martha's husband, George, became too ill to defend his seat in the House of Commons, so Martha campaigned throughout Yukon and became, at sixty-nine, Canada's second female parliamentarian.

When the two guests were settled at the Blacks' in the late afternoon, their hostess inquired whether Lady Eaton followed Timothy's ways: "Do you yourself still adhere strictly to those principles? Or do you use a little stimulant now and then?"

Lady Eaton allowed as how she did on occasion enjoy the odd libation. Martha called to her husband in the room beyond, "George, bring in the rye! The girls drink." [20]

In her declining years, such excursions ceased. Fewer people cared what she thought and Lady Eaton became a lonely figure. Like many a wealthy widow, she seemed to spend most of her days dressed and coiffed, reliving the glory days and waiting for something to happen.

As she had written in 1937 to O.D. Vaughan, Lady Eaton hoped that Eaton Hall would be a gathering point for the family, but other than Christmas, family members rarely came calling. Other guests were just as uncommon. In her splendid isolation, she would call the downtown Eaton's beauty salon and request that a hairdresser be sent to the house to do her hair, more for the pleasure of conversation and the comfort of human touch than for her coiffure.

Memory's Wall was the title of her 1956 autobiography, but memory's wall can become something other than a reverent surface upon which to pin recollections. It can also be a barrier. After a time, people no longer cared to peep over the ramparts or walk the great gardens within, even when invited.

After a time, her birthday became the only occasion when anyone paid attention. In 1965, when she turned eighty-six, she wore shoes with gold heels and announced: "I am celebrating my ninetieth birthday because it's more dramatic that way. From now on, on each birthday, I may jump two years." [21]

In 1969, when Eaton's celebrated its one hundredth anniversary with a special ceremony at the Queen Street store, Lady Eaton was too frail to attend with the other members of the family. All the Eaton wives were given a copy of the ceremonial key used to open the front door that January day. Lady Eaton's key was dispatched to her house, a sad reminder of how removed she'd become from the festivities that had once so dominated her life.

On July 9, 1970, at ninety-one, Lady Eaton died. At the service in Timothy Eaton Memorial Church, her pew, the ninth on the west side of the church, was left empty, marked by a cascade of pink roses. "The Holy City," one of her favourite hymns, was sung. "Lady Eaton believed that privilege means responsibility," senior minister C. Andrew Lawson told the six hundred assembled. "She had nothing but scorn for those who sought an easy or free ride through life." [22]

Said an editorial in the *Telegram*: "The helpless, the hopeless, the dispossessed, the downtrodden found in Lady Eaton a sympathetic and understanding friend." [23] The *Toronto Daily Star* declared: "Our Canadian upper class has always been a bit grey and conventional, too concerned about their status to play the obvious public role in our communities which has traditionally gone to the very wealthy in other societies. There have been few exceptions to this rule and one of those exceptions died yesterday."

Lady Eaton's jewellery and some other personal belongings were shared among her children, but there were no specific bequests to friends. She had never had money of her own, just trustees who paid bills using family funds she never saw. The contents of her homes were sold at auction; Signy bought a few items for people she knew would cherish her mother-in-law's memory. Forty-eight oil paintings by her brother, Harold Wellington McCrea, were donated to the Art Gallery of Ontario. None of the works, showing Canadian scenes from coast to coast, is currently on display.

The next Toronto Symphony Orchestra annual rummage sale took on a decidedly higher tone than usual when an Eaton's truck arrived stuffed to the gills with her clothing and old lace, plus sundry keepsakes and one-time treasures the family did not want. Her prize dairy herd had already gone to the University of Guelph in 1966 following a $250,000 barn fire; ten cartons of Inuit art gathered on her Arctic trip had been donated to Trent University in 1968 to be housed in Lady Eaton College. Seneca College paid $1.5 million for Eaton Hall to create a conference centre for student training in hospitality programs.

After the church service, mourners gathered at the Eaton mausoleum in Mount Pleasant Cemetery. Among the onlookers was magician Johnny

Giordmaine. When members of the family emerged from under the orange rain canopy, several came over to say hello to the unofficial court jester.

As the limousines prepared to depart, John David called out: "What time is it, Johnny?" The little man hesitated briefly, then reached for his oversize pocket watch and pulled out the cookie. "Time for lunch," he chirped. John David laughed and the cars drove away, the old joke told one last time for Johnny's deceased benefactor and friend. [24]

CHAPTER SEVEN

THE BOYS: BORN TO RULE

~

From the moment they were born, the world of the Eaton boys was cashmere-lined. They were fawned over at family events. Servants picked up after them, cooks catered to their every taste. If the sky had opened up and rained pennies, a butler would have collected the manna on their behalf.

The trouble with having everything done for you is that an individual's capacity to learn is stunted. When everything comes so easily, no work ethic is instilled. With neither a guiding hand nor obvious motivation, the days are filled with little more than self-indulgent aimlessness.

John Craig, the eldest, could play hockey well and so believed he could skate through life just as easily. Fred, the brightest of the four boys, could fathom no reason for using his brain to its full capacity. Thor, whose interests seemed to develop slowly, failed to become attached to anything. George, the youngest, had trouble with school so hid his embarrassment by becoming a renegade.

John Craig attended Harvard where he played hockey and was an indifferent student. In June 1959, at the end of his second year, John Craig married Catherine Burdick Farr. Kitty, as she was called, was swept into the family. In their honour Lady Eaton held a party for seventy-five couples at Eaton Hall. The theme was Italian and there were miniature gondolas in the pool, strolling minstrels and waitresses in peasant blouses.

The ceremony at Timothy Eaton Memorial was attended by five hundred guests. The bride wore a diamond-and-platinum locket set with a miniature of Sir John, a gift, along with a family Bible, from Lady Eaton. The grande dame herself wore the same lace-and-taffeta gown in rosy beige that she'd worn to the 1940 wedding of her daughter, Florence.

The newlyweds honeymooned in Europe, spent the summer at Georgian Bay, then lived in Cambridge, Massachusetts, so that John Craig could continue his studies. But he soon failed his fourth subject and was forced to withdraw; he joined Eaton's on a permanent basis on March 2, 1960. "I've never really thought about what else I'd do," he said. "I was born a merchant." [1]

Kitty gave birth in July 1960 to the first child of the fifth generation of Eatons, John David II, followed by Signy Catherine in 1961 and a second son, Henry (named after Kitty's father) in 1963. The family lived at 49 Highland Avenue in Rosedale and threw parties that became legendary. Guests' cars lined the street; the loud music was carried far. Unhappy neighbours used to call the police and the fire department in search of peace and quiet.

McGill University had accepted Fred's grade-twelve diploma, but he worried that Montreal would offer too many temptations. The out-of-the-way location of the University of New Brunswick in Fredericton appealed. "You have to come to a conclusion at some point in your life that you are responsible for what you do and you better settle down if you want to accomplish anything," he says.

Being far from the glare of the Toronto spotlight also meant anonymity. The only Eaton who mattered in New Brunswick was *Cyrus* Eaton. Born next door in Pugwash, Nova Scotia, Cyrus Eaton was no relation to the Upper Canada Eatons. He had moved to the U.S. in 1900, established Republic Steel, and later sponsored international peace conferences in his birthplace. "People were only interested in an Eaton if you were a relative of Cyrus," said Fred. "If you weren't, you were nobody." [2]

Fred shared a room with fellow freshman Douglas Bassett in the Lady Beaverbrook residence, the only male dorm on campus. Bassett lost the coin toss and drew the upper bunk. "It was the worst goddamned room in the whole residence," recalls Bassett. "It was a small little room. There wasn't much action other than sleeping, I'll tell you." After first year, Fred rented an off-campus apartment.

Like all the Eatons before him, Fred loved fast cars. At sixteen he was given a Morgan. During his first evening behind the wheel, a drunk driver struck him from the rear, shoving the Morgan forward into a Simpson's truck. After that, he drove his mother's Kharmann Ghia, which was later passed

Founder Timothy (inset) and in his office with son Jack. (Canapress; Archives of Ontario)

Timothy and Margaret with chauffeur in their 1906 Packard landaulette.
(Archives of Ontario)

Jack, circa 1911 (inset),
and in uniform as
benefactor of the
Eaton Machine Gun
Battery for which he
was knighted in 1915.
(both City of Toronto Archives)

Ardwold, Sir John and Lady Eaton's fifty-room mansion in Toronto, built in 1911 and demolished in 1936. (City of Toronto Archives)

The *Florence*, Sir John's 172-foot long ocean-going vessel, donated to the war effort. (Archives of Ontario)

Robert Young Eaton, president from 1922 to 1942, increased Eaton's outlets tenfold. (Toronto Sun)

Lady Eaton and second son, John David (right), at the 1930 opening of the College Street store in Toronto. (City of Toronto Archives)

The First Family in 1929: (from left) John David, Gilbert, Lady Eaton, Timothy, Edgar; (sitting on grass) Florence and Evlyn. (Toronto Sun)

Kawandag, Lady Eaton's summer home on Muskoka's Lake Rosseau, destroyed by fire in 1973. (Archives of Ontario)

Lady Eaton shares a pre-hunt toast with a fellow rider at Eaton Hall. (Toronto Star/J. Russell)

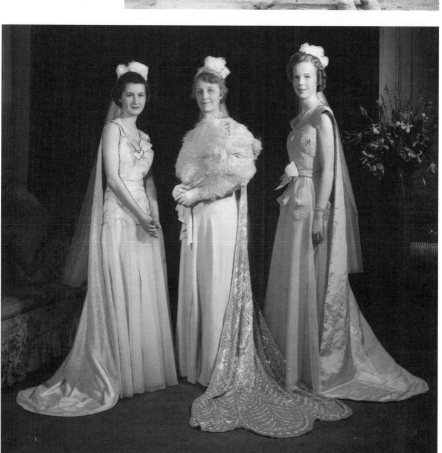

Begowned for their 1938 presentation at Buckingham Palace, Lady Eaton with daughters Evlyn (at left) and Florence. (Tunbridge-London)

The 1933 wedding party of John David and Signy Stefansson: (from left) Gilbert, Harald Stefansson, Timothy, John David, Signy, Lady Eaton, Florence, Evlyn, Jock Riddock, and Ross Jenkins. (Toronto Sun)

Lady Eaton (right) and a fellow protester picket a decrepit hospital in 1944. (Toronto Sun)

John David in 1947 before his health failed. (Karsh of Ottawa)

John David and Signy in 1949 with their four boys: (from left) John Craig, Thor, George (with his six-guns), and Fred. (Toronto Sun)

Signy circa 1962 in her art-filled home on Dunvegan Avenue
in Toronto's Forest Hill. (McKague)

The family celebrates Eaton's 1969 centennial with founder Timothy looking on. Front row, Fredrik D'Arcy and Flora Catherine with John David; John David II; Signy Catherine and Henry Craig with Signy; back row, John Craig and Kitty, George, Thor, Nicky and Fred. (Archives of Ontario)

John David and Signy's Caledon hideaway northwest of Toronto, where Queen Elizabeth II stayed in 1973. (Toronto Star/J. Goode)

John Craig, flanked by George (left) and Fred, meets the press after a failed 1976 kidnap attempt. (Toronto Sun/David Cooper)

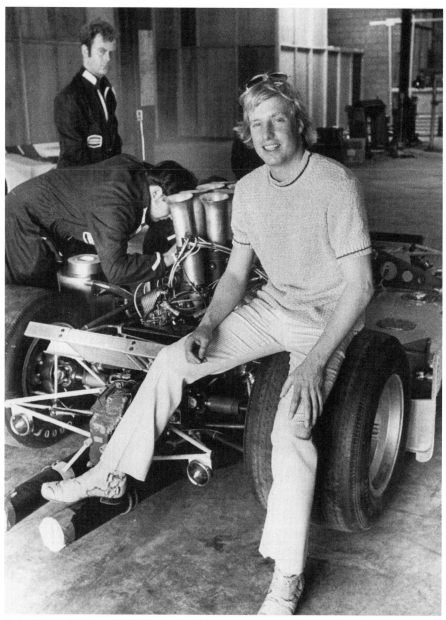

Rebellious George in 1970 with his Can-Am car from British Racing Motors.
(Toronto Star/D. Darrell)

Sherry, John Craig's second wife.
(Toronto Star/F. Lennon)

John Craig, and his third wife, Sally, with, at left, Ontario Premier Bill Davis.
(Toronto Star/R. Bull)

Landau bears Henry, younger son of John Craig, and wife, Victoria, after their 1987 wedding at Timothy Eaton Memorial Church. (Toronto Star/E. Combs)

George's former Forest Hill home, sold in 1997 for $4.98 million.
(Toronto Star/P. Power)

George's Caledon mansion, shown under construction in 1989, was offered for sale in 1998 at $18 million. (Toronto Star/R. Eglinton)

The boys, just before the 1977 opening of the Toronto Eaton Centre: (from left) George, Fred, John Craig, and Thor. (Toronto Sun)

George at the February 27, 1997, news conference admitting Eaton's insolvency.
(Financial Post/Peter Redman)

The Eaton mausoleum in Toronto's Mount Pleasant Cemetery.
(City of Toronto Archives)

down to George. At UNB Fred owned a stolid Plymouth for two years, then moved up to a black Corvette convertible.

Fred was assistant manager on the varsity hockey team, contributed to the student newspaper, and served on the student council for two years. He ran for president but was defeated. "He was an intellectual," says Bassett, "as he is today. Christ, I just drank Seagram's VO and Hart's Lemon Gin and completely fucked up my life down there." While all four Eaton boys attended university, only Fred graduated.

Both Thor and George tried university briefly then dropped out. In 1965 George became an arts student at Simon Fraser University, in Burnaby, B.C., where he shared a house with, among others, Wayne Kinnear, son of Eaton's CEO David Kinnear. "It was a pretty free-form pad, people coming and going and dropping in at all hours. I don't think George had ever been exposed to that type of atmosphere and the freewheeling discussions that went on. But he adjusted quickly," said Wayne. "In the semester he was in school, I think I saw George's car on campus five times at the most. But he passed three of the five courses he was taking in the Christmas exams before he dropped out of school. It just wasn't his thing." [3]

Their working experience at Eaton's followed a similar split. John Craig and Fred got involved as teenagers. Thor worked for one summer, and George stayed away. John Craig's first role at Eaton's had been as a driver's summer helper. Fred, then thirteen, desperately wanted to work, too. "Take it easy," cautioned his older brother. "There's lots of time. Once you're in the store, you're in." [4]

While that may have been true, there was no planned approach for the boys' retailing education as there had been for previous generations. What they learned was that time-honoured traditions were everything, efficiency a lesser consideration. Deliveries were interrupted by friendly chores. "On one truck route, the driver stopped at a home where the family was away on holiday," John Craig recalled in 1977. "He put the sprinkler on the lawn and turned on the water. He came back again to move it. Then before we left the neighbourhood he turned it off." [5] Through the 1960s John Craig spent time in a variety of departments, including women's wear, fashion accessories, and personnel. He worked in group sales at the Don Mills store and spent a year in the London, England, buying office.

To listen to John Craig, life was all about responsibility, and he was not above pontificating to a reporter: "I guess that for a short time a playboy's life might seem attractive. But that's not the real world. The real world is work.

You get your satisfaction from achieving goals."[6] His performance, however, did not match his fine words. Merchandising manager Ed Walls was twice asked to train John Craig and took him on buying trips to Europe and New York. "Both times they ended up such disasters I had to cut short the visits and bring him home. He would act up, drink too much, spend too much, upset the people around," says Walls.

During the New York trip, Walls and John Craig were invited to spend the weekend as house guests on Fire Island. "He went down to the local bar, down the beach about two miles, got very drunk. I had to go down and get him in the middle of the night, bring him back," says Walls. "He went to bed. About half an hour later I hear windows breaking all over the bloody place and I went into John Craig [and said] 'What the hell is happening?' He said, 'I'm too hot. I broke all the windows.'"

The next day Walls bundled an angry John Craig on to the plane bound for Toronto. "He told me never, ever to call him anything but Mr. Eaton again as long as I lived." That was the end of Walls's tutelage. "You try twice. I wouldn't ever try a third time."

In 1968 John Craig and his family moved to London, Ontario, where he was manager of the Wellington Square store for a year. "I think he just sort of lost interest," says David Kinnear. "He spent more time back in Toronto. We had to take him out of there."

Fred seemed eager to learn all he could from every seasoned hand, but first he took a few summers to travel and try other things. In the summer of 1959 Fred was a go-fer on the police beat at the *Telegram* and helped monitor police and fire department radio calls. He received no bylines, but one of his stories was posted as best of the day. He'd written about a truck with a too-tall load trying to travel under a low bridge. The headline was: "Thirteen into twelve won't go."

In the summer of 1960 Doug Bassett and Fred started in Rome and drove a red Volkswagen Beetle through Italy, France, Belgium, Scandinavia, and on to Moscow. Of the four brothers, Fred is the most intellectual. He's a prodigious reader and inveterate visitor of museums and galleries. "I wanted to go out and try to get laid every night and drink booze, lie on the beach and sleep in in the morning," says Bassett of their junket. Not Fred. He made sure the two rovers soaked up culture. "I was never interested in Toulouse-Lautrec. He dragged me to the Louvre, for Christ's sake. *Mona Lisa* was such a letdown. I wanted to go to the Crazy Horse Saloon and places like that." At night they did frequent such bistros; sometimes Fred would sing and play guitar, attracting other young people for a hootenanny. Accommodation was often luxurious. In Paris, they stayed at the Plaza Athenée hotel with Lady Eaton. In London they checked into the Dorchester and quickly ran through a standing credit established by John David.

Upon graduation in 1962 Fred received the Gold Student Activity Award for extracurricular activities, a gold signet ring that he has worn ever since. (The university conferred an honorary doctor of laws on him in 1983 and he has been chancellor since 1993.) On June 16, 1962, he married Catherine Martin, the daughter of D'Arcy Martin, one of Hamilton's top lawyers. Catherine, known to everyone as Nicky, gave birth to a son, Fredrik D'Arcy, the following April; a daughter, Flora Catherine, was born in 1965.

As John Craig and Fred entered the business on a full-time basis, the colossus was growing. In 1962 Eaton's opened a store in Brentwood Shopping Centre in Burnaby, B.C., as well as two stores in suburban-Toronto malls: Shopper's World and Don Mills. That same year the downtown-Halifax store at Barrington and Prince Streets was closed after thirty-four years and was replaced by a store in the new Halifax Shopping Centre on Mumford Road. At 150,000 square feet on three levels, it was the largest store in Atlantic Canada. Fred and John Craig attended the official opening, then repaired to the Lord Nelson Hotel with Don Cameron, whose firm had installed the fixtures. The three consumed every bottle of champagne in the hotel.

Among the topics that celebratory night was how best to manage the empire. "Fred was on the delegation side of the argument. He wanted hired guns," recalls Cameron. "John and I took a more traditional approach; members of the family should run it on their own."

Fred and John Craig were different on other counts as well. It soon became clear that Fred was good with people and possessed skills that would mean he could be a leader. He had a way with him that was received quite differently than John Craig's manner. Where John Craig would alienate, Fred would make friends.

Fred's first job at Eaton's was selling shirts in the Queen Street store. One summer he travelled around Ontario by car with Harold Tait, who was head of the Ontario branch stores, soaking up knowledge about retailing.

After a stint in Victoria, Fred was back in Toronto in November 1963 as assistant department manager in infants' wear, then was manager at the newly opened Rexdale warehouse. As part of his training, Fred, then a stationery buyer, accompanied Bill Hughes, a buyer of notions, art, and needlework, on a trip to Asia. The two were flying into Taiwan on a JAL flight that, without warning, began to bounce crazily. Glasses and liquor bottles at the front of their first-class section were falling and breaking; passengers' items were skittering around the cabin. After a few fearful minutes, there was an announcement. "This is Captain Johnson," said a firm voice from the Chuck Yeager school of in-flight broadcasting. "I don't want you to be alarmed. It's just a little turbulence."

The flight continued, and as the passengers deplaned safely the captain was on hand to say his farewells. He was Japanese. Hughes and Fred realized that JAL pilots must carry a series of suitably reassuring and previously recorded English-language messages for every occasion. Hughes spent another thirty years as an Eaton's buyer, and every time Fred saw him he'd salute Hughes and say: "Well, Captain Johnson, how are you tonight?"

During their visit to Japan, Hughes and Fred were invited to tour the facilities of Sakimoto and see cultured-pearl production. Hughes begged off, so Fred went alone. That night, Fred insisted that they eat in the rooftop dining room of the Palace Hotel in Tokyo. Fred ordered a dozen oysters and, lo and behold, found a pearl in the first one he ate. "Here," he said, handing it to Hughes, "take that home to your wife." When a second pearl showed up in Fred's next oyster, Hughes knew he'd been had. Fred had bought a dozen pearls earlier that day and had the Palace chef "seed" his entire serving. He gave the full dozen to Hughes. The dining room was in an uproar as everyone ordered oysters hoping for the same Irish luck.

In October 1965 Fred was sent to the London, England, office where he organized trips for buyers, shepherding them around Europe and the Soviet Union. In April 1966 he was made manager of Scarborough's Shopper's World store, then in August 1966 became manager of the store in the Toronto suburb of Don Mills, where he gained a reputation for standing by his troops. One day an unusually husky woman returned a bulky knit sweater that she claimed was damaged and demanded a refund. The clerk pointed out that it was an all-sales-final item. Moreover, the damage seemed to have been inflicted by the purchaser. For both those reasons no refund would be issued.

The woman persisted and Fred was called in to mediate. He backed his employee. "If you don't give me a refund," insisted the shopper, "I'll tie you in knots." Fred stuck to his guns until she finally departed. Only later did Fred learn that the irate shopper probably could have carried out her threat: she was a professional wrestler.

"I didn't dislike any of them," said their cousin Robert, Jack's son, who, as a worker Eaton, toiled further down in the organization, "but I had a different value system." Even when John Craig and Fred had worked in the stores, their roles did not involve normal duties. "Their day was totally different from mine. They would move into jobs that were specifically created for them. When it was time [for them] to move, the job was amalgamated with someone else's job. They never really did anything."

John Craig preferred dabbling with the family money. A friend from UCC, Andy Hutchison, had an opportunity to buy a wire-and-sheet-metal plant. He approached John Craig, who'd already bankrolled a photo-arts studio and a modelling agency run by two other friends, Doug Wheeler and Chris Scott. Hutchison was given start-up funds and retained a piece of the business, which was named Burdick Metal Industries; despite the use of Kitty's middle name, she had no involvement. Burdick, which the four friends co-owned, produced in-store metal shelving for General Electric, card stands for Coutts Hallmark, and newspaper boxes for both the *Telegram* and the *Toronto Daily Star.*

"In the whole group [of companies], mine was the only operation that was showing in the black," says Hutchison, who is now the Anglican Bishop of Montreal. "I paid for that dearly because they were keen to have some of that offset their losses in other parts of the group. In the course of two or three years they lost something like a million bucks on operations that were really not high-overhead operations. One might say, 'How do you do that in the sixties?' You could stand at the door and hand out dollar bills and not lose that much."

Hutchison found himself doing battle with his partners over expenses that were being charged against Burdick that he believed belonged elsewhere. There were other sore points. "Part of the game was that you did everything possible to get yourself locked in socially with those you depended on for your benefit," says Hutchison. "Chris really did nurture a friendship with John and spent as much time personally with him as he could. That's where he found a certain kind of security. My scruples didn't exactly move in that kind of direction."

Losses in the group of companies continued to mount until 1963, when John David's lawyer and business adviser stepped in. "Swatty Wotherspoon blew the whistle and said the boys had lost enough money and were to pull in their horns. So they did a whole lot of liquidating very quickly. We blew apart, and I stepped out," Hutchison recalls.

John Craig had less merchandising savvy than Fred, so he took on those honorific roles that required a public profile. The time he spent representing the family and touring the stores away from home eventually cost him his marriage. He and Kitty separated on January 1, 1970, and were divorced July 13, 1971.

Of the four boys, John Craig is the only one to be divorced and is now married to his third wife. "John has a tendency to divorce and remarry," says his Aunt Florence. "He likes to wander." Kitty was a bit of a wanderer herself. Her marriage to John Craig collapsed after she had an affair with businessman Peter Munk, whose island summer home was near theirs on Georgian Bay.

Susan Swan also summered on Georgian Bay and published a novel in 1989, *The Last of the Golden Girls*, that portrayed a fictionalized version of that dalliance. There are parallels between the characters of Jonah Prince and Peter Munk, Bull Cape and John Craig, Bobby Cape and Kitty. There are nighttime trysts between Bobby Cape and Jonah Prince in his speedboat, *Thunderbird*. "He paddles the *Thunderbird* over under cover of night. That summer they shared a private joke: if the islanders listen carefully . . . they will hear the swish of paddles . . . see a boat cross the gap between the two islands . . . behind the silhouette of the landscape, lovers are making the eternal journey to the shrine of each other's bodies." [7]

"[Kitty's] marriage to John Craig had been a shaky one for a long time," says Swan. "I remember seeing him at parties and he, John Craig, frankly, could act very boorishly. I remember being at one party up there when he was being very loud and belligerent to her. So I always used to think it was a good thing that she'd left. He's not my favourite Eaton, John Craig."

"When the honeymoon's over," explains Kitty, nearly thirty years after the breakup, "the honeymoon's over." She looks back and realizes she blundered in seeing Munk on the side. "It was a mistake. You can quote me on that. He left Linda, I left John. He dumped me a year later."

The Eatons not only turned their backs on Kitty at the time of the divorce, they wanted her publicly shunned. As far as they were concerned, Kitty should wear the scarlet letter of the adulteress.

Initially Kitty asked for a lump-sum settlement of $250,000. John Craig countered with $30,000 a year. Kitty's mother urged her to have the annual payment adjusted for inflation. John Craig agreed, as long as she didn't remarry or live with anyone. During the last few months of their marriage, they had moved to 82 Chestnut Park Road, which she received as part of the settlement and later sold for $285,000.

In 1976 John Craig discovered that Kitty had retained a half interest in the summer home. He asked her to sign over the deed and Kitty agreed, but in return asked him to renew her membership at Caledon Ski Club. He refused and the matter went all the way to the Supreme Court. In 1980 the court ruled that at the time of their divorce both thought the property was in his name.

While Kitty may have lost that skirmish, she won the war. When the annual payments, with their inflation escalator, hit $70,000, John Craig claimed that she was living with a man so the alimony payments should end. Kitty had certainly dated. Among the gentlemen callers were Duff Scott, a friend of the Eaton boys from UCC, and Alex Trebek, who has since gone on to fame as host of the television game show *Jeopardy*. In 1980 the Ontario Court of Appeal dismissed John Craig's claim, awarded Kitty $122,697 in withheld payments, and told John Craig to continue paying alimony with the promised adjustments for inflation. Kitty has never remarried and her alimony now runs to $130,000 annually. In addition to her Toronto house, Kitty has a farm property near Georgian Bay and a Florida condo she inherited from her father.

"[John Craig's] gotten a little pompous through the ages. That's sort of disappointed me a bit," says Kitty. "He started getting that way towards the end of our marriage just because everybody was patting him on the rear end. It's very difficult. People do that and I can't stand people doing that, [but] that's what happens."

While John Craig's first marriage was coming apart, Fred and Nicky were building a life together. They lived first at 102 Kilbarry Road, then in the early 1970s moved to 104 Forest Hill Road, a mansion built by steel magnate Sigmund Samuel that overlooks UCC's front campus. Nicky wore clothing from Balenciaga, Guy Laroche, and Chanel. The *Toronto Daily Star* named Fred as one of Canada's eleven sexiest men, along with, among others, dancer Frank Augustyn, poet Irving Layton, Argo running back Terry Metcalf, and CBC anchor Knowlton Nash.

In 1968 Fred began construction of a $300,000 summer retreat on a seven-acre island of black granite near his parents' Georgian Bay residence. Discussions with architect Blake Millar were brief. He told Millar the number of rooms he wanted, but Fred's only other instruction was that the place should be "open to the sun by day and the moon by night."

Millar created a T-shaped structure with glass walls and twenty fortresslike towers that support beams of cedar and red oak. On the main floor are the living room, dining room, kitchen, a guest bedroom, and six thousand square feet of sundeck punctuated by pines thrusting through the boards. A circular staircase leads to four bedrooms on the second floor. Everything is push-button electric with an underwater cable supplying power from Parry Sound eighteen miles away. Construction was so spectacular, says Nicky, that "people used to come by in their boats, anchor, and drink cocktails while they stared."

"Fred's splendid retreat has caused some good-natured gibes among the competitive Eaton clan," reported *Time*, which featured Fred's place in its architecture section. "Elder Brother John Craig, 31, who manages the family's London store, makes do with an unpretentious prefab cabin on an island of his own nearby. On learning that the living room of 'Fred's damned Taj Mahal' has a 20-ft. ceiling, John announced plans to build a mainland retreat in the Caledon Hills northwest of Toronto with a ceiling of 50 feet. The older brother may win the ceiling battle, but will have to do well to top Fred's hideaway in any other respect. 'The great thing about the project,' summed up Architect Millar, 'is that lots of bread was spread, but the crumbs don't show.'" [8]

While John Craig and Fred were marrying and erecting monuments to their wealth, Thor and George both remained single and stayed away from the family business. Thor's only experience actually working at Eaton's came in the summer of 1960 when he was a student employee at the Toronto warehouse store. He was a stockbroker at Dominion Securities and became a partner with George and a friend, Ken Walker, in Eaton-Walker Ltd. With offices at 221 Victoria Steet, one block east of the store, the company promoted concerts, such as the Toronto Pop Festival, which attracted fifty thousand fans to hear rock bands and singers at Varsity Stadium in July 1969. Thor also launched Grand Entertainment Corp., a record-distribution company. First artist on the Grand label was Nana Mouskouri. Her album *Come With Me* went platinum in five weeks.

Thor rebelled in a modest fashion compared to George, who always seemed to have something to prove. In 1965 George bought a Sunbeam Alpine that had been raced by Toronto car dealer Eppie Wietzes, took some instruction, and entered his first race at Harewood Acres near Lake Erie. He finished third. In 1966 he paid $10,000 for a white Ford Cobra with a 427-cubic-inch engine, entered seventeen regional and national races, and won his class.

During those two years, George also worked as a stockbroker at Doherty Roadhouse, but his real interest was weekend racing. In 1967, at twenty-two, he quit his day job and moved up to big-league racing by entering the Canadian-American Challenge Cup series with a McLaren MK3. He qualified for his first race at Mosport Park in eastern Ontario by finishing twenty-fifth in a field of twenty-eight with a speed of ninety-nine miles an hour, ten miles an hour slower than Denis Hulme, who won the pole position.

George was like a diminutive jockey riding those powerful steeds. While

John Craig is the tallest of the Eaton boys at five foot eleven, George is the shortest at five foot eight; at the time he weighed only 140 pounds. He was so skinny that one writer said he could tread water in a test tube. George called himself "the beautiful whippet" and wore Edwardian suits. His shoulder-length hair was the colour of corn silk, causing one racing magazine, which pictured him beside a beautiful blonde, to describe him as "the world's wealthiest hippy."

"The hair is long because I like it that way," George told *Toronto Daily Star* sportswriter Frank Orr for his 1970 book, *George Eaton: Five Minutes to Green.* "There's a great deal of speculation that I wear it that way to assert my individuality or because I'm a rebel. Amateur psychologists have a field day with it. No one has ever written that maybe I wear it that way because I like it." [9]

Orr struck a deal to write a book based on a year in the life of George as a race-car driver. Orr was paid a $1000 advance on royalties and gave $400 to George who became a frequent visitor to Orr's house, often helping himself to food from Orr's refrigerator. Once, George sat underneath the kitchen table sulking because, he claimed, Orr had been mean to him. The Orrs often invited George to stay to dinner. Then twenty-four and still living with his parents, he'd phone home first to see what the chef was cooking, then decide where to eat.

One time when Orr and George got drunk together, George said: "When my daddy dies, he's only going to leave me a set of blocks: Yonge and Queen, College and Yonge . . ." Says Orr, looking back at the young man who would become president: "I really liked the guy, but it was a bit of a surprise when he showed up as the head of the stores."

John David was so little involved and interested in the life of his boys that he never once watched his son race over the six years George was on the various circuits. Signy came twice, once to St. Jovite, in the Laurentians north of Montreal, and once to a Can-Am event in Bridgehampton, New York. "All racing ever meant to me," she once said, "was a little chill down my back every time the phone rang on a weekend."

Fred was at Mosport Park in eastern Ontario one day to watch George in a McLaren that was performing poorly. A tire lost pressure, the throttle got stuck in the open position, he spun out three times, and the temperature in the cockpit reached sixty degrees Celsius (140°F.), but George somehow endured and finished ninth. He looked like a boiled wiener when he climbed out of the car and vomited almost instantly. Fred shook his head in admiration and astonishment, saying: "Geez, I didn't know it was that tough."

In 1968 George participated in the United States Road Racing Championship. In his first race in Mexico City, he finished ninth and won $700 in prize money. At the end of the season, he was well back in the pack with four points compared with champion Mark Donohue's forty-five points.

George also raced that year in the Canadian-American Challenge Cup series and had his best finish at Laguna Seca on California's Monterey Peninsula. Laguna Seca means "dry lagoon," but that day torrential rain fell and George turned in a virtuoso run. He finished third, only eighteen seconds behind winner John Cannon. In the press room afterwards, George took swigs from a magnum of champagne and told reporters: "The reason Canadian drivers make such good mudders is that the intense cold of the Canadian winters tends to paralyze that portion of the brain that normally tells a person to come in out of the rain. As a result, we dash about in the worst possible weather without really knowing any better. It gives us a great competitive advantage over better-adjusted drivers." [10]

In retrospect, Laguna Seca not only ranked as that year's best performance, it was one of the highlights of his racing career. He finished the Can-Am season in eleventh place and won $11,000. His handlers urged him to press ahead. Said Teddy Mayer, Team McLaren manager: "If you have the money to support all this and you don't have to worry about where your next meal is coming from, then what are you worried about? There's nothing to stop you from doing it." [11]

By 1969, when he was racing in the Canadian-American Challenge Cup Series, George was paying for a five-man crew. His bright red McLaren Mark 12 with a 427-cubic-inch Chevrolet engine was worth $25,000, the price of a decent three-bedroom home at the time. There were no sponsorships and prize money was limited. In all, travel, fuel, parts, and crew for that year's two dozen races cost George $300,000.

"At first, the old bull about all my money bothered me," George confided to biographer Frank Orr. "Many people viewed me as a spoiled, rich punk, a feeble-minded playboy, racing cars because I didn't know what else to do. They figured I just raced for kicks. Even when I did a good job, I'd hear I succeeded only because I could afford a good car and first-rate preparation. Nobody ever bothered to say that maybe I'd done a good job because I had some ability to drive a race car." [12]

George's high-handed attitude caused problems. "He's the only person I've ever met whom I could love and hate at the same time," Orr was told by Paul Cooke, fired by George in 1969 from his position as team manager and chief mechanic. "He has one side that I admired — independent, tough-minded, and determined. But, on the other hand, he could be thoughtless, rude, careless, and totally oblivious to anyone else's feelings."

Orr, who spent a year interviewing George on a regular basis, concluded that he raced because it offered him a field of his own where he wasn't measured against his brothers. As the youngest, everywhere else he went, his competitive siblings had already been. Even such minor matters as the tab for a restaurant lunch could set off a fierce debate among them. "It took us longer to figure out who was going to pay than it did to eat the lunch," said George, describing one argument. "John Craig claimed it was Fred's turn and Fred said Thor was a cheapskate. We argued for half an hour about who was going to pay this fourteen-dollar lunch tab."

Between racing seasons, George relaxed at the family compound in Antigua, skin-diving. Or he'd head north in the winter to the cottage near Parry Sound and practise his moves. He'd take a car out on the thick ice, then do spins at eighty miles an hour because the conditions were like racing in the rain. In the city he'd do doughnuts in a supermarket parking lot on a Sunday after a snowfall.

In 1969 George took a gamble. To gain more experience quickly, he decided to enter both the Formula A series and the Can-Am series, twenty-four races in all. In the first Canadian championship at Mosport that May, George led the field for a while but seemed to lose focus and finished second to Bill Brack. Thor had been so confident of the outcome that he and best friend David Bassett had put champagne on ice in the restaurant at the nearby Flying Dutchman Motel in Bowmanville. Brack drank it instead.

George learned not to dwell on his failures or his triumphs. Once, when he won a medal for finishing third, he wore it briefly, then gave it to a friend. "George has a tendency to forget yesterday," said Paul Cooke. "In fact, he has a tendency to forget this afternoon. He claims now is all that matters and he practises it very well. Tomorrow, to him, is much more important than yesterday." [13]

While George looked like he was plunging into the guys-together world of racing, he was really a lone wolf. His pit crew grumbled that he didn't spend much time hanging out with them after a race. What George really wanted was to move up to Formula One racing. While such ambition is to be admired, it's no substitute for experience. "You can't expect miracles," says Ludwig Heimrath, now a Toronto Porsche dealer, who was racing when George arrived on the scene in 1965. "George wasn't lacking in money, but in my opinion he had the wrong guidance from people who liked his money but really couldn't care less about George. They took his money and didn't do anything for it."

After less than four years in the sport, in 1969 George was talking to British Racing Motors (BRM) about Formula One, despite the fact that in four of his recent five Can-Am events, he'd failed to finish. He had only one eighth-place finish to show for his money, but the public-relations campaign he mounted had raised his profile with BRM, a racing firm conceived after the Second World War as a national project funded by industrialists; in 1950 it became involved in world championship racing. George did a trial run with BRM at Watkins Glen, New York, and had the slowest qualifying time. In the race itself he was in eighth place, but his engine blew at the three-quarters mark. In the Mexican Grand Prix, he was sidelined with a broken gearbox.

Racing is not a big-league business like other professional sports. Hot young prospects are not always paid to drive for a factory team. BRM was attracted to George not just because he showed promise but also because he could, in the parlance of the business, "buy the ride." He could afford to pay the $500,000 it would cost him to join the BRM team and participate in Grand Prix racing for a year.

He finished out the Can-Am season at Texas International Speedway, placing second in that race. Bruce McLaren was the season winner with 165 points and $160,960 in purses. George was fifth with fifty points; he earned $51,300. The results were good enough for BRM; they were ready to take his money. On December 2, 1969, his one-year contract was announced at a Toronto press conference. Other Canadian drivers, like Eppie Wietzes, had done rent-a-ride deals during the Canadian Grand Prix beginning in 1967, but George was Canada's first full-time Formula One driver. "Everybody thought I was pushing too fast," George told *Time*. "But I've been able to escalate my own program at my own speed. Frankly, that's one of the benefits of being rich." [14]

George joined Pedro Rodriguez and Jackie Oliver on the BRM Formula One works team, but BRM's cars that year were mediocre and plagued with mechanical problems. "BRM had been big in the 1950s and 1960s, and had ties to people with titles, but it was in a bit of a decline at the time," recalls Orr. "He bought the ride and they also built him a car for the Can-Am series. It was a dismal flop. It was the only car I ever saw that fish-tailed in the front end."

George's first race was the 1970 South African Grand Prix. He had to quit after fifty-eight of the eighty laps because the engine was losing oil following a missed gear change. In the next race the ignition system quit after twenty-three laps. He failed to qualify for Monaco, missed Belgium because of the flu, and did only twenty-six laps in the Netherlands before the oil-cooler tank gave out. Finally, at Clermont-Ferrand, in the French Grand Prix, George had his first finish. He came twelfth, two laps behind the winner, Jochen Rindt.

In order to participate in both Formula One and Can-Am, George commuted back and forth across the Atlantic. But the Can-Am project was also plagued by mechanical and other problems. An exhaust pipe fell off at Mosport, and the suspension gave out at Watkins Glen. The only bright spot was a third-place finish at Le Circuit. George qualified for the British Grand Prix, but engine trouble meant that he did not race. He finished the Austrian Grand Prix, but was lapped twice by winner Jack Ickx. In the Canadian Grand Prix, held at Mont Tremblant, Quebec, he finished tenth, but was five laps behind Ickx, the winner again.

Danger is every driver's copilot. Jochen Rindt, himself heir to a fortune, was killed at Monza in 1970 after a mechanical failure caused his car to strike a barricade. He was awarded the World Championship posthumously. In the very next race the same part gave way on George's car, but George was lucky. His car spun out onto a long grass verge that eventually slowed the vehicle to a full stop; he was able to climb out, unscathed. Piers Courage, a member of a prominent British family, was also killed racing that same year. There had been twenty-one drivers in the first Grand Prix in Canada at Mosport in 1967. By 1973 only nine were still alive. "He was frightened that he was going to get killed," recalls Susan Swan. "It was just a matter of time in a sport like that."

As a team, BRM wasn't even close to having a Formula One winner that year. George won no points on the circuit. "BRM was not a highly financed company so I'm sure they were looking to have George's money," says Heimrath. "I'm sure that George said, 'Screw you, I've had enough of that. How much money do you think I'm going to give you guys to make it work?' He was so disappointed and he just left." George's final F1 fling was in the 1971 Canadian Grand Prix at Mosport. Jackie Stewart led from start to finish; he lapped George five times.

George then switched to the U.S. Auto Club championship series with its Indy-style cars. His car was prepared by a pair of Hungarian brothers, George and Rudy Fejer, and he was named top rookie for 1971. In racing, there are drivers and there are constructors. In an unusual and expensive decision George decided he would be both. In the 1970s each car typically cost $1 million to build.

In 1972 George was entered in the Indy 500, but the partnership with the

Fejers dissolved before the Memorial Day event and he did not race. His high-speed career sputtered to a stop. "I have no great explanations to offer. I've retired from racing to pursue other interests," he told Orr. "I've enjoyed my years in the sport and met many great people. Now it's time to move on to something else." [15]

The tab for George's six-year racing career was substantial. In the years before signing with BRM, he spent at least $500,000 on his machine shop, four mechanics, business manager, and racing manager. The BRM year cost a similar amount. Indy car development with the Fejers, another $500,000. Travel would have added a further $500,000. The entire fling likely cost him $2 million.

The money let him in and the money let him down. "Everybody who was connected with George liked to have his money," says Heimrath. "George had the killer instinct, the feeling for it, but wasn't guided properly. He wouldn't listen to anybody, because he thought he knew. Everybody has to live and learn. All the money in the world sometimes doesn't make you who you want to be."

CHAPTER EIGHT

LOST IN THE SIXTIES

⬱

T HE T. EATON CO. WAS AS RUDDERLESS AS THE lives of the boys. John David's business guidance seemed to occur only in fits and starts. His personality was such that he could not motivate; his health was beginning to fail and his interest flag. The team that John David had assembled did little to pick up the slack caused by his lackluster leadership. Senior executives spent the entire decade of the 1960s dithering about what to do with the empire.

John David's only ambitious international foray occurred in 1958 when he joined a group who journeyed to the Soviet Union at a time when the Soviets were beginning to seek trade with the west. Even then, his time was spent more in merriment than merchandising.

Toronto insurance broker Edgar T. Alberts organized a twelve-day tour in 1958 for twenty-nine business leaders, including W. R. McLaughlin, president of Orenda Engines Ltd.; Oakley Dalgleish, publisher of the *Globe and Mail*; A. C. Ashforth, president of the Toronto-Dominion Bank; and Harold McNamara, president of McNamara Construction Ltd. The businessmen shared the $100,000 cost. The group visited factories, aircraft and steel plants, and saw ballet and opera at the Bolshoi Theatre.

John David was accompanied by Eaton's vice-president and friend Ross Jenkins. Jenkins had had a charmed career ever since he had introduced John David to Signy. He joined Eaton's in 1935 selling hosiery, was sent to British Columbia as a director and general manager at the time of the

Spencer's purchase, and in 1953 had been made a vice-president and director. John David and Jenkins inspected GUM, the state department store, but pronounced themselves unimpressed.

At the end of the day, the official schedule over, the business leaders would gather for drinks and dinner. Festivities would run until three in the morning, the hotel staff replenishing glasses throughout. During one banquet Jenkins and John David asked the members of the string quartet that had been playing if they knew "Volga Boatman." The musicians had never heard of the song, so the two visitors undertook to teach them. Jenkins gave up after a while, but John David persisted, and the group was eventually able to manage a passable rendition.

With the trade balance overwhelmingly in Canada's favour, Nikita Khrushchev, who that year had been named chairman of the Council of Ministers, spent most of the one-hour-and-forty-minute meeting with the businessmen promoting Soviet goods. "Who is ready to give us credit to make good money?" *Time* quoted Khrushchev as asking. "I want a mutual profit. That is a business approach."

Continued the article: "His attentive listeners signed no contracts, but some bought a bill of Krushchev's goods. Glowed Department Store Magnate John David Eaton on his return: 'We know now the people in Russia want peace more than anything.'" [1] John David made another prediction: "Before 15 years Russia will surpass the United States and that is their target." [2]

At the office, John David was equally easy to convince. By 1962 Ross Jenkins was senior vice-president and Alan, R.Y.'s son, was a director, but nothing of consequence was decided at the weekly board meeting. "We had a little thing called the executive committee which met to discuss things of importance we didn't want John David to know about," says Alan who is now retired. "The executive committee would send O.D. [Vaughan] in to John David to tell him what we wanted done." If that strategy didn't work, Jenkins would be dispatched to see the owner. "He was the only one who got along with John David. He could handle him, sort of, more than O.D. could."

Eaton's was no longer the corner store John David had once stated it to be, but no one seemed to have the knowhow to run it any other way. So far was Eaton's from modern ways that senior executives were still being remunerated using cash in pay envelopes, rather than company cheques. "The corporate style that John David Eaton represents is what made Eaton's a national institution and one of the world's great department stores. But by the mid-1950s it was becoming embarrassingly apparent that Eaton's could no longer continue pretending it was a corner grocery," wrote Alexander Ross in a 1968 *Maclean's* story with the delightful title, "What It's Like to Live in Toyland."

"It lagged behind its competition in the race to the suburbs. In a rapidly urbanizing country, it was beginning to suffer from its Stanfield-underwear image. Warehousing and distribution were chaotic, and there was little long-range planning. Buildings tended to sprout new wings and annexes in improbable directions, as though the prospect of expansion had been totally unforeseen." [3]

The rule about Sunday window coverings had been eased briefly in 1951 when the windows along Ste-Catherine in Montreal remained uncovered at Christmas so the public could view the nativity scenes. But it wasn't until 1968 that the neutral-coloured drapes were removed from windows across the country. The novelty was such that in the east-end Montreal suburb of Ville d'Anjou, fifty-five thousand people showed up on Sunday just to peer in the windows.

Imaginative development deals brought by others to Eaton's were dismissed out of hand. Leo Kolber, representing Fairview Corp, approached the retailer to become a tenant in Cedarbrae Plaza, a mall slated for the east-Toronto suburb of Scarborough. He got nowhere; Eaton's was not interested in ideas from pesky developers. "There was a kind of arrogance through the organization that said, 'Hey, we're Eaton's,'" says Kolber. The developer's representative went across the street to Edgar Burton at Simpsons (the apostrophe was dropped in the 1950s) and cut a deal in ten minutes. Cedarbrae opened in 1960. "He made money from the day it opened and it didn't increase his ad budget three cents," recalls Kolber.

Eaton's preferred to follow its own plodding course. In 1954 Eaton's had bought one hundred acres of land on the northwestern outskirts of Toronto for $1.4 million. In 1961 Eaton's offered Simpsons as much of that space as it wanted — up to half — for the same amount, $1.4 million. The plan was to build Yorkdale, the first regional shopping centre in Canada. Simpsons asked for about nineteen acres on the west side of the property but demanded that the purchase price include sewage and water connections, roadways, and said that the site had to be "ready for blacktop surfacing." Eaton's agreed and then proceeded to spend $1 million preparing its competitor's site.

Eaton's eventually got to where it should be; it just took longer. In its day Yorkdale was a consumer's world of wonders. The mall was fully air-conditioned and boasted a two-storey inner court with two fountains. The windows had curtains automatically activated by the sun to let in just the right amount of light. Twenty-foot trees were planted on the roof. One shop, a beauty parlour for little girls called Ponytails, had hobbyhorses rather than chairs for the young clients.

The shopping centre concept was becoming well established in Canada: a department-store anchor at each end and the smaller shops in between. Simpsons convinced Eaton's to come to the seventy-store Fairview Shopping Centre in the western Montreal suburb of Pointe Claire. When Fairview opened in 1965, it was Eaton's eleventh mall location.

Just as Eaton's had been slow to go into the malls, so store operations were equally unresponsive to Canada's changing ethnic mix. The European immigrants who began pouring into Canada in the 1950s were often treated with disdain by clerks. "Eaton's sales help did not look favourably upon New Canadians," said an internal Eaton's report prepared in 1957. "They lack courtesy in their treatment of them and are impatient with them because of their language difficulties and the reluctance of a New Canadian shopper to make up his mind as quickly as a Canadian." Italians in particular were singled out as "most likely to antagonize staff because of language difficulties and inherited indecisive shopping habits." [4]

The anti-Semitism of the 1930s remained unchanged. In 1950 the Canadian Jewish Congress complained that the Montreal Eaton's store's travel department was advertising resorts that excluded Jews. Eaton's agreed to remove references to so-called "restricted" resorts. [5]

After ninety years of decentralized operations, where every store and every region controlled its own buying and merchandising, management was finally beginning to realize that such a structure did not function well in the modern era. Suppliers had grown larger, there was consolidation in manufacturing, and Eaton's buyers found themselves at a disadvantage. Other retailers were able to negotiate better prices because they could place one order to cover all stores.

"People in the industry were baffled," says Ray Luft, an economist who joined Eaton's in Vancouver in 1965. "It was not uncommon to find two to five Eaton's buyers in one supplier's office all at the same time as if they were representing different companies." Finally, in 1968, the autonomy of the four regions (eastern, central, western, and Pacific) was ended. Operations were placed under the direction of a six-member management committee that reported to the board of Eaton's of Canada.

Some aspects of the past remained untouchable. Eaton's no-arguments return guarantee was continued even though fourteen out of every hundred items purchased were brought back, often after shoppers had used them. In an attempt to discourage such returns from the wealthy who were just as likely to abuse the policy as anyone else, Eaton's went so far in the late 1960s as to take photographs of socialites at the Queen's Plate. Said John David: "When we showed them to the ladies who returned the clothes, they said: 'How could you stoop so low?'"[6]

In spite of such episodes and Eaton's antediluvian management style, there were flashes of the former brilliance that had engendered such customer loyalty. After a March 1966 blizzard in Winnipeg, 1482 people actually bedded down and stayed overnight in the store.

Much of the corporate problem flowed from the fact that John David's merchandising skills were more quirky than visionary. If anyone mentioned a city with an Eaton's store, John David could reel off the names of all the local competitors. As for what should actually be done to stay ahead, well, that wasn't his forte. He preferred word games, had a prodigious vocabulary, revelled in using arcane terminology, and enjoyed catching colleagues in verbal faux pas. He kept dictionaries and reference books close at hand to buttress an argument or provide an apt quotation. Salty phrases were sprinkled throughout his speech. "Bloody" was a favourite; politicians were "leather-lunged bastards." The farther he was from the office, the coarser his language became.

John David did not bestride the earth. He was not one of those owners who drew the best from people through the sheer force of his personality. His usual mode of transportation was as modest as the man himself. In the 1950s he drove a Volkswagen; in the 1960s he had a sporty light-blue Ford Mustang convertible. His explanation for driving a small car was that he didn't like the bother of parking a large vehicle. But there was another reason for driving a Volkswagen. John David had been offered the VW distributorship for Canada but turned it down because he couldn't imagine abandoning Eaton's "goods satisfactory or money refunded" policy to run a car dealership. (John David wasn't the first Eaton to misjudge the automobile market. His uncle, William, had been invited some fifty years earlier by Sam McLaughlin to join McLaughlin's fledgling business in Oshawa. Colonel William declined McLaughlin's offer in favour of running an Eaton knitting mill. By 1918 McLaughlin's factories had been acquired by General Motors, and McLaughlin was president of General Motors of Canada.)

Not only did John David miss a money-making opportunity, he wasn't even attuned to one of the main reasons for owning a Volkswagen. He exchanged pleasantries about the car one Christmas while greeting an employee in the receiving line at the annual party. When asked, "How's the mileage?" John David seemed startled by the question. "I never thought about that," he replied. "Pretty good, I guess."

Away from the responsibilities of the store and out of sight of Signy, John David was a different man. No penny-pinching economy car for him. While visiting London in the 1960s, he announced that the office in England needed a new car. He visited the Daimler showroom and quickly settled on the same top-of-the-line model favoured by the Queen. Staff were uppity toward someone they regarded as no more than a colonial bumpkin. "You wouldn't be interested in that vehicle," he was told. Eaton's London office had to send over a cheque before Daimler was convinced John David had the wherewithal. By the early 1970s some buying offices had been closed and there were attempts to reduce expenses in those that remained open, like London. The cutback strategy was undermined by another visit from John David, who decided London needed a *new* Daimler.

John David was not a happy man at heart. Despite all his wealth, he was mired in a role he didn't want, one he was carrying out only because it was expected of him. As he reached middle age, his face became weathered by drink and disappointment. At root, John David simply preferred life away from the office pursuing personal pleasure.

John David played a middling game of tennis and could shoot a round of golf in the nineties, but his real loves were hunting, yachting, or just holing up for weeks in his Georgian Bay retreat. In 1959 he had the *Hildur*, a 104-foot-long ketch-rigged yacht, built in Vancouver. Designed by William Garden of Seattle, the *Hildur* was radar-equipped, and had three guest cabins and a crew of seven. It took him to destinations like the Caribbean, the Galapagos, and deep-sea fishing on the U.S. West Coast.

Naming his ship after his wife did not make her any more enamoured of the extended cruises John David favoured, although she did accompany him once on a trip to Greece. He sailed at least six weeks of the year and also went on several duck-hunting trips during which he'd put on a turtleneck sweater and a pair of old slacks, then keep everyone up all night, drinking, singing songs, and swapping stories. The next morning he'd be the first man up, gun at the ready.

Among John David's buddies on seagoing voyages were Vancouver architect Charles Van Norman; Duncan, B.C., store manager John Lawrence; Clayton "Slim" Delbridge, a six-foot-six former semi-pro pitcher and publisher of the Vancouver *News-Herald*; Eaton's carpenter Laurie Davis; and Parry Sound lawyer Frank Powell, with whom he started Georgian Bay Airways.

(The airline's takeoff was almost aborted in 1960 when the Air Transport Board rejected the application. High-placed allies intervened when Transport minister George Hees was able to obtain cabinet approval, thus overruling the agency. The airline, headquartered in Parry Sound, started as a scheduled passenger operation, but there were too few travellers. They soon abandoned that business and did only charters.)

John David was devoted to those he liked. Ralph Spradbrow, John David's personal pilot since 1938, was seriously injured in a traffic accident while holidaying in Jamaica in 1959. Spradbrow had just arrived on the island and forgotten to drive on the left-hand side of the road. John David collected blood plasma and an oxygen tent, then flew south, but Spradbrow died before help could arrive.

"He liked his pals around," said Big John Bassett. "He liked to drink, have a few belts, and tell stories. That was the Irish in him. He liked to hear stories, what was happening, what was going on, he liked to get the news. He invited me on the yacht one time. He wanted to go somewhere, I don't know, northern Canada or something. I said, 'Nah, I'm not going to go. You and Frank Powell [can go]. I'll tell you what to do. Lend me the yacht, you go with me and I'll pretend it's my yacht and I'll fill it with beautiful babes and we'll go down to the islands, we'll go to the Bahamas.' Oh, he roared."

The closest Bassett came to his fantasy cruise was once in the Bahamas, when he did sail with John David, and the *Hildur* tied up at Lyford Cay. There was a reception on board and Bassett told everyone that the yacht was his. Most of the guests were friends of both men, so they knew otherwise. John David played along with the joke; but there were no babes.

In addition to the *Hildur*, his three residences in Canada, and his corporate jet, John David also had a house on Antigua, now owned by French movie actor Jean-Paul Belmondo. John David also acquired a two-seater Hughes helicopter in 1966. He and a Hughes pilot spent ten days bringing his new toy back from California. After one hundred hours of flying, he acquired his helicopter licence in 1967, and used the chopper for quick hops to and from Georgian Bay.

"The joyful thing about a helicopter is that you don't have to go up very high," he once said. "You're like a bird. You can fly in all kinds of weather. I guess I like helicopters because I like to see what's on the other side of the hill." [7] Flying at five hundred feet, he'd spot boys playing in a field below, decrease altitude, hover above them and wave, then buzz away. It was hard to know for whom the connection mattered most.

In his Toronto office, he was equally in control. Although his office had no door, no one approached the king without an appointment made through his secretary, Marlene Josiak, who guarded the inner sanctum. The office itself was decorated with pale yellow broadloom, a mahogany desk, some of carpenter Laurie Davis's African-style sculpture, and a scroll attesting to his membership in the Eaton's Quarter Century Club. One wall had a grouping of photographs showing the various boats he'd owned over the years. There was also a model of his beloved *Hildur* in a four-foot-tall glass case. Like him, it seemed trapped, straining to be free. (The model is now displayed in the lounge of the Royal Canadian Yacht Club's midtown Toronto facility. It's one of the few stinkpots, as sailors call motorized vessels, on display.)

In his desk drawer John David kept letters from customers, including several well-thumbed favourites he'd pull out and read to visitors. One had been written by a farmer who'd ordered a pump. When he and his son unpacked the box, there was no handle. The letter ran to four angry pages, cursing Eaton's for being so slipshod. At the end of the missive, the farmer wrote: "Never mind this letter. My son just found the handle in the bottom of the box." Another letter that became legendary was from an Inuit living on Herschel Island who'd ordered a dress from the catalogue. After it arrived, he wrote to complain: "Where is the woman?" [8]

Just as John David's legend was larger than the man himself, it was sometimes hard to separate fact from fiction at Eaton's. Details included in the lore were so specific. An oft-told tale concerned a man who walked into the store in Edmonton with a wedding ring still in its satin-lined box and bearing the price tag $10. He said he'd bought the ring forty-one years earlier, but his intended had changed her mind. Only now had he decided he wanted his money back. The refund was paid without question.

John David liked to lunch in the Round Room at College Street or the Georgian Room at Queen Street when there were fashion shows. Among the models there would always be some starry-eyed tryouts who were hopeful of making the big time. Their responses to comments from diners — some of whom were store executives — would test the poise and apparel knowledge of the models.

"I made my Round Room debut in a week of showings which featured me in a hooded red coat," wrote former-model-turned-newspaper-columnist Joan Sutton in 1977. "Every day, some man would smile at me and say, 'Well, now, who is this? Little Red Riding Hood?' And I would giggle and simper and go on my way. Until the last day, Friday. Five days of men, all asking what they thought was an original question, was I Little Red Riding Hood?

"On the fifth day, I sallied out and did my pirouette beside a table crowded with men. One of them smiled at me and said the inevitable, 'This must be Little Red Riding Hood.'

"Something snapped. 'I suppose,' I answered, 'and you must be the Big Bad Wolf.'

" 'No dear,' said one of the men. 'He's John David Eaton.' " [9]

Others who approached his throne often found themselves ensnared in one of his practical jokes. Once, when an American boater asked about a marker buoy in the waters of Georgian Bay, John David told him it was a lobster pot and suggested that the unwitting visitor come back the following day when freshly captured crustaceans would be available. According to John David's version of events, the gullible traveller did return, his mouth watering.

Another favourite prank required an unsuspecting city dweller visiting the island for the first time. The head of the grocery department at Eaton's, a Miss York, was once just such a stooge. John David told her that the family's food shipment that weekend had not included the meat order, so she would have to hunt and kill her own game. Fortunately snipe inhabited the island, he said, and were easy prey.

As darkness fell, she was taken down a narrow path by Ted the boatman, who told her to crouch on top of a box holding an open sack. At the mouth of the sack was a stick to trip any snipe travelling along the path. All she'd have to do was close the sack and the bird would be trapped. Miss York was provided with a lantern, told to remain very still, then left alone. The lantern held little oil and soon stopped burning; the hapless huntress was plunged into pitch-black darkness. Of course, no birds came and after a time she began calling softly for help. Her subsequent embarrassment and ire when the gag was revealed only caused John David to laugh all the harder.

In Toronto John David liked to end his workday early and be home by four-thirty, then call a friend to come around for a drink. A frequent visitor was Allen Lambert, who was appointed chief general manager of Toronto-Dominion Bank in 1956, then president in 1960. In the more than fifteen years Lambert was John David's main banker, they never met at John David's office. Nor did John David care much for the bank's board meetings. When the Bank of Toronto and the Dominion Bank merged in 1955, John David chose not to continue as a director of the merged institution.

"Basically, John David was a pretty private person," says Lambert. "Some might say shy. I don't think it was so much shy as he had his own way of life. I don't think being a corporate director was very exciting to him — you know, you sat around for a long time listening to other people talking." Nor was he much interested in spending time in his own office. "He wasn't one to sit behind a desk," says Lambert. "John was very open and very relaxed, talking about turning over responsibility to the boys. He wanted to spend less time in the business."

John David also enjoyed talking about the good old days when everybody knew his or her place. As far as he was concerned, even the Great Depression had its good side. "Nobody thought about money in those days, because they never saw any," he reminisced in 1968. "You could take your girl to a supper dance at the hotel for $10, and that included the bottle and a room for you and your friends to drink it in. I'm glad I grew up then. It was a good time for everybody. People learned what it was like to work." [10]

⸺

When Eaton's tried to change, sucess was rare. By 1965 Eaton's CEO Ross Jenkins was in failing health after suffering a stroke. He was replaced by David Kinnear, who decided that the company needed a new, more activist strategy. Kinnear had a free hand to do what he wanted; by then John David's management style could only be described as studied indifference. "He didn't really get his nose into it very deeply, to tell you the truth. He left it to his 'pros,' as it were," says Kinnear. The trouble with such a hands-off attitude was that much of management was deadwood. John David just didn't have the heart to get rid of many of the old standbys, despite the fact that some were earning as much as $300,000 a year. "He just had to let them run their careers out," says Kinnear. "I gave early retirement to quite a few of the senior executives, just so we could get some new blood. They were used to sitting on their behinds and getting big salaries. I wasn't very popular."

Before he retired, Jenkins tried to recruit as secretary-treasurer A. J. "Pete" Little, a partner at the accounting firm of Clarkson Gordon. The firm, which traced its origins to 1864, was more than just the largest accounting firm in the country. It was also the unofficial finishing school for young men of the upper class. Little had joined Clarkson Gordon in 1935 after graduating from the University of Western Ontario and was made a partner in 1945. A longtime confidant and counsellor of Lady Eaton's, Little was one of the firm's leading tax experts and would have been a superb addition. But Little was not interested in joining Eaton's. Jenkins's second choice was Osler, Hoskin & Harcourt lawyer Swatty Wotherspoon. Founded in 1862, Oslers, as the firm was known, was typical of an old-line Toronto WASP law firm. The partners were all male until Bertha Wilson, later a Supreme Court justice, joined in 1958. There were no Catholics in the firm until the 1950s, no Jews until the 1960s. Most of the lawyers had attended one of the prep schools known as the Little Big Four — Trinity, UCC, St. Andrew's, or Ridley College — and many were invited to join the firm by a family member who was already there.

Wotherspoon's manner was gruff and militaristic, as befitted a man who was educated at the Royal Military College, served with the Royal Canadian Armoured Corps from 1941 to 1945, and with the Canadian Militia from 1930 to 1952 before retiring with the rank of brigadier. As secretary-treasurer of Eaton's and a member of the board of directors, he was to help run the firm and prepare the boys for the day they would take over. Others at the law firm, including Allan Beattie, would continue acting for the family and the firm.

When Ross Jenkins was asked by a colleague why he hadn't recruited accountant Little instead of lawyer Wotherspoon, Jenkins replied: "He said, 'No, thanks.' Swatty said, 'Yes, please.'" Eaton's would make do with Swatty. Such a leap from law to business was rare. Lawyers get paid to recognize risk and list the options; few have the talent to take the business decisions that must follow. But Wotherspoon needed to make a move. He'd found himself in a potential conflict of interest; his wife owned land that was involved in litigation. Moreover, power at the firm was flowing to the next generation of lawyers; Wotherspoon's clout was diminishing daily.

Like so many of his fellow Eaton's executives, new CEO David Kinnear was an Ulsterman; he was born in County Down and arrived in Canada at nineteen with experience in a Belfast drug firm. He landed in Toronto on March 7, 1928, was interviewed by Eaton's the following day, and joined the day after as a ledger keeper in Toronto. He was sent to Hamilton after eighteen months, transferred to Vancouver in 1948, became general manager of British Columbia in 1952, and was named a director in 1960. One of Kinnear's more successful ideas was signing hockey legend Gordie Howe in 1964 to a ten-year exclusive contract as sports adviser to Eaton's. Howe toured the country, refereeing games, playing charity golf events, and signing autographs in the stores.

Under Kinnear, one long-running problem was finally fixed. Canadian Department Stores, the money-losing chain acquired in 1928, was sold in 1965. Eaton's now had forty-nine stores, down from sixty-nine three years earlier. There were also thirty-nine heavy-goods stores and 336 catalogue outlets. The catalogue was getting creaky, but it continued to be a major part of Eaton's merchandising approach. Explained Kinnear at the time: "We feel we can better serve smaller Canadian communities with our catalogue operation. We can offer thousands more items in our catalogue than we could ever stock in a small branch department store." [11] In 1965 Eaton's total sales were about $700 million; upstart Simpsons-Sears was closing the gap with nearly $500 million. Because the arrangement Sears had with Simpsons did not allow stores in Toronto, Eaton's senior management had no regular contact with the U.S. interloper and seemed oblivious to its phenomenal growth in the rest of the country.

The enemy was not only outside the walls; there was continual warfare within. Executives, who had responsibility without authority, expended too much energy trying to circumvent John David, causing strained relations. Small victories mattered above all; big-picture vision was impossible. Typical of the small-minded gamesmanship was an occasion when public-relations consultants Charles Tisdall and Joe Clark were asked to make a presentation to the executive group. On their way to the meeting, they met John David in the hall. He asked them why they were there and, when told, decided to join in. The officers, who did not want to involve John David, quickly cancelled the session. "They made fun of him, patronized him," says Tisdall. "He was brighter than they thought he was."

On some matters executives would simply disregard his views. There was a move to update drivers' uniforms, but John David was opposed, saying: "Leave the goddamn uniforms alone." [12] After a time new uniforms were quietly introduced anyway. Store hours were another battleground. When Yorkdale opened in 1964, John David wanted normal closing at five-thirty or six, just like in Timothy's time. Everyone else wanted nine-thirty, the same as the other stores in the mall. "John David was a very nice fellow, but he wasn't very bright," says Alan, R.Y.'s son, who was by then corporate manager, research and development. "He thought he knew what he was doing but he didn't. We had the dead hand of the grave running everything. He'd listen to his mother." John David agreed to the later closing only after repeated assurances that no one would work unduly long hours as a result.

On larger questions Eaton's seemed lost, lurching from one new plan to another as if looking for the magic bullet. Two thousand upper-level managers and supervisors were shuffled for no apparent reason or benefit, causing widespread chaos. The groceterias were closed and Eaton's began to abandon its longtime position in manufacturing. In 1964 the Guelph Stove Co., owned by Eaton's since 1919, was sold to the Minneapolis-based Franklin division of Studebaker Corp.

Some steps towards modernization were costly calamities. In 1965 Eaton's decided to install a giant mainframe computer to handle customer-credit-card billings. Simpsons had already moved to computerization three years earlier. Eaton's belated attempt at catch-up was disastrous. Not only did they install a new computer, they tried to change everyone's account number and move to a form of descriptive billing that replaced so-called country-club billing, in which actual sales slips had been returned by mail to customers.

Chaos ensued. Debits would mysteriously appear as credits. Even when honest customers wrote to correct mistakes, nothing would happen. Many buyers got a free ride. A University of Toronto professor told his students about one customer he knew who'd made $600 in purchases and wasn't billed for six months. Of the 750,000 customers at the start of the program, 100,000 cancelled their accounts because of the confusion.

An eighteen-acre warehouse opened in 1967 in Toronto's east end, meant to be a modern miracle with an electronic sorting system for fifty thousand orders a day, was a mess for months. Eaton's had mistakenly erected a six-storey edifice; the vertical design hampered the easy in-and-out flow of goods.

In some regions there was rot and ruin. Managers had been given so much power that some of them regarded themselves as potentates. "Throughout the Prairies guys had harems within the stores. During the year, the most important job in the store was to make sure there was liquor available. There was a lot of emphasis on the entertainment and social part," says John Williams, an MBA from Northwestern who started with Eaton's in Victoria in 1959 and was sent to Edmonton in the 1960s as part of a process to clean house.

Some store managers would prey on female clerks. The manager maintained a suite at a local hotel for afternoon trysts and told an underling to make sure that the room was always in a state of readiness. "You got more trouble for having the wrong scotch in the room than your store results," says Williams. At Christmas managers would give their assistant managers a shopping list with the names of half a dozen women and their designated gifts, which could be as lavish as a mink coat.

Petty scams were rampant, not just in the Prairies, but throughout the organization. Draperies and other items used as floor displays were sometimes removed only to reappear in a manager's cottage. Store carpenters might even do the installation. Discount favours were traded. The usual employee discount was 10 per cent, rising to 20 per cent at Christmas. Individuals arranged trade-offs with colleagues in which they reduced by 50 per cent the cost of an item purchased in their department if similar savings were given to them when they bought goods from their colleague's area. Senior executives had entire kitchens installed in their homes "on approval." When a new line of appliances was introduced, the more up-to-date models were shipped out to replace the older units.

There was one brief attempt to modernize the firm under Eaton's corporate personnel manager Tony Peskett. Born in England, Peskett was an engineer who had done postgraduate work at the American University of Biarritz before joining Eaton's in 1948 in Vancouver, then moving to Toronto head office in 1960. He believed in management by chaos. "The minute you establish an organization," he'd say, "it starts to decay." [13]

The "Pesketteers," as this new, young band of guerrilla managers called themselves, set out to tweak the nose of authority and reshape the empire using as their theme the Bob Dylan line of that day: "He who's not busy being born is busy dying." They made little headway. "I thought a lot of it was just baloney," says Alan Marchment, who joined in 1965 and was named treasurer the following year. "It was razzle-dazzle. Anything that couldn't have a sizzle wasn't important."

Hired in 1964 was F. Ross Johnson, who went on to notoriety as president of RJR Nabisco in the 1980s and was featured in the book *Barbarians at the Gate.* Johnson later cited three lessons learned in his rise to the top. At General Electric he'd learned patience; at General Steel Wares he was schooled in the tough side of management; and Eaton's, he said, showed him how to play corporate politics. His mentor, Eaton's corporate personnel manager Tony Peskett, taught Johnson how to get power and what to do with it. "He made me aware of the political maneuvering, and the handling of people," said Johnson. "He showed that there are certain power spots in a corporation and that you can take any job and build it. If you get control, you don't have to be the boss, you run the place." [14]

Little was accomplished. "Change started, but there wasn't enough support at the top. The people that Peskett brought in just didn't last," says John Williams. "John David was not a driven man. We weren't the street fighters our competitors were. We were way behind the industry best practices. The key values were to protect the assets rather than to grow."

When Kinnear came in as CEO in 1965, he had his own ideas. Peskett soon fell out of favour and departed in 1968 to become president and CEO of the Employers Council of British Columbia. Johnson left the same year. Whether Peskett had the right idea or the wrong idea hardly mattered. Eaton's would have none of it. The top executives didn't want to change and rebuffed any new concepts.

Nothing more exemplified John David's personality and the corporate culture of the company than how Eaton's dealt with municipalities. In 1958 Project Viking, as it was then known, was supposed to replace the Queen Street store in Toronto with low buildings and formal courtyards. Two years later there was a new plan by world-renowned architect I. M. Pei — he designed four geometric buildings that would contain office and retail space. That project idea was in turn replaced by one from Toronto architect E. L. Hankinson, who first used the descriptive label "Eaton Centre" in a 1963 proposal that included a store, office tower, galleria, and new Stock Exchange. In 1964 Canadian architect James A. Murray and Victor Gruen, the father of American shopping centres, suggested a modification that added various cultural and social activities to the mix.

John David took no decision until September 1965 when he finally announced that Doug Haldenby and Andy Mathers, sons of the two men who had designed his residence on Dunvegan, had been selected as Canadian architects working with the New York firm of Skidmore, Owings, Merrill. Their proposal was huge: an office-retail twenty-acre super block that would include 1.3 million square feet of department store, two shopping arcades, three office towers ranging in height from forty storeys to sixty storeys, and a five-hundred-suite hotel. The plan included demolition of the nineteenth-century Church of the Holy Trinity and the Old City Hall, leaving only the clock tower. Also slated for the wrecker's ball: a printing plant and clothing factory, mail-order buildings, the budget-goods Annex, and the main store on Queen Street.

In 1966 David Owen, who had worked with real estate developer William Zeckendorf on Montreal's Place Ville Marie, became managing director of the project. Zeckendorf's company, Webb & Knapp, had successfully carried out urban redevelopment schemes in New York, Philadelphia, and Washington, D.C., among other U.S. cities. Owen was both a dreamer and doer. On redevelopment projects he'd tear down buildings that Zeckendorf hadn't even acquired yet.

There was no such accelerated approach in Toronto. Opposition to the Eaton Centre quickly centred on Holy Trinity, which had existed cheek by jowl with Eaton's since 1907, when the excavations for the mail-order building had been dug by hand. The Tudor Gothic church was erected in 1847 following a donation of £5,000 from a woman living in Yorkshire, England. Although it was the fourth Anglican church in Toronto, Holy Trinity was the first where pews could not be rented. The working-class residents of what was then the outskirts of Toronto could worship for free.

More than a century later citizens rallied to defend the past. One group cleaned soot off a portion of the Old City Hall, erected just before the turn of the century, to show the beauty of the russet rose-and-beige sandstone underneath. John David, whose home phone number was listed in the telephone book, was besieged by irate calls. Frustrated by the lack of community support, John David cancelled the project in May 1967. He told associates: "Let's walk across the street and tell [Mayor William] Dennison he can shove the Old City Hall up his ass." Two years later, when asked if he were powerful, he snorted. "If I were so bloody powerful, the Eaton Centre would be a going concern today." [15]

"My greatest failure, I think, has been in my dealings with city politicians, especially in my hometown of Toronto," he said in 1969. "For years we've been trying to improve our downtown image, yet City Hall has consistently thwarted us, even though it would mean we'd pay far more taxes than we do now. How the hell does a storekeeper combat that kind of mentality?" [16]

Eaton's downtown-planning difficulties were not limited to Toronto. A $125 million redevelopment on a twenty-acre Montreal site bounded by University Avenue, Ste-Catherine, Sherbrooke, and Mansfield streets was also declared dead in 1968. Construction on the $75 million Pacific Centre in Vancouver began in 1969 and it opened in 1973 — twenty-five years behind schedule.

The biggest problem was not intractable politicians in each of those cities, but Eaton's arrogance. "Eaton's is the biggest stumbling block to progress in this city," wrote developer Zeckendorf in his 1970 autobiography. He was particularly dismissive of John David. "Mr. Eaton is a merchant prince, but in pride of city or sense of service, no Medici."

Zeckendorf acknowledged Eaton's market dominance but could discern no rationale for that prime position. "Almost by happenstance, Eaton's had a geographic stranglehold on the natural growth of Toronto, by virtue of the land space they owned in and around their store. A greater part of this land lies idle, either as parking lots or as dusty, truck-choked warehousing. Sprawled out like a great patch of crabgrass on a lawn, the Eaton holdings effectively choke any new growth trying to get underway alongside." [17]

John David's final year at the helm did not begin auspiciously. Eaton's was one hundred years old in 1969, an anniversary that called for the family to be out in force. And so, on January 2 at 9:30 a.m., they arrived at the Queen Street store in limousines accompanied by a police escort.

There were John David and Signy, John Craig and Kitty (in their final year together as a couple), Fred and Nicky, Thor, a bearded George, and a gaggle of five grandchildren. Granddaughters Signy and Catherine put a gold-plated key into a conveniently low lock as fireworks exploded on the roof, one boom every four seconds to mark the years since Timothy had opened the first store.

The family was greeted inside by a thirty-two-voice children's choir, as well as hundreds of employees and pensioners. Bells rang throughout the store. There was a six-foot-square Eaton's logo made from 750 lamps surrounded by green foliage. The official party gathered at Timothy's bronze likeness and John David was formally introduced. There was a hush as everyone craned expectantly to see the great man and hear his grand words. "First of all a very Merry Christmas — I mean a Happy New Year." Then he paused and added, almost to himself: "That's a good start." [18]

Other celebrations throughout the year were more carefully controlled. A new pink hybrid tea rose, named after Timothy, was sold in every store. Eaton's hired William Stephenson to write an illustrated history called *The Store that Timothy Built*. Stephenson, an author and writer of television screenplays, described Eaton's as "the unselfish, dedicated friend of all Canadians." He quoted John David as saying: "Retailing is such a pleasant and stimulating way of bringing people together."

Without the smoothing influence of public relations, John David was more unvarnished in media interviews. One writer asked John David whether or not he'd ever used his power to have a newspaper story killed. His reply was brief but instructive: "Wouldn't you?" [19]

He also seized the occasion to vent his views on immigration. "Take those Czech refugees who came in — there were a lot of doctors, a fine type of immigrant to get, only they can't be doctors here, they have to go to school. There's every reason to believe at least one or two of them are as good as any doctor in Canada." [20]

John David could perhaps be forgiven for his intemperate statements. After nearly forty years in the business, his patience had long since been exhausted and he was in miserable health. He decided to take early retirement on August 6, 1969, two months short of his sixtieth birthday.

In December four hundred suppliers, bankers, and friends gathered at St. Lawrence Hall for a final centennial salute. Everyone signed a seven-foot-tall birthday card just inside the door. Four models, wearing dresses costing $1200 each, circulated among the guests. Another attendant, her midriff bare, handed out cigarettes. Mayor William Dennison presented an illuminated, framed scroll thanking Eaton's for contributing "immeasurably to the enhancement of Toronto as the merchandising and commercial centre of Canada."

John David did not attend. Guests were greeted by John Craig and Fred. As quietly as he'd come, John David was gone. "He said good-bye and that was that," commented Fred a year after his father retired. "He hasn't been back to the office since." [21] As an epitaph for a career, it wasn't much. He hadn't even bothered to establish a succession plan.

Canada's own Centennial year in 1967 had been a halcyon time, the like of which the country has not seen since. That year, John David and Signy sponsored a lavish coffee-table book of photographs by Roloff Beny entitled *To Every Thing There Is a Season.*

Eaton's own season in the sun ended at 3:30 a.m. on November 22, 1968, when a bomb exploded in a locker on the Métro level of the Montreal store. In the weeks that followed, other devices were discovered and dismantled. The Montreal Santa Claus Parade was cancelled in 1969, never to be held again. Eaton's store windows were fitted with wooden shutters that could be quickly bolted in place against bombs or riots. Violent times had arrived and a more fractious future lay ahead. The country and the company had lost their innocence together.

CHAPTER NINE

BOB BUTLER: THE COMMONER

—

J0HN DAVID MIGHT BE GONE, BUT THE NEXT generation was far from ready. John Craig and Fred, then in their early thirties, had only modest retailing experience; Thor and George, still in their twenties, had none at all. Timothy had devised a successful transition that followed his death in 1907. When Sir John died prematurely in 1922, at least R.Y. was available to step in. This time, no "worker Eaton" would be seriously considered, even though there was no member of the "owner Eatons" with the maturity and talent to take the reins.

Even the boys freely admitted what everyone knew to be true. "There was a general consensus amongst the executives and ourselves that we weren't ready," says Fred. "So we devised a method to remove ourselves from the day-to-day."

That meant going outside the family for the first time ever to find a president. Likeliest candidates were Bob Butler and Don McGiverin. A third possibility was R.Y.'s eldest son, Jack. As manager in Montreal, he'd expanded the 400,000-square-foot store by 600,000 square feet and within two years had sales per square foot back to previous levels, a phenomenal achievement.

Merchandising is all about "turns" — how many times an item sells in a given twelve-month period. Other merchants might get eight "turns" a year in a department like women's dresses. Jack got sixteen. Jack didn't want any "aged" stock, unsold items still hanging around months later. His preferred position was best demonstrated by the menswear manager who once flipped a hat onto Jack's desk and reported, "That's my aged stock."

In 1958 *Maclean's* had tipped Jack as a "man to watch" and called him the "fastest rising member of the merchandising family and strongest candidate in sight to succeed T. Eaton Co. president (since 1942) John David Eaton." [1]

Such accolades did Jack no good. He might well have made an excellent president, but he enjoyed too little support among the owner Eatons and their flunkies. When Jack returned to Toronto in 1968, he'd become just another worker Eaton to whom the family paid scant attention. When John Craig was manager of the London, Ontario, store, Jack scheduled a visit. When Jack arrived, he found that John Craig had taken the day off to golf.

Calgary-born Don McGiverin was a gold medallist in commerce from the University of Manitoba and received his MBA from Ohio State University in 1946. As a student, McGiverin worked part-time selling shoes in the Winnipeg store and joined the Toronto operation after graduation.

By 1961, at thirty-seven, he was named a director, the youngest nonfamily member ever appointed to the board. So young was he and so fast his ascent that John David called him "Kid." In 1966 McGiverin was sent to Winnipeg as group vice-president. After decades of dominating the local scene, Eaton's had been slipping rapidly. Decor, design, advertising, and merchandise mix were all out of date. Simpsons-Sears had arrived in 1959 and was taking market share away from Eaton's. McGiverin launched the turnaround process, but it would take six years, as well as the work of others who followed, to produce any improvement.

Bob Butler was also a long time Eaton's employee. Born in Toronto in 1923, he inherited his love of retail from his mother, who was the first female buyer for the British menswear store, Austin Reed Ltd. Butler had worked in Eaton's at fifteen after school. Following war service with the Royal Canadian Air Force as a navigator on bombers, he joined Eaton's full-time and rose to become vice-president, planning and development in 1968.

In that role Butler travelled across Canada visiting stores with John David and saw first hand the depth of Eaton's problems. Once, at the end of their rounds in Sudbury, they found themselves near the candy counter. Said John David: "Bob, I wouldn't mind some chocolates." Butler asked the clerk for a specific type. "We decided not to carry those," said the clerk. "They sold too well and we couldn't keep them in stock." The men looked at each other in despair. Butler bought something else.

Taking the easy way out had become typical of the entire organization. The Queen Street store received a new coat of paint in 1968. "We wanted to do something that would be clearly visible to our patrons and yet not spend millions in the process. Somebody suggested a coat of paint, so we got right to it," explained Butler. [2]

Succession was divisive. McGiverin and Butler both had backers. Some executives who were there at the time say that McGiverin had the support of John David and Wotherspoon, and claim that the four Eaton boys preferred Butler because John Craig and Fred had worked most closely with him. "I recall it as a very collegial kind of discussion and a collegial decision," says Fred. "We were consulted. There wasn't a big huge fight. Certainly my brother and I did not carry the day."

Butler was chosen over McGiverin. Looking back, Butler says he felt both lucky and flattered — but ill-equipped. "I wasn't smart enough. I was a merchant. That's my strength, that's my interest. What Eaton's needed was a massive reexamination of costs. I questioned whether I had the right background." He considered the offer carefully for several weeks before finally agreeing to become the first nonfamily president of Eaton's.

Coinciding with Butler's appointment as president, outside directors were named to the board of Eaton's of Canada for the first time. They included Allan Beattie, managing partner at Osler, Hoskin & Harcourt; Dick Thomson, chairman and CEO of the Toronto-Dominion Bank; and Thor Stephenson, Signy's younger brother, an aeronautical engineer who was president and CEO of United Aircraft of Canada Ltd. of Montreal.

Alan Eaton became vice-president, administration, but didn't last long. "The boys didn't want me around. They didn't want any of R.Y.'s progeny around." In June 1972 he took early retirement. Brother Jack thought about quitting his merchandising role but hung on for another five years. Lady Eaton was vindicated; the worker Eatons were vanquished.

David Kinnear was made chairman. Even twenty-five years later the frigid relationship between Butler and Kinnear remains fresh in their minds. "He was not my kind of guy. He was one of those go-go boys," says Kinnear. "He went off in all kinds of developments without getting proper research." Butler held Kinnear in equally low regard and rarely consulted him. "Kinnear was simply a survivor. He just kissed asses," says Butler.

Despite the title of president, Butler felt powerless. "I never really took over. I was a holding pattern until the boys came of age and could take back their company," he says. "Fred was learning. I saw my role as helping to get the family ready. I understood that. I had no illusions about becoming a shareholder."

Runner-up McGiverin was asked to move to Toronto as vice-president, corporate development, but his personal life had been haunted by tragedy.

After their four-year-old son drowned in 1957, his wife never fully recovered and she died in 1968. The next year their eleven-year-old daughter, Mary, was found to have a serious spinal condition and spent four years in a body cast. With his wife dead less than a year and his daughter ailing, he rejected the move east. He had turned down a job offer from The Bay a year earlier, but now he was ready to accept a job in Winnipeg with the competition. In September 1969 he moved to The Bay as managing director, retail stores, where he went on to become a successful leader.

There was surprise in the ranks when Butler was chosen. "The beginning of the end came when Butler was chosen over Don McGiverin. History will record he did a far better job at The Bay than Mr. Butler did for Eaton's," says Albert Plant, who was an Eaton's executive from 1970 to 1975. "I would have a struggle trying to determine what Bob Butler's talents were and I worked with him extremely closely."

Moving the boys out of the day-to-day operations meant giving them honorific roles in the family holding company, Eaton's of Canada Ltd. John Craig, then thirty-two, was named chairman, and Fred, then thirty-one, became president. The appointments to the holding company meant they no longer had operational responsibilities in the retail arm, T. Eaton Co. Scant though their merchandising experience was, their learning curves in the business were abruptly curtailed.

They'd been "kicked upstairs" to Eaton's of Canada as directors with no line responsibilities, no staff roles, nothing to do. The two would arrive at their offices over the former stables on Terauley Street around nine, read the newspapers, walk through the tunnel to the main store, and take another elevator to the ninth-floor Georgian Room for coffee at ten. After that, they'd return to their offices using the same circuitous route, make a few phone calls, maybe deal with some mail, then go for lunch. The afternoon would pass with equal aimlessness.

"They'll have a rough row to hoe," said John David of his sons' prospects. "But they'll have lots of help and a hundred years of experience to draw on. They'll get by." [3] But was getting by good enough?

Getting by seemed to permeate the whole company. Even Butler seemed unperturbed that some aspects of Eaton's were no longer first-rate. "If you asked 100

customers today, the [money-back] guarantee will be a very important reason why they shop at Eaton's. They sometimes put up with less than satisfactory service because of that integrity," he told interviewer Dean Walker in 1971. [4]

Yet, as president, Bob Butler faced an almost insurmountable task. A 1971 article in *Forbes* entitled "Corporate Rip Van Winkle" detailed Eaton's many failings. "Eaton's was slow to modernize and upgrade its in-city stores, letting applications for expansion drag along endlessly as they were debated by city governments. Worse, it failed to follow its customers to the suburbs. What Eaton's failed to see, Sears Roebuck clearly grasped. In partnership with Simpsons Ltd., Sears invaded Canada.

"From a standing start in 1952, Simpsons-Sears climbed to sales of $647 million, much of which could have been Eaton's for the taking. 'We have been followers rather than leaders,' admits Robert J. Butler, Eaton's 48-year-old president." [5]

The Butler era would last six years and was marked by too many bad ideas that were poorly executed. Butler tried valiantly to be the modern motivator. In his first three months on the job, he spent half his time on an airplane, crisscrossing the country, meeting seven hundred managers. He'd gather Eatonians in groups, take off his jacket, park himself on the edge of a desk, and say: "Talk to me." Eaton's was not profitable, he told them, and hadn't been profitable for years. Most were hearing the bleak message for the first time. He also delivered a call for change they didn't want to hear. "We had not taken advantage of the opportunities that existed," he recalls. "We were playing catch-up."

Eaton's had centralized its operations just prior to Butler's appointment; now Butler proceeded to decentralize. The pendulum swung between the two strategies for another decade, draining energy with every oscillation. "Once the pendulum got going, it threw the equilibrium out of the organization for a long time," says Stan Shortt, who became vice-president, merchandising, in 1973.

Butler's plans included the hiring of 125 new members in management over a five-year period. "It was the end of the era where management all had grown up through the company," says Alasdair McKichan, who was recruited as public-relations manager in 1971 after eight years at the Retail Council of Canada, first as general manager, then president. "There was a clash of cultures with the old-line traditional managers who were merchants who had learned on the job. There was tension between the two sides. You couldn't say either side won."

Both groups spent more time conniving than seeking consensus, more time manoeuvring than merchandising. "I didn't know which way the doors were swinging," says economist Ray Luft, who'd been hired in Vancouver in 1965, left Eaton's briefly, rejoined and was transferred to Toronto in 1971. "There were an awful lot of people around. Some of them were on their way in and some of them were on their way out."

Butler had never worked anywhere else, so he had no practical perspective on how to change an organization. "Innovation was not encouraged," says John Williams. As national merchandise manager he lunched with Butler during the early part of his regime as president and suggested a raft of ideas. "No, no, I just want you to run the stores," Butler told him. "We'll do the creative thinking." But profitability did not improve. "They weren't making the numbers," says Williams. "Year after year when I was there, there'd be a drive: 'This is the year we gotta make the numbers.' We were never making the numbers."

At least some new stores were coming on stream at last. In the first three years of Butler's reign, Eaton's opened more than 1.5 million square feet of retail space. More followed: Sherway Gardens and Scarborough Town Centre in Toronto's suburbs; Guildford Town Centre in Surrey, B.C.; and Laval City in north Montreal. There was also Vancouver's Pacific Centre in 1973 — the first large downtown store to open in Canada in forty years — then Calgary South Centre in 1974.

Butler's downtown strategy was his greatest legacy. Establishing Eaton's in prime urban locations was a brilliant stroke that remains successful. But any major centre can only support a certain number of large stores. Eaton's was still playing catch-up in the suburbs, so there had to be another leg on which to run. In response, in 1972 Butler launched Horizon, a chain of discount stores meant to battle competition from new arrivals such as Sayvette, Woolco, and K-Mart.

Horizon was intended to be a national chain of 122 discount outlets. Each store would occupy sixty thousand square feet and focus on soft goods like clothing, as well as hardware, health and beauty aids, and small appliances. Horizon store specifications and locations were meticulously planned. Each store required two hundred thousand people living within a ten-minute drive. The first to open, at Victoria Park and Sheppard in Toronto's northeast end, came in right on target with $52,500 in opening-day sales. The only other successful outlet was at the densely populated intersection of Yonge Street and Eglinton Avenue in midtown Toronto.

Initial success almost seemed to make Eaton's sloppy about the rest of the Horizon stores. Most of the other locations did not hew to the carefully researched specs. "They believed that because they were Eaton's they'd figure out a way to make it work," says Luft, who had done the advance calculations about size and population. "Engineered to fail, I used to say. I spent twenty-five years with that."

Site selection became haphazard. The two Horizon stores in London, Ontario, for example, were in malls with insufficient population in the market area. Other stores had too little available parking. Someone decided that Horizon should carry heavy appliances. It was a foolish strategy because Horizon was self-serve, so there was no floor staff to explain the different features on something such as a line of refrigerators. That foray wasted another six months as heavy goods were moved into all the stores, then had to be wheeled out again when they failed to sell. Of the fifteen Horizon stores that were eventually opened, thirteen lost money from day one. Horizon construction was halted in 1974.

The stores created an entire new orphan division bolted on to a contraption that was already showing signs of flying apart at the seams. Every selling season seemed to bring a new management theory about how Eaton's should be reaching the public. The organization was paralysed by infighting over the future course. Could Eaton's be a downtown retailer, have suburban stores, *and* run discount outlets? Should the strategy change from being everything to everybody in favour of a Macy's format that was more upscale and focused on fashion? Should the catalogue be closed? Or should the catalogue carry on, but, like Simpsons-Sears, offer the same goods as the stores?

As if the juggling act didn't already have enough flaming torches in the air, in 1971 Eaton's launched Viking Fund. The group of mutual funds slowly built up assets of $14 million over the next two years, but for many at Eaton's the foray was an embarrassment. Among the companies purchased was an affiliate of I.O.S. Ltd. Former I.O.S. chairman Robert Vesco and other individuals were charged in the United States by the Securities and Exchange Commission with fraud.

Eaton's also blundered badly by taking an ownership position in a supplier, a rare step into entrepreneurialism. Rapid Data Systems & Equipment Ltd. started out in 1961 as a Montreal-based distributor and merchandiser of office equipment. In 1972 the company acquired world rights to manufacture a Canadian-designed pocket calculator. Rapid Data president Clive Raymond concluded that mass merchandising was the way to go, and Eaton's agreed to sell his Rapidman mini-calculators. The four-function $99.95 model could add, subtract, multiply, and divide. First-year sales targets were an ambitious five hundred thousand units.

After the pocket calculator was introduced in the spring of 1972, Rapid Data's stock price soared to $27. But prices for components were falling so fast that inventory bought one week wasn't worth as much the next. As competitive pressures grew, retail prices kept dropping and other models with better technology appeared. By October Rapid Data share price had fallen to $8.

Pressed by his bankers, Raymond found new financing, but the firm continued to lose money. Eaton's had not only backed the wrong horse, they kept betting on the horse even as it fell further behind. In all, Eaton's Retirement Annuity Plan lent Rapid Data $6.5 million.

Trading was finally halted in January 1974 with Rapid Data share prices at $1.79. The company was declared bankrupt four months later. As secured creditors, Bank of Montreal and First National City Bank were paid back $6.9 million of the $9 million they were owed. Eaton's received nothing except some out-of-date Rapidman models, a fitting reminder of a money-losing venture.

"The image of dowdiness was being changed, but a change of that magnitude really needs to be managed carefully. It's pretty hard to retain the best that you had when everything you have is suspect," says Alan Marchment, who was a vice-president in the early 1970s. "This led us into making mistakes." Butler believed that 80 per cent of the profit came from 20 per cent of the business. "It's easy to take a trite saying like that and adopt it holus-bolus as if it's the new secret," says Marchment.

⟶

A key reason for the debilitating debate about direction was that there were far too many groups cluttering the decision-making process. There was management, the board of T. Eaton Co., directors of the family holding company Eaton's of Canada, and the trustees of the Eaton estate. The first three groups might try to exercise their influence, but major decisions were the sole prerogative of the five trustees: Signy, her brother Thor, Swatty Wotherspoon, Allan Beattie, and TD's Dick Thomson.

The core dilemma rested in the very makeup of that star chamber — two family members, two lawyers, and a banker. "The trustees were not familiar with merchandising," says Stan Shortt. "Their main focus was on survival, not on rebuilding or repositioning. It was a pretty tense time from a financial point of view. Bob Butler had the vision, the ability, the confidence, to do all of that *and* carry the whole organization through — but was not allowed to."

The family's indifference about Eaton's infected all their thinking. If Eaton's was a corporate Rip Van Winkle, as *Forbes* put it, the *Telegram* was Robinson Crusoe, about to be stranded by its owners. In 1971 the *Tely* was in its final days, losing $1 million a year. Big John Bassett wanted to kill the paper, a step that would throw 1350 *Tely* employees out of work. The owners gathered in the library of 120 Dunvegan Avenue on a September evening. Lawyers Wotherspoon and Beattie, who were also directors of the Telegram Corporation Ltd., were there, as was Signy and all the Eaton and Bassett boys except David.

John David did not attend. He was spending more and more time on his own at Georgian Bay or sailing. His absence didn't make any difference. Whatever Big John wanted was fine with John David. Johnny F., the eldest of John Bassett's three sons, was the only one arguing to keep the paper alive and had developed a plan to turn it into a tabloid. Conrad Black was keen to buy the *Tely*, but when Fred heard that Black's partner, David Radler, was prepared to fly to Toronto to table a takeover proposal, Fred told him the family was not interested in seeing the *Tely* survive. Instead, they preferred to see the paper killed and the assets sold off. "No thanks," said Fred, "we'll grab the cash and run." [6]

On Thursday, September 16, the newspaper guild voted to go on strike. Bassett decided to close the paper. He sold the circulation list and leased the presses to the *Star*, then sold the building to the *Globe*, generating $19 million in all. After debts were paid, there was a $7 million profit to be split among the four Eaton boys and the three Bassetts.

While the boys knew exactly what to do with the *Tely*, they had no particular vision for the department store chain. John Craig was barely interested. When John Craig was named chairman of Eaton's of Canada in 1969, Andy Hutchison, his friend and former fellow investor in Burdick Metal Industries, was baffled. He couldn't understand why the boys were removing themselves from the retail operations. He called John Craig. "What the hell are you doing?" he asked point-blank. "I'm not a retailer," admitted John Craig. "That's not where my interest is. I want to play with money."

With the *Tely* gone, fresh funds were available for his pleasure. John Craig, who had just divorced Kitty, was busy squiring many of the available women in the city. "If it moved, he hit it," says investment banker and longtime friend Peter Eby. "And they were lined up." That era showed John Craig at his worst, behaving like the nickname he'd given himself, Pig. "I have heard John described as arrogant, because he can be brusque, but it's done in sort of a fun way," says Eby. "He liked things in excess. But he's always joked about it; he'll wear a pig hat every now and then. It's not something that he gets excited about. He can dish it out or take it with the best and was able to laugh at himself."

What John Craig did best was have a good time. He revelled in the camaraderie of a black-tie evening, a club lunch, or an all-night booze-up with the boys. He loved joining a group of merrymakers, and if one didn't exist he'd create one, as he did in 1964 when he was in charge of ladies' wear at the newly opened Don Mills store. John Craig, store manager Jerry Shier, and Don Cameron, of Cameron-McIndoo Construction, the firm that had done the store fittings, had a pre-Christmas celebratory lunch. After a few too many drinks they decided to start a group called the 4872 Club. The sole purpose was to gather every December for lunch, then double the group every two years so there would be forty-eight members in 1972. At that point they'd invite as speaker the prime minister of the day.

As the years passed and the numbers grew, the lunches became ever more riotous affairs, spilling into the late afternoon, on into the evening, often continuing until the following morning. Attendees ate, drank, and entertained each other with tall tales. "Not only do you stand in your place, but the tradition is to stand on your chair and occasionally on the table," recalls Gordon Gray, who joined in 1966. On one occasion, as a new member held forth, someone made a rude comment. Without missing a beat, the speaker stood on the offending party's steak, and carried on with his remarks. When membership reached twenty-four, expansion was halted because it was becoming difficult to hire a room for the unruly crowd. No club would have them back. Forty-eight rapscallions would have been unbookable. And the prime minister was never invited.

John Craig and Johnny F. soon found a sinkhole for their $1 million windfalls from the *Tely*: sports. They played hockey Sunday mornings at George Bell Arena in Toronto's west end for an industrial-league team known as the Sahara Desert Canoe Club. Among the other players were Roy McMurtry, who later became attorney general of Ontario then high commissioner to the U.K., and McDonald's founder George Cohon.

Sports were such fun to play, so why not invest in them, too? Johnny F. was the most entrepreneurial of Big John's three sons. One of his first adventures was to obtain the rights to *Hair*, the quintessential 1960s musical, for Toronto and Montreal runs in 1969-70. The two formed Can-Sports Inc., with Johnny F. as president and CEO and John Craig as chairman, then set out to round up another two dozen investors.

In 1973 a few people were invited to a downtown lawyer's office and thirty eager participants showed up, chequebooks at the ready. Bassett had nothing on paper; he simply made an oral presentation that called for individuals to invest units of $50,000 as a way of raising $2 million for a hockey team.

The group paid $1.8 million for the Ottawa Nationals of the World Hockey Association, then moved the team to Toronto to play as the Toros during the 1973-74 season. Not satisfied they could lose money fast enough in hockey alone, the investors acquired the franchise for World Team Tennis, a league that included both male and female players. The Toronto Royals were the only Canadian team; the other teams were from such U.S. cities as Boston, Phoenix, and Chicago. Crowds were sparse; the Royals lasted one pathetic season.

The loss budgeted for the Toros' 1973-74 season in Varsity Arena was $800,000, even if every game was sold out. John Craig didn't much care. For him, the team was just another excuse to carouse. *Toronto Star* sportswriter Frank Orr once walked into a Winnipeg bar after a Toros away game. "I hear somebody yelling at me and it was John Craig and he really had a snootful. He was walking like he was born on the side of a hill. I don't know how the hell he stood up. It was gravity-defying. He said, 'Oh Frank, come on, I gotta buy ya a drink.' And then he said, 'No, no, I can't buy ya a drink. If I make it to bed before I hit the floor I'm gonna be lucky.' And away he went."

The following year the team moved to Maple Leaf Gardens for its home games. Broadcast revenue was supposed to boost income, but on the day of the first game the necessary lighting had not been turned on. John Craig and Allan Beattie visited Gardens owner Harold Ballard to remind him of the arrangement. Ballard denied that the deal included lights. Even when Ballard's own lawyer told him that lights were part of the deal, Ballard was adamant, telling his lawyer, "Well then, you made a mistake." Ballard demanded an extra $18,000 for lights. John Craig wrote a cheque on the spot.

Former Leaf great Frank Mahovlich signed to play for the Toros at $235,000 a season. Even so, the Toros didn't amount to much. At Christmas the team and the owners held a skating party. "I realized we were in trouble," said Eby, "when it became evident that John could skate faster than a good half of the Toros team." In 1976 the team moved to Alabama and became the Birmingham Bulls.

Professional football was equally parlous. In 1973 Johnny F. obtained one of the four franchises in the newly created World Football League and spent $3.3 million to sign three stars for the Toronto Northmen from the Super

Bowl champion Miami Dolphins: Larry Csonka, Paul Warfield, and Jim Kiick. The trio celebrated their signing a little too long in the hotel suite and Csonka arrived at the news conference drunk.

The nationalistic Trudeau government turned thumbs down on the idea. "The future of Canadian football is too large and too important a question to be left to the tender mercies of a few entrepreneurs out for a fast buck," said then health and welfare minister Marc Lalonde. [7] In April 1974 legislation was introduced in Parliament to ban U.S. football leagues. The bill was never passed, a July election intervened, but Johnny F. and John Craig got the message. In May the team signed a five-year stadium deal in Memphis, Tennessee, where the team played as the Memphis Southmen and eventually became the Tampa Bay Bandits. As they left Toronto, most of the local investors dropped out, but not John Craig. Ever one to back a loser, he carried on.

Everybody knew that Johnny F. and John Craig were bound together in the Telegram Corp., and there was a widespread belief that they had a bottomless pit of money. Milt Dunnell of the *Toronto Star* introduced Johnny F. as Sportsman of the Year at a 1974 B'nai B'rith banquet by saying that at the rate they were spending money, "there's a danger they'll run out in 100 years." [8] In all, the investor group lost $4.5 million, of which $1 million was John Craig's.

—▬—

In July 1973 alcohol was offered for the first time in the cavernous Round Room at the College Street store. John David was not on hand to toast the occasion. Gravely ill since February, he lay in bed at home, dying.

Eaton's was building a restaurant and bar scheduled to open in 1974 on the second floor of Winnipeg's Polo Park store. The new establishment was to be called Timothy's, but there was some debate about how appropriate it was to name a bar after a teetotaller. The boys agreed to ask their father what he thought. "Why don't you call it Sir John's?" he said. "My father would have loved to have a bar named after him." Sir John's it was. It was John David's last official act involving the business. On Saturday, August 4, 1973, he died at sixty-three.

Simpsons graciously published a full-page advertisement in the *Globe and Mail* that, in the words of the competitor's chairman and CEO Allan Burton, was "a tribute we usually reserved for the death of the monarch." [9]

According to his will, John David was worth $16,142,833.77.[10] Of that amount, $13.9 million fell into the catch-all category of "book debts, promissory notes, mortgages and other monies on loan." Stocks and bonds were worth $635,241.87; 120 Dunvegan was valued at $580,000, boats at $481,275, and the Georgian Bay summer home at $192,000.

Signy received $2 million. In a May 25, 1973, codicil to the will, John David designated a number of bequests to staff and servants. The largest sum, $25,000, went to his secretary, Marlene Josiak. Three others were given $15,000 each, other servants each received $5000. Those at the Antigua residence each got $2500. John Craig moved into 120 Dunvegan; Signy tried apartment living for a time, didn't like it, and bought a house at 105 Poplar Plains Road.

The announced $16 million was far from John David's total net worth. As with many tycoons, his wealth was stashed away in trust funds that had already moved ownership of the stores, worth an estimated $500 million, out of his hands. In his case there were four such funds with the decidedly unimaginative names 1958 Trust Fund A, B, C, and D, known collectively as the Children's Trust Fund. Signy served as the nominal head of the trusts, but did not have voting control. Through what's known as an "estate freeze," the holdings were given to her at John David's death. When she died, the assets could move into the hands of the boys without attracting capital gains tax.

Once an appropriate period of mourning was over, Signy returned to the social swim. She saw something of architect John Parkin and was often on the arm of Don McGiverin, who had moved to Toronto in 1972 when he was appointed president of The Bay. "She was one of the nicest, smartest, kindest women of talent, artistically knowledgeable people, I've ever known," McGiverin said shortly before his death in 1998. "Maybe the most. Signy never got her feet off the ground. That was a great influence on the boys, for good."

Under McGiverin, The Bay bought Zeller's in 1978, acquired Simpsons in 1979, then that same year was itself swallowed up by Thomson Corp., headed by Ken Thomson. The Bay had 22.7 per cent of the department-store business; Sears led with 27.5 per cent. Eaton's by then was running a poor third with 15.5 per cent.

In one sense, McGiverin and Signy made for an odd couple, coming as they did from opposing sides of the retail landscape. But each had lost a spouse and he could be her "walker," a safe and respectable escort who knew and was known by everyone wherever they went. In the end, McGiverin had won more than he ever could have as president of Eaton's. Not only was he becoming the victor in the store wars, but he'd also replaced John David at Signy's side.

—

Eaton's remained a captive of its own history. The generational lore and everyone's love for the organization held many executives in a stranglehold. It wasn't that they wanted to go back so much as they didn't know how to go forward.

For its part, the family was no help in putting on pressure for change; they believed their own public relations. They saw themselves as being above the usual corporate realities where tradition is important but new ideas matter more. As far as the Eatons were concerned, they were pre-eminent retailers who could match anyone's prowess.

Outsiders who were invited into the inner sanctum took a sharply different view. In 1973 Butler hired Air Canada vice-president of finance Earl Orser. As the new vice-president, administration, Orser found an institution that was still living in the Dark Ages, a slack outfit that demanded precious little from its managers. The catalogue had lost $40 million in the previous decade and was showing no signs of returning to profitability.

TD banker Dick Thomson and Pete Little of Clarkson Gordon met with Signy and Fred early in 1974 to discuss the catalogue and how the whole retail operation was suffering as a result of this festering sore. Their message was clear: "If you don't get rid of the catalogue, we're no longer going to support you as your auditor or your banker."

The catalogue had become a huge operation. A permanent staff of 130 created the nine editions published annually; 8500 employees in 250 offices handled $300 million in annual sales. But the rural consumer, once the mainstay of the catalogue, was disappearing. At the turn of the century three-quarters of Canadians lived on farms; by the 1970s the proportion was less than one-quarter.

But, oh, the history! The catalogue was viewed as the very heart of the operation and the hand that reached out to the country. There were stories galore. American aviator Cy Caldwell had visited Newfoundland in 1927 and reported that the catalogues made the locals yearn for a better life. "The girls read Eaton's catalogues, and other bits of uplifting literature, and right away they get a hankering to beat it out of here so fast that the codfish and the salmon disporting themselves in the bay will stand on their tails asking each other who it was that passed them so quickly." [11]

In the 1940s a Saskatchewan farmer decided to buy a new suit. His wife took his measurements using a length of binder twine and a carpenter's square. In due course a letter arrived from Eaton's: "We suggest that the measurements given in your recent order be rechecked. We suspect that a suit made to these measurements would not fit any living human. If the figures are correct, we will be glad to have the suit made to measure." [12] New measurements were submitted.

A 1952 letter from Hamilton was particularly plaintive. "I am told the T. Eaton Co. can furnish anything asked for. Now I lost my wife over a year ago and I am very lonely living alone. Can you send me a woman not too old. I have my own house here. I have $67 a month income." [13]

"The mail order catalogue became a book of dreams wherein hardworking fathers and mothers, as well as their eager children, found things that they craved which could be brought within their reach by extra endeavour and rigid economies," wrote G. R. Stevens in his 1965 book, *The Incompleat Canadian: An Approach to Social History.*

That worshipful view was not universally held within Eaton's, where many merchants saw the catalogue as "farmerish." In 1965 Eaton's attempted a revamp. After much debate, the overall size was reduced from 9¾ by 12 inches to 8 by 11 inches. The reason? The committee believed that when the woman of the house stacked up the many catalogues she'd received, she'd put Eaton's on top, it being the smallest, and therefore use it more often.

There existed a mañana attitude about the catalogue. Fixing it was always being postponed even though there were deep-seated problems. Long catalogue deadlines meant that fashion had to be conservative so that goods weren't out of style partway through the book's lifespan.

Moreover, Eaton's often had trouble collecting payment from far too many of its customers. Goods would be shipped to Newfoundland, and Eaton's could whistle for its money. "The bad-debt situation there was terrible," says Kinnear. "These fishermen would buy an outboard engine and boat and they'd be out in the wilds someplace. They made a down payment and you never found them again."

Costs had gotten out of whack because of two long-standing policies. First, if an item ordered was no longer available, the customer was sent a more expensive item for the same price. Second, abuses of the money-back guarantee were legion. The policy was costly enough when items were brought back to a store, but in the case of the catalogue, Eaton's paid return shipping costs of items that often could not be resold. The dress worn several times. Tea sets after several parties. A broken toy. Shoe returns in Toronto ran to 40 per cent of sales. In one catalogue, Eaton's went so far as to say that the return of a used tube of toothpaste "should not be necessary." But the policy remained unchanged.

Production expenses had skyrocketed. Eaton's annually spent $12.50 per household printing and delivering to each household the two major catalogues and other clearance books. Those costs had to be added to the usual sales and overhead expenses on goods. For Eaton's to break even on the catalogue, orders per household had to be $125 a year. In Toronto, the average was $80, in Montreal a mere $30. Only in Atlantic Canada, where the average household order was $170, and in the West, where it was $200, was the system profitable. But profits in those regions were not enough to offset losses elsewhere. Starting in the mid-1960s, the catalogue operations lost between $2 million and $10 million annually. By contrast, sales of the Simpsons-Sears annual catalogue were about the same as Eaton's — $300 million — but they managed to make an $18 million profit.

Eaton's could only hope to find a deep-pockets partner prepared to bail them out and solve the problems. If Simpsons could cut its 1953 deal with Sears Roebuck & Co., maybe some other American retail partner could come to Eaton's rescue. Butler approached Donald Siebert, chairman and CEO of JC Penney Co., who had run the Penney catalogue division for nine years. Siebert was intrigued. Six months earlier Penney had signed a Japanese joint venture with Dai'ei Inc. and C. Itoh & Co. that would see ten Penney's stores open in Japan during the next five years. Why not go next door to Canada?

The lives and leadership styles of the men who headed Eaton's and JC Penney couldn't have been more different. Where the Eaton family was media shy, J.C. Penney, who founded the U.S. chain in 1902, was ubiquitous. He not only attended every store opening, he'd appear on television to tell his entrepreneurial story, even on such unlikely programs as "Queen for a Day."

In the early years at JC Penney, every store manager was an owner; Penney was known as "the man with a thousand partners." When that structure became too cumbersome, the department-store chain went public, issuing shares in 1929 just before the market crashed. A Miami bank of which Penney was chairman failed, and Penney was almost wiped out, but he fought back in the 1930s and soon prospered again.

In 1957 when management suggested accepting credit cards, Penney was against the move. He wanted to retain the cash-only concept. But unlike John David, who fought progress, Penney heeded the advice of others and cards were accepted. He came into the office daily until he was in his late eighties, keeping three secretaries busy. "My sight is gone," Penney would say, "but my vision is better than ever." He died in 1970 at ninety-five.

Penny's style still suffused the firm when, in April 1974, Bob Butler issued a terse news release saying Eaton's was studying a joint venture with the U.S. giant. What Eaton's had in mind was to replicate the Sears deal with JC Penney buying 50 per cent of Eaton's catalogue. If JC Penney would also buy thirty of Eaton's smaller, money-losing stores, including the Horizon chain, so much the better.

Eaton's certainly had picked a powerful potential partner. JC Penney's annual sales were $6.2 billion through two thousand stores and 1140 catalogue sales centres. To head the project, Eaton's appointed Albert Plant, a commerce graduate from the University of British Columbia who had joined in 1970 as manager of Toronto operations. His assessment was as bleak as Thomson's and Clarkson's. "Eaton's," recalls Plant, "was headed for bankruptcy." Plant assembled a small team and gave the project a code name, VX, short for Venture X.

It quickly became apparent that JC Penney wasn't interested in buying any of the stores. "The old, small Ontario stores were not a lot of interest to them because they were the wrong shape. They were multi-storey; Penney operated on a single-level," says Alasdair McKichan, who had been promoted to vice-president, consumer and corporate affairs, and was on the task force with Plant. "In the case of the catalogue, they realized, as did Eaton's, that there would be a substantial investment required to bring Winnipeg and Moncton distribution centres up to any standards of operation."

In 1974 Eaton's catalogue lost $17 million. "The catalogue was in such bad shape it couldn't be fixed," says Al Lynch, then a JC Penney systems-department consultant who later became president and CEO of JC Penney International. "The deeper we dug, the more apparent the problems were. There was no way to make it work." A recession in the U.S. that year hurt JC Penney sales; the Christmas season saw no improvement. The anticipated costs of the joint-venture project were enormous — $550 million split between JC Penney and Eaton's. JC Penney also concluded that a new management team would have to be sent from the United States. JC Penney decided it wasn't prepared to supply either the money or the manpower.

Plant was at JC Penney headquarters in New York on February 14, 1975, to hear the verdict: there would be no joint venture. He immediately flew back to Toronto and relayed the bad news to the Eaton's of Canada board.

At the end of Plant's presentation, TD President Dick Thomson turned to John Craig and said: "I'm calling the *Star*."

"Today?" asked John Craig.

"Yes. Remember, that's the deal. If Penney's doesn't buy the catalogue we shut it. I'm phoning the *Star* and telling them the catalogue's closed."

Everyone talked at once until Earl Orser finally was able to interject: "There are some huge financial ramifications and people ramifications that we haven't even thought of. There would be chaos in the marketplace, they might boycott the stores, the retail business might suffer if this thing's not properly handled. God knows what could go wrong." The board decided to postpone any decision for two weeks.

The board needed a whipping boy, someone to blame for this fiasco. A report from JC Penney describing Eaton's management as weak gave them all the ammunition they needed. On March 12, a month after JC Penney pulled out, Bob Butler was fired as president.

As a face-saving device, Butler was given the largely figurehead role of chairman that Kinnear had vacated in 1973. "They expected me to drive the Penney deal and I couldn't do it," Butler says. "I was called over one day and told, 'You're going to be chairman and Orser's the new CEO. Sorry it didn't work out.' [There was] no board discussion, no professional way of doing it. That's because of the arrogance of ownership."

Fred wrote Butler a glowing letter telling him that he'd always have a job at Eaton's. It was as if they didn't bury their dead.

CHAPTER TEN

EARL ORSER: THE EXECUTIONER

—

THERE WAS NO TIME TO LOSE. THE CATALOGUE had to be killed. Fortunately a hit man was at hand. While Bob Butler had been trying to keep the loss-making operation alive, Earl Orser had come up with a plan to close it in a way that minimized shutdown costs and switched $100 million in catalogue sales to the stores.

"Butler was doing a helluva lot of stuff that made the trustees uncomfortable. Orser's loyalty was to the trustees," says Ray Luft, the economist who had been assigned to assess costs on the JC Penney joint venture. "The number-one person Orser had in mind was Orser. Butler got it, not by accident, but by design. Orser did a better job of manipulating the trustees."

In mid-March 1975 John Craig and Allan Beattie invited Orser to Beattie's downtown law offices and offered him the job as president and CEO of the T. Eaton Co. Unlike Butler, who wavered for weeks when the same proposition had been put to him, Orser accepted on the spot. The salary was $160,000, with a performance bonus of up to $40,000. The official announcement claimed that the appointment of Butler as chairman and Orser as president reflected "the division of the increasingly heavy duties of Eaton's senior management responsibilities which the company's growth dictates."

Except for the fact that the two men lived on the same street in suburban Don Mills, the forty-six-year-old Orser had little in common with Butler. Butler had been a merchant for three decades; Orser's background was finance. His only retailing experience was selling socks for The Bay in Edmonton.

By 1975 Eaton's annual profit was a paltry $39 million on sales of $1.3 billion. Orser vowed to double profitability, said he would reduce the number of suppliers by half, and promised to deepen relationships with Eaton's credit-card holders. In fact, he had only one job: close the catalogue.

A detailed study completed in May estimated total costs of the closure at $70 million for inventory write-downs and severance pay. There was one final, tension-filled meeting of the board of Eaton's of Canada. The path was obvious; no one any longer argued to keep the catalogue alive. Losses in 1974 were $17 million; in 1975 they were headed for $35 million. Add the $40 million lost in the previous half-dozen years and the total was nearing $100 million.

The catalogue had become like gangrene. If amputation wasn't performed, the disease would spread. But the boys couldn't bring themselves to wield the scalpel. "They recognized that the company's and the family's reputation was going to be different because it was the first apparent confirmation of a much-rumoured weakness in the enterprise," recalls a participant at the meeting. Tempers flared and the usual public solidarity among the brothers crumbled.

"We'll be seen to be responsible for this," whined one.

"Well, of course we are," shot back another.

Finally the decision was taken to close the catalogue. There were two windows during the next twelve months when a public announcement was possible: August 1975 and January 1976. At both of those times the next catalogue would be printed and ready for distribution with all the listed goods in stock. If an announcement were made in October, for example, Eaton's would be awkwardly in the middle of the cycle. The merchandising risk would have been higher because more goods would have been ordered but might never be sold because there'd be no "next" catalogue.

Picking between the two choices was up to Orser. As the August possibility approached, senior management urged him to make the announcement then. Orser concluded they weren't ready, designated January 1976, and assembled a team from various departments that expanded through the fall to include ninety employees. Everyone worked offsite and was sworn to secrecy. Details were hammered out that covered severance pay, employment counselling, inventory clearout, and communications.

The boys spent a week at a hotel, the Inn on the Park, undergoing media training so they'd be ready for the expected onslaught of interviews. An elaborate plan was devised to provide advance warning to specific politicians. Job losses in Manitoba and New Brunswick meant that those two provinces were of greatest concern. The New Democrat government in Manitoba might kick up a fuss against big business; New Brunswick could cause difficulties because of the already weak economy in Moncton, where the catalogue employed one thousand.

On January 6 John Craig and Orser visited Ed Stewart, principal secretary to Ontario Premier Bill Davis; Fred and Orser then flew to Ottawa to inform Robert Andras, minister of manpower and immigration. The next day Orser, Fred, and Greg Purchase, senior vice-president of the western division, called on Manitoba Premier Ed Schreyer. His response was more than understanding: "It's nice to see someone else having problems, too." On January 8 Orser and Fred flew to tell New Brunswick Premier Richard Hatfield, then, as a courtesy call, went to New York to inform JC Penney's Siebert in his Avenue of the Americas office.

Once the political bases had been covered, the seismic decision was announced at a news conference on January 14, 1976. The 1976 spring-summer catalogue would be the last. Nine thousand employees would be out of work. After ninety-two years the social compact between Eaton's and Canadians was dissolved.

The public's reaction startled Eaton's officials. Instead of widespread anger, there was an outpouring of nostalgia. Unlike the federal government's cancellation of the Avro Arrow interceptor jet program in 1959, there were no repercussions, political or otherwise. "What I had anticipated, a backlash, didn't happen," says O.J. Reynolds, a former staffer at the Canadian Radio-television and Telecommunications Commission, whom Orser had hired as manager of consumer and corporate affairs to handle the closing. "It astonished us because people got on this nostalgia trip about what the catalogue had meant to them. We got off very lightly as far as the media was concerned."

Despite all the advance media training, Barbara Frum managed to knock Orser off guard. Her opening question that evening on CBC Radio's *As It Happens* was as simple as it was cutting. "Mr. Orser," she asked, "how could you?" Orser sat in stunned silence for several seconds before he was finally able to get his tongue in gear and use some of the pat responses he'd practised.

Most journalists got caught up in the keening. Far easier to praise the past than investigate the business fiasco. Eaton's chronic incapacity to be efficient went unnoticed; everyone was overpowered by tearful recollections. "A day without Eaton's is like a day without Canada," lamented the usually curmudgeonly Gordon Sinclair on his "Let's Be Personal" radio commentary.

"By rights, Eaton's last catalogue ought not to be interred into the ground," eulogized John A. Edds in *Canadian Business*. "Instead, it should be cremated and its ashes scattered over the length and breadth of Canada. For there is scarcely a square mile of Canada or a segment of Canadian society that hasn't felt the impact of 'The Book,' 'The Homesteaders' Bible,' 'The Wishing Book' — all synonyms for Eaton's mail order catalogue."[1]

"Its influence can only be guessed at," said Philip Teasdale in the *Toronto Star*. "But there are few Canadians who don't include the Eaton's catalogue among their early memories. Stuffed into stockings, it made good shin pads for hockey-crazed youngsters. Boiled, it made a passable Easter-egg dye. Soaked in salt water, rolled and tied, it became a Yule log. With scissors, it became a cut-out book; with crayons, a coloring book. Its ads for lacy underthings made it, in a more innocent era, a sort of *Playboy* magazine. And everybody has heard the jokes about how useful the Eaton's catalogue was in the john."[2]

In its day Eaton's catalogue operations had been innovative. "The really great achievements of Canadian public life have not been those of industrial management or the organization of labour," wrote Hugh Hood in his novel, *The Swing in the Garden*. "They have been those of the wholesale distribution of goods. The true epic of Canadian life might be told in the story of . . . the Eaton's catalogue."[3]

But those accomplishments were in the distant past. Hidden by the thicket of praise was the fact that the closing of the catalogue represented a colossal marketing blunder, another tumble downward in the long slide that began in the 1930s. For decades Eaton's had reached the growing urban market through its stores, while the catalogue had provided the rural route to sales. But for the previous twenty years Sears had made inroads in both those markets. Eaton's couldn't determine how to fix the catalogue, so they just closed it. Eaton's had never figured out how to defend itself and now had departed one of the fields of battle.

Since then Sears Canada Inc. has capitalized on Eaton's waving the white flag of surrender. In 1997 Sears distributed five million copies of what has become the largest general-merchandise catalogue in North America. Its 1-800 number is the most frequently called in Canada, with eighteen million calls annually. Although Sears does not reveal what portion of its total $4 billion in annual sales in Canada comes from the catalogue, the amount is estimated to be about $800 million, almost triple the level it was before Eaton's quit the business.

In 1976 Fred received a handwritten note from his uncle Timothy, the train buff, then living at Northfield House, Langton Green, Kent, England. "My sympathy lies with the nine thousand employees," he wrote. "I recall my grandmother Eaton quoting an old Irish proverb when I was a boy (from shirt-sleeves to shirt-sleeves in three generations) so enjoy yourself while you can." [4]

In 1967 residents of Rathnelly Avenue, a leafy enclave in midtown Toronto, decided they'd have some fun for their Centennial Project. They declared they were seceding from Canada, crowned a queen, and called their neighbourhood the Republic of Rathnally, adopting a different spelling for the mythical domain. It was here that royalty of another sort had settled. On November 26, 1975, John Craig married his second wife, Sherrill Taylor Reid, then thirty-one and a divorcée.

Although the stores were no longer the powerhouse places of old, the family continued to represent aristocratic wealth. That reality was reinforced in the worst possible way at about 1:30 a.m. on June 15, 1976. The Eatons' next-door neighbours, Phil and Anne Lind, were still awake. From the window, Anne saw a shadowy figure scuttling across their front lawn. Worm-pickers were common in the area, but this man did not look typical. He was carrying a bag and heading for John Craig and Sherry's red brick home next door. The Linds called police to report a prowler and also alerted John Craig by phone.

John Craig put on pants and shoes, stuck a Luger in his belt, and began searching the house. When he got to the basement, he called: "All right, my friend, come on out of there." A man emerged wearing what John Craig later described as "a type of Castro hat," as well as a kerchief that covered the lower portion of his face. He was carrying a rifle, somehow took command of the situation, and ordered John Craig upstairs. John Craig complied and hid his gun under a coffee table.

The intruder pulled rough twine from a duffel bag and bound the wrists of John Craig and Sherry. John Craig's daughter, Signy, who usually lived with her mother, was staying with the couple that weekend because the rest of the family had gone boating, a pastime Signy didn't enjoy. The intruder placed tape over Signy's eyes, but botched the job. The tape kept sticking to his fingers, and when he finished, she could still see.

The man had done such a poor job of tying Sherry up that she'd surreptitiously freed herself. The paper shopping bag that had been placed on her head had shifted and Sherry was able to watch the intruder. It crossed her mind to grab his gun, lying nearby. "He's so short and light," she thought. "I could push him over." Just then a shaft of moonlight shone into the room, reflected off the blade of a knife she didn't know he had, and she abandoned her plan.

"This is a kidnapping," he announced. "We'll contact you in twenty-four hours." He shuffled through some papers and left a ransom note that demanded $600,000. The note also warned he would offer no proof Signy was alive once she was out of their sight. "It's a chance you will have to take. But just remember, we're not in this business for murder, if we can help it, but for money. As a businessman yourself you will understand that. However, like businessmen everywhere, we hate to be double-crossed. Remember that too."

The intruder led Signy from the room, heading downstairs.

"Take it easy and relax," he told her. "It's just like going home from a date."

"Daddy," implored Signy.

"Dear, don't worry," said John Craig.

At 1:54 a.m. police, summoned by the Linds, arrived. Constables Shawn Clarke and David Linney split up. Clarke approached the house, opened a side door and spotted Signy, wearing a long nightgown, being led by a masked man carrying a rifle in one hand and a flashlight in the other. The kidnapper waved his rifle and ordered a surprised Clarke to drop his service revolver.

"Don't shoot," shouted Clarke, and took cover outside. With her captor's attention distracted, Signy was able to break away and dash back upstairs. The masked man fled through the open door. Realizing that the perpetrator was now alone, Clarke fired six shots into the darkness after him.

Two dozen members of the Emergency Task Force, wearing bulletproof vests and carrying shotguns, arrived and began combing the area. At 3:19 a.m., police found the suspect, clutching an ammunition clip and lying facedown in a seven-inch-deep trench that he appeared to have dug himself. They also found his car and a .30 calibre M-1 military rifle.

The crime was a shocking event in Canada. John Craig's parents had feared just this kind of kidnapping since the 1930s. Four decades later, an armed intruder had finally fulfilled the family's worst nightmare.

John Craig made direct appeals to newspaper publishers and station owners for a news blackout, but the incident was widely reported. Deputy Police Chief Jack Ackroyd would not reveal the identity of the family at an 8 a.m.

press conference, but the Eaton name was soon known. John Craig promised a midmorning statement at the house, then went off to play tennis.

By the time he returned home from the courts in his purple Rolls-Royce, journalists and photographers had begun to arrive. They chased him for comments, but he eluded them by vaulting a rear fence. Shortly after 10 a.m., flanked by George and Fred, John Craig stood in front of his house and read a brief statement. "The Metropolitan Toronto Police Force are to be congratulated for their promptness and efficiency in apprehending a suspect so quickly. As a parent, it is most gratifying to know we have such efficient law enforcement within our city." There was no other comment except for a passing reference to the suspect as an "insignificant-looking bald guy."

The accused refused to speak to officials and had to be identified through his fingerprints. He was Ernest Caron, a forty-seven-year-old native of France with a police record that included armed robbery and attempted murder. He had twice been deported from Canada but had returned both times. He spoke not a word during his September trial and was sentenced to life in prison.

A few months later John Craig became the target of another attempted crime. Harry James Woiski, a thirty-three-year-old businessman married to a former Miss Aruba, arrived from the Caribbean island with bonds he planned to pledge against a loan for a supermarket development. Banks would give him only sixty per cent of their value, not enough to improve his tenuous financial situation with unhappy creditors. He hatched a plan to extort money from John Craig by calling Eaton's in January 1977 and claiming that a group of Cubans had planted four bombs in the downtown store. The devices would be exploded unless John Craig delivered $500,000 to him at a prearranged location.

Bill Kerr, a staff sergeant with the Toronto police force, had the same stocky build as John Craig, so was designated to meet Woiski. Kerr wore John Craig's clothes and memorized a few personal details in case Woiski tried to confirm his intended victim's identity. The first encounter was botched when Woiski realized the bag Kerr had brought was filled with newspapers, not banknotes. Kerr convinced Woiski he'd been duped, too, and a second rendezvous was staged. This time Kerr drove John Craig's Rolls-Royce and had $15,000 in bills covering the newspapers. Woiski was apprehended.

The two incidents forever transformed how the family viewed the world. To this day the Eaton boys retain the round-the-clock services of a security firm for themselves and their families. Some of their friends are more blasé. After Forest Hill had been hit by a raft of burglaries, Fred decided he'd speak

to his neighbour, George Cohon, about his protective practices. Fred was surprised to learn that Cohon, chairman of McDonald's, did nothing.

"You mean to say that you don't have any alarm, that you don't have a
guard dog, no protection whatsoever?" Fred quizzed Cohon. "That's right,"
replied Cohon, tongue in cheek. "Before I go to bed every night I just hang
this little sign outside my door." And with that, he produced a notice that
read: "Fred Eaton lives two doors south of here." [5]

⟶

Under Earl Orser, stodgy Eaton's was desperate to appear new. Marketing took
on a brash tone. A full-page ad in the December 12, 1975, issue of the *Globe and
Mail* showed, as Barbara Amiel wrote in *Maclean's*, "four brooding gentlemen
rigged up in caftans and summer whites staring in a somewhat somnambulant
manner into space. In between them, on the floor, was a thin bikini'd girl
halfway into a pushup showing some of her limited bosom and a great deal of
her substantial palate."

Simpsons that same day offered the same old stuff. "Dad was decked out
in his knee-length leather trench coat with a Christmas present gift-wrapped
under his arm. Mom, snappy in her wool knit dress was looking blissfully
vague next to a Christmas tree sprouting from the wall-to-wall oriental rug.
Teen-age son was breaking out in a big smile getting ready, it would seem, to
try his first complete sentence. It was Canada as usual." [6]

The racy Eaton's ad touched off a public debate. "Group rape fantasies,"
charged Laura Sabia, chairman of the Ontario Status of Women Council. But
the external noise was nothing like the fighting within Eaton's itself, where the
swingers briefly seemed to be winning. Lifestyle television spots promoted Timothy E., the new menswear boutique. Signy happened to see one of the ads,
showing models dancing in undershorts, and complained. The ad disappeared.

For the most part all the changes were superficial. Amiel quoted Gordon
Ryan who had recently been wooed away from Bloomingdale's, where he'd
been director of design. "Here was a store that needed me," he told Amiel.
"Everyone in the boondocks would think they died and went to heaven if they
woke up on Eaton's fashion floor. My God! The biggest problem since I'm up
here is that there's no one to talk to about merchandise. They have this corporate level who buys merchandise for the stores and you just don't know what it
is till it arrives. What this company needs is more than two token Jews." [7]

Concluded Amiel: "Eaton's is like a barometer showing with unerring accuracy yesterday's weather. Knowing too much about tomorrow would be, well, just too fast."

The boys seemed blissfully unconcerned. "Some Horizon stores are pulling their weight but not all," Fred admitted during a 1976 visit to Winnipeg. "Earl Orser will have to decide what to do about them. That's his job." [8] The newspaper report quoting his comments also noted that he was deeply tanned, just back from an African safari. No Horizon stores in trouble there.

The Toronto Eaton Centre, declared dead during the reign of John David, was about to be resurrected. Ah, the Eaton Centre! Salisbury Cathedral took less time to build. Nearly aborted on half a dozen occasions, the downtown redevelopment scheme was now in its second decade of discussion. In 1968 Eaton's hired Brian Magee and Gordon Gray of real estate firm A. E. LePage Ltd. to push the project forward. Gray was a chartered accountant who had started A. E. LePage in 1955 with thirty-five people, made his name assembling land for the Toronto-Dominion Centre, and saw his firm eventually grow to twelve thousand employees. The firm quietly acquired, on Eaton's behalf, the key twenty properties that were needed, in addition to those the family already owned.

LePage, in turn, brought in Fairview Corp. Ltd. (later Cadillac Fairview Corp.), the real estate arm of Cemp Investments, founded by Sam Bronfman as a trust for his four children. Cemp was managed by Leo Kolber, who laid down three conditions for Fairview's involvement in the Eaton Centre. First, Eaton's had to demolish its Queen Street store and move north to land that Eaton's owned on Dundas Street. By so doing, Eaton's and Simpsons would create two "anchors" with other shops in between just like in the suburban malls. Second, the Old City Hall was to remain untouched. "I didn't want to see my name in the Toronto papers as destroying a heritage building," Kolber told them. Third, Eaton's had to become the lead tenant in the office tower planned for the north end of the development.

Eaton's agreed to leave Old City Hall untouched, but refused to move the store. "They were appalled at the idea," recalls Kolber. The family had been badly burned when it strayed north to build the College Street store in 1930 and did not want a repeat. Magee stayed at Kolber's house in Montreal's Westmount until 2 a.m. one morning trying to change his mind. "I'm not trying to be stubborn," Kolber told Magee. "It's the only way to do it. It's only the straight line that works."

A decision was urgently needed. The Queen Street store was decrepit. In the words of John Craig, it was "held together by paint and prayer." [9] After a year's consideration, the family finally relented. Eaton's would locate the new store near Dundas Street and agreed to be the major tenant in the new office tower. At the same time, the new plan did not involve demolition of the Old City Hall or the church.

The next tough sell was the name of the development. "We can't call it the Eaton Centre," Fred said. "If someone goes into another shop in the centre, and is badly treated, they'll blame us." His attitude was reminiscent of Jimmy Muir, who was chairman of the Royal Bank during construction of its cruciform-shaped forty-five-storey Montreal headquarters. Royal Bank was the major tenant when the building opened in 1963, but Muir didn't want the bank's name on the building, so it was called Place Ville Marie. Kolber had seen how Muir's successor, Earle McLaughlin, fought unsuccessfully for years to raise the bank's profile as a result.

Toronto-Dominion Bank took the opposite route. In 1967 when the first tower of what would eventually be a six-building complex opened in downtown Toronto, it was called the Toronto-Dominion Centre. "Phone [TD chairman] Allen Lambert," urged Kolber. "Ask him why he called it the TD Centre and what it did for him. It gave them a boost they didn't believe." Fred finally relented.

Lord knows, Eaton's needed a boost. Sales at Simpsons-Sears Ltd., a firm that had been in existence for less than fifteen years, were $1.5 billion, almost as much as Eaton's. With fewer stores (fifty-three versus sixty-two) Simpsons-Sears had sales of $134 per square foot — the highest in Canada; Eaton's was running at about $100 per square foot. "Almost all Canadian developers prefer Simpsons-Sears Limited as their key anchor tenants," wrote Ira Gluskin, an analyst with brokerage firm Brown, Baldwin & Nisker Ltd., in a research paper prepared in 1976 for the Royal Commission on Corporate Concentration. [10]

The Eaton Centre project was massive. Municipal approvals required one hundred visits to City Hall. Architects Bregman & Hamann and Zeidler Partnership designed the 866-foot galleria with 1.6 million square feet of space for three hundred stores, all under a 127-foot-high vault modelled on the Victor Emmanuel Galleries built in Milan in 1867. "I'm like a shipbuilder," said architect Eberhard Zeidler. "I build the ship. Someone else sails it away." [11]

The complex, on a fourteen-acre site that included a nine-level Eaton's store, was built in three phases over five years. There was provision for moving goods into the store at night using the Toronto Transportation Commission subway tracks. A removable wall was built where the "two below" level meets the subway, but the "underground railway" has never been used.

A few months before the official opening in February 1977 of the $250 million retail complex, Eaton's merchandisers suddenly realized that the floor-space figures they were using did not add up. They somehow had too many goods ordered for the retail area actually available. Everyone had assumed the store was one million square feet when, in fact, it was only 900,000 square feet. Designs for each department had been based on the belief that a "bay," the space contained within four pillars, measured thirty by thirty feet, or nine hundred square feet. So, if a department wanted 1800 square feet, two bays were requested. But the pillars were only twenty-eight feet apart, which meant two bays yielded just under 1600 square feet. Display cases had to be altered and less merchandise was needed. But which department would give in?

Forty managers assembled at a downtown Toronto hotel for an all-day meeting convened by Jack Eaton, vice-president operations, and Stan Shortt, vice-president merchandising. No one was allowed to leave the room until everyone had given up sufficient space so that all departments could fit. At noon there was no give; by four o'clock they had reached a consensus to avert the behind-the-scenes disaster.

With the Eaton Centre store set to open in February at its new, more northerly location, some old standbys closed. On Christmas Eve 1976 last suppers were served in the Round Room at the College Street store and the Georgian Room at Queen Street. There would be no more Easter Bunny lunches, breakfasts with Santa, or Violet Ryley's chicken pies. On December 29 the one-and-a-half-ton bronze statue of teetotalling Timothy was moved to a new site that was as central as it was ironic: the northern entrance to the store near the Patio Restaurant, a licensed café.

On Saturday, February 5, 1977, John Craig and George stood for an hour at the doors of the Queen Street store pumping shoppers' hands as that location closed for the last time; Fred and Thor did the same at the College Street store. "Don't ever go out of business forever," said one little old lady. "Don't worry," said John Craig, "we never intend to." [12] Hazel Snape, who was in the Eaton's accounting department in 1941 and earned $592 for the entire year's work, brought in her income-tax slip for the boys to sign.

The Queen Street store was torn down to make way for the galleria and other retailers. College Street was purchased for $35.6 million by a consortium consisting of London Life Insurance Co., Markborough Properties Ltd., Canadian

National Railways pension fund, A. E. LePage Ltd., and Eaton's. A $25 million renovation created a mixed-use complex that reopened in 1979 combining retail boutiques, provincial court services, and office and residential space.

On Thursday, February 10, the Eaton Centre was officially opened with a ribbon-cutting ceremony involving Signy, Ontario Premier William Davis, Lieutenant-Governor Pauline McGibbon, Toronto Mayor David Crombie, Cadillac-Fairview president Neil Wood, and TD banker Dick Thomson. There were pipers from the 48th Highlanders, a seventy-piece band from Malvern Collegiate, and eight members of the Fort York guard.

Long after the Eaton Centre was opened, controversy continued. Suspended above shoppers at the south end of the galleria is a Michael Snow sculpture called *Flight Stop*, consisting of sixty Canada geese looking as if they're about to come in for a landing. Red ribbons were tied around their necks by Eaton Centre management as part of the 1982 Christmas marketing campaign. An irate Snow felt his artistry had been besmirched. He hired Toronto lawyer Julian Porter, who argued before Supreme Court of Ontario Justice Joseph O'Brien: "I'm in no doubt that on Halloween there will be jack-o-lanterns hanging from all the geese and green ribbons on March 17." What next, he asked, bells on Timothy's toes? The court ordered the ribbons removed.

For Eatonians, the world suddenly changed. Employees moved into spiffy quarters in the north tower. "We took people out of all kinds of funny offices and buildings all over downtown Toronto," says O.J. Reynolds, the woman who was in charge of communications. "It was unbelievable because they'd had doors and walls and suddenly we put them all in open landscape. The angst over that!" The boys went through their own metamorphosis. "Once they got out of their offices above the manager's garage and suddenly were on the twentieth floor, things were vastly different," says Reynolds. "They looked around and looked out at everything. I think they were ready then to play store."

With the Eaton Centre open, the boys no longer needed mercenaries to do the family's bidding. Chairman Butler was already meeting informally each week with other business leaders for lunch with Ontario Premier William Davis to talk about issues of the day. Davis encouraged Butler to join the Ontario government and in April, Butler became deputy minister of consumer and commercial relations at a salary of $75,000 a year, less than half what he'd made at Eaton's. When Butler told his family, they were shocked. Asked a daughter: "Daddy, does this mean we'll have to give up desserts?" "No," he replied, "but you can only have three helpings from now on." [13]

Earl Orser was equally expendable. In April Orser began to realize that for the previous few weeks, he'd been treated as if he had the plague. There was little communication or contact with the family, the trustees, or the board. He became so concerned with the change in his status that he retained counsel from the law firm of Campbell, Godfrey.

His suspicions were well founded. On May 17, 1977, Allan Beattie and Fred told Orser that his services as president were no longer required. They claimed he had not been sufficiently forthcoming with the board on a variety of topics. Orser complained that the allegations were as trumped-up as they were transparent, but it was obvious that his brief retailing career was over. Both sides agreed that severance arrangements should be tidied up quickly.

Orser's team of lawyers, led by Claude Thompson, arrived within fifteen minutes. Beattie and Fred were taken aback both by his efficiency and his selection of counsel. Unknown to Orser, Thompson had acted for Kitty when she divorced John Craig. Eaton's did not want a messy wrongful-dismissal suit; they were willing to pay handsomely for Orser's quiet departure. Within two hours the two sides had drafted a handwritten agreement that gave Orser two years' severance, or about $400,000.

Orser also demanded an opportunity to address the board of Eaton's of Canada one last time. A special meeting was duly called and he told the directors forcefully that the action taken against him was unfair. At the end of his monologue, there was a ritual "Thank you, Earl," then the room fell silent.

In a family business, ownership is all. Hard-nosed managerial talent is irrelevant. Orser didn't own a single share, so he had no leverage. Once the Eaton Centre was successfully opened and there appeared to be clear sailing ahead, the boys decided they could take the helm.

"Orser was the best we ever had," says Ed Walls, one of the top merchandisers of the day. "He had a terrible mess on his hands between the credit business and the catalogue. And he fixed the credit business, he closed the catalogue, and he did it very well. He was a good team player. I have nothing but good things to say about Earl Orser. The worst thing the company ever did was let him go. It was rather typical of the family — once the dirty work is done, they will appear." (Orser went on to success as a consultant to Brascan Ltd. and in 1981 was named CEO of one of the conglomerate's companies, London Life Insurance Co.)

The old guard felt equally unwelcome. Jack Eaton, the last son of R.Y. in the business, retired that same year. He seized the occasion of his farewell reception in the fifteenth-floor boardroom to let the twenty-five attendees know exactly where they stood in his mind. Gathered for the occasion were John Craig, Fred, several members of the Eaton's of Canada board, and a few other senior officers, perhaps fifteen men in all.

About ten women from various lower-echelon positions also attended. Jack paid no attention to the men; he spent all his time talking to the female employees. As the event sputtered to its conclusion, he left the room briefly and returned with an armful of long-stemmed red roses. He gave a rose to each woman, then departed, having spoken not a word to any of his male colleagues.

Ray Luft, who had worked closely with Jack for the previous three years, caught up with him at the door. As they left the room together, Jack commented: "Some people leave in a cloud of dust. I'll leave them with a good smell."

With Earl Orser out of the way, the trustees had two choices about succession and the future of Eaton's. They could pick one of the four boys to be president and sole owner, then pay the rest off, as had happened when John David was chosen in 1942, or they could designate all four as equal owners and pick a president from among them.

The reality was that none of the boys was up to the job on his own. There wasn't enough royal jelly among them to spread on a piece of toast. First possibility was the eldest, John Craig. He was charming but he also had a mean streak and a short fuse. Of the four sons, he was the most like his stubborn father. At dinner parties he'd often get into a heated discussion with any woman who happened to be sitting beside him. If she disagreed with his opinions, or — *gasp* — had strongly held views of her own, John Craig could become belligerent, although he'd been known to apologize later for his outbursts.

The parallel with his father also included a fondness for drink. "John is either on the wagon or not on the wagon — there's no halfway with him," says investment banker and friend Peter Eby. "Basically, we all like our martini and our glass of scotch. The last time I saw John he was more into the wine. He said he wasn't drinking and then you'd notice two or three bottles of wine. That doesn't count."

Of all the brothers, John Craig was also the most generous with praise to employees. "John Craig is the one who says thank-you," comments Eaton's archivist Judith McErvel. "Fred's not a warm person. He's okay, but John Craig was the one you felt a connection with."

Fred, despite his intelligence, could act just as much the schoolboy as John Craig. After the *Toronto Sun* was started in 1971, following the demise of the *Tely*, the new paper tried unsuccessfully for years to land Eaton's as an advertiser. Founder Doug Creighton's longtime friendship with both Fred and John Craig made no difference. Eaton's argued that the audience reached by the *Sun* was too down-market. Nevertheless, the boys were avid readers of the tabloid. Whenever there was an article critical of the store, Fred or John Craig would call Creighton and take him to task. If the paper published a photo of a scantily clad Sunshine Girl who looked particularly luscious, they'd call and salivate.

John Craig's jock talk was macho and juvenile. Even a locker-room phrase like "getting laid" wasn't descriptive enough for him. He'd refer instead to "getting your ashes hauled." The act of urinating was known as "bleeding the turkey." John Craig was Peter Pan with an attitude.

Of the four boys, Thor always had the least involvement in matters retail. He never took on the public profile of John Craig and did not work in the stores. Like John Craig, he had an interest in politics, but his involvement didn't go beyond attending the odd fund-raising dinner.

Thor preferred to be around his horses. If one of them won at the track, he'd happily leave the stands for the traditional photograph with the horse, jockey, and trainer, but those photos were not public monuments; they remained private mementoes.

His pride and joy bearing the red, blue, and white silks of Eaton Hall Farm was the filly Bessarabian. Thor was once offered $2 million for her but declined to sell. Lifetime earnings, including eighteen wins, were $1,032,640. Bompago, bred by Eaton Hall Farm, was placed in the 1981 yearling sale, fetched $25,000, then went on to win the 1983 Queen's Plate. When asked why he'd sold Bompago, Thor replied: "If you don't sell something, there's nothing to pay for the farm." [14] Thor hasn't had a horse in the Queen's Plate since 1981. Winnings in 1997 at Woodbine for his entire stable were a modest $93,519, hardly enough for hay.

Thor was too busy about other matters to be considered for a top retailing job. Moreover, he didn't have the people skills. "Thor's a more remote personality than George," says Susan Swan. "He was engaging to talk to, but he didn't show you his heart, which George quite often would do. He was an enigma. He didn't really seem to be impressed with his status as an Eaton. He had his own very private take on things." "He's a funny kid," agrees his Aunt Florence. "Nicky Thor's quite a go gal, and Thor isn't terribly."

That two brothers both ended up marrying women with the same name was unusual. Fred's wife's Christian name is Catherine, but everyone calls her Nicky. Thor's wife's name is Nicole, so among the family, the accepted short-hand everyone uses is Nicky Fred and Nicky Thor. Both Nicky Thor and Terrie, George's wife, are Catholics, what John David, father of the boys, used to call "salmon snappers."

In 1968 Nicole Courtois joined CFTO-TV, the Baton Broadcasting station in Toronto, as a researcher on Fraser Kelly's half-hour Sunday public-affairs show, *Fraser's Edge*. "I never knew anyone who worked harder and didn't need to," says Kelly. "She was clearly from privilege, but she treated everyone with courtesy — camera people, studio people, everybody."

Thor's boyhood friend David Bassett introduced Thor to Nicole after she'd moved to Toronto. David had met her in North Hatley, south of Montreal, where both families had summered as they grew up. Nicky is the daughter of Jacques and Joan Courtois, ranking members of the Montreal establishment. He is a partner with the law firm of Stikeman, Elliott, and is one of the few business leaders in Quebec who openly admitted to being a member of the federal Progressive Conservative Party even in the 1970s when Pierre Trudeau and his Liberals dominated the ballot boxes in Canada and the watering holes of Montreal.

Thor and Nicky were married in 1977 at Montreal's Mary Queen of the World Church. Of all the Eaton wives, she has the most moxie. "She is quite ambitious and wants to have her own identity within that Eaton umbrella, and it was for a while very hard for the wives to have their own identities," says Swan. "They were Mrs. Eatons. The family was quite traditional in its expectations."

George surprised everyone. After refusing for years to join the business and rebelling by racing Formula One, he went through a major lifestyle change that coincided with his turning thirty in 1975. He'd been living the bachelor's life in a condo in the Manulife Centre on Bloor Street before marrying twenty-two-year-old Terrie Ann McIntosh in March. He bought a Buick, moved to Forest Hill, and began coming into the office daily.

There had always been high hopes for George's retailing future. His father had told banker Allen Lambert twenty years earlier that the likeliest candidate to succeed him was George. "The tradition in the family was to appoint one. I think he was not prepared to appoint one at that time. He said maybe the youngest will prove to be the best choice, but he avoided trying to make that decision too soon," says Lambert.

By 1977, with the Toronto Eaton Centre — the jewel in the family crown — built, the time for decision had finally arrived. The Eaton boys had always tried to portray succession as part of the competitive spirit of their lives. "It's a friendly contest," said John Craig in 1968, "but it's kind of deadly. You know — winner takes all. I guess it's something I've grown up with all my life." [15]

But in 1977 when the five trustees interviewed each of the four possible heirs individually, there was no fight to the death. The boys all held the same view; ownership should be shared. "The decision not to break it up was made by the trustees on the recommendation of the four of us," says Fred. "We believed that we were four equal sons." As a trustee and their mother, Signy certainly could not choose one among them. "She wanted us to make our minds up," says Fred. "[My parents] loved all of us with equal intensity."

After Orser had made his final, hopeless plea to the Eaton's of Canada board and left the room, the directors realized that corporate continuity demanded they must designate a new president immediately for the T. Eaton Co. The choice was quickly narrowed to either Fred or George. They had been the most active; they had led the revolution to get rid of Orser. Of the two, Fred had far more retail experience; he'd been in the business fifteen years. George had only been around full-time for two.

One of the directors spoke up, saying: "Fred, you're the president of Eaton's of Canada, you've got to be the president, CEO, and the chairman of this company because the company has to understand that one person is running it. It cannot be run by more than one person." He so moved, everyone else said aye, and the selection process was over in the blink of an eye. One month short of his thirty-ninth birthday, Fredrik Stefan Eaton, second son of a second son, was installed as chairman, president, and chief executive officer of T. Eaton Co. Ltd. George was made second-in-command as deputy chairman.

Butler, who suffered self-confidence problems when he became president in 1969, tried to be reassuring. He told Fred it was impossible for anyone picked to be a president to know his own capacities because he had never done the job before. "In his case that was true and in my case that's true," recalls Fred. "It's not true of people who travel from company to company being the CEO. They have proven records. But if you come up through a company and they give you the big job, who knows?"

Across the empire there was support for the board's choice of Fred. "He was the strongest of the four," says Stan Shortt. "He had been in the stores, he had run a store, he had a very good sense of people, he was intelligent, he had good taste levels. He wouldn't necessarily have driven the company, but he would have allowed the company to move with a professional team under him."

George was not perceived in anywhere near the same light. "Fred's an educated person. George is an intelligent person, not necessarily educated. He's a very fast learner, but then whatever goes in stays exactly as it went in. [There's] not much flexibility in thinking," says Shortt.

Fred didn't wait long to show his muscles. He fired the vice-president responsible for an advertising slogan the boys didn't like: "At Eaton's you're more than welcome." Of the hapless executive, Fred quipped: "At Eaton's you're no longer welcome." [16]

To the family, only one aspect of the business really mattered: control. With the conclusion of the Butler-Orser era, the second interregnum of Eaton's was at an end. When asked in June 1977 about the philosophy of the Eaton Centre, which had by now become the boys' playground, Fred replied: "My father, who expanded all across Canada, always said Toronto was the source of our good fortune and now it was time for the rest of the country to pay for downtown Toronto." [17]

Arrogance was back. The rightful heirs had returned to the throne.

CHAPTER ELEVEN

FOUR BOYS, ONE BRAIN

—

THE ESTABLISHMENT BREATHED A SIGH OF RELIEF when Fred became the fifth Eaton to wear the ermine mantle. At the Toronto Club there were martinis and Montecristos all round. If the Eatons could make it into the fourth generation then maybe the past *was* prologue; perhaps change wasn't quite as necessary as some of those whippersnapper MBAs claimed.

But Fred's ascension to the throne was nothing like his father's crowning. In 1942 when John David became president, his siblings were paid off and had nothing further to do with running the stores. This time around, all four brothers remained partners. Even though they had varying degrees of expertise and interest in retailing, each had an equal say, an awkward arrangement that was bound to complicate the business affairs of the family.

In the beginning, it looked as if Fred would be first among equals. He carried all the job titles that mattered — president and CEO — and was named to a variety of outside boards. When Conrad Black's mentor, J.A. "Bud" McDougald, expanded the board of Argus Corp. in 1976, Fred was named a director. In return, Fred offered blind loyalty to Black. In 1978 Fred backed Black when he seized power at Argus following the death of McDougald. Black was lining up board support and tracked Fred down in Minneapolis, where he was visiting a Dayton's department store. Fred's response: "I don't really understand all this, but you've got my vote." [1]

Just as Black had put Fred on his board, Fred returned the favour. Black was invited to the Eaton's offices in Toronto whereupon he was met by all four brothers. In an attempt at humour, and before any Eaton had a chance to speak, Black said: "I accept." The offer followed.

Doug Bassett had received a similar summons to appear before the throne and accepted his knighthood just as readily. He soon learned his place as an Eaton courtier. A *Financial Post* interviewer asked him whether Eaton's would ever go public; Bassett allowed as how one day it might. Bassett was called in for a second audience with the boys; this conversation was far less convivial.

"You keep your mouth shut, Douglas," he vividly recalls being told. "You don't speak for us. So don't think or assume that you know we might do something or might not do something. It's not for you to open your big mouth." Suitably chastised, Bassett slunk away and never again offered an opinion about the Eaton state of mind. The next chance he had, he was quick to correct himself publicly: "What I meant was that they may be going public in the next several years. But I don't know quite frankly. There's no talk of going public. I'm just the new boy and they don't make the new boy prefect." [2]

Dick Thomson, who'd been on the Eaton's of Canada board since 1969, named Fred to the Toronto-Dominion bank board from which John David had resigned in 1955. The ancestral seat, first granted in 1899 to great-grandfather Timothy, was warmed once again.

There was just one problem. The good ship Eaton's was listing badly. Simpsons was making a respectable profit of 3.2 cents on each sales dollar. Eaton's profits were running at only half that. "It's a tough time and we're not looking for any major changes," said Fred in his first interview following his elevation. "We'll just be fine-tuning the business." [3]

Fine-tuning! Fred did not lack for challenges — the Horizon stores, for instance. "The biggest problem was that we didn't know what we were doing when we went into the business," he said. [4] The eventual fix-it step showed an astonishing lack of imagination. In 1978 Ontario Horizon stores were converted to Eaton's outlets; those in Quebec kept the Horizon name but continued to be operated by Eaton's. A new label could hardly be enough to fix a long-running problem.

As for the T. Eaton Co. merchandising office, created less than a decade earlier, it was closed and regional buyers were given more freedom, thus setting in motion the decentralization-centralization pendulum again. Every new direction came only after lengthy political infighting that drained energy from the real business: buying the right goods and selling them at the right price.

Other aspects of the retailing empire remained frozen in time. In 1978 The Bay began accepting bank-issued credit cards. Eaton's did not follow The

Bay's lead, preferring its own operation with 1.3 million cards and $2.6 million in annual profit. The stolid approach generated cash for the boys, but showed a high-handed attitude toward consumer choice. It wasn't until 1981 that Eaton's finally accepted American Express; VISA was allowed in 1984, MasterCard not until 1985.

With Fred as president of T. Eaton Co., John Craig continued as chairman of Eaton's of Canada, a titular role that included representing the family at public events. The very furniture in his office bespoke his traditional views. The desk was his father's, the chair the one his grandfather, Sir John, had occupied as a director of the Dominion Bank. One personal touch was the cast of a blue marlin weighing almost three hundred pounds that he'd caught off the Bahamian island of Bimini.

Although Fred had commandeered all the important job titles, George quickly became the power behind the throne. Within eighteen months, Fred began deferring to George, who went so far as to maintain two offices for himself, both on the executive floor, the only brother to do so. The one he used for Eaton's of Canada matters was formal and filled with fine family furniture. For business pertaining to the retail arm T. Eaton Co., the surroundings were starkly modern.

Because George oversaw day-to-day matters, Fred was free to enjoy the honorific aspects of his role, like touring with Nicky the Potteries in England where fine china had been made by Royal Doulton and Wedgwood, among others, for centuries. "They were very well received by all of the old pottery people because they had long and wonderful memories of association with the Eaton Company going back decades," says Stan Shortt, who accompanied the couple on two such trips. "Fred was very gracious. It was as close to travelling with royalty as we would get."

For George, life at the top was a far cry from his previous incarnation as a sixties swinger. "There's a guy who's had a metamorphosis," said Conrad Black in 1978. "My God, his evolution is incredible, like a religious conversion. He never dresses less conservatively than me." [5] Whenever members of senior management met with Fred, George would often sit in and play bad cop. "Anything I wanted to do as far as communicating with the employees, George would just say no," says O.J. Reynolds, the woman who stayed on to handle communications after Earl Orser left.

The Eaton boys weren't even interested in the findings of the consumer panels that had been established to elicit shoppers' views, preferring the family's own instincts instead. "They already had Mother. I certainly read the writing on that wall," says Reynolds. "I couldn't honestly take Mother seriously, but she was on the board. Signy was a very nice woman, but . . ."

Reynolds quit in 1979 but not before she noticed one more signpost in the continuing deterioration of the empire. The wives of the boys ceased shopping at Eaton's. "They even stopped using the beauty salon, where I used to see them. Mother would buy things abroad and bring them in to have them fitted."

What Fred seemed to enjoy most was his wealth, although he denied being a playboy. "You don't have to be a playboy to enjoy life," he said in 1986. "We enjoy our jobs, getting a sense of accomplishment, just like anybody else." [6] He belonged to all the upper-crust clubs: Royal Canadian Yacht for sailing, Caledon Ski and Caledon Mountain Trout, Queen's and Badminton & Racquet for tennis, Lyford Cay for a Caribbean getaway, Griffith Island and the Long Point Company for hunting, as well as two downtown lunch clubs, the Toronto and University.

Fred was baffled by the eccentricity of someone like Hal Jackman, who despite his wealth, drove the same clapped-out car for years. The then controlling shareholder of National Trust once parked his elderly vehicle in the lot behind the 10 Toronto Street headquarters of Conrad Black's Argus Corp. When Fred joined the meeting, he said, "Did you see that wreck in the parking lot? I've had it towed." Jackman borrowed subway fare from Fred's chauffeur to get home. [7]

Although there was much to do at Eaton's, Fred seemed to be more interested in connecting to the world outside. He joined the Young Presidents Organization, an international group restricted to those who become presidents before the age of forty. In 1979 he was named International Retailer of the Year by the U.S.-based National Retail Merchants Association.

Fred foresaw few changes on his watch. In a May 1979 speech he told the International Council of Shopping Centers that he just couldn't "see shoppers of the future doing all their shopping over television or by computer. Traditionally people went to bazaars and markets. They simply like to go to them. People like to be with people. There will always be some people who want to shop by telephone or television or from a catalogue, but I just don't see it having much of an impact on us." [8]

"Management will be as it has been," he said in 1977 interview. [9] Stay the course. It was good enough for his father and, by gum, it was good enough for him. Typical of the upper-level lethargy was the case of Juan José de Madiraga, longtime chief buyer in Spain. De Madiraga was from a royal family and had hunted with John David in Europe. He always took every opportunity to remind others at Eaton's about his friendship with John David, describing him as "*mi amigo.*"

There had been a time when such foreign buyers were Eaton's great strength, supplying Eaton's with merchandise that was unavailable in other Canadian stores. But the world had shrunk. Exotic and unusual goods had become readily available to most retailers. No buyer had seemed more beyond head-office control than de Madiraga. When at last he was fired, although Fred had been unable to pull the trigger himself, he pronounced himself pleased: "I was waiting for somebody to get rid of that guy."

Fred's regime was marked by two problems that had plagued Eaton's for years: the deadwood stayed and talented merchandisers who saw no future for themselves at Eaton's fled in droves. "They weren't given free rein," recalls Charles Tisdall, a consultant to Eaton's at the time. "They all fought with the family. That's why they left." Departees in December 1976 included W. H. Evans, general merchandising manager and a twelve-year employee; J. Stewart McCowan, general manager of Ontario and Toronto stores; and Jules Chatoff, group sales and merchandising manager. The spring of 1977 saw more: Don Beaumont, group sales and merchandising manager and a twenty-year veteran, who went to Towers Department Stores; Hy Rosenstein, general merchandise manager, hard goods, and a ten-year employee, who joined Bad Boy Appliances; Ralph Peck, senior VP in charge of Toronto and Ontario stores, who went to Bowring's and later became president.

Fortunately for Fred, the Toronto Eaton Centre was immediately success-ful. He'd arrived at the top at just the right time. The newly opened store revitalized a moribund business. Although the retail space occupied by the new store contained only two-thirds of the company's previous downtown selling area, total sales increased by thirty-eight per cent in the first eight months. Customer traffic in the complex averaged 500,000 a week, 750,000 at Christmas. Says Kolber: "The Eaton Centre probably saved the company."

The real money, however, was not generated by retail operations. The most substantial profits came from the other operations controlled by the family. In 1978 T. Eaton Realty Co., which owned about one-third of the company's twelve million square feet of space, paid a dividend of $17 million to Eaton's of Canada. Eaton's vice-president Michael Spohn had single-handedly built a land bank from which the family would benefit for the next twenty years. Spohn had left Eaton's before Fred took over, but his foresight meant that joint-venture deals for malls could be financed by putting raw land into the deal, land that had been bought cheap by Spohn.

"When people say, 'Did Eaton's make money?' I always said, 'It never had to,'" says Albert Plant, who saw operations up close during the 1970s. "It received its financing from T. Eaton Acceptance Co., which ran the credit card, and T. Eaton Realty Co., which owned the real estate. The real estate rent to the retail company was rigged to create a profit for the real estate company. The acceptance company rigged the credit charges to the retail company in order to run a profitable credit company."

Profit in the retail arm? Who cared? That was where all expenses and charges got dumped from everywhere else. For example, the boys' compensation and expenses were paid by the holding company, Eaton's of Canada, and the total of those items was charged to the retail arm, T. Eaton Co. There was no need for the Eatons to expend effort getting retail right when the very ground the stores stood on generated income and produced wealth. For the Eaton boys, the legacy of a hired hand like Spohn just created more family jewels.

⟶

Such an effortless flow of funds meant that the boys were free to pursue other pleasures. The Benmiller Inn near Goderich, Ontario, was the setting in 1981 for a policy conference called by Ontario Premier William Davis. The semiannual sessions, held at a rotating list of resorts, were attended by a handpicked group of cabinet ministers, members of caucus, government bureaucrats, and individuals from business and academe.

Although some among the thirty attendees were only invited once in a while, John Craig had been a regular for half a dozen years, as was his sidekick, J.J. "Joe" Barnicke, a Toronto commercial real estate broker. They were not summoned because of the brilliance of their ideas, but because they were bagmen for the provincial Progressive Conservative party.

Then deputy minister of health Tom Campbell delivered a presentation about the growing problems caused by rising health-care costs. Afterwards the floor was thrown open for discussion. When John Craig's turn came, he launched into a rant. "There's clearly a lot of waste. Have you ever seen photographs or movies of an operating theatre? Look at all the people who are standing around doing nothing. Clearly you could be cutting back. You don't need one guy doing all the work and everybody else standing around watching."

The old hands cringed. They had grown accustomed to John Craig's right-wing views, but this description of a lifesaving surgical team was even more bizarre than most of his beliefs. One of the regular participants decided to test the depth of his conviction. "Look, there's more waste than that," said the participant, his tongue planted firmly in his cheek. "Think of the Hospital for Sick Children. We spend loads and loads of money fixing kids up when they're ten or fifteen years of age. What happens thirty-five or forty years later? They get sick again." John Craig, who thought he'd found a kindred spirit, immediately embraced the sentiment, saying: "You're absolutely right."

There was a stunned silence as everyone in the room realized John Craig didn't understand that he'd been hit on the head with a joke about as subtle as a two-by-four. As chairman, Premier Davis gently intervened. "John, thank you for that," he said, then looked studiously around the room and asked: "Are there any other views on the matter?"

"It stood as an example within the Davis circle of the degree to which raw business acumen or instinct could be seriously misplaced. [The intervention] became a teeny burden on John Craig," says one of the attendees that weekend. "Among the Red Tory faction, he wasn't highly regarded," says another. "They thought of him as less than an intellectual giant."

Poor oblivious John Craig. If his last name weren't Eaton, you'd never have heard of him. His money not only bought access to the inner circle but also produced a forgiveness factor not available to ordinary folk. He was the Prince Charles figure among the Eaton boys: the firstborn, the highest profile, and the only one to be divorced. He liked to pilot aircraft and revelled in wearing military uniforms, just like his grandfather and namesake Sir John.

He and Barnicke first became involved in fund-raising for the Ontario Tories in the 1960s under Premier John Robarts, when solicitations were mostly by mail. The two men transformed the technique by establishing a corporate campaign that included personal calls on chief executive officers. By the time Davis was elected premier in 1971, the pair had built a Big Blue money machine. In nonelection years, they'd collect $1 million to $1.5 million, rising to as much as $2 million in an election year. John Craig and Barnicke would visit CEOs no matter what their political stripe, because businesses never knew when they were going to need a favour. "They would all give, but the CEOs wanted the visits, they wanted the personal attention," says Barnicke. "The fact that some of them were leaning heavily the other way politically was not a big issue."

In 1980 John Craig was chairman of the first Premier's Dinner, which two thousand people each paid $150 to attend. The fund-raising event became an annual affair. "There's a certain credibility to the Eaton name," says Bill Davis.

"He certainly added something that John Jones wouldn't have. The reality is that he was able to get a response where other people might not. People paid attention. People liked him and still do."

Barnicke's wife died in 1971, leaving him with five young children to raise. He and John Craig became inseparable. They'd carouse together at night, hunt on weekends, or hang out at John Craig's Georgian Bay summer home. The two would often travel the forty miles south by boat on a Saturday and show up at Bill Davis's cottage near Honey Harbour, unannounced and uninvited. Many was the Monday morning when the premier would phone his Toronto office to say: "I may be a little delayed. I lost most of my Saturday doing some work for the party. *They* dropped in." He didn't need to tell any of his staffers who *they* were.

John Craig also became ensnared in the politics of religion. In 1980 Barnicke, a Catholic, suggested to Emmett Cardinal Carter that he should copy the Bishop's Dinner, a successful annual fund-raiser in Detroit, Michigan. Carter agreed and Barnicke corralled John Craig to share the cost of a black-tie dinner at the York Club for 160 business leaders. The next year about a hundred of those attendees each bought tables of ten for $1500. The money was used for Southdown, a rehab centre for priests north of Toronto. The event has become an annual affair and attracts about 1400 luminaries from business and politics.

Rubbing shoulders with Carter made John Craig and the other Eatons feel like the moneyed Irish families of Boston or New York. Barnicke, John Craig, and Carter took annual June fishing jaunts to Oak Lake near Kenora for pickerel or went to a fishing camp John Craig and George own in Quebec, northeast of Mattawa, for brown trout. Being in the presence of a premier or a prince of the church offered an endorsement from someone with real standing in society. While those who are born rich don't appear to need any-thing or anyone, in fact they do. Because they never know whether or not their success is simply because of their name, they collect movers and connect with shakers as a way of telling themselves that they must be more than mere stewards of an inheritance.

⟶

At Eaton headquarters Fred increasingly came to rely on two people: his brother George and Greg Purchase. Purchase was born in Winnipeg in 1931 and worked at Eaton's briefly in 1954 before obtaining his MBA from the University of Western Ontario. He rejoined Eaton's in Winnipeg and was transferred to Toronto in 1976 to head up what was known as central division — the stores in Ontario. Purchase was legendary for his cheese-paring ways. After Earl Orser was fired in 1977, Purchase in turn fired the former president's eight secretaries. "He liked lots of girls," says Purchase. "I got rid of all of them."

Other key line managers soon felt his presence, because Purchase had two very powerful tools. For one, he was running Eaton's Ontario operations, so he was in close physical proximity to the family and the trustees. The other, and perhaps the more important, Purchase enjoyed good personal chemistry with George. As a result Purchase slowly brought the rest of the country under his control. In 1980 he was given Winnipeg. Shortly after he was named executive vice-president and chief operating officer and put in charge of everything. Centralization was back in vogue again.

Fred gave Purchase a free hand. "General George Patton had a saying, 'Give a man a job, don't tell him how to do it. He'll surprise you with what he does, but you won't be disappointed,'" says Fred. "I was the good guy who brought the good news. He was the guy who sometimes brought the bad news. We worked together very closely and we travelled extensively." Purchase certainly had an incentive to reduce costs and increase profits. In addition to his $100,000 base salary, he earned a bonus equal to 1 per cent of annual profit. If he could get profit levels to $50 million, for example, his bonus would hit $500,000.

The initial strategy was to reverse the loss in market share by adding floor space. By 1981 Eaton's had 114 stores with a total area of about twelve million square feet. In that year alone two floors were added to the five-storey Pacific Centre in Vancouver, and new stores were opened (some replacing older locations) in Edmonton, Calgary, Red Deer, Hamilton, Regina, Nanaimo, and Quebec City. Four more were under construction in the Ontario cities of Markham, Mississauga, Sarnia, and Guelph. Another twenty-five stores were planned over the next five years.

But the expansion added to the inefficiencies because inventory control across the system was almost nonexistent. There was no rigorous way to know what was selling well so that those goods could be restocked. Eaton's had come to a fork in the retailing road. One path was to follow the merchandising-marketing growth strategy already under way by spending more money to expand. The other path was to cut costs by reducing sales staff and hope to achieve higher productivity from those who remained.

The growth strategy was backed by senior executives such as Don Hudson, Ralph Peck, and Stan Shortt, all of whom had merchandising backgrounds. The cutback scenario was promoted only by one person: Purchase. George, whose say on such major decisions had grown in importance, understood and supported Purchase. Moreover, a recession had arrived in 1981 and retail sales were down. Constraint became the chosen path.

But staff cutbacks did more than just reduce expenses; the approach totally altered Eaton's corporate culture. "When sales wages on an operating statement changed attitudinally from an investment into the business [and became] an expense line, that was a watershed," says Shortt. "It set an entirely different attitude as to how you looked at the front line, the employees. For a retail company, that was death."

The decision caused another outflow of talent. In 1981 merchandise manager Ed Walls, son of Fred Walls, a longtime Eaton's vice-president, left to become chairman and CEO of Jas. A. Ogilvy Ltd., the Montreal department store. In 1982 Stan Shortt joined The Bay. Don Hudson, who had successfully turned around the Pacific division, left to become president of the Vancouver Stock Exchange. Hudson's successor, Bill McCourt, a hotshot in his forties, fled to BC Tel as vice-president of network marketing.

Purchase had corralled all the power using a remarkable technique; at all times he kept his colleagues guessing about what he was thinking. If a good negotiator keeps his cards close to his vest, Purchase kept his entire deck in the secret pocket of a suit hidden at home. He'd call someone into his office for no stated reason, then sit sucking on his pipe, saying nothing for minutes on end. "He was a very taciturn individual," said Alasdair McKichan, himself a laconic Scot who worked at Eaton's between 1971 and 1975 before rejoining the Retail Council of Canada and becoming president. "Even I noted it. He never used two words when one would do."

Departmental managers grumbled that under Purchase the fun of the good old days was gone. No more wacky and successful promotions like the "pet fairs" previously held in the basement of the Queen Street store. One event had featured piranhas and a promotion in which a child could pay a penny, scoop a net in the goldfish pond, and keep whatever was caught. At night, any leftovers were fed to the piranhas. Another pet fair sold dogs from the Toronto Humane Society pound. The idea proved to be so popular that the supply of canines dwindled. After a couple of nights of sweeping the city there were no more strays to be found, so the pet fair turned to homeless cats.

The Winnipeg store had been equally innovative. When the roof on the company curling rink collapsed under the weight of snow in 1966, nothing remained but the ice-maker. In 1968 the machine was used to install a rink in the Donald Street annex for a week-long show that featured a headliner from the Ice Capades, a barrel-jumper, and an on-ice fashion show. When the promotion ended, the ice was cut up using saws and the pieces smuggled outside at night to melt in the streets.

Centralization of everything in Toronto hurt such local innovation. Winnipeg's food services were providing 50 per cent of Eaton's profits from 20 per cent of the national food sales, but Toronto wanted to homogenize everything by imposing menus and ideas. Purchase didn't care about protests from staff or customers. His constituency was the Eatons. "Greg knew how to manage the family," says merchandiser Jim Chestnutt, who joined Eaton's in 1959 and stayed nearly forty years.

With Purchase as master puppeteer, the family could relax and go back to reigning. "How well I remember the difficult times we had been through, and were still suffering under, when you arrived from Winnipeg," Signy once said in a handwritten note to Purchase. "You truly saved us, turned things around and delivered us into new prosperity." [10]

Unlike the days when Lady Eaton's high-profile comments were regularly reported and her store tours were top-to-bottom affairs, President Fred was all but invisible. Media appearances were rare, walkabouts few. Despite the fact the boys had offices in the Toronto Eaton Centre, even those store employees saw them only every six weeks or so. Moreover, those sightings were always carefully choreographed with a day's notice for what was a most perfunctory inspection. Around the store they became known as "four boys, one brain."

If 1982 had been a fish, Fred would have thrown it back. The recession had arrived with a vengeance; consumer spending had collapsed. And then, on January 30, a nasty incident reignited a long-smouldering francophone backlash against Eaton's. Claude Charron, government house leader in the Parti Québécois government of René Lévesque, was shopping in the downtown Montreal store. He tried on a jacket, put another jacket over his arm, then proceeded to the cash register where he paid for only one item.

Once Charron was outside, a security officer stopped him to ask about the $120 tweed coat for which he had no bill. Charron bolted down Ste-Catherine

Street with two members of Eaton's security in hot pursuit. One of them caught up with Charron, but the footing was slippery and both tumbled to the sidewalk. Charron scrambled to his feet and ran off again, past Place Ville Marie and across Dorchester Boulevard, before he was finally apprehended.

Three weeks later Charron held a news conference in which he revealed the incident and announced his resignation from cabinet. He claimed that as soon as he'd been challenged outside the store he'd realized his mistake. He said that Eaton's security officers had assured him: "We won't prosecute you." The statement exploded across the province. Why had they spoken to a prominent Péquiste politician in English?

Charron had adroitly hung his guilt on his accusers. Eaton's had been pilloried for years because clerks refused to deal with francophone shoppers in their mother tongue. It wasn't until August 1968, when the two-storey Eaton's store opened in east-end Montreal's Les Galeries d'Anjou, that store signage said "Eaton" for the first time. Eaton's had increased the number of bilingual clerks before the passage of Premier Robert Bourassa's 1974 language legislation, Bill 22, but Charron's accusation demonstrated the chasm between the smug anglo stereotype and a company struggling to be responsive to changing times. Charron further charged that security officers had been overruled by executives in Toronto. "Monday morning I got a summons," he told the press. "That means there was a higher-level consultation, and they decided to execute me." [11]

Execute! Eaton's countered by saying that the decision to prosecute was taken in Montreal; Charron had been treated no differently than any other shoplifter caught red-handed. The media fed the flames. An Aislin cartoon in the Montreal *Gazette* showed a contrite Charron with both arms awkwardly stuck in a jacket that was still on its hanger, saying: "Pardonnez-moi, Timothy." Declared a letter to the editor published in *La Presse*: "France has its [celebrated martyr of anti-Semitism] Dreyfus, we have our Charron." Charron pleaded guilty and was fined $300.

Other problems were less public. Five hundred employees were fired: Winnipeg, Toronto, and Montreal were the hardest hit. Greg Purchase was mockingly called "Mr. Sunshine" because of his dour demeanour in videos communicating bad news to employees.

There was worse to come. In 1982 Fred announced that he would be the Grinch who stole Christmas. For the first time since 1905 there would be no Eaton's Santa Claus Parade in Toronto. Begun modestly, the parade had taken on mammoth proportions. Annual costs had reached $250,000 and

Eaton's concluded that the event did not promote sales, despite the fact that up to one million people lined the route and a further thirty million watched the televised version in Canada and the U.S.

From 1928 until he retired in 1963 the parade had been the private preserve of Jack Brockie. As head of public relations, he walked the five-mile route every year with the marchers to keep an eye on proceedings. One year, a Felix the Cat costume split down the back revealing far too much of the young woman inside. Brockie spied her embarrassing situation and swept her into a tailor's shop on Bloor Street shouting "Santa Claus Parade" as they burst through the door. She lay facedown on the counter, the tailor made quick repairs, and she rejoined the parade.

Santa, the focus of attention, often suffered some calamity. One year his pants fell down; another year it was raining so hard that his foam tummy took on cumbersome extra weight. A low branch almost knocked him unconscious on another occasion. Santa's sleigh was always followed by a car with darkened windows. Inside were a doctor and nurse in case St. Nick suddenly became ill. The car also contained a backup Santa, fully bearded and ready to go.

By the 1950s the parade had grown to one thousand costumed marchers leading Santa and his helper, a gold-mopheaded bear named Punkinhead. The simpler the humour, the better. In the tradition of the English pantomime, Mother Goose was often a man wearing earrings that lit up for laughs. Vulgarity was avoided. "Anything about pants has been funny since Adam," said Brockie. "But they're dangerous. A pair that gets a laugh by coming down an inch is going to come down two inches for twice as big a laugh. We keep clear of that kind of gag." [12]

Fred said: "I'm forty-four years of age, and I remember at least forty Santa Claus parades. It has been a long and happy association, and I, with a lot of other people, have enjoyed it immensely. Times are difficult, and it seems silly to be spending money on a parade when we are having to let people go." [13] (The 1982 Toronto parade was taken over by a nonprofit organization that still runs the six-kilometre event with floats, bands, and 1300 volunteer participants. A celebrity clown program means any corporate executive who pays $1000 can be a clown for a day and walk in the parade.)

Fred also cut out some personal perks. Eaton's sold its Lockheed JetStar to the government of Canada. "We have now moved from corporate jets for executives — first class for senior management and connoisseur or empress for others — to skybus for all," said Fred in a speech. "It's quite comfortable back there, and the back of the plane will arrive at the same time."

All retailers were feeling the pinch. In the first six months of 1982, department-store sales in Canada fell to $4.27 billion, down 2 per cent year over year. Eaton's gamely insisted that it was doing better than the competition. "We are winning the race of the snails," said Purchase. [14]

With retailing offering no fun, the boys turned their attention to their broadcasting interests. In 1984 they consolidated the family positions in Baton Broadcasting by buying Douglas and David Bassett's 20.6 per cent portion of Telegram Corp., in which their Baton shares were held. Because Johnny F. had already sold his position to the Eatons in 1976 for $5 million, the Eaton boys now controlled Baton with more than 60 per cent of the shares.

Douglas and David each received approximately $15 million. David parked his money in an offshore account of the Canadian Imperial Bank of Commerce in the Bahamas, where he lives. Of the two surviving Bassett brothers (Johnny F. died of cancer at forty-seven in 1986), David now has the most wealth, once boasting that if he took the interest he earns annually and reinvested only that portion, he could live quite comfortably on the interest earned by his interest.

Greg Purchase had done many things right, but he'd also created a monster that began to bite back at its master. During the recession, he'd imposed a wage freeze that lasted twenty-six months. "The firm continued to expand while at the same time severe staff and wage cutbacks were employed to rationalize the operations of the stores and to finance the expansion," wrote Sandra Elizabeth Aylward in her 1991 doctoral thesis about Eaton's. "For the most part, it was the women who were laid off. Management also used sexual harassment and intimidation to control the work behaviour of the women. While strict rules dictated company policy on firings, evaluations, discipline and promotions, management wielded considerable arbitrary power in the implementation of those rules." [15]

When the freeze was finally lifted in January 1984, some employees were given a 4 per cent raise, some received a measly five cents more an hour, and others got nothing. Half the staff were converted into part-time employees. Eaton's was gambling that any lower sales levels that were the result of reduced customer service would be more than offset by diminished payroll costs.

Feeling betrayed, employees were roused to action. In 1948 the union had come seeking employees. This time, Eaton's staff approached the Retail, Wholesale and Department Store Union. The Eaton's store in Brampton was the first to be organized, followed by two more locations in Toronto, then London, Bramalea, and St. Catharines. Pro-union advertisements gave details about the paltry pensions of retired Eaton's employees. One told of a woman who had a monthly pension of $70 after sixteen years' service. Some ads were so contentious that many radio stations refused to air them. "The workers were outraged at Eaton's breach of the paternalistic contract and wanted to 'get back at them'. Despite their perception of unions as 'anti-family', communist, terrorist organizations, they envisioned joining the union as a way of shaking the company up," wrote Aylward. [16]

Eaton's responded with handbills saying: "Would you enjoy seeing Eaton's develop the same reputation as other union-dominated industries and services like the post office, or the UAW? Do you appreciate what they have done for you, the consumer?" Negotiations towards a first contract produced no results, and so on November 30, 1984, 1300 employees went on strike. Most of the strikers were part-time workers and female employees earning $6 an hour. Strike pay was $70 a week.

On the first day of the strike Fred crossed picket lines to work in the stores alongside the clerks who hadn't joined the union. When he showed up in a battered hatchback at Scarborough Town Centre, some militant organizers urged those on the picket lines to chant antimanagement slogans, but the strikers fell silent, then began to applaud his regal presence. After working behind the counter for an hour, Fred departed to help out at another store.

Six months later the union caved in. The result was little better than what striking Eaton's cloak makers had achieved in 1912. A first contract provided for wage increases that were no different than those received by non-union employees. So embarrassed was the union that no vote was held and the contract was simply sent to New York headquarters for ratification. A year later all unionized employees, except for one small group, voted for decertification by a two-to-one margin.

Middle managers also had complaints. "As long as I worked there, we were always informed that the company was performing poorly; bonuses and raises were always restrained," said Andrew Vajda, who held various executive positions at Eaton's from 1977 to 1991. "Being a private company we had no way of knowing if this were correct, although, due to the departments I managed, I had a fairly good barometer of daily activities. To the contrary, at one point Eaton's was profitable." [17]

Who was responsible was a matter of some debate. Eaton's was being run by what was called the Office of the President, a triumvirate consisting of Fred, George, and Greg Purchase. "We didn't go around saying, 'I think this and do that.' That wasn't the way," claims Fred. "Everybody was free to say whatever they thought. We very seldom disagreed on anything, and if we did disagree on it, we would meet privately, the three of us, and discuss these things, so that we were never in conflict in front of the management. The final decision was always mine." Others disagree. "Fred never called any shots. Even Fred would not argue with Greg," says Ray Luft. "To the extent anyone was running things, it was George."

George's control increased after illness felled Purchase. While visiting Winnipeg in 1984, Purchase gathered with some cronies for an evening of bridge. As he picked up his cards, he realized he had no vision in his left eye. Purchase was diagnosed as having multiple sclerosis, a progressive disease that affects the central nervous system and eventually causes immobility. "It went on so fast. I couldn't believe it," says Alan Finnbogason, who had worked with Purchase in Winnipeg. "He lost his grip almost immediately."

For a while the disease was kept secret to all but a select few until Purchase was forced to get around the stores on a small four-wheeled scooter. In 1987 Fred gave up his office and moved down the hall so that the space could be used to expand Purchase's office for a therapeutic whirlpool. "It's physically so shattering. It's a horrible disease," says Fred. "To have that happen to anybody is just horrible. We worked as long, and maybe too long, but certainly as long as we possibly could to make sure that he felt needed and wanted."

Executive vice-president Tom Reid was filling part of the vacuum left by Purchase, but the boys needed more help. Why not do what daddy did? Just as John David had hired Swatty Wotherspoon in 1965, the boys reached into the family law firm of Osler, Hoskin & Harcourt for Allan Beattie. When Wotherspoon joined Eaton's in 1965, Beattie had taken over his clients, the Eaton and Bassett families.

By the mid-1970s Beattie had become managing partner at Osler, the top position in the firm. Law firms are very political; there's continual infighting and jockeying for position. In such a milieu Beattie was the consummate corporate warrior. "Allan Beattie never had a meeting of the partnership or the executive committee that he didn't know what the outcome was going to be," said fellow committee member Harry Boylan in 1995. "He'd have felt it out and sounded it out before." [18]

Beattie would fit right in on the Byzantine landscape of Eaton's. He'd been on the board of Eaton's of Canada since 1971, and now he was ready to take on a new full-time role, for he'd lost his powerful position at Oslers. In late 1986, the firm decided to replace him as managing partner with a four-person management committee. Beattie served on the many-headed beast for a few months, then jumped to Eaton's of Canada as vice-chairman.

Eaton's was little changed from the days when Wotherspoon had made the same move. "The company was adrift," said one old Eatonian. "To replace Greg's ability to get around and meet people, we had an operations committee that met every Tuesday. There was no agenda. You'd go in and talk about problems, and the discussion would be all over the place. Nothing would be resolved. So you'd get up and leave the meeting and come back a week later and talk about the same things all over again." [19]

In 1988 Fred ceded one of his titles, president of T. Eaton Co. Ltd., to George. It was the family's ultimate indulgence. Baby brother was about to take over in name, as well as deed. "Fred was tired of running the company and he felt it would be wonderful if George would run it for him," says Purchase. To Purchase, the appointment of George was a mistake. "I don't think he had enough experience to be a good merchant."

Fred had become bored. As George assumed complete control, Purchase retired and Fred did less and less. In September 1991 relief finally arrived for Fred when Prime Minister Brian Mulroney named him Canadian high commissioner to the United Kingdom of Great Britain and Northern Ireland. In June Mulroney had called Doug Bassett to have him ask Fred if he'd like to replace Lincoln Alexander, whose five-year term as lieutenant-governor of Ontario was coming to an end. Bassett raised the matter with Fred in a roundabout way by saying he'd heard a rumour that Fred would be taking on the role. "I wouldn't accept lieutenant-governor of Ontario," said Fred. "The only job I would accept is High Commissioner to the Court of St. James's."

Bassett reported to Mulroney that Fred wasn't interested in being lieutenant-governor, but he did not pass along Fred's stated aspiration. Bassett was angling for just such an appointment himself. In July Mulroney did offer Bassett London, but by then Bassett had undergone a change of heart. He'd had surgery for melanoma, the same deadly skin cancer that had killed his brother Johnny F. Life suddenly seemed to be about living, not stuffy receptions in far-off lands. He turned Mulroney down, then told the prime minister about Fred's interest in London.

Mulroney offered Fred the posting and he accepted with alacrity. Shades of Sir John! Fred would be in his element. The appointment might not have quite the cachet of a knighthood, but in the modern era, it was the next best thing. "I wanted a change," says Fred. "Both jobs are highly cere-monial, but I thought I'd rather be out of the country. By that time I was not the chief executive of the company and it's an easier thing to get out of peo-ple's hair [and] not be there."

The anointment called for a celebration by his closest friends in the most extravagant fashion. Eight couples, who all owned farms north of Toronto, had been partying together as "The Cross-Country Club" for nearly a decade. In addition to Fred and Nicky, the group included Senator Trevor and Jane Eyton; investment bankers Latham Burns and Leighton McCarthy, and their respective spouses, Paddy-Ann and Brenda; *Toronto Sun* founder Doug Creighton and his wife, Marilyn; Royal LePage Chairman Gordon Gray and his wife, Pat; McCarthy Tétrault lawyer Jim McCutcheon and his wife, Brenda; Hollywood producer/director Norman Jewison and his wife, Dixie.

In 1982 the first day-long event began at 9 a.m. at the Eytons' with a champagne breakfast, followed by flights in gliders. Next, everyone climbed on a bus for lunch at Fred and Nicky's. The bus, arranged through Jim McCutcheon's brother Doug, who owns Rosedale Livery, had previously been used by a rock band on tour. On the side of the bus were emblazoned the mys-terious letters "DILLIGAF," which, apparently, stood for "Do I look like I give a fuck." The in-joke not only set the tone for the day, but also for all other such happy-gang gatherings in the future.

When the revellers arrived at Fred and Nicky's, they were greeted by a man dressed in traditional Swiss costume sounding a ten-foot-long alpine horn. There was a treasure hunt and a contest that involved hitting golf balls at a tire floating on the pond. Next was high tea at the McCarthys' with cro-quet played in whites and flannels. The festivities concluded at the Grays' with dinner, dancing, fireworks, and entertainment by two comedians. The earliest anyone left for home was 3:30 a.m.

For Fred and Nicky's 1991 sendoff, the DILLIGAF crowd rented Stop 33, the dining room atop the Sutton Place Hotel in midtown Toronto. Red carpet was laid from the curb through the lobby to the elevator. Another piece was placed in the elevator for continuity, and there was a final length in Stop 33, leading to two thrones. Everyone knelt before the royal couple who had been supplied with crowns and capes. A special edition of the *Toronto Sun* was printed and delivered before the evening was over. It featured a page-one coronation photo of Fred and Nicky.

There was also a telephone call broadcast over speakers from an actress who could mimic perfectly the plummy tones of the Queen. She told Fred: "My husband and I need you immediately." The well-briefed caller expressed concern that Fred's 120-foot yacht, *Brave Wolfe*, might dwarf the Royal yacht *Britannia* on the Thames River. Some minutes passed before Fred came to realize that he was not conversing with Her Majesty.

The final hurdle was Fred's appearance before the House of Commons External Affairs and International Trade committee. The session was more ritual than real, but the parliamentarians' queries could be embarrassing. Fred faced a fusillade of questions, not about his credentials, but about whether or not the clubs he belonged to accepted female members. MPs pounced on the fact that there were no women in the Long Point Company, a century-old hunting club with eighteen members. "I do not know too many women duck hunters," lamented Fred, who said he would not quit the club. [20]

"I do not think it would be wrong to say that our family has been blessed with a lot of strong women," added Fred. "I know a lot of strong women: my mother, my grandmothers. Mrs. Timothy Eaton was a strong woman. These are strong, vigorous, outspoken women. I know about them. I admire them. I like to have them working with me." [21] Within limits, of course. The only woman on the Eaton's board was Signy. There were no women among the senior executives.

The Commons committee could only review Fred's appointment during the seventy-five minute session, not reject it, and Fred was already scheduled to take up his duties the next day in London. (In November, when committee members raised the matter again with External Affairs Minister Barbara McDougall, she announced that Fred had quit Long Point Company after all.)

The posting came with a staff of three, a residence in Grosvenor Square, a driver, and an elderly Mercedes-Benz. Fred thought a Rolls-Royce would be more suitable in London than a German-built car, so he shipped his vintage 1950 Rolls-Royce Silver Dawn, first purchased by Algoma Steel Corp.'s Sir James Dunn for Lady Dunn. Fred and the Japanese envoy were the only two ambassadors in London at the time with Rolls-Royce automobiles. (When Signy died in September 1992, Fred inherited her more up-to-date Rolls. He had it shipped to London to replace the vintage vehicle, which was sent back to Canada and in 1995 was donated to the National Museum of Science and Technology in Ottawa.) *Brave Wolfe* was moored at Portsmouth for trips along the Scottish coast or was dispatched to the Mediterranean where Fred and Nicky would fly to meet the yacht for getaways.

Fred presented his credentials at Buckingham Palace wearing a morning coat that hadn't been on his back since his wedding almost thirty years earlier. In a lunch speech at the Savoy Hotel he joked that he was just trying to even the score with Donald Smith, who drove the last spike in the completion of the CPR in 1885, became Lord Strathcona, and served as both Governor of Hudson's Bay Co. and High Commissioner for Canada in the U.K. from 1896 until his death in 1914. Fred admitted that Eaton's was a relative newcomer compared with The Bay, which had been founded in 1670. "We never thought HBC meant Hudson's Bay Co.," he said. "We thought it meant Here Before Christ."

He also told the audience of two hundred guests that he was a bit baffled about why he was picked for London. "No one was more surprised than myself when I was asked by the prime minister to accept the position. Many people ask me why the prime minister chose me to represent the country. Modesty prevents me from telling you why I think I was chosen and, frankly, he didn't tell me the process by which he arrived at his choice. Perhaps it's better I don't know."

Wrote columnist Allan Fotheringham: "If Fred Eaton, high Tory and generous fund-raiser for the party, really doesn't know how he got the job, it is clear he should never be allowed out of the house without his mittens secured by a string. Do we really want him wandering around Britain without a keeper if he believes what he said? Do we wish to expose to the worldly Brits such an innocent child, who apparently believes in the Tooth Fairy and that babies are found under cabbage leaves? I worry about our country." [22]

Fred had certainly been a generous Tory supporter. He gave $1000 a year to the party out of his own pocket; Eaton's contributed a hefty $81,463 in the election year of 1988, and $40,000 in the two subsequent years. [23]

Other Canadians posted to Britain watched the newly arrived diplomat with concern. "Early in his tenure, he was learning the ropes. His speaking style was painful but, as time passed, he improved," said George Hutchison, then director of public affairs at Ontario House. "On the business side, he was received well. But within the Canadian community, for people who were accustomed to a high-profile, more outgoing high commissioner, it was a difficult transition. He was low key."

"I quite enjoyed being 'your excellency,'" admits Fred. "It's not a hugely difficult job to do. There's no day-to-day worry in a job like that." That's the trouble with London; there is precious little official work. Canada's ambassador to the United States has a wide range of trade issues to manage and is an active lobbyist on Capitol Hill. Although there are 250 Canadian companies with British operations, few firms need much help from the High Commission. Tricky bilateral treaties are rare.

With little of substance to do, Fred carried on just as he would have at home: he raised money and paid attention to his social life. Fred and Conrad Black, owner of the *Daily Telegraph*, raised $2 million for the Canadian War Memorial, a red granite monument erected in 1994 in Green Park adjacent to Buckingham Palace, to honour the one million Canadians who came to Britain's aid in two world wars. Fred also joined Britain's Polite Society, which, among other activities, encourages drivers to be considerate.

Before his arrival, he knew several members of the House of Lords and so was often invited for a weekend of shooting on some peer's estate. He cultivated the friendship of Lady Goldsmeed, an eccentric in her eighties who would swim in the sea naked but for her pearls because she felt they needed salt water. Fred called her Rosie; she called him Freddy dear. When her ladyship died her funeral was delayed to accommodate the schedule of Prince Charles.

Fred also committed a few diplomatic faux pas that were more unintentionally humorous than internationally harmful. At the opening of an exhibit at the Tate Gallery, Fred was introduced to someone but didn't catch his name. All Fred heard was "Spain," so he asked: "Have you ever lived in Spain?"

"Yes," came the slightly quizzical reply.

"How nice," said Fred. "Perhaps you speak a bit of Spanish, then?"

"I hope so," the man answered. "I *am* the Spanish ambassador."

When Sir Nicholas Bayne was appointed Britain's High Commissioner to Canada, the German ambassador to Britain, Dr. Hermann Freiherr von Richthofen, hosted a lunch for Sir Nicholas and invited Fred. Herr Richthofen gave a tour of his residence and happened to comment: "You know, English homes are beautifully done on the street side, but the back walls are filled with nothing but rubble." Sir Nicholas maintained a polite silence, but not Fred, who blurted: "Probably caused by you chaps in World War II!"

In a mistaken attempt to fill the awkward silence that followed, Fred blundered all the way back to the First World War by asking his host if he were related to Manfred von Richthofen, the infamous "Red Baron" who shot down eighty enemy aircraft.

"Why, yes," said Herr Richthofen, "I'm a direct descendant."

"What a coincidence," said Fred, who had a war ace up his own sleeve. "My brother's godfather was Billy Bishop," citing the Canadian fighter pilot who shot down the most German aircraft during the First World War. Fortunately for Fred there were no more wars to remember.

Among Fred's official forays was a trip to Northern Ireland in 1992. He attended a dinner in Belfast, then he and Nicky made the pilgrimage to Bally-mena, birthplace of his great-grandfather. They visited the shop in Port-glenone where Timothy had carved his initials on a door. They stopped at the old family homestead to inspect a small historical plaque erected in Timothy's honour, spoke to the current owner, and searched a cemetery looking for Eaton headstones. Like touring royalty, they also did a walkabout at Eaton Park Pavilion, a local recreation area and sports field supported by the firm and family.

This was not the first such pilgrimage home by an Eaton. In 1907 Jack and Flora visited the graves of Timothy's parents, John and Margaret, at Kirkinriola. In 1949 R.Y.'s daughter, Margaret Dunn, attended the official opening of the Eaton Park playing fields. Eaton's had given £1000, R.Y. another £500, of the overall £14,000 cost. In the years that followed, there were various expansions, for instance, new club rooms in 1968 to which Eaton's contributed $1000 of the £20,000 cost. R.Y. made several trips, including one in 1954 when he was made a Freeman of the Borough. In June 1969, as part of the Eaton's centennial celebration, John Craig unveiled a plaque on the shop in Portglenone where Timothy had apprenticed. (A second plaque was attached to the homestead in 1987 by the Ulster History Circle.)

In spite of all those family visits, Fred was the first to make a surprising discovery. During a lunch sponsored by municipal officials, local historian Eull Dunlop told Fred that, according to church records of Timothy's parents, the correct spelling of his surname was actually Aiton. Quipped someone, to laughter all round: "It's going to cost you a lot of money to change the name on all those stores."

Meanwhile, what George was doing at home would not only cost a lot of money, but also make the boys want to take their name off the door, however it was spelled.

CHAPTER TWELVE

GOING DOWN WITH GEORGE

GEORGE HAD BOUGHT HIMSELF ANOTHER WILD ride. This time the Formula One spectators were replaced by thousands of employees and suppliers who were swept along on a high-stakes run that would end in disaster. During the 1980s, Fred had given up job titles, Greg Purchase had been stricken with multiple sclerosis, and George had been taking charge.

Some Eaton's executives doubted the family's prowess. "I don't know that any of the Eaton boys have what it takes," says Graham Clark, who was both an administrator and a merchandiser in Toronto from 1959 to 1995. "John we used to call 'The Playboy of the Western World.' Fred was the best. Thor never showed any interest. When I first saw George it was out at King in the summer when they had the big parties and George was there with his six-guns on his hips. He never grew out of being a kid with his six-guns. Greg [Purchase] was the one that held it together. When he got sick, the boys took it over and it just went downhill at an accelerated pace from that point on. Once Fred pulled out, it went downhill like a bobsled."

As George's hold on power grew firmer after being named president in 1988, he busied himself building monuments. The final phase of the Eaton Centre, completed in 1989, included a second office tower south of the first. Eaton's took three hundred thousand square feet, and the usual standards for office size were disregarded even for low-level positions. Although buyers spent much of their time out meeting suppliers, each buyer had a 175-square-foot office, often with a window.

On the executive fifteenth floor, grand epithets were etched into glass walls. "Only those who risk going too far can possibly find out how far one can go," declared one. "All work is God's work. Honour your creator and fulfill yourself. Be the best you can be," said another. Author of the first was poet T.S. Eliot. Author of the second was George.

George was also building a mansion in Caledon and decided that he should be able to flit back and forth by helicopter so he had the office super-structure and rooftop strengthened. Because nearby hospitals had air-ambulance helipads, special approvals were required. Transport Canada and the office of then prime minister Brian Mulroney were both involved. Once built, George never did use the rooftop landing.

Although the boys possessed complete control of the stores, they did little. There were just too many personal distractions. Every whim could be, and was, indulged. Even after his Caledon residence was complete, George retained his sixteen-thousand-square-foot house at 135 Dunvegan Road. The living room and private courtyard could accommodate 350 for a reception. The grand ballroom could hold up to 125 for a sit-down dinner. On the second floor there was a study, music room, master bedroom with his and hers baths and dressing rooms, as well as four other bedrooms, each with an en suite bath. On the third floor was another guest bedroom and staff apartments. In the basement was a cinema with a hidden screen, a fitness centre and massage room, two wine cellars, and a wine-tasting room, along with a manager's office. He sold that property in 1997 for $4.98 million.

The gothic-and-gingerbread confection he built in Caledon was 50 per cent bigger again than Dunvegan and contained 25,000 square feet. A long driveway winds through manicured grounds, past a tennis court and five spring-fed ponds. Designed by New York architect Thierry Despont, Hawkridge Farm has eleven bedrooms, mahogany window frames, wall-to-wall walkouts, seven framed fireplaces, plaster cornice mouldings, and a double-height trophy room. Barely four years after construction was completed, George decided to sell. When the estate appeared in Christie's November 1998 catalogue, the price was eroneously shown as $12 million. In fact, George wants $18 million, making his house the most expensive ever brought on the Canadian market.

Terrie and George have three boys, James, Michael, and David, ranging in age from twenty-five to seventeen. James lives in Boulder, Colorado; like his father, he races cars. Michael showed promise as a tennis player and attended special camps, but recurring back problems have limited his progress. All three have inherited George's dyslexia, so learning has been a struggle.

George belongs to Griffith Island, a hunting club in Georgian Bay, where he once took Bank of Montreal chairman and CEO Matthew Barrett deer hunting. Members' guests are allowed to shoot fawns and does, but not bucks. Such trophies are restricted to members. Barrett paid no attention to the house rule and shot a magnificent twelve-point buck. To compensate for his overzealous guest, George contributed $1000 to help replenish the club's stock.

When it came to houses, only Thor competed with George. Of all the wives of the Eaton boys, Thor's Nicky was the most socially ambitious and enjoyed grandeur. They used to live at 232 Forest Hill Road in what the neighbours jokingly called the "retailer's house." Ted Burton of Simpsons sold it to Ira Gerstein of Peoples Jewellers, who in turn sold it to Thor. Thor then moved to 103 Poplar Plains Road, which was part of a small enclave of three houses, one of them Signy's at the time.

Nicky can also be outrageous. The vanity plate on her four-wheel drive vehicle says "Froggy," an allusion to her Québécois background. Her speech is peppered with four-letter words, whether by habit or for shock value, no one can be sure. "She's solid, cuts through the b.s., and she's not afraid to ask for money," says Frank Potter, chairman of the Royal Ontario Museum Foundation on which Nicky serves. She will often preface her comments at meetings by saying something like, "I know you'll think I'm a bitch, but . . ."

Although appointed, like other such charitable board members, for her capacity to raise money, Nicky also understood the museum's innermost workings better than most volunteers. "She has a very good grasp of the politics of a not-for-profit institution," says William Withrow, director of the AGO for thirty years. "There are forces at work that are very much like a political party, the manoeuvring around power, who's doing what to whom."

Thor and Nicky have two children, Thor Edmond, eighteen, and Cléophée, sixteen. Both handle horses well; Thor was junior Canadian jumping champion. Cléophée attended Havergal; both are now at boarding schools in the United States. Thor Edmond suffers from dyslexia, like his Uncle George.

Thor now lives on a four-hundred-acre farm in Caledon. Arriving guests often mistake the stables and staff quarters for the main house. The mansard-roofed main chateau stands about 150 metres deeper into the property. Inside, the decor is formal with artwork that includes gouaches by Picasso and, like George's home, wildlife paintings by George McLean.

Thor is a crack shot and raises pheasant for hunts on his property with invited friends. His gun dog is an apricot-coloured purebred standard poodle.

Thor's city pied-à-terre is a $1 million townhouse. When he's not at the track watching his horses, Thor is likely hunting or fly-fishing. "He's smart enough to know that he didn't need to bother with the folly of work," says Bill Ballard, son of Harold.

⟶

For all the luxury he allowed himself, George has a tightwad reputation. Tony Fell, chairman and CEO of RBC Dominion Securities Inc., gives a speech laced with one-liners at his firm's annual black-tie shareholders' dinner. Many of Fell's jibes focus on his demands to keep a lid on costs. But Fell also finds fodder in clients. "Sometimes we make light of it but some of the wealthiest and most successful business entrepreneurs in Canada make it a religion," he said in his 1988 speech.

Fell quoted Harrison McCain, of McCain Foods, who told Fell he hadn't replaced worn carpets because "carpets don't make money." Fell also cited legendary skinflint Roy Thomson, Lord Thomson of Fleet, who "used to fly regularly across the Atlantic economy saying it was the cheapest money he ever made." George fell into the same category. "When asked why he did not keep racehorses like so many of his friends, he replied he did not like race-horses 'because they eat while you sleep.'" Fell liked the line so much that he recycled it in his 1991 speech.

Maybe it was those cheapskate views that led George to launch Eaton's most disastrous strategy: everyday value pricing. In June 1990 about forty-five field and marketing managers gathered in the fifteenth-floor boardroom to hear Ray Luft present marketing plans for the following year. Luft had hung on the walls the complete schedule, which included four-colour newspaper inserts, Trans-Canada Sale flyers, and off-price coupon deals. After one look around George said: "Take them down."

George declared that henceforth there would be no off-price promotions and no advertised sales. Consumers were suddenly supposed to believe that whenever they shopped at Eaton's, they would be getting the lowest price possible. Luft was flabbergasted at the abrupt change. "After George got involved, everybody knew better. It was amazing how smart everybody got. If Fred had been there, it never would have happened."

Bill Hughes, the Eaton's buyer who thirty years earlier had taught Fred the ropes in Asia, accosted George, saying: "You can't run Eaton's like a Wal-Mart."

"Oh yes, we can," snapped George. "We don't have to advertise."

"But Wal-Mart advertises," replied Hughes. "I know. I go to South Carolina twice a year."

"Oh, no, no, no."

"Well, you can kiss my business goodbye," warned Hughes. "That's how I live — advertising."

Six months later Hughes retired. "I was glad to leave," he says today. "I never had too much use for George. I don't think he had a business sense."

Prior to launching everyday value pricing in the fall of 1990, George outlined the concept to a gathering of 150 key merchandisers and store managers. "They presented it to us, then sat at various tables at dinner and asked us our reaction," says Graham Clark. "We said, 'What the hell are you asking us for? You've already told us this is what you're going to do and you're not going to change it.' Nobody approved it but they went ahead and put it in."

"Unless you get a fashion merchant that's smarter than God, you're going to make mistakes," says Luft. "When you make a mistake, you're going to have to lower prices. In the customer's mind that's a sale. If it's not, you'll have to mark it down again. You can't be in the fashion business and do everyday value."

Eaton's marketing consultant, Martin Goldfarb, also raised the alarm. "Everyday low pricing could never work. We told them it would be very difficult. We used the term 'thrill of the hunt.' People want sales. They walked away from Trans-Canada Sale, which was the most powerful sales tool in this country."

"It is a bit of a nebulous phrase," admits Peter Saunders, a longtime Eaton's merchandiser who became chief operating officer in 1995. "Is it the lowest price? No. Is it the lowest price of the season? No. It is lower than the regular suggested retail by a manufacturer, but it's not necessarily as low as their promotional price. There was a decision that you could not have sales and everyday value pricing, that that would confuse the customer. We became too pure. Sometimes you have to be first. Sometimes being first doesn't work."

But Eaton's was not first. Sears Roebuck had tried everyday value pricing in 1989, pronounced it a failure, and quickly dumped the concept. Eaton's was copying a similar program begun in the U.S. by Dillard's Inc. in 1990, but Dillard's did not abandon all the other merchandising methods. Dillard's semiannual sales, the Tuesday specials, and other off-price offers continued in parallel with everyday value pricing.

George wanted no such blurring at the edges. The announcements were uncompromising: "Not once a week," they said, "Not once a month," and "Not once a year." Not a chance. Canada was wracked by a recession; household income was shrinking. If Eaton's held no sales, customers would go elsewhere. The session when George announced everyday value pricing to managers was the last such gathering where he was front and centre. Subsequent national meetings, held every January, turned into stilted, pro forma affairs. With no promotional program to present, there wasn't much to discuss.

⟶

In March 1992 a creditor group led by the Bank of Montreal seized the Eaton Centre in Montreal. Because they were not owners, there were no financial implications for Eaton's. Eaton's had simply licensed its name, but rumours arose just the same that Eaton's was in trouble. In June the company issued a statement that said such speculation "is a fabrication and is totally denied." Huffed executive vice-president Tom Reid: "We're store builders, not store closers." [1] Two months later Reid was named chief operating officer and became George's right-hand man. But Reid was no merchant; he was a former banker who'd joined T. Eaton Acceptance in 1970 to oversee credit-card computerization.

Reid's power had been waxing during the years Greg Purchase's health was waning. Reid's appointment was George's second major mistake. "The family really didn't want the responsibility, but they never gave their management the total authority," says Martin Goldfarb. "They were not good operators. They began to trust their finance guys more and more and walked away from merchants and marketers."

Many of Eaton's executives were perplexed by the appointment of a bean counter like Reid. "That helped put the grease under the skid," says Clark. "He's a great talker," says Andrew Vajda, who, as corporate purchasing manager, reported to Reid. "He was very proud of the fact that he had only a grade nine education. He thought he was a motivator but after you went to the third meeting you'd heard it all before."

"It was hard to take him seriously," says human-resources officer Marc Newman. "Tom Reid is a brilliant man. He just thinks he's about twice as brilliant as he is." Adds David Kinnear: "Tom Reid didn't know the business. He got to be a feisty little guy and so people didn't like him. He got so that he acted like he owned the place." Counters Peter Saunders: "There's a lot of people who would have felt that Tom was an accountant, not a merchant. I don't think Tom would disagree with that, but that didn't say Tom didn't have any merchandising abilities."

Reid's appointment was meant to quell concerns by the banks about the financial health of Eaton's, but his arrival achieved little. George himself had to deny rumours of trouble early in 1993. "Talk is cheap," he said. "They were wrong then and they're wrong now. Downsizing is not in our plans." He also denied that the family was pouring its money into the stores to keep the business afloat. "We prefer to take money out of it," he said. "We think that's a much better way to have it go." [2]

Indeed. In 1992 T. Eaton Realty and T. Eaton Acceptance managed to turn a combined profit of $27 million. The family seemed to be more in the credit business than in retailing. Even as they floundered on the store floor, *Forbes* magazine's authoritative annual list of the world's wealthy families reported that the Eatons were worth U.S. $1.2 billion in 1992, down only a titch from U.S. $1.3 billion in 1990 but behind the scenes the family's financial deterioration had begun in earnest.

"They should have been looking for more qualified people," says David Kinnear, pronouncing a damning indictment. "The reason they didn't was because they didn't think they needed to. They thought the company ran itself." Former Ontario premier Bill Davis, who knows the boys, agrees: "I don't think they had the capacity of their father, any of them."

In August 1992 Signy suffered a stroke. "I certainly don't want to be drooling and in a wheelchair," she had told Frank McEachren a year earlier. "I hope they let me go."

"They remembered," says Florence McEachren. "Thank goodness the boys had the courage to let her go." After a week in hospital, Signy was brought to her home on Poplar Plains Road to await the inevitable.

There were round-the-clock nurses. Unable to speak, Signy could only respond by squeezing a visitor's hand. Two weeks after suffering the stroke, she died on September 10, at seventy-nine. She was serene right to the end, her skin still smooth and smelling of the Joy perfume she had always favoured.

At her funeral there were four long-stemmed pink roses on the casket, one from each of her boys. Signy was interred with her husband, bringing to fourteen the number of family members in the Eaton Mausoleum at Mount Pleasant Cemetery. [3] Signy's estate was valued at $32.9 million, an amount that included $2.3 million in real estate. [4] Under the terms of her will, her ten grandchildren each received $250,000. Four of them had already received their legacies when they were married. Ashley and Alexandra, the adopted children of John Craig's second marriage, were specifically mentioned by name; they were to receive nothing. Clearly, blood lines mattered to Signy. And yet, the three children of Evlyn Payton, John David's adopted sister, each got $100,000.

Most nieces and nephews were each given $100,000 or $150,000 outright. Two other nephews and three sisters-in-law were to receive the annual income generated by a series of separate funds in the amount of $250,000 invested on their behalf. The church Signy attended as a child, Winnipeg's First Icelandic Lutheran, got $50,000. The Betel Foundation in Selkirk, Manitoba, received $100,000. Five members of staff were given sums ranging from $10,000 for a maid to $100,000 for longtime secretary Marlene Josiak. Fred's Nicky inherited all Signy's clothing and furs. The Caledon farmland was to be sold to George at a price agreed upon by the trustees of the estate. All remaining assets, including all paintings, sculpture, jade, pottery, and other works of art, were divided among the four boys. [5]

Signy's death caused another significant turning point in George's life. "When Mrs. Eaton died, it had a hell of an impact on George," says Ray Luft. "He changed, really dramatically. He went from being very cocky, 'We're going to make this work,' to 'Get somebody else to run this place, I'm not interested.'" With Fred in London, Eaton's lacked hands-on family leadership more than ever.

For all their supposed sense of tradition, the Eaton boys saw no value in the past; they felt little need to cherish family heirlooms. Art Gallery of Ontario curators had urged Signy on more than one occasion to bequeath something to the gallery in her will. A Picasso was particularly prized. "She could be very enigmatic," says William Withrow, gallery director from 1961 to 1991. "There was no answer." In 1985 Signy donated a gouache by Bram van Velde and in 1987, two wax crayon works by Jan Groth, but that was it.

Fred, whose taste in art was the most enlightened of the boys, had donated one item, an acrylic by London, Ontario, artist Greg Curnoe entitled *Zeus 10-Speed*. According to Withrow, the Eatons don't qualify as true collectors. "They didn't have the disease that real collectors have. They liked the things and appreciated them, but they were part of their living environment, not a collection. It's visual pleasure."

After Signy died Fred kept several items from her collection, including two pen-and-ink drawings by Thomas Gainsborough, a landscape of southern

France by Pierre Bonnard, and an abstract work by Fernand Léger. The other three brothers had less love for her art. They auctioned off eleven of Signy's works through Sotheby's in New York. The items were sold at three different sales in 1995 and 1996, fetching a total of US $4,179,500. Kandinsky, Picasso, Braque, Pisarro, all gone. Despite her long association with the Art Gallery of Ontario, the family gave the institution nothing to grace the walls and honour her name. [6]

The same indifference marked the family's attitude towards Eaton's corporate archives. Beginning in 1956, the store maintained archives under the direction of Kittie Fells, then latterly, Judith McErvel. In 1987 the family lost what little interest it had in such matters and decided to donate the entire collection to the Province of Ontario. "It was not a sophisticated family," says McErvel. "They were not into the arts."

In a world where the trend was to privatize government services, Eaton's did the opposite. They took a private-enterprise function and made it part of the public sector. When Eaton's first offered papers and artifacts to Ontario, head provincial archivist Ian Wilson urged Eaton's to continue maintaining its own archives. "In giving away its archives, the company is distancing itself from its heritage and its corporate memory," he wrote in a January 15, 1988, letter to Eaton's.

Eaton's persisted and in April the province relented and agreed to house the Eaton papers. For months the skid loads flowed from the archives at the Yorkdale store and a warehouse in Scarborough, Ontario, where documents had been stacked helter-skelter for decades. Eaton's wanted to obtain a tax deduction for the gift, but was unsure exactly where the archives came under the corporate umbrella. "Because the organization of Eaton's companies is very complicated, the company has not yet identified the corporate entity that is the actual owner of these records," wrote G. Lee Muirhead of Osler, Hoskin & Harcourt in a letter dated April 8, 1988. Two months passed before T. Eaton Holdings Ltd. was named the appropriate "owner." The National Archival Appraisal Board and the Cultural Property Review Board set a value of $1.5 million on the archives, and Eaton's received a tax receipt for that amount. The transfer was made official in October 1988.

Doing an inventory and organizing the material took two years. Among the dozens of collections of business records at the archives, Eaton's is by far the biggest. At 1764 cubic feet it is ten times the size of the next largest, Maclean Hunter Ltd. Included in the Eaton collection are 1500 linear feet of boxes, film of every Santa Claus Parade since 1922, 100,000 still photographs, drawers of microfilmed material, and copies of every catalogue ever issued. There are sales and order books, newspaper clippings, architectural renderings and blueprints, leather binders filled with memos from head office about hours, dress codes, and travel arrangements, even lists of provisions for the *Eatonia* right down to the number of cigars required on a trip. When the items first arrived, personal material was mingled with the professional. "It was very hard to distinguish between what was family and what was Eaton's. All the secretaries, lawyers, and accountants worked for both the family and the business," says senior archivist Larry Weiler, who oversees the collection.

While few documents held in the archives relate to personal wealth, one memo does reveal the extent of one family member's holdings and the interwoven nature of home and office. A communication dated January 27, 1967, from Eaton official C. M. Beattie to Swatty Wotherspoon noted that Gilbert, John David's brother, owed Eaton's $171,300. The amount was comprised of various items, including a sum promised to son Timothy Craig for a house, bills from the store, and two purchases at Birks on Portage Avenue in Winnipeg for $32,250 worth of loose emeralds and a pair of earrings. The Birks bills had been submitted directly to Eaton's at the request of Gilbert's wife, Marjorie.

"During the current year we have transferred to his account about $130,000," wrote Beattie. "It is apparent that Mr. Eaton is living on a combination of income and a substantial amount of capital." The $1.5 million in securities owned by Gilbert generated an after-tax income of between $50,000 and $60,000 a year. Neither Wotherspoon's response nor the outcome of the dispute is included in the file. [7]

The reason so few personal documents are contained in the collection is that once the initial inventory was completed by archival staff, Eaton's executives were allowed to remove items that the family did not want to be available for public viewing. In many other cases Eaton's severely restricted access to papers that were allowed to remain. Files about the 1976 catalogue closing are unavailable until 2006; all labour-related material is sealed for seventy-five years. Moreover, Eaton's retains copyright on everything, which means that nothing in the public archives can be reproduced or republished without Eaton's permission. (Archival rules have changed since the Eaton's bequest. Now, copyright on donated documents is assigned to the province. As a result, a donor firm can no longer control use in perpetuity.) "Eaton's is very conscious of its image," says Weiler. "They consider it their collection despite the fact that we own it."

Some aspects of the past were not so easily jettisoned as Signy's art or Eaton's papers. In 1993 the racing community created the Canadian Motorsport Hall of Fame. Twenty nominees, George among them, were invited to a dinner at the Four Seasons Hotel in Toronto where the first ten inductees were to be announced. George dutifully attended, but when the honorees were named he was not among them. Lapped again.

"He was disappointed and a little embarrassed that he wasn't inducted in the first year," says Len Coates, who serves as Canadian racing's unofficial historian. In 1994 the system was altered to eliminate such surprises. The next ten Hall of Famers were carefully informed in advance. This time George made the cut, but he did not attend the ceremony.

The citation gives and it takes away. "Canada's first full-time driver in Formula One was George Eaton." So far, so good. "No one could have mistaken the 1970 Formula One BRM for a winner." Oops. The wording then heads for the more laudatory landscape of the earlier years, saying: "George quickly proved before going to Formula One he was also a standout in the Can-Am circuit and absolutely unbeatable in a Shelby-Cobra."

"They were different days," says Coates. "Had he been racing today and had the wherewithal that he obviously has, he probably could have gone a lot farther. George would have been talented enough to make it with a top team eventually. It will always remain a question mark how good George really was and how good he might have been had he stuck at it."

Other circumstances were easier to control. In 1993 the Retail Council of Canada named George as a Distinguished Canadian Retailer. In his June acceptance speech he defended everyday value pricing, by then in place for almost three years, as "sensible — different, forward thinking — certainly a necessity for being on the leading edge of the retail scene today."

Andrea Kuch, editor of the Council's magazine, *Canadian Retailing*, assigned a writer to prepare a cover story on the recipient. "George refused to be interviewed altogether and insisted that his PR flack do the job," says Kuch. "We were hardly doing an exposé. The understanding was clear to begin with that he would have approval of the story. Not an intimidating arrangement.

"I had this story delivered to me by an ancient, withered chauffeur, who probably had served the family for about 150 years and may have been the only trusted employee. The guy was pretty scary. He looked like he came out of a Dickens novel. He came creeping into my room, handed me this disk, and said: 'This is the story that is to be run.'

"The story stunk. Big time. It was real bad, I mean PR writing at its absolute worst. It was completely ungrammatical but it came with the instructions that I wasn't allowed to change a comma. Tough task for someone in my business. I was pretty pissed off."

Kuch tried to rally support within the Retail Council for a more professional approach, but no one would back her. "Eaton's was such a cherished member that they couldn't afford to lose them." The puff piece ran in the July/August edition, word for word, as supplied by Eaton's.

More difficult to gloss over was the sales downturn caused by George's pricing strategy. Since specific promotions were not possible, Tom Reid decided to raise the profile of Eaton's itself. Late in 1992 he recruited Darcia Joseph, whose previous experience had been with advertising agencies, for vice-president of marketing. When Joseph was ushered into George's office for the final interview and a lengthy silence ensued, she finally realized she was expected to kickstart the conversation.

Nervous, she blurted: "What's it like to be famous?"

"I don't know," he said. "What's it like not to be famous?"

Despite the exchange, she was hired and soon realized that Eaton's was trapped in a time warp. "You walk into that environment and you walk into 1968. The organization was still the Great Mother Eaton. You never actually addressed people issues, you just moved them around. There was a lot of talent there, but there were also a lot of unguided, lost souls."

Bad strategy though it was, everyday value pricing was not even being carried out consistently. Nobody was too sure what the phrase meant, so some departments would match prices at The Bay, others would try to be 10 per cent below The Bay's regular price, and still others would try to meet the competitor's sale prices. "You have to be efficient to have everyday low pricing," says retail analyst George Hartman, of Dundee Securities Corp., a Toronto investment firm. "Eaton's wasn't efficient."

Reid spent an inordinate amount of money on consultants, much of it to no avail. Ernst & Young did a "change management" study that resulted in Eaton's forking out $12 million for a computer system that few employees used. McKinsey & Co. became the merchandising-idea generator for Eaton's, as if Reid had no confidence in any member of his own executive. A team of McKinsey consultants that numbered several dozen, led by Nora Aufreiter and David Court, spent months on the premises. Fees ran to $15 million.

McKinsey's key recommendation was that Eaton's create a series of "destination" stores. These renovated locations would focus on "softer" goods with high profit margins, such as fashion. The first four stores designated were Erin Mills in Mississauga, Calgary Southgate, Edmonton Millwoods, and Montreal Anjou. Joseph said the executives often wondered: "Can we actually execute this? Will we ever have the cash to pull this off?"

The company was starved for capital. The destination strategy was supposed to produce profitable locations that generated cash for more makeovers. The family seemed unwilling to invest the necessary money. "Their preference was to see if it could be done through more efficient operation as opposed to marketing programs, through more productive use of wages, and that's not just cutting staff, it's increasing productivity per hour," says Peter Saunders.

When a store did undergo a revamp, the approach was often half-baked. Hamilton's Lime Ridge Mall, for example, was known as a "partial." The original plan was to pull out furniture and heavy goods, then build a freestanding store to sell those items. The first part of the plan was executed, but the second location was never built. Annual sales at Lime Ridge fell from $30 million to $25 million.

The destination solution was causing three new problems. First, the designated stores were getting out of popular items that Eaton's had always sold, like candy and toys. While margins might be slim on those lines, their disappearance meant that certain shoppers stopped coming to Eaton's. Every time Eaton's exited another product category, store traffic dropped.

The second problem was that Eaton's was positioning itself to be what's known as a "moderate-to-better" store, aiming for a more upscale consumer than they had attracted in the past. "Every time Eaton's tried to go upscale, they didn't succeed," says retail analyst George Hartman. "There weren't enough wealthy people. There weren't even enough pretty wealthy people."

Third, the McKinsey strategy was focused on twenty suburban stores each with 120,000 square feet. But Eaton's had sixty other stores. Twenty of those were deemed important, but the bottom forty on the list were described in such quaint euphemisms as "freestanding" and "opportunity." "The feeling in those stores was 'What's the use?'" says Marc Newman, who worked for Eaton's from 1978 to 1997, the last twelve years in human resources.

The best money spent on consultants was a $2 million systems-and-logistics project conducted by Arthur Andersen. The Toronto warehouse was a major beneficiary. The warehouse handled all goods for Eaton's stores east of Thunder Bay. Suppliers would ship everything to the warehouse where each box was opened, all contents checked, and, in some cases, price stickers added before the goods were repacked and sent on to individual stores.

In a world where successful retailers such as Wal-Mart either had suppliers ship direct to stores or allowed items to sit only for a matter of minutes on a loading dock, Eaton's handling system was a fossil. At Christmas 1992 the travel time for goods to move from a supplier to an Eaton's store was six weeks. Trucks delivering to the warehouse were backed up, unable to unload, because previous shipments were still stacked inside awaiting action. Once the recommended new system was installed, the pace quickened. By 1994 travel time was down to two weeks.

Even so, Eaton's was light-years behind the competition. For decades all Canadian retailers had hidden behind tariff walls. Following the launch of the Canada-U.S. Free Trade Agreement in 1989, three dozen U.S. retailers invaded Canada, many of them category killers or big-box stores such as Gap, Banana Republic, Talbot's, Starbucks, Home Depot, Sport Authority, Michael's, and Wal-Mart. Grand old names began to disappear. The Bay took over Simpsons in 1991 and Woodward's in 1992. Woolworth closed 240 stores in 1993. Kresge was gone in 1994. Consumers Distributing went into receivership.

"Eaton's response to such trends was to position itself where it has always been — everything to everybody, stuck in the middle in terms of price, merchandise, quality, assortment and service," wrote Donald Thompson, professor of marketing at York University's Schulich School of Business. "Eaton's came to stand for nothing — not the lowest price, not the best depth in merchandise assortment and not the best service." [8]

The only good news came in 1994 when Canada Post issued a stamp to commemorate Eaton's one hundred and twenty-fifth anniversary. The stamp featured Timothy and a montage of items from the past. But those glory days were gone forever; the final downhill slide towards insolvency was about to begin in earnest.

George was presented with a financial statement in January 1995 that was the worst any family member had faced since the dark days of the depression. Behind the honour of the stamp, there was a horror story. Eaton's sales were usually stronger in the run-up to Christmas than at any other time during the year. Such results normally provided the retailer with the necessary revenue to reduce bank operating lines — the short-term loans established to smooth out the peaks and valleys of Eaton's cash-flow needs.

Christmas 1994, however, was a disaster. Consumer spending was far lower than expected. So little money had come in that Eaton's was unable to pay back very much of what it had borrowed. In January, the operating line continued to hover near the $200-million ceiling. The banks wouldn't raise the ceiling so there were no funds available.

George faced a cash flow crunch. Eaton's could not follow the typical pattern and order necessary items for sale in the coming season. He was forced to order a 10 per cent reduction in inventory levels, a step that only made matters worse because that decision drove sales down further. Consumer choice was reduced and shoppers went elsewhere.

Then, in March, George received a very clear, and immediate, warning. Michael Rayfield, executive vice-president of corporate banking at Bank of Montreal, told Eaton's the bank wanted to reduce the line from $200 million to $160 million. The message was unmistakable: Eaton's needed to get its house in order. Instead of heeding the bank's warning, Eaton's decamped, and ended the Bank of Montreal relationship that started with Timothy in St. Marys in the 1860s. Toronto-Dominion, which had backed Eaton's since before the First World War, was joined by a newcomer, the Bank of Nova Scotia.

George was in total denial. "Don't tell me how to run my store," he'd say. "I'll run it any way I want." If he chose to take the ship right onto the rocks, then he damn well would. Even the lighthouse keepers on shore were supposed to be silent. On several occasions consultant John Williams was quoted in the media criticizing Eaton's retailing strategy. George grew increasingly angry and asked Alasdair McKichan, president of the Retail Council of Canada, to tell Williams to back off.

The Council, meant to represent all retailers, was an unlikely route for such a message, but George's clout carried the day. Williams was baffled that McKichan, a man he regarded as a friend, would be so beholden. "It was," says Williams, "a dysfunctional culture."

With sales falling at Eaton's stores across the country, specific locations were losing strong market positions that had taken years to build. In 1989 Eaton's Vancouver Pacific Centre was doing $125 million a year; The Bay's sales were $85 million. Four years later those numbers were reversed. Annual sales at the Toronto Eaton Centre flagship store fell from $150 million to $100 million in the same period.

In addition to poor inventory control and low levels of available goods, staff layoffs meant poor customer service. Shoppers who did manage to find what they sought had trouble locating anyone to take their payment. Employee morale was at an all-time low. "There was a lot of frustration on the part of the staff. There wasn't enough help. They were feeling the pressure of the customer. The amount of emotional energy put into the job was somewhat waning," recalls human resources executive Marc Newman.

Programs meant to involve employees in a search for solutions turned out to be counterproductive. In 1992 George had launched a process called "guaranteed customer service," led by Jeffrey Gandz, head of the MBA program at the University of Western Ontario. Gandz had participated a decade earlier in the turnaround at General Electric under CEO Jack Welch. The transplanted idea was to ask employees in town hall meetings how to improve the business, then have those same employees do what they said needed to be done. In the first year, fifty town hall meetings were held; in the second year, 150.

"We had a very hard time with the second stage of having employees do what they thought they wanted to do," says Fred's son, Fred, Jr., who worked on the program. "A lot of what they wanted to do was quite ambitious. The company wanted to be quite progressive about trying to work with what the employees wanted to do and yet wasn't able to deal with some of the issues."

The project created traffic jams in management and exasperation among employees. The same idea would be proposed in various meetings across the system, so several groups would be established to wrestle with that one thought, thus causing time-wasting duplication. Problems arose when employees suggested new ways of dealing with suppliers who, when contacted by those same employees, were unresponsive to suggestions coming from such low-level personnel.

Referring tough questions up the line didn't seem to help. A matter would eventually reach someone in management for whom that issue was not a priority, so nothing would happen. Only about one-third of the ideas generated by employees were actually carried out, and most of the changes that occurred were modest. "I don't know if it moved us back, but it didn't move us forward," admits Fred, Jr.

Transformation was no easier at the top. Among senior managers, the wrong people occupied some key roles, but even when duds were identified, getting rid of them was a glacial process. George attended a two-day planning session in the Yonge Street office tower and later said to two participants: "You know, I don't think that ——— knows what the hell he's doing. I think he's the wrong guy. We're going to have to do something about that." Replacement of the designated individual took a year.

Other family members were of little help. John Craig's role continued to encompass only public duties, so he continued his personal pursuits and play. Sometimes the two intermingled. In 1982, he had been appointed chairman of the Trillium Foundation to oversee the annual distribution of $15 million a year from Ontario Lottery Corp. to charitable organizations. The foundation's executive director was Sally Farr, a registered nurse with twenty-five years' experience in voluntary services. Sally had previously been married to Dickie Farr, who had not only worked at Eaton's but was the brother of Kitty, John Craig's first wife. Both Dickie Farr and Sally Horsfall, as she was then known, were in the wedding party in 1959 when John Craig and Kitty were married. Dickie and Sally lived in the coach house when Kitty and John Craig lived at 49 Highland Avenue.

By the 1990s John Craig was gearing up for wife number three: Sally. "I guess I knew that there was something going on with John and Sally because he left Sherry on a Thanksgiving weekend," says Kitty, the first wife. "And then Sally left Dickie about two or three months later and I said, 'Uh-oh.' And of course my brother had no clue. He wouldn't have believed me even if I'd told him of what I suspected."

After a while, however, Dickie wised up. "We both sort of think that Sally always was interested in John," says Kitty. "We were a pretty tight little foursome there. She just wanted the lifestyle maybe, and maybe she's in love with him, and maybe she always was."

If only Sherry, the second wife, had known. After the 1976 kidnap attempt on daughter Signy, John Craig and Sherry lived briefly on Ardwold Gate, the housing development on the grounds of Ardwold, the home of John Craig's grandfather. They then moved into the former family home at 120 Dunvegan. (Current owner of 120 Dunvegan is venture capitalist Martin Connell.) John Craig hosted many a dinner meeting for the Trillium board at their Dunvegan residence, and Sherry would join the volunteers for a predinner drink, unaware that her eventual replacement, Sally Farr, was supping under her very roof. John Craig and Sherry were separated in 1986.

John Craig's third wedding caught even their closest friends by surprise. He'd filed for divorce from Sherry in July 1993. On December 8, 1994, he and Sally hosted what had been billed as a 6 p.m. to 8 p.m. reception at their Rosedale home. Guests were still arriving when John Craig rang a spoon against a glass to get everyone's attention and announced: "This is going to come as a bit of a surprise, but Sally and I are going to get married here today. I hope you'll join in the ceremony with us." John Craig was marrying his first wife's brother's ex! He was marrying his kids' Aunt Sally!

A minister was produced, and during the exchange of vows John Craig stumbled over the phrase "to thee all my worldly goods I endow." Laughter rippled across the room; many had heard the rumour that Sherry had received a $30 million divorce settlement. When John Craig flubbed another phrase, Fred called out: "You'd think by now you'd get it right."

Guffaws at his expense did not bother John Craig. "It's very hard to faze John," says friend Peter Eby. "He can sit there and take quite a shelling and never know what happened. He's not oblivious. He's just used to letting things roll off him."

Two ex-wives meant a lifestyle change, even for an Eaton. His Georgian Bay island property was listed for sale in 1997. Built on a bluff looking west, the four-thousand-square-foot main house has seven bedrooms, all with en suite bathrooms. There is also a private bay with docking and a boathouse, as well as two guest cabins, all on fifteen acres. Asking price: $2 million.

"Why are you doing that?" Kitty asked him. "Why don't you just give it to the kids? Sell it to them for a dollar."

Replied John Craig: "I need the money. I have to pay Sherry."

"Well, I always told you not to marry her. She wasn't your type," retorted the first Mrs. Eaton.

The decision to wed under the guise of a reception was so sudden that neither Thor nor George was able to attend. John Craig's eldest, John David, had been told about the wedding the day before, but the other two children, Signy and Henry, learned just that morning.

John David stood up for his father, delivered a brief speech, and gave his father a pitchfork for mucking out the barn. "John David is an Eaton, true and blue," says Kitty. Henry was less pleased about the turn of events. After the ceremony was over, he left.

Henry wasn't the only family member who was miffed. "Quite frankly, I was not amused, shall we say. Me and Queen Victoria," says John Craig's Aunt Florence. "I don't think that's the way to treat a wedding."

Unlike John Craig, for whom retailing holds little interest, Fred might have been able to help halt the downward spiral, but George wouldn't let him. As Fred's three-year term as High Commissioner was coming to an end in July 1994, there were those in the Jean Chrétien government who said Fred might be reappointed even though it had been his Conservative friends who'd picked him and were by then out of office.

Nicky would hear none of it. She missed her children and granddaughter. During their time in London, her father had died, and she'd contracted breast cancer and undergone a mastectomy. "That's when you realize that being a billionaire doesn't matter," says Fred.

Back in Toronto Fred was shocked at the sorry state of Eaton's. "It was changed," he says, "and I was disappointed."

"It was very clear to him that we had not kept pace," says Peter Saunders, who was named COO in 1995. "He was aware that there were issues of not having put money into the company and [competitors] had. The Bay and Sears had already started their renovations. In the three years he had been gone, there was certainly quite a change in the retail environment with power centres having evolved."

Fred was also made to feel like an outsider in the family business. During an interview in April 1995 about executive shuffling at Baton Broadcasting, Fred noted that Douglas Bassett had just been appointed chairman of CTV Television Network Ltd., a position that conferred an elder-statesman status.

When the talk turned to Fred's own function at Eaton's, he admitted his duties as chairman of the executive committee at Eaton's of Canada were hollow. "After I left here and went over to England, I mean, I come back here and I don't have a role. They gave me an office and — if you're talking of elder statesmen — they let me go and talk to the boys and give fatherly advice, that kind of thing."

Like a lot of other empty-nesters, Fred and Nicky downscaled; the Forest Hill mansion was sold in favour of a smaller townhouse in Toronto. But they retained their property in Caledon, with its skeet-shooting facilities, baronial mansion and three-storey entry hall hung with hunting trophies from Fred's safaris to Kenya, Zimbabwe, Zambia, and elsewhere in Africa. (The cost per week of one of Fred's safaris is US $10,000. Accompanied by a friend or his son, he would hunt all day with a professional hunter who carried a backup gun in case of danger. An entourage of eight included trackers, guides, and a chef who prepared meals of antelope and other animals they killed. Half a dozen Land Rovers moved people, tents, and equipment.)

Fred had also invested in a Florida gated community developed by real estate friend Gordon Gray. In 1981 Gray and longtime partner Brian Magee bought 750 acres near Jupiter, twenty minutes north of West Palm Beach, a mile and a half inland from the Atlantic coast. Jack Nicklaus designed the development's eighteen-hole golf course, Loxahatchee, which opened in 1985.

One hundred founder members paid US $75,000 for a golf membership and a building lot. When Magee decided to get out in the late 1980s, the number of partners was increased to six — including Fred — in Restigouche Inc., which owns both Loxahatchee and Maplewood, the residential and commercial community. Fred built a $1.5 million residence that features a swimming pool with a waterfall. Other Canadian Maplewood residents include Conrad Black's brother Monte, Toronto lawyers John Finlay and Jim McCutcheon, former IBM chairman and CEO Lorne Lodge, former Nabisco Brands Ltd. chairman and CEO Jack MacDonald, and investment banker Peter Eby.

Restigouche has been a money pit. "It's not profitable," admits Gray. "It's more a labour of love. You get carried away." Even in 1997, twelve years after opening, Loxahatchee still needed twenty more members to reach its reduced target of 315. Nicklaus, who lives nearby and plays the course regularly, is a perfectionist. That means maintenance costs of $1 million a year. Revamps of holes add a further $1 million annually. Until recently, when revenue from members finally reached the break-even point, Loxahatchee was a drain on the six partners.

Maplewood sales have been slow. The community was only about 60 per cent complete when the recession hit in 1990-91 and buyers dried up. Fred's losses are in the $5 million to $10 million range. "Fred obviously came in, as we all did, at a time when it looked like we would make money," says Gray. "No one could have imagined the downturn. I think we should get our money out, but I doubt there'll be a profit."

Those losses have not crimped Fred's lifestyle. *Brave Wolfe* was sold upon his return from London and a new forty-seven-foot sailboat, *Volunteer*, designed by naval architect Mark Ellis, of Oakville, Ontario, was launched in 1996. *Volunteer* has teak decks and mahogany joiner work, and cost $800,000. There's room in the cockpit for four guests, but the advantage of this design are hydraulic devices that raise or lower the sails so that Fred can sail solo.

Fred chose the name *Volunteer* not only because he liked the rhythm of the word but also because he had spent many hours serving the community, a role his mother had taught him. A good number of Fred's charitable interests overlapped with hers, including York University and the Art Gallery of Ontario, where both served as trustees. Signy was active at the AGO beginning in 1949, Fred since 1968. He served as gallery president from 1984 to 1986.

There were other changes in Fred's life on his return to Canada. After having been rewarded the prime minister's juiciest patronage plum, in 1995 he turned his back on the Progressive Conservative Party to become a fundraiser for Preston Manning's Reform Party of Canada.

"I am still a philosophical conservative," he told Peter C. Newman in a *Maclean's* interview early in February 1997. "But I happen also to be a card-carrying member of the Reform Party. I like what it stands for and I like Preston Manning. People ought to look at the history of who they're dealing with. His father was premier of Alberta for twenty-five years and was never touched by scandal. Ernest Manning was a man of considerable probity and I believe Preston is too. I've chaired a couple of dinners for him and found that when people stop and listen to what he has to say, they agree with him."

For all his efforts, Fred has not been able to garner much support from his establishment friends. In October 1997 he was chairman and master of ceremonies at a $250-a-plate Toronto dinner that featured Preston Manning and drew 450. Few business stars attended. The audience contained the same decidedly middle-of-the-road constituency that already supported Manning. Doug and Susan Bassett were there, but their tickets were paid for by Fred. So was Hal Jackman, but with the exception of Garrett Herman, chairman and chief executive officer of brokerage firm Loewen, Ondaatje, McCutcheon, most other executives fell into the "former" category, such as Jack Leitch, onetime president of Upper Lakes Shipping Ltd., and Dick Sharpe, who had been chairman and CEO of Sears Canada Inc.

Friends and colleagues in the Conservative party were upset at Fred's becoming a turncoat. Barbara McDougall badgered him at a social event, saying: "You were with us in the good times, why not in the bad times?" Fred just laughed at his former boss and told her to join Reform, arguing that the right must unite. Even George has taken a shot at his brother. In 1997 George supported Peter Atkins, who ran for the Progressive Conservatives in the Toronto riding of St. Paul's. In a speech to a meet-the-candidate reception held at a house in Forest Hill, George said: "Some of us Eatons remain loyal."

Of the four boys, Thor continued to be the most detached from the business.

He also faced health problems. He contracted peritonitis in the late 1980s and recently lost partial sight in one eye. In the early 1990s, when Eaton's troubles were well under way, Maple Leaf Gardens occupied much of his time. After owner Harold Ballard died in 1990, several new directors were appointed to the Gardens board, including Rogers Communications Inc. president and CEO Ted Rogers and former vice-chair of Toronto-Dominion Bank Ted McDowell.

Grocery magnate Steve Stavro was positioning himself to take control. He wanted Fred to become a director, but Thor assumed the role. The ensuing battles over ownership were controversial. Said Thor of one of his opponents, in a phrase as colourful as it is typical: "I hate him so much I wouldn't piss on him if he were on fire."

Beyond his horses, Thor was more likely to get caught up in wife Nicky's pursuits than help out with the stores. In 1989 Nicky and Hilary Weston, now lieutenant-governor of Ontario, produced a coffee-table book, *In a Canadian Garden*. They surveyed two hundred gardens across Canada to choose the thirty-five in the book photographed by Freeman Patterson.

Among the gardens featured was Nicky's own, created on the windswept rock face at their Georgian Bay summer home. One of the few patches of earth on the rugged outcropping was turned into a huge perennial border containing 350 daylilies behind a stone retaining wall overhanging the bright blue water near the main dock. The other gardens on the island, including plots producing vegetables and herbs, exist alongside the stately jack pines and birches only because compost and soil were brought in.

According to *Frank* magazine, Nicky's coauthorship arrangement with Hilary almost fell apart in 1994 when the two women were meeting with others involved in the project at the Weston mansion in Forest Hill. Hilary was running late as usual, and Nicky decided to start the meeting before Hilary came downstairs. When Hilary did arrive, she was so incensed at the slight that she turned on her heel and phoned her husband Galen. He berated Nicky over the phone for not showing Hilary the proper deference.

Frank had that part of the story absolutely right. What the gossip sheet did not report was the conversation that occurred later that same day when Galen phoned Thor to smooth ruffled feathers. Putting on his best aristocratic English accent, Galen burbled: "Hello, hello, hello. I hear our lovelies have had a spat." Replied Thor: "Spat? You rude son of a bitch," and hung up. Thor immediately ordered his horses moved out of Weston's Florida stables, where they'd been boarded, and had them trucked elsewhere.

Outraged as he was on Nicky's behalf, Thor was secretly relieved. Weston was marketing an upscale enclave and seaside community called Windsor on four hundred acres in Vero Beach, Florida. "Thank God," Thor confided to a friend, "I've saved two million bucks because now I don't have to buy a lot and build in Windsor." When Nicky and Hilary's second book, *At Home in Canada*, was published in 1995, the ladies were barely speaking. At the launch they held court in separate rooms. [9]

By late 1993 Eaton's marketing vice-president Darcia Joseph had been in her role for a year. From the beginning of her time at Eaton's, she had been hearing the frustrations expressed by merchants who felt their hands were tied by everyday value pricing. Finally she prepared a memo for George recommending that Eaton's move away from that straitjacket and return to a normal promotional schedule. Tom Reid approved her suggestions, but told Joseph to submit the memo directly to George under her own name. If the idea didn't fly, Reid didn't want to be any part of it.

To everyone's surprise, George did an about face on his cherished strategy. Responding a day later in a manner that was almost matter-of-fact, he told Joseph that he'd never intended that his views on everyday value pricing be interpreted as stringently as they had. Any change in direction, however, had to be executed carefully. No one could admit that everyday value pricing hadn't worked, and they certainly couldn't use the s-word. Recalls Joseph: "We had hours of painful discussions about things like whether the word 'clearance' means the same thing as 'sale.'"

The first tentative step back to the old way was to resurrect a former favourite of the midwinter retailing doldrums, an event called "Eaton's Uncrates the Sun." The problem was that no institutional memory seemed to exist about the nuts and bolts required for such an event. Specific items were advertised at 50 per cent off, but the fine print failed to mention exclusions; so customers were demanding and receiving those deep discounts on high-ticket items, like big-screen televisions, that were at regular prices. The promotion was a money-losing disaster, but at least it was a step on the road to normal merchandising methods.

Customers quickly cottoned on to the new strategy. When specials were advertised, sales would be strong for those few days. Once regular pricing returned, so would the dismal numbers. Annual sales totals continued to fall by $100 million each year. After losing a total of $50 million in the 1992-94 period, matters became worse. Eaton's lost $80 million in 1995. The modern-day business was mimicking the store's first passenger elevator in 1886. Like Fenson's "plunger," there would be no stops until the boys reached the bottom.

George took solace from the fact that no customers were phoning him to complain, as if somehow that was proof the strategy was working. He'd pull out the phone book, open it to the page with his home listing, and say: "Look, I'm right there. Customers never call."

As the situation worsened, Tom Reid maintained his optimism while attempting to motivate the executive team and maintain the family's confidence. "He's a very convincing human being," says Joseph. "That's why the company continued to spend money it didn't have. There was this optimistic belief that there was a nirvana solution."

But Reid could also humiliate and belittle. He loved to stir the pot and get fights going among underlings. "He had an ego that was bigger than a bus," says Ray Luft. "I never heard him say anything good about people who weren't in the room. If it was store guys [in the room], the merchants were stupid. If it was merchants, the store guys were stupid. Once in a while he'd get mad and call you all stupid."

George had decided to bring in a new chief operating officer for the T. Eaton Co., but balked at the pricetag he'd have to pay to import outside talent. Rather than bring in any new blood, Peter Saunders, a twenty-three-year employee with a merchandising background, was promoted to replace Reid in 1995.

Perhaps stinking pride was another reason why Eaton's did not hire outside savvy. There were certainly examples where such a strategy worked. In 1992 Sears, Roebuck lost US $2.7 billion, then hired Arthur Martinez, the former Saks Fifth Avenue vice-chairman. Martinez sold nonretail assets, closed more than a hundred stores, fired tens of thousands of employees, and targeted female shoppers aged twenty-five to fifty-four. By 1996 Sears was healthy again, with a U.S. $1.7 billion annual profit.

"It would look like a cop-out if they went out and hired a star. It would become *his* business," says Robin Korthals, who watched the deterioration of Eaton's from his position as president of the Toronto-Dominion Bank from 1981 to 1995. "It's a huge burden for a family to have its name attached to a business. There are two risks. If a member of the family gets into trouble, it rebounds on the firm. Second, if the company underperforms, the family is on a floundering ship."

Fellow retailers were dismissive of the boys' talents as sales lagged and the stores began to look run-down. "They don't spend any time on the selling floor," said menswear retailer Harry Rosen in 1997. "The Eatons walked through their stores with blinders on. They don't want to see those awkward people known as customers." [10]

With Saunders's elevation, Reid was made chief operating officer of the Eaton group of companies, putting him in charge of real estate and credit operations. Fred, Jr., was named as his assistant, a staff role that had been recommended by another of the many management studies that substituted for executive thinking. Reid was no mentor. "I had a difficult relationship with Mr. Reid. We didn't work very closely," says Fred, Jr. "If I worked on it, he didn't work on it. If he worked on it, I didn't work on it. It was a frustrating job."

Saunders brought little fresh thinking to his new role. "He was a bit more like Tom Reid than you really would've liked him to be," says Marc Newman. "He changed a lot when he became COO. He'd always been self-confident, but the frustration of running the whole show — and seemingly nothing ever working — took its toll on him." Neither Reid nor Saunders was an inclusionary leader. "Tom and Peter were primary proponents of a management style that didn't invite conversation or discussion," says Joseph. Once Saunders was promoted, Reid fired Joseph from her $150,000 job, only three years after she'd joined.

An executive management committee was created, and a more awkward arrangement for day-to-day operations is hard to imagine. Members included Saunders, George, chief financial officer John Anderson, and Dale Brewster, who was head of credit. Fred and Allan Beattie were ex officio members.

George oversaw a store-renovation plan, dubbed Eaton 2000, that called for the expenditure of $300 million over five years. But the losses had increased debt and there was insufficient cash to service the debt and pay for all those upgrades, so in June 1995 Eaton's put its real estate up for sale to raise money. Such a sell-off was a tragedy. The family's wealth had been for decades tied to real estate as much as retailing. Now the boys decided to dump prize assets at the bottom end of the real estate cycle. In the late 1980s, the portfolio, which included interests in twenty-five shopping malls across Canada, might have been worth $1 billion, but by 1995 real estate values had fallen by as much as three-quarters. The family had never sold property in this manner before, but over the next eighteen months, Eaton's raised $286 million through asset sales and used $198 million of that to pay down debt. Sold were Pacific Centre Ltd., Peterborough Square, Midtown Plaza, Le Carrefour

Laval, Les Promenades St-Bruno, Les Galeries de la Capitale, Carrefour de l'Estrie, Calgary Northland and Calgary Eaton Centre, Winnipeg's St. Vital Centre, and Victoria Eaton Centre.

In 1995 everyday value pricing was officially and finally dumped. A sixty-second self-mocking television spot about the fiasco featured a man saying: "Just to prove Eaton's does have sales, we're having a sale." Inexplicably he was shown standing in an empty warehouse. Perhaps that image was intended to represent the ten thousand jobs — about 40 per cent of the staff on hand at the beginning of the decade — that had been cut during the 1990s to reduce payroll costs. Eaton's hired Cape Breton grunge fiddler Ashley MacIsaac in a misguided attempt to woo younger shoppers. Shortly after signing the contract with Eaton's, MacIsaac admitted in a magazine interview that he liked unconventional sex. The Bay was using squeaky-clean Anne Murray and megastar Céline Dion.

For George, the end was nigh. The economy was still slow and the money-losing retail arm could no longer be supported by real estate sales and profits from Eaton Credit Corp. At this rate, all assets would soon be gone, drained away by the sinkhole the stores had become. One-third of the chain's eighty-five stores were losing money.

Then, in November 1996, there was one final turn of the screw by Scotia-bank and TD when Eaton's $200 million line of credit came up for annual discussion and renewal. Eaton's chief financial officer John Anderson and accountant Hap Stephen, from Ernst & Young, asked TD vice-president Paul Douglas and Scotiabank executive vice-president Dennis Belcher for an increase to $300 million.

In the months leading up to Christmas the banks had allowed Eaton's operating line to bulge to $250 million as a way of covering costs of seasonal inventory. Eaton's wanted to have that kind of money available on an ongoing basis without feeling the pressure of the banks, but the lenders were becoming uncomfortable. Losses were mounting and the banks had no security on money Eaton's already owed. Eaton's agreed that real estate could be used as collateral, but balked at the banks' demands to use inventory as security, too. Pledging goods could upset suppliers, who would assume that Eaton's was in trouble and stop shipping.

By Christmas there had been little progress toward new banking arrangements. Eaton's was beginning to see the two banks as unlikely partners in any business resurrection and began to consider a total restructuring of its finances. "The conclusion was that it was not going to work," says Hap Stephen.

"The company would not survive. It would have got weaker." The unprofitable stores were not only draining cash resources, but also stood in the way of finding a buyer or outside investor. "We didn't think that people would be attracted with an unrationalized chain," says George.

As negotiations with the banks stalled, both Stephen and Eaton's lawyer Chris Portner of Osler, Hoskin & Harcourt, began discussing alternative restructuring solutions. The two most likely were the Companies' Creditors Arrangement Act (CCAA) or the even blunter Bankruptcy and Insolvency Act (BIA).

"The family was initially aghast at the concept of actually having to go and do this sort of thing publicly and have the world scrutinize everything that was transpiring — not for want of disclosure, but just simply because this was not something they ever conceived of as eventually having to be necessary," says Portner. "And, of course, it then becomes a carcass at which dozens and dozens if not hundreds of people rip very savagely to try and achieve either commercial opportunity or protection of an interest."

In January the banks softened. They waived their demand for security on inventory and agreed to lend $360 million. Eaton's argued that that amount was at least $100 million short of what was needed. "Workouts are fundamentally objectionable to people on the receiving end of our advice," said Scotiabank's Belcher, "often because it's the first time in their lives that they're not in control and they have to listen to other people. Sometimes there's a fine line between being businessman of the century and being a goat." [11]

George had no desire to be the goat. CCAA and BIA were now debated in earnest. CCAA offered the advantage of a "stay" period to work with creditors, including landlords. BIA was more powerful and would have allowed Eaton's to cancel leases immediately. On February 5 Eaton's launched a parallel game. While talks with the banks continued, other lenders were invited to bid on a new financing deal. The original code name used by Ernst & Young for the restructuring Eaton's had in mind was Project Renaissance. With the change in tactics, Eaton's decided that a better name was Project Beaver.

Despite that patriotic ring, the potential new players included two American firms, GE Capital and Citibank, and only one Canadian possibility, Royal Bank of Canada. For Hap Stephen, GE Capital was a natural choice. In 1995, when Stephen was the court-appointed monitor for a restructuring by Dylex Ltd., GE Capital had supplied the funding.

The three parties were told that the firm coming up with the best deal first would win the business. They were further informed that negotiations were continuing with TD and Scotiabank, although the two banks were never told that the ground had shifted. Three weeks later a $555 million refinancing proposal from GE Capital had been proposed and accepted.

With new deep-pockets backers aboard, the boys concluded that same day, February 26, 1997, that they would seek court protection under CCAA. After 128 years of privacy, the unthinkable had suddenly become inevitable. Eaton's was not only insolvent but would have to make that frank admission to the world. "You don't rush to that outcome. That's what you do when you feel that you really have come to the end of your rope and still have enough strength in your organization to restructure," says George. "We obviously tried to turn it around without using that strong a measure and perhaps we should have been trying alternatives earlier.

"There is a realization process that you go through that that is the best route. It's not easy. There was some strong soul-searching and a real period of discomfort for all of us [in the family] as we went through that, then a recognition of the magnitude of the challenge and an absolute determination to carry it out as best we could."

On the morning of February 27, 1997, with the court appearance scheduled before Ontario Court Justice Lloyd Houlden for later that day, Scotiabank's Belcher and TD's Douglas were informed that they'd been scooped by GE Capital. The two banks, owed a total of $168 million, were irate. "We had been advised that this filing was not going to be made. It turns out that we were misled," Charles Scott, of Tory, Tory, DesLauriers & Binnington, who acted for Scotiabank, told the court. The banks were angry not just because they lost the business, but also because they were left stranded with unsecured loans. Scotiabank chairman and CEO Peter Godsoe was particularly miffed; he'd regarded himself as a close friend of the family.

"Eaton's has come before me today and requested the protection of the court," said Houlden to the bank's lawyer. "The company has been around for more than one hundred years, it's got thousands of employees in dozens of communities, and I want to see it succeed. So, unless your client wants to bankrupt the company today, I'm going to do what they've asked me to do."

Houlden granted the T. Eaton Co. Ltd. protection under the Companies' Creditors Arrangement Act and gave Eaton's until June 15 to draft a restructuring plan. "We didn't get into trouble because we did a lot of things right," says Peter Saunders. "People who do things right don't get into trouble." It wasn't bankruptcy, but it sure was close.

CHAPTER THIRTEEN

SUNSET ON THE EMPIRE

—

GEORGE EATON ARRIVED FOR THE EARLY-evening press conference at a Toronto hotel on February 27, 1997, and blinked as the strobe lights from a dozen cameras revealed his grim demeanour. He looked somewhat baffled, like a hedgehog newly awakened from a long winter's nap, and not at all happy to be on hand.

Little wonder. The Eatons had enjoyed four generations as the most private of families, and now one of them was about to confess his sins on live television before the nation. George was the only one of the four boys present. The official explanation was that the other three were busy visiting the stores, reassuring the staff. Or maybe they were just letting George have this moment alone to explain the inexplicable.

A two-inch-thick binder filed with the Ontario Court of Justice (General Division) that afternoon detailed the failings of the family's business acumen in excruciating detail. "The applicants," said a sworn affidavit, "are insolvent." With those four words, Eaton's admitted the unthinkable. They couldn't pay their bills. Two banks were owed $160 million and 4200 suppliers were owed $170 million.

During the previous five years, annual sales in the eighty-five-store chain had fallen from $2.1 billion to $1.6 billion — about the same level as twenty years earlier. The stores had lost $250 million during the same five-period period. Only one-third of the stores were profitable, another third were barely breaking even, and one-third were losing money. Intercompany debt was

$224 million. When one arm borrows from another in an attempt to use the same money in two places at once, that's a sure sign of trouble.

The photographers were shooed away, George moved behind the podium, and began with his best news. "Eaton's is open for business, so come on in and shop with us. All customer policies and services are in effect, including our famous guarantee: Goods satisfactory or money refunded."

In addition to the media, the audience included a smattering of suppliers worried about their money and a pride of investment bankers sniffing for work. The ensuing questions only confirmed the family's primal fear about the press. Three times during the twenty-two-minute question session that followed the brief opening statement, George was asked what his great-grandfather Timothy Eaton, dead for ninety years, would think. The first two times his reply was identical: "He'd be as disappointed as we all are. It's very tough." The third time the question was put, a journalist, desperate for some show of emotion, foolishly implored: "Could you cry?" George did not.

For all his reluctance about public appearances, George had previously shown a capacity to sell his own wares. There was an evening in the mid-1980s when he lay prone on the quarry-tile floor of Fenton's, a fashionable downtown Toronto restaurant. A chic woman knelt at his side, running her hands back and forth over the length of his body, never touching him, always staying two inches away. When asked what she was doing, she replied: "Feeling his aura."

A patron, unaware at first whose aura it was, called a waiter over and said: "If that man's dead, I'll give you $5 for his tie." Within two minutes a grinning George appeared at the patron's table, collar button undone, a red-and-black-striped silk tie draped over his hand. Why let someone else sell his goods? An Eaton always closed a deal himself. On this day in February 1997, however, the family at last cried out for help.

The Eaton boys were not alone. Many other grand old Canadian families had lost their businesses: the jewellery Birks, the grocery Steinbergs, the eyewear Hermants, the newspaper Southams.

"Companies become big and then they usually become bloated and then they usually become dinosaurs," says Michael Bliss, professor of Canadian history at the University of Toronto. "They either learn to slim down and become mobile or they get destroyed. Individuals come and go. Families come and go. Some do a better job of surviving than others.

"The Eaton family was extraordinary in its survivability. There used to be two exceptions in Canada to the notion 'shirtsleeves to shirtsleeves in three generations.' One was the Masseys and the other was the Eatons. In the 1960s and 1970s Massey went down. The Eaton firm simply lost its competitive zeal and began to stagnate. It went the way of people who don't stay up in the competitive system," says Bliss.

At the press conference George offered plenty of excuses. "First, there was an economic contraction at the end of the eighties and early nineties. There were new entrants in the marketplace which were very aggressive that impacted on [market] share. We also moved into a strategy of 'everyday value pricing' which did not work and we stayed with it longer than we should have. It did not appeal. I would have thought it would, but I was wrong. I accept responsibility as the prime motivator. I guess [shoppers] like the chase of the sale and the hunt."

In response to a question George admitted that Eaton's would have been wise to go public in 1988 when the stores were profitable and Eaton's market share had clambered back up to 22 per cent. Yet throughout the 1970s and 1980s the family had stoutly insisted on staying private. Peter Eby, the investment banker who took Baton Broadcasting public in 1971, regularly recommended they take the retail chain public, but engendered no interest.

"Fred told me at one point they'd never go public," says Eby, who quotes Fred as saying: " 'Even if it was the right thing to do, do you think my brothers and I are going to be responsible for ending the legacy? I don't think so.' "

"That was the attitude, that there was almost a higher calling than pure dollars and cents," adds Eby. "But business has changed. It's dog eat dog."

During the weekend that followed the Thursday press conference a television ad showed George standing beside Timothy's statue. He thanked Canadians for their support, told them to come in and shop, then rubbed the toe of his great-grandfather's left boot for luck.

Commentary about Eaton's insolvency was lethal, far from the nostalgic nattering that greeted the catalogue's closure two decades earlier. "Eaton's a national icon? You must be joking," railed hotline host Rafe Mair in the Vancouver *Courier*. "If ever there were a department store of choice in this town it was David Spencer & Co. When Eaton's bought out Spencer it was, to my sainted grandmother (who, being a Cape Breton Islander, had her own Toronto axes to grind) . . . an outrage. She never set foot inside the Spencer's-cum-Eaton's store again and I must confess I have only rarely." Eaton's, said Mair, was "probably the worst employer of white-collar workers in Canada. If it spent as much on employees as it did on union-busting, it might be thriving today."

In the Montreal *Gazette*, snide editorializing crept into the news report.

Under a page-one headline "Eaton's facing huge cuts," the first sentence read: "The fat English ladies are clearing their throats at the T. Eaton Co. Ltd." The stinging reference embraced not just a well-worn figure of speech transported from opera to sports ("It ain't over until the fat lady sings"), but it was also an allusion to the fact that many Quebecers still regarded Eaton's as a throwback with English-only service. In 1989 Quebec Industry Minister Pierre MacDonald had complained that some of his colleagues were "fed up with going to Eaton's and being served by a big, fat, damned English lady who doesn't know a word of French." (The *Gazette* ran a page-one apology the next day for what was termed an "inappropriate lead" sentence.)

Eaton's became the butt of jokes. Toronto radio station CHFI announced a top ten list of ways to know Eaton's was closing. Among them, new advertising tag lines such as: "We want to be your store, and for a small down payment, we can be." Another was: "Goods satisfactory until next week." A further indication of trouble at Eaton's: "You're met by a Wal-Mart greeter." But the number-one reason your local Eaton's was closing: "You didn't know you had one."

⟶

The clock on the federal building in downtown Brantford, Ontario, strikes eleven even though the hands say quarter-past. Everything's a little out of kilter in the Telephone City, where the federal building was erected in 1919. A block away, Eaton Market Square lasted but a blink by comparison, only fifteen years. Eaton's, Shoppers Drug Mart, and a branch of National Trust are the only national retailers in the mall. The rest are locally owned outlets like Crazy Lee's, Everything for a Dollar Store, and Value Furniture. Of the ten stores near the main entrance of the Eaton's store, half are vacant. The only merchant thriving in Eaton Market Square seems to be a tough-looking dude in his late thirties who's moving a lot of small packets into the hands of passing youths.

The semiannual Trans-Canada Sale is billed outside Eaton's as "the one and only," but inside, at least three other promotions are under way. Signs also announce "Eaton's Uncrates the Sun '97" with 25 per cent off fashion; banners and balloons identify today's "Surprise Sale" with 50 per cent off specific items; and there's a buy-six-get-one-free deal on children's clothing. Despite all the razzmatazz, by actual count there are but ten shoppers sprinkled throughout the two floors of Eaton's on this sunny spring morning.

The Brantford Eaton's is poised at the halfway point between February 1997 when George Eaton admitted insolvency and June 1997 when it is scheduled to close. The fifty employees seem to have given up. On the office reception counter are two bowls, one marked "positive thoughts," the other labelled "negative thoughts." Both bowls are empty. So's the office. The manager and his assistant are away for the day.

Brantford is one of twenty-one money-losing stores that will close over the next twelve months. Stores in Brantford, Sarnia, Guelph, and Peterborough were all opened in the early 1980s as part of a wrong-headed Ontario-government experiment that drew Eaton's in to help revitalize downtown urban cores that had been disembowelled by suburban malls. The idea was a miserable failure, another situation where Eaton's paid little heed to the fact that there was no business case to the strategy it decided to follow. The four cities still owe almost $40 million because loan repayment was to be based on profits that never materialized.

In downtown Sarnia, the scene is sadly similar to Brantford. The four stores beside Eaton's in Bayside Mall are vacant. "We're trying to keep positive," says manager Nadine Lasenby. Each day she's conducted a ten-minute meeting with her fifty employees to buck them up, but she's feeling a bit blue herself. She just joined Eaton's the previous fall, after twenty years elsewhere in retail, and this location is closing at the end of June.

George's announcement shocked Ron Longo, too. He and his brother Lou bought Bayside Mall two months earlier from developer Cadillac Fairview. "Downtown locations are tough," says Longo. "They haven't changed with the times. It wasn't no secret by no means that Eaton's was in financial difficulties." Still, Longo would like to have known that Eaton's would be closing its Bayside Mall location. Almost one-third of the eighty-four retail units in the mall are already empty. When Eaton's departs, vacant space will triple to 130,000 square feet — half the space available to lease. "We would have gone through with the sale," sighs Longo, "but we would have bargained a lot harder."

A mere thirty minutes farther west in Troy, Michigan, a retail complex called the Somerset Collection is not just in a different country, it's in a different world. This is what Eaton's could have been but never was. At 10 a.m. Nordstrom has just opened its doors and Millicent Leigh Schneider is at the keyboard of a Steinway baby grand playing "Somewhere over the Rainbow."

Somerset does seem like the pot of gold at the rainbow's end. Imagine a huge H with the middle bar of the letter a seven-hundred-foot enclosed "skywalk" linking two giant malls. On the south arm of the H are department stores Saks Fifth Avenue and Neiman Marcus; on the north arm are Nordstrom and Hudson's. In addition to the four anchors, Somerset Collection contains 181 stores, 1.5 million square feet of vaulted gallerias with skylights, palm trees, nineteen restaurants, six thousand employees, parking for seven thousand cars, and sales of US $450 a square foot.

Shoppers look as if they've spent time at home getting dressed especially for the outing. Prestigious retailers abound: Liz Claiborne, Ann Taylor, Burberry's, Laura Ashley, The Disney Store, Waldenbooks, Crate & Barrel, The Limited, Tiffany & Co., Mont Blanc, Henri Bendel, Abercrombie & Fitch, Polo/Ralph Lauren, Gucci, FAO Schwarz, Brooks Brothers, Rodier Paris. Even the restaurant, the Capital Grille, boggles the mind as it empties the wallet. A menu the size of Prince Edward Island contains prices to match. Beluga caviar is $39.95, a 24-oz. dry-aged porterhouse is $27.95. There are a dozen ports and as many cognacs available by the glass.

Beginning at 7 a.m., three hours before the stores open, all the public spaces are alive with people — squads of seniors, a bevy of boomers, chatty mothers pushing tots in strollers — all members of the year-round "Walkabout Club." Wednesdays is for frequent walkers. The concierge punches membership tickets for credit toward a free gift after ten strolls. Once the day's exercise is concluded, participants can linger for a cappuccino, a manicure, or a new pair of shoes. Welcome to retailing, American-style. And this ain't South Beach or Scottsdale or Rodeo Drive. This is Troy, Michigan.

Canadians exposed to the glitzy world of American supermalls feel like goods-starved East Germans encountering the bounty of the West after the 1989 fall of the Berlin Wall. If Eaton's had copied such savoir faire from the United States instead of everyday value pricing, maybe, just maybe, Canadian shoppers would have responded.

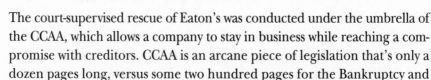

The court-supervised rescue of Eaton's was conducted under the umbrella of the CCAA, which allows a company to stay in business while reaching a compromise with creditors. CCAA is an arcane piece of legislation that's only a dozen pages long, versus some two hundred pages for the Bankruptcy and Insolvency Act, thus giving judges flexibility to approve any deal that the company and creditors negotiate. Even the time available is flexible. Eaton's was initially given until mid-June 1997 to come up with a plan, then obtained a sixty-day extension to mid-August.

But should Eaton's really have been able to use CCAA and obtain the help of the court in this belated attempt to repair mistakes and catch up to the competition? In January 1996, just thirteen months before the desperation filing, the boys seemed to have access to plenty of funds when they announced they would buy all the shares in Baton Broadcasting they didn't already own. The offer to shareholders would, if accepted, have cost the family $166 million. Some large shareholders of Baton, notably Ontario Municipal Employees Retirement Board and Ontario Hydro pension plan, refused to tender. Because the Eaton boys needed, but did not receive, commitments totalling 90 per cent of the shares, the offer expired.

The Eaton boys were also active on other financial fronts. They were smart enough to take care of themselves. T. Eaton Co. had paid Eaton's of Canada a $10 million dividend on November 8, 1996, the same year the ailing company lost $120 million. After the payment was revealed in the February 1997 court filings, it was voluntarily returned on March 10, 1997.

The two creditor banks, Scotia and TD, demanded an investigation to flush out any other such unusual transactions. On March 10 the court appointed KPMG Inc. to conduct a study that was supposed to report in four weeks but took more than three months. By the time the results were available at the end of June, the information was far too late to be of any use.

The report disclosed a series of convoluted intercompany transactions. Among the most interesting was the January 29, 1990, sale by T. Eaton Co. (TECO) of T. Eaton Acceptance Co. Ltd. (TEAC) to Eaton Credit Corporation (ECC). In payment TECO received preferred shares in ECC, then ECC redeemed the shares by issuing a demand note for $200 million.

That amount, $200 million, was not the product of any impartial, fair-market evaluation. It was a number arrived at in May 1988 by Tom Reid, then vice-president of finance at TECO, an amount that the report said "may have been excessive."[1] Intercompany shuffles followed, then there was a partial repayment of the loan in 1994. Dividends flowing from the shares were paid to Eaton's of Canada (EOC), then were lent back to TECO. KPMG concluded that TECO — remember, this is the same entity that was declared insolvent in 1997 — lost $78 million as a result of all this paper shuffling.

Throughout the 1990s TECO managed all cash resources for the Eaton Group and paid the majority of expenses incurred — including management fees for EOC, the family holding company. EOC management fees charged to

TECO in the two years prior to TECO's insolvency totalled $8.8 million. "Did TECO receive fair-market value for the management fees charged to TECO by EOC?" asked the report. Despite its court-appointed clout, KPMG could not discover the answer. "We have requested specific details of the management services provided, including the persons involved, but such details have not been supplied." [2] The report urged that the court do a further review of management fees, as well as "the allocation of other expenses between the various entities," but there was no follow-up.

The two creditor banks didn't wait around for KPMG's findings. On March 26 they sold the $160 million debt Eaton's owed them to a vulture fund led by Bear Stearns & Co. Inc. of New York for about ninety-one cents on every dollar owed. The banks had decided to cut their losses and let the vulture funds try to extract full repayment of one hundred cents on the dollar. Many of Eaton's former suppliers and trade creditors were equally quick to sell to other vulture funds.

The Eaton boys could now no longer negotiate a deal through the courts and pay back creditors at, say, sixty cents on the dollar as often happens in CCAA proceedings. The vulture funds weren't interested in such measly returns. They needed the full one hundred cents on the dollar to cover their purchase costs and provide a quick profit.

But where would Eaton's raise such a sum? Real estate was worth perhaps $150 million, and Eaton Credit could be sold for $100 million. The rest would have to come from selling all or part of the retail chain, but what was it worth? Sales were $1.6 billion, but the stores were losing money so any value in the enterprise could only be realized after several years of improved balance sheets.

The other choice would be for the vulture funds to share ownership in T. Eaton Co. with the boys. A new CEO could be installed, given a lucrative incentive package, and all the partners, including the vulture funds, would benefit from any turnaround. Even if this was successful, such a process might take two years or longer. Vulture funds prefer quick payouts that involve no ownership duties.

By May George had come to realize that he should step down as CEO and hire someone with retail experience to replace him. The searchlight very quickly fell on George Kosich. He seemed perfect for the job. At sixty-two, the president and CEO of Hudson's Bay Co. was preparing to retire. He'd put his Toronto house on the market, planned to move to British Columbia, and teach at the University of British Columbia. In 1985, when Don McGiverin's career at The Bay was over, two executives had been promoted to take his place: Iain Ronald at Zeller's and George Kosich at The Bay. Both companies saw improved results. Drastic action had included selling the Northern Stores Division and the fur-sale business, the very foundations on which the centuries-old firm had been built.

In 1987 Kosich was named president of Hudson's Bay Co. and oversaw a downsizing at The Bay and Zeller's that was so bloody he was called Carnage Kosich. He slashed middle management, centralized buying, upgraded computer technology, and refurbished stores. "He surpassed Eaton's, starting from a weak position," says retail analyst George Hartman. "Eaton's was way behind on logistics, systems, and store appearance."

In the ten years Kosich was president sales grew from $4 billion to $6 billion. During the same period the market value of Hudson's Bay, a public company, tripled to $1.5 billion. After a while, however, the boost he gave to The Bay began to dissipate. Wal-Mart arrived in 1994 and by 1996 had become the biggest retailer in Canada with a 24 per cent share of the department-store market. Zeller's was in second place at 23 per cent, Sears had 18 per cent, The Bay 15 per cent, and Eaton's was mired in fifth place with 12 per cent and falling.

"He's a very good store merchant. From that point of view, he is probably a good transition person. At least he understands store operations. He's also tough-minded enough to make decisions," says Stan Shortt, who saw Kosich in action at The Bay. But Shortt also sees a weakness; Kosich is no team player. "George is very controlling. An awful lot of people who work for him don't have the freedom of decisions that they could have under a different kind of leadership."

It was to this saviour that Eaton's turned. On June 5 George Kosich, who four days before had retired from The Bay, was named president and CEO of T. Eaton Co. Ltd. George Eaton was openly relieved. The appointment, he said, "leaves me more time for fishing." For Kosich, the leap was lucrative. The Bay had given him a departure package that paid $1 million a year, plus benefits, until August 1999. He also cashed in $3.6 million in stock options. Foolishly his former employer did not have Kosich sign a no-compete clause, so he was free to go to Eaton's for a signing bonus of $1.25 million and an annual base salary of $1 million.

During a visit to the Montreal store, Kosich revealed the depths of his concerns about Eaton's. He said that the strategy of selling real estate and closing stores reminded him of a scene from Jules Verne's *Around the World in Eighty Days.* In the novel a ship departs from Japan and reaches its destination only by burning everything on board, from furniture to the rigging. "By the time it gets to

San Francisco, it's one big furnace," he said. "I wonder if that might be the fate of a company that sells off some of its best assets to keep the company afloat." [3]

Yet the sales continued. Among the deck chairs the Eaton boys sold that summer was their 10 per cent interest in Desjardins-Laurentian Financial Corp., the last gasp of the financial-services business launched more than twenty-five years earlier. The sale realized $68 million. Sold, too, was the Eaton Tower — complete with George's unused helipad. Cadillac Fairview paid $40 million for Eaton's 60 per cent stake. Some asset sales were for specific purposes, not general corporate health and well-being. Proceeds from Eaton's 20 per cent stake in the Toronto Eaton Centre were used to help create a $50 million defence fund for George and the other directors in the event of lawsuits arising from the insolvency.

But the highest octane fuel for the good ship Eaton's demanding boilers came from the company pension funds. All company pension funds are supervised by actuaries who make assumptions about employee mortality, disability rates, spousal survival, turnover, and future salary increases. Those assumptions usually err on the conservative side; in most cases, less is paid out to recipients than was originally predicted and a growing surplus is the result.

When Eaton's declared insolvency, initial financial information showed pension surpluses of $284 million. Eaton's had already been nibbling at a smaller fund for executives, the Eaton's Superannuation Plan (ESP), and had drawn out $6 million. Approval by ESP members was not required. Tapping into the larger Eaton Retirement Annuity Plan (ERAP) was a different matter. That would need approval by the fourteen thousand participants.

Susan Rowland, of the Toronto law firm Koskie Minsky, helped provide the key that unlocked the vault. Just prior to the CCAA announcement, Marc Newman, an Eaton's human-resources officer who'd been let go, had retained Koskie Minsky on his own behalf because he was concerned about his benefits. Within hours of the CCAA filing, Rowland correctly analyzed what happened and realized there was potential for her firm to become more involved in the proceedings, so she scrutinized the court documents and financial statements. "I kept shaking my head and saying, 'There's no insolvency here.' What they had was a cash-flow crunch. I figured something had happened with the banks. Somebody had tried to tell the Eatons how to run their business. Sometimes the arrogance of individual bankers can really put businesses off. My guess was that George and the bankers had been like oil and water. The bankers had demanded extra security and George had said, 'Pee up a rope.' As a result, the CCAA filing had happened."

During the previous two decades, Rowland had been involved in many major corporate bankruptcies. She had worked at the Pension Commission of Ontario, the Ministry of Labour, and been counsel to employees in high-profile liquidations such as the 1994 collapse of Confederation Life Insurance Co. The day after the CCAA filing, Rowland called Hap Stephen, of Ernst & Young, who'd been appointed by the court to oversee the rescue operation. Thinking she must still be with the Ministry of Labour, he came on the phone and said: "We've paid all the wages, there's no problem."

"I've got something better for you," she said. "How interested are you in doing a pension deal? I'll bet you want to get your hands on it and so would the employees."

"Well, you can appreciate we've been over the pension plan left, right, and centre, but we can't figure out how to do that."

"I know how," Rowland said. "Are you interested in doing a deal?"

"I'll have to talk to everybody, but I'll certainly be interested in whatever you have to say."

Surplus-sharing arrangements involving insolvent companies are not easy. Deals take years while pensioners die off. Ontario legislation was changed in 1991 to encourage such agreements, but never had employees come to an understanding with a company that continued in business.

To spread the word among ERAP pensioners and sign them up, Koskie Minsky conducted meetings in church basements, legion halls, and hotel meeting rooms across the country. Those sessions, plus a telephone campaign by former employees, brought together three thousand pensioners by the end of March. It was a surprisingly large number, given Eaton's paternalistic legacy. "The anti-union animus is so strong that the store managers were trying to discourage us even though it was to the Eaton family advantage," says Rowland.

Typical of those ERAP members who came out to the meetings was a Hamilton woman who'd worked at Eaton's for fifty-two years and received a monthly pension of only $21.40. She approached Rowland after the information session and said: "Now, what you're going to do, it's not going to hurt the Eatons, is it? Because if it does, I won't have any part of it."

At the end of April, Koskie Minsky was officially appointed by the court to represent members of ERAP. Two weeks later Eaton's and the pensioners had agreed in principle to a fifty-fifty split that still left a surplus in ERAP for future beneficiaries. The final agreement was okayed on September 12. Not only had the two sides agreed to do something that had never been done before, they'd taken far less time to do it than in situations where a company was liquidated.

For example, after Confederation Life was seized by the federal government in 1994, the surplus-sharing agreement took more than three years. Moreover, the amounts both sides received were far beyond initial expectations. Eaton's got $208 million; the pensioners $237 million. The minimum payment for an ERAP member was $1500, although some long-service individuals received more than $100,000. The average was $11,000. Three hundred former and active Eaton's managers and company directors, who were in Eaton's Superannuation Plan (ESP), split $49 million, or an average of $160,000 each.

For someone like Eaton's human-resources executive Marc Newman, declared redundant in 1997, the deal made a huge difference. After nineteen years with Eaton's, the forty-one-year-old Newman had been offered a lump-sum pension settlement of $83,000. With the pension-sharing agreement, his lump-sum payout tripled to $246,000.

Since the insolvency crisis became public, Eaton's had been approached by American retailers such as Federated, Dillard's, May Co., and JC Penney. The Eaton boys flirted with the possibility of selling the firm, but interested parties wanted only the two dozen trophy locations that were profitable. Eaton's would have been left with the dregs. Four possible Canadian buyers were not interested in much more: Sears; a group led by Joe Segal, former chairman of Zellers Inc.; Caisse de dépôt et placement du Québec, the Quebec public pension fund; and Dundee Bancorp Inc., a Toronto merchant bank. None of the talks got very far. The windfall pension deal was like winning the lottery and provided almost half the money the family needed to pay off creditors. Emboldened by this turn of affairs, the family decided to pay off the vultures and remain 100 per cent owners. The paupers were princes again.

There were two U.S. vulture funds to deal with, one led by Bear Stearns, which represented the former bank debt, the other, Rothschild Asset Management, which represented the trade creditors.

In mid-July, Toronto-based investment banker Nesbitt Burns Inc. and law firm Fasken, Campbell, Godfrey, advisers to the vulture fund led by Bear Stearns, proposed a restructuring plan. The negotiating strategy was simple: make the Eaton boys believe that the vultures wanted to own the company. That outcome was the one the family feared the most.

The proposal to Eaton's saw the Bear Stearns group fare far better than the trade creditors. For every dollar the trade creditors were repaid, the Bear Stearns group wanted $1.60. The counterproposal by Eaton's was even more generous. Rather than the $1.60-to-$1 ratio, the Bear Stearns group would get $3.50 for every dollar paid the trade creditors. "It was extraordinary from our perspective," says a source close to the negotiations. "We were at a loss to explain it. We puzzled about it and could only assume the company knew what they were doing." Despite their mystification, the Bear Stearns group did what any good negotiator would do: they asked for more. They demanded more cash up front, better security, and improved covenants.

By August Wilbur Ross of Rothschild Asset Management, New York, joined the game and began negotiating in public on behalf of trade creditors who'd sold their debt to other vulture funds. "One hundred cents on the dollar — that's our mantra."

For once, Eaton's had a plan. They were willing to pay both vulture funds whatever it took and now had the money to do it. The busy fall retailing season was fast approaching. If consumers were going to be convinced that Eaton's was there for the long haul and if suppliers were going to believe Eaton's could order and pay for goods, Eaton's had to have a plan by mid-August.

———

The loyal Eatonians pour off the down escalator in the atrium of the Toronto Eaton Centre on August 15, 1997. Another cadre of stalwarts spills from the up escalator arriving from a lower level. A six-piece Dixieland band tootles the Bobby Gimby theme "Ca-na-da" as the two human tributaries converge. Everyone is carrying white placards bearing the names of different store locations and the slogan "We've got the plan."

Within minutes several hundred employees, flown in from every store across the country, have filled the atrium and are chanting: "Eaton's, Eaton's, we've got the plan." On the raised stage, flags of the provinces and territories flank the Canadian flag and the Eaton's flag with its white background and red-and-black stripes. There's a lineup of Eaton's executives, plus three of the four brothers, John Craig, Fred, and George. Thor is absent. Everyone from executive to employee is wearing a blue-and-gold lapel button bearing the phrase of the day. The sign bouncing nearest to John Craig bears the name of the store in Guelph, one of those set to close in February 1998. These loyal Eatonians seem thrilled to be invited to dance on their own graves.

Around the edge of the throng stand some keenly interested participants: Hap Stephen, the court-appointed monitor overseeing the restructuring; Tom Long, the headhunter who recruited George Kosich two months earlier as new CEO; Douglas Bassett, longtime family friend who lunched that day at the Toronto Club with Fred, Sr., and Fred, Jr.; Tom MacMillan, public relations strategist and former political organizer who conceived the day's theatrics. And, wandering lonely as a cloud, John David Eaton II, son of John Craig and at thirty-seven the eldest member of the family's fifth generation.

All that's required for this to be a political rally is for the band to play "Happy Days Are Here Again." Indeed, the warm-up music did range from the decidedly upbeat, "Grab your coat and get your hat, leave your worries on the doorstep," to the religiously fervent, "Just a closer walk with thee."

The celebration is being held to coincide with the filing by Eaton's of its restructuring plan with the court that afternoon. In his speech to the throng Kosich declares how the plan includes new merchandising ideas (more brand names, more stock, and renovated stores) as Eaton's bids to recapture its position as "the dominant traditional department store in Canada." Fred delivers an emotional pitch about family and fairness, a theme that worked for his father and his father before him. He quotes a Winston Churchill speech from 1942: "'Now this is not the end. It is not even the beginning of the end. But it is, perhaps, the end of the beginning.'"

Fred concludes with what sounds very much like a benediction: "On behalf of the current generation, and all of those who preceded us, and all who love this company, I thank you from the bottom of my heart." Then he fires his final salvo. "And remember this: We've got the plan!" With those words he pumps his right arm straight up, the fist clenched in triumph, to cheers all round. Fred and George plunge into the crowd, grabbing outstretched hands; John Craig autographs placards thrust toward him.

Behind them, the business of the store goes on. At cosmetics counters, women perch on stools while clerks fuss with expectant faces looking for makeover miracles. Too bad corporate change isn't as easy. Too bad there isn't a Lourdes to which insolvent firms could go on pilgrimage and come back whole. Too bad today's energy can't be bottled as the Elixir for All Ills.

⟶

At the news conference that followed, George made it plain that the pension surplus had saved the family. Indeed, the surplus had provided a double whammy. Not only did it inject cash but it also acted like a poison pill. If the creditors vote against the plan, the pension surplus would not be available and the creditors and vultures would be forced to accept less than one hundred cents for every dollar owed.

"Our goal from the outset has been to present a restructuring plan that is fair, reasonable, and in the best interest of our associates, suppliers, customers, and other stakeholders," said George. "We are pleased that, unlike other restructurings in the retail sector, this plan provides our creditors with full recovery."

The family has come some distance from earlier in the year. "I've heard George say, 'Let the thing go,'" says Gordon Marantz, one of four insolvency lawyers from Osler, Hoskin & Harcourt who acted for Eaton's. "It's like a roller-coaster ride — you had the peaks and the valleys. By the time we saw there was significant value in the pension surplus, we realized there was something to hang on to. The picture changed. Real estate value [alone] wasn't going to solve the problem. The real key on this thing was being able to unlock the pension funds."

The total amount owed to all creditors had grown to $419 million but could be fully repaid, with interest, using $208 million from the pension fund, $100 million from real estate sales, and $100 million from selling the credit card division, Eaton Credit Corp., to Norwest Financial Capital Canada Inc. The Eaton family also contributed $50 million.

Mr. Justice Houlden was just as crucial as the pension money to a positive outcome. Eaton's occupied a particularly warm place in his heart. He and his wife had bought their first kitchen-table-and-chair set from Eaton's. One of the chairs didn't match; Eaton's promptly exchanged it. Court approvals in mid-September came just a week before Houlden was set to retire at seventy-five, a deadline of no small import. At the final hearing he talked about what he termed "that dreadful night" in February when he'd permitted Eaton's to seek protection under CCAA. Scotiabank, he recalled, was playing dog-in-the-manger and threatening to send back Eaton's cheques. "I was almost on my knees asking the bank not to do that," said Houlden. Lawyers in the court gave him a standing ovation.

Some members of the bankruptcy and insolvency bar believe that courts have become too lenient with companies operating under CCAA and make too much law on the fly with no appeal possible. "The court has gone too far," says David Baird, of Tory, Tory, DesLauriers & Binnington. "Houlden has always been known as a pro-debtor judge. He gave them a couple of wrinkles." For example, a mall tenant often has a lease that allows cancellation if an anchor store closes. In cases where Eaton's closed its mall store, Houlden did not allow other tenants to exercise their contractual right. "In my view, he didn't have the authority," says Baird. "Does the end justify the means?"

There were also raised eyebrows about the speedy appointment of Hap Stephen as chief financial officer of Eaton's only eighteen days after creditors approved the very deal he'd overseen as court officer. In fact, he had grown so close to the process that in mid-August when Eaton's held its "We've got the plan" rally, he sat beside George at the news conference that followed and participated actively. (Within weeks, CFO John Anderson and COO Peter Saunders both departed with severance packages.)

A celebratory dinner, held in November at the Art Gallery of Ontario, was emceed by Lyndon Barnes, the Oslers lawyer who'd stickhandled negotiations with creditors on behalf of Eaton's. In attendance were the Eaton boys, store executives, lawyers, and representatives from investment firms. Because the deal had been code-named Project Beaver, George was given a three-foot Haida carving of a beaver. Participants not only received the usual commemorative "tombstone" — a four-inch marble replica of the announcement detailing the financing — but also a small pewter beaver.

The program after the meal of seared tuna and beef tenderloin included a twenty-five-minute video. Clips of George from the news conference were intercut with suggestions about how he should handle himself. One piece of advice was: "If you get a question you don't like, pretend you didn't hear it." The video then showed George holding a cupped hand to his ear and saying, "Excuse me?"

The video also featured a running gag about Barnes and his colleague Chris Portner trying to write their participation in the script, a spoof on the time the lawyers take while charging $400 an hour. The video ended with Barnes walking away in frustration, leaving Portner alone, still trying to come up with the right words, the meter running the whole time.

When the Eaton Irregulars met for their annual dinner that same month at the Badminton and Racquet Club in Toronto, suspicion had replaced reverence. The group of sixty-five men had been formed twenty years earlier to gather each fall for drinks, dinner, and reminiscences about Eaton's glory days. Membership is limited to merchants who actually pushed a cartload of goods through the tunnel between the Annex and the Queen Street store in

Toronto. No pointy-headed financial guys or marketing gurus are invited. And no women, no matter what their role.

"Most personally have had something unpleasant happen to them as a result of structural changes," says Stan Shortt, a member of the Irregulars who was fired by Eaton's in 1982. "But riding through it all is a unique bond of values expressed not by the company, but through the company."

While they still regarded one another with respect, by the fall of 1997 the loyalty the Irregulars felt for the family and the empire was waning. The pension surplus had caused a rift. They were happy to receive the extra money, but wondered why it had not been paid to them years earlier. "If the outside group hadn't hired the lawyer to go after the undistributed surplus," says Al Boothe, one of the four founding members of the Irregulars, "it might never have come to light."

With creditors and pensioners paid, in spring 1998 Eaton's released its latest financial results. For the year ended January 31, 1998, Eaton's lost $153 million on sales of $1.7 billion. Twenty-one stores had been closed, leases had been renegotiated on eight others, and the chain had shrunk to sixty-four outlets. [4] A further twenty-one stores no longer sold entire product categories such as furniture, appliances, and electronics.

After a more than a year of surprising revelations about the previously private company, the Eaton family dropped one final bombshell in April 1998. The retail arm, T. Eaton Co., would go public in June. So much for Sir John's declaration in 1920: "There is not enough money in the whole world to buy my father's name." Anyone with a few dollars would be able to buy shares and learn more about the ongoing finances of the retailer than even the most senior company officials had ever been told in the past.

In preparation for seeking a listing on the Toronto Stock Exchange, Eaton's announced a new eleven-member board of directors. A majority of those named were outsiders who were not Eaton's executives. They included: as chairman, Brent Ballantyne, who retired in July 1997 as chairman, president, and CEO of Beatrice Foods Inc.; Philip Orsino, president and CEO of Premdor Inc.; Joe Segal, former chairman of Zellers Inc.; Louise Roy, president and CEO of Telemedia Inc.; Kathleen Taylor, executive vice-president, Four Seasons Hotels Ltd.; and John Evans, a partner in the law firm Osler, Hoskin & Harcourt. Eaton's officers on the board included president and CEO George Kosich and CFO Hap Stephen. Fred, George, and Thor also became directors, but John Craig decided not to join his brothers. His son Henry asked his father why he had not joined. Henry reported: "He just said he wasn't that interested."

For the first time in more than twenty years, an Eaton was not in charge. As had happened so often during past decades, Eaton's made the right moves, but too late. In this case, ten years too late. A CEO with retail experience aided by a strong board would have served the boys well back in 1988. Eaton's predicted that the twelve months ending January 31, 1999, will show a profit of $52 million, a turnaround of massive proportions. Whatever happens, the family will never revisit the heydays of 1930 when they had 58 per cent of the department-store market share. Nor are they likely even to enjoy 1988 again, when a brief flurry took them up to 22 per cent. By 1997, that number had slipped all the way to 10.6 percent.

Call it the history of lost opportunities. For the past fifty years, the company coasted on what was created in the first half of the twentieth century. Eaton's ignored social and economic change and expected customers to continue to act like vassals enthralled by the royal mystique of the Eaton family.

But that world seems as distant as medieval times. Retailing today is increasingly divided into two main camps: high-end stores and niche specialists. Inventory systems and superior service are the new monarchs. Little place is left for the all-in-one mass-market emporium, no matter how honoured the name in some bygone era.

CHAPTER FOURTEEN

BANKRUPT

―

The notice posted on the doors of the flagship Eaton's store in the Toronto Eaton Centre on the morning of August 23, 1999, is not the usual professional presentation. The 8½" by 11" document has been photocopied and hung in place with Scotch tape. The typescript statement, evocative of the words carved on a tombstone, reads: "The T. Eaton Company Limited, an insolvent person, pursuant to subsection 50.4(1) of the *Bankruptcy and Insolvency Act*, intends to make a proposal to its creditors."

Eaton's. An insolvent person.

A clutch of expectant shoppers stands and stares at the death-knell notice as they await the 10:00 store opening. When the doors are unlocked, they scuttle inside, but are sorely disappointed to find that the deep-discount liquidation sale has not yet begun. They gape at the surroundings rather than gather any goods, then depart empty-handed.

Ten steps from the same doors, unnoticed by the eager bargain-seekers, is the bronze statue of Timothy Eaton unveiled in 1919 on the occasion of Eaton's fiftieth anniversary. None of the visitors bothers to rub the toe of his left boot for luck as countless thousands have done in the past. Eaton's heydays are long gone. Timothy's legendary genius did not make it to modern times.

At the south end of the Eaton Centre, near the crosswalk where hordes of shoppers used to surge back and forth across Queen Street between Eaton's and Simpsons, there is another sign. This one, erected by Eaton Centre landlord Cadillac Fairview Corp., has a large colour photograph of the Yonge Street office tower once occupied by Eaton's executives. Half a dozen floors are circled. "Space for your people," declares the poster. The top of the building, home to George's helipad and the high-profile location where once the Eaton's logo was proudly displayed, is also circled: "Space for your name." After 130 years, everything is up for grabs at the former Canadian icon.

That afternoon, in a Toronto court room, the company makes its second cap-in-hand appearance in little more than two years. This time Eaton's has no hope of continuing; the pension fund surplus cannot bail them out again. "The company is out of cash. The company has no ability to borrow and fund operations, including payroll," declares Gordon Morantz, of Osler, Hoskin & Harcourt, the law firm that for decades has acted for the family. Documents filed with the court show that Eaton's owes $329 million, almost as much as it did the first time round in 1997.

Mr. Justice James Farley approves Eaton's beseeching plea for bankruptcy protection; liquidation can begin in earnest. Quips his honour as the hearing concludes: "No doubt everyone will want to rush over to Eaton's to get those good bargains." If only those shoppers had shown up sooner.

Family businesses are unwieldy beasts at the best of times. There's no certainty that an aging founder will hand over the reins at the right time and there's no guarantee that an able successor exists among the offspring. If there's power or money involved, sibling rivalry can quickly escalate from dinner-table bickering to public donnybrooks. That's why only 70 per cent of family businesses survive into the second generation and a mere 10 per cent make it to the third. The Eatons fared far better than most; at the end, members of the fifth generation were working in the organization.

In another era the family and their advisers would have even now been preparing for the crowning of a new heir. The Eaton boys have a total of ten children ranging from John David, thirty-nine, to Cléophée, who is seventeen. This time around there will be no royal succession. The family business has gone bust. Perhaps it's just as well that no choice must be made. The gene pool has become thin gruel.

As the eldest of Timothy's great-great-grandchildren, John David would have been first in line to inherit the throne. If ever there was an Eaton who could live with the harsh reality of losing that prize, it is this child of John Craig's first marriage. In a family of boasters, John David is bashful; amid grating arrogance he is gracious and self-deprecating.

After graduating from the University of Western Ontario in 1982, he became a management trainee, sold sporting goods, and worked in the outdoor shop. In 1987 John David married Lisa Belton, a Ryerson marketing graduate. His divorced parents, John Craig and Kitty, came together long enough to host the Toronto Club rehearsal dinner prior to the ceremony at St. Michael's Cathedral. (Like his uncles Thor and George, John David married a Catholic.)

In January 1995 John David was named official spokesman for Eaton's, but they parked him in an office far from the action of the executive floor. John David lacks one job skill demanded of PR flacks: he is unable to lie. The night before the February 1997 insolvency announcement, word had leaked that something might be happening. A journalist stationed herself in the lobby of the Eaton's office tower in hopes of ambushing John David on his way home. That evening, however, he needed to buy a birthday present, so he took another route through the store. He later admitted that if he'd run into the reporter, he might not have been able to deny what was about to occur. In 1998 Eaton's moved him out of PR back into the stores, as group business manager in charge of several lines at Yorkdale.

John David's sister, Signy, married Jeffrey Shier, whom she met while summering on Georgian Bay. Signy stays home with their three children: Reilly, Stefan, and Buster. Shier is president and chief operating officer of his family's firm, OSF Inc., a Toronto-based store-fixtures company that started life in 1926. The business nearly disappeared in the 1960s after a misguided foray into real estate, but today it's the biggest customized-fixture maker in North America with annual sales of $200 million. Shier is Jewish. What John David, the grandfather who called Catholics "salmon snappers," might have said about such a marriage can only be imagined.

John Craig's younger son, Henry, did his undergraduate degree at the University of Western Ontario, worked for eighteen months in the retail branch training program at Toronto-Dominion Bank, then returned to Western for his MBA, graduating in 1988. Some say that, unlike his unassuming elder brother, Henry has a permanent chip on his shoulder. "He has a mouth and an attitude," says a family friend. "He can be arrogant in a family known for its arrogance." Longtime family friend Peter Eby disagrees, saying that Henry is simply more reticent than his siblings. "Henry has always been much more serious when he was growing up, much more quiet, and much more reserved," says Eby. "I don't think that's an attitude as much as it is just being more reserved. The kids are surprisingly good. You'd think having had the name and all of that there'd be some smart-asses in the group and I can't think of one." Henry is married to Vicky Gordon, daughter of a Toronto architect. They have two children, Robert and Laurel.

After graduation Henry joined Gordon Capital Corp. as an associate in investment banking, doing the usual grunt work with small teams on corporate bond issues and initial public offerings. Except for summer jobs, he has carefully avoided Eaton's. According to family lore, George once asked him to come work at the store, but Henry replied: "I'll come when I can have your job."

Henry has not, however, completely severed the umbilical cord. In 1991 he started work in advertising sales at the "other" family firm, Baton Broadcasting, then became vice-president, strategic planning and business development. John David, Signy, and Henry all live in Toronto and have stayed close to their mother. "I don't think they're getting high on the hog," says Kitty. "I think they're pretty down to earth. I raised them that way. Now, if anyone told me differently, I'd be up there with my witch's broom, but I think they're okay.

"I've kind of raised them alone most of those years. They always saw the Eatons for their big holidays, Christmases, of course. But they lived with me and I don't think there was anything ever snobby about me. I was basically a slob and still am."

Fred and Nicky's only son, Fredrik D'Arcy, was born in 1963 and attended Upper Canada College, where he was an average student who participated in house sports such as soccer, hockey, and cricket. When he worked in the stores as a teenager, he used an assumed name, Fred Smith. He enjoyed many of the same interests as his father and they went on two safaris, one in 1980 to Botswana and South Africa, followed by Zambia in 1983. In all, Fred, Jr., has fifteen "trophy" kills, including buffalo, leopard, lion, and antelope.

He graduated in 1986 with a degree in economics from Williams College, in Williamstown, Massachusetts, a small liberal arts school in the northwest corner of the state. In his final year he was on the Ontario biathlon team, a gruelling sport that combines cross-country skiing and target-shooting over ten- or twenty-kilometre distances. He spent 1987 with the Canadian team, but after participating in several events, including the World Cup, where he placed in the top fifty, and the North American championships, where he placed seventh, he quit.

He continued sailing competitively in his fourteen-foot international-class dinghy. He raced in the world championships in England in 1991 and Kingston, Ontario, in 1993. In 1996 he suffered a herniated disc, underwent surgery, and has since limited his sailing to less strenuous roles such as serving as a tactician on someone else's boat.

"He's a good hunter, he's a good sailor, and he's a nondrinker," says his father Fred, Sr. "He has never, ever been a drinker. Don't know whether that's a comment on his father or not. He went through a whole bunch of years when his body was a temple. And of course, unfortunately, I think he figured it out at that time that unless you're prepared to take [performance-enhancing] drugs, you're finished, you can't compete."

Although Fred, Jr., felt no family pressure to join the business, he did have avenues unavailable to others. In the summer of 1987 those family connections took him to the U.S. department store Dillard's Inc. for two years. In 1995, after he returned, he became assistant to Tom Reid, then chief operating officer, using his real name. "It was time to deal with it at that point. That was my name." Being an Eaton often meant special, but not always favoured, treatment. "Senior management gave me more time than they would give a typical person in my position. Some of the people working in the department were intimidated by the name and who I was and weren't sure why I was there."

By then Fred, Jr., who is single, had learned to cope with being an Eaton. "It's more of an issue when you're younger. As you grow older, you're more comfortable with who you are and more able to adapt to that. But it's always there, even today. There are lots of people who presume they know a lot about me who really wouldn't know very much.

"At the same time, knowing who you are, you do have a role to play, even as a child. You go along, you wear the right clothes, you stand there politely, and you do what you're supposed to do. It's not really that tough. Some things you have to do and you get to do a lot for doing it. It's a pretty good deal, all in all. You have to do stuff in your own right, for which you're responsible, and choose what those things are and go and do them regardless of your father or great-grandfather. It's not really relevant to you. You don't get credit for it and you shouldn't take credit for it." With the collapse of the stores, he's become chairman of the Eaton Foundation, the family's charitable arm.

His younger sister, Catherine, graduated from Bishop Strachan School in 1984 and followed her brother to Williams, where she was captain of the women's ice hockey team. There, she met and later married fellow student Rob Coakley, an American. He's in media sales, the couple lives in New York, and they have a daughter, Fred and Nicky's first grandchild. "As far as I can tell, there's only one downside," quipped Fred, Sr., after the blessed event. "Realizing that you're going to bed with a grandmother."

——

On April 30, 1998, the afternoon sun streamed through the stained-glass windows into St. Paul's Anglican Church in midtown Toronto. Among the glowing gothic memorials is one to Iris Burnside, the twenty-year-old granddaughter of Timothy Eaton. She drowned in 1915 when the *Lusitania* was torpedoed by a German U-boat and sank.

Hundreds gathered to mourn the death of John White Hughes Bassett at eighty-two. With family and friends were cardinals, judges, former premiers and prime ministers, lieutenants-governor past and present, and numerous chief executive officers. The last special guest to be seated was Bobby Kennedy's widow, Ethel.

Pallbearers on the four corners of Big John's casket were the Eaton boys: John Craig and George on one side, Fred and Thor on the other. They were aided by *Daily Telegraph* publisher Conrad Black and *Toronto Sun* columnist Peter Worthington. While he lived, Big John was a surrogate father to the Eaton boys. His death served as a vivid reminder: it was Bassett's strategic vision and savvy move into broadcasting that created most of wealth retained by the Eaton dynasty today. With their mother and father both dead, now their other great benefactor was gone, too.

The public humiliation of Eaton's near collapse in 1997 had poisoned relations among the family. Disharmony had been rare among the Eaton boys in the past, but finger-pointing now replaced fraternal loyalty. Fred, in particular, was bitter about what had occurred during his three years in London as High Commissioner. "We let things get away from us," he told a friend in the summer of 1997. "Some of the stores were a fucking disaster." By the end of that year, Fred's harsh views had moderated somewhat. "Thank God we've finally got some decent management in here running this place," Fred told another friend that Christmas.

As a result of the trouble in the retailing empire, each of the boys decided to go his own way and disentangle their various business interests. The most obvious candidate for quick sale was their 40.3 per cent jointly held position in Baton Broadcasting. Established in 1960, when Big John Bassett obtained a Toronto television licence, Baton became a major force in

Canadian broadcasting with twenty-five stations, ownership of the CTV Television Network, and interests in seven specialty cable channels. After languishing in the $8 range for several years, share price of Baton reached an all-time high of $25.60 in January 1998.

Baton had until then been an interesting but not highly significant part of the Eaton-family wealth; at those values it had become a key component. "[I]n terms of emotional attachment, it's a second company, rather than the first," says Fred, Jr. "It doesn't have your name on it. It doesn't have the history. It isn't the reason why everybody is aware of who you are."

Suddenly there were plenty of reasons to sell Baton. Share price was running well ahead of earnings and a strong bull market was feeding investor greed. Neither condition was likely to last. Baton needed more capital for equipment and facilities, but the Eatons were unwilling to invest additional money. The third compelling reason to get out, and perhaps the most important, was the rancour that had developed within the family. By selling Baton, each brother would be able to create financial independence for his own family. If one of the four boys wanted to mismanage his own money, that was fine; the others did not want to become penniless in the process.

George and Fred represented the family investment on the Baton board. After Eaton's declared insolvency, their fellow Baton directors detected problems in the relationship. "There was tension between the brothers," says one director. "You could see it at board meetings, one not listening to the other. The unity was fraying. They would agree at the end of a board meeting, but they would have different views during the meeting. This was a huge change. The fact that they disagreed in public was a sign that there was tension."

Over Christmas 1997 the boys decided to sell Baton and divvy up the proceeds four ways. "There will always be disharmony but there's no huge disharmony. There's more to the fact that the money was good," says Fred, denying any family discord. "There was no big argument. Nobody stood up and said 'Hey, don't sell that company.' There was basically harmony on that point. I think everybody has to get their estate in order and one of the ways that that can be done — and I think that all my brothers would agree with this — is that you can realize [value] on some of the things."

In January 1998 Newcrest Capital Inc., a Toronto investment banker, shopped the Eaton boys' block of fifteen million shares, asking $25 apiece. There were no takers. Baton directors gathered for a board meeting at 9:00 p.m. on January 27 in the Toronto offices of Osler, Hoskin & Harcourt to get moving on a planned issue of treasury shares to raise capital. Newcrest was handling the deal, and the Eatons agreed to sell their control block at the same time for $22.35 per share. Newcrest assured the board that it could find buyers for all the shares involved — the 4.5 million treasury shares, as well as the Eaton block — using what's known as a "bought deal." Under this method Newcrest bought the shares in concert with other investment dealers, then immediately resold parcels to pension funds and other institutions, as well as to individual investors.

As the meeting continued past midnight, much of the time was spent huddling with advisers trying to figure out how best to structure arrangements to minimize taxes owing. George was present; Fred was consulted by phone. Other directors were left with the clear impression that the boys needed the money, either for investment in the stores, for themselves, or both. Directors approved the deal once the Eatons agreed to place $50 million of the family proceeds in a trust fund until all tricky tax implications were approved by Revenue Canada. The meeting finally broke up at 4:30 a.m. When the stock market opened five hours later, all the shares were gone within ninety minutes.

After commissions, the Eatons received $330 million, half of it immediately, the other half in February 1999. The booty was divided among four numbered companies, one for each of the boys: 1274527 Ontario Inc. through 1274530 Ontario Inc. There would be no more joint investments of that scope among the four Eatons.

Over the nearly forty years they'd been involved in Baton, the monetary investment by the Eatons was minimal, yet the value had grown to the point where it was worth as much as the department stores, which had been around for more than three times as long. There were two reasons the family fared so much better in broadcasting than in retailing. First, television was a faster-growing industry, but second, and more important, the boys never tried to run Baton. As majority owners and directors, they certainly had their say, but professional management always made the key decisions.

They saw the stores differently. Because their name was on the door, they just assumed they knew what they were doing. That's not an unusual failing in any family business. But being a member of "the lucky sperm club" doesn't necessarily mean brains, just breeding.

Cash-out value was not so easily realized at Eaton's. After the 1997 court-supervised restructuring, the retailer appeared to be doing everything right in order to pull off a successful corporate resurrection. Debt was paid down, the private company went public and raised $175 million in equity, new management was hired, and the board of directors was buttressed. But few companies can lose as much money for as many years as Eaton's did and still survive. "Once a retail concept starts to decline, its financial performance can tumble rapidly, making recovery increasingly difficult," said a *McKinsey Quarterly* study of retailers suffering three consecutive years of losses. "Almost half went bankrupt and most of the others took at least another four years to recover." [1]

Eaton's had lost money for more than three years and had particular problems that the steps taken did not come close to solving. Despite all the changes, the corporate culture of Eaton's was unaltered; core elements of the 130-year-old family business remained as ossified as ever. "The present generation and their parents did not manage the enterprise, resulting in an organization that was bloated with managers and out of sync with its customers," said Richard McLaren, professor of law at the University of Western Ontario in London, Ontario.

Nor was Eaton's much-touted new retailing strategy, focusing on high-end fashion and the youth market, necessarily the best approach. "The restructuring then tried to create an entirely new enterprise, turning it into a fashion clothing store, not a department store. Eaton's went out of fashion with the buying public and tried to get back into fashion with product that it didn't understand how to market. It had the brand 'Eaton's' but not the merchandise to go with the brand image," said Mr. McLaren, who is an expert in commercial law and corporate insolvency. "The message is: stay with your core business. I can't think of a successful restructuring, in any sector of the economy, where the company did not stay with its core strategy," he said.

"Eaton's was a nightmare to run; stores ranged in size from 90,000 square feet to 1 million square feet. You don't change corporate culture from where they were to a high-powered place in a couple of years," said John Williams, a senior partner at the Toronto office of J.C. Williams Group, a retail and marketing consulting firm.

The hiring in June 1997 of George Kosich, who was retiring as CEO of competitor Hudson's Bay Co. to become CEO of Eaton's, was a risky step. After more than three decades at The Bay, the abrasive management style of Mr. Kosich was well and widely known within the industry. So, too, was his retailing philosophy of loading stores with lots of inventory, an approach aptly captured by his motto: "Pile 'em high and watch 'em fly."

Such wretched excess may have worked in the 1980s, but not in the 1990s when pricing and inventory control are crucial. Retailers such as Wal-Mart succeed because they always know the status of in-store stock, how much is on the shelves, and what's on the way from the warehouse. Staff can order items right from the store floor using hand-held scanners. By contrast, Eaton's closed for a morning in January 1999 to conduct an old-fashioned count of goods.

The high levels of inventory required by the Kosich strategy demand equally high levels of cash flow from daily sales to pay suppliers. Eaton's didn't enjoy that kind of cash flow, so lines of credit with GE Capital were twice increased. GE Capital became so fretful about Eaton's deteriorating health that interest rates on some of the loans reached 13 per cent, a level perilously close to that of credit cards.

The high inventory levels also demanded lots of customers, yet Eaton's decided to abandon many of its popular product categories. Heavy appliances, electronic goods, toys, candy, and books were eliminated from the stores. In so doing, Eaton's reduced customer traffic and turned its back on the empire's traditional shopper.

To replace those loyal consumers a new advertising campaign dubbed "Diversity" was devised to capture the youth market. But two years is the minimum amount of time required to attract a new customer, and bringing youthful buyers into a department store is particularly tough. Fashion trends tend to be spotted early by smaller niche retailers. By the time a stodgy department store has begun to stock "hot" items, the youth market has long since moved on to the next look.

Kosich's retailing strategy was further hurt by the fact that both the high-fashion clothing market and the youth market are shrinking. Moreover, the full range of the highly promoted goods was available only in a half-dozen locations, thereby causing shoppers further confusion. The depth of Eaton's problem became evident at Christmas in 1998 when December sales were 12 per cent lower than the previous year. The following month saw a 31 per cent drop from the same period twelve months earlier. Even the top location in the chain, Toronto Eaton Centre, had sales of only $151 per square foot, about half what Wal-Mart achieves in Canada.

Sales during that make-or-break season were hobbled by renovations that weren't finished until well into November in the four top-selling stores, Montreal downtown, Vancouver Pacific Centre, Toronto Eaton Centre, and Toronto Yorkdale. The $70-million spruce-up was a modest outlay. Marshall Field and Co. recently spent US $115 million to renovate one store, State Street, in Chicago.

For all his failings, however, George Kosich did play a valuable and essential 'front man' role through the court restructuring and the process of taking Eaton's public. Through that critical period he reassured suppliers and investors that, maybe, Eaton's was getting back on track. "Bringing George Kosich in was the right thing to do. They needed someone to jump-start the company, but they should have used him as 'the Marines' and used that time to find a knowledgeable president," said Williams, the retail analyst. Instead, when Kosich was fired in November 1998, Eaton's named as his replacement Brent Ballantyne, chairman of T. Eaton Co., a man with no previous retailing experience. Kosich sued Eaton's over his abrupt departure and won a $1 million settlement.

Employee layoffs seemed to be the only cost-cutting exercise carried out by the company, as employment fell from 15,000 to 13,000 during the final two years. Eaton's did not, for example, contract a third party to handle any aspects of the business such as warehousing or delivery, a step taken by most companies trying to trim back expenses. Eaton's should have closed more stores in its attempt to restore health. The initial plan that would have seen the closure of thirty-one stores was altered and only twenty-one were shuttered, leaving sixty-four outlets, many of which were unprofitable. When the public announcement was finally made May 18, 1999, that Eaton's was seeking a buyer for all or part of the chain, there were at least thirty orphan stores that even Eaton's realized no one wanted.

The code name for the sale was Project Flower but there were few blooms. By July there was only one interested bidder, Federated Department Stores Inc., of Cincinnati, Ohio, the largest operator of department stores in the U.S. with US $15 billion in annual sales through four hundred stores in thirty-three states under such banners as Bloomingdale's, Macy's, Burdines, and The Bon Marché.

During the month-long negotiations that followed, the number of Eaton's stores in which Federated expressed interest was constantly changing and at one point the total reached twenty-five. Although Federated never said as much, there was an underlying concern about the political future of Quebec, but Montreal-area stores were part of the possible package until the last minute when all Quebec stores as well as the two Eaton's outlets in Edmonton were dropped.

Federated intended to use the Macy's name, the company's middle-to-upper price banner (Bloomingdale's is more upmarket), and appeared willing to pay $100 million for the leases on sixteen downtown and suburban

Eaton's stores in four cities: Toronto, Calgary, Vancouver, and Victoria. Eaton's had hoped to attract simultaneous interest from Sears and The Bay for a further ten locations, but those two retailers did not want to be part of any deal involving Federated, arguing that anything they did at that point would only speed the arrival in Canada of a powerful new competitor.

Talks with Federated got far enough along for Cadillac Fairview and Cambridge Shopping Centres to be included. As landlords they were delighted with the prospect of Federated's interest. They believed that if Macy's was successful, Federated might bring in others among its banners as well, thereby broadening the number of mall tenants available. For Eaton's part, the Federated deal would not have saved the company from the eventual debacle, but at least the music for the final act would have been more triumphal and there would have been additional funds for creditors.

Ron Tysoe, Federated's vice chairman, finance and real estate, was the biggest fan within the Federated hierarchy of expanding into Canada. But support from the board of directors was lukewarm at best. There was even less enthusiasm from operations personnel at Macy's East, the corporate division that would have managed the new Canadian locations. In particular, Macy's East president James Gray, a thirty-seven-year veteran at Federated and former president of Burdines, remained unconvinced that expanding to Canada was anything close to a good idea.

Beyond such specific concerns by individual directors and officers, Federated was also taking a pessimistic view about weakening retail sales in North America in 2000. The more Federated analyzed the spending habits of Canadian consumers, the less they liked what they saw. Average wages are lower in Canada than in the U.S. and the Canadian public is more value-oriented. Federated feared that annual sales at Macy's Canada might not be as high as required to make the foray profitable, taking into consideration the hefty investment of money and management time required. Federated planned to spend $380 million, with landlords paying as much as half that amount, to renovate the sixteen stores to their liking.

There was one final problem hovering over the negotiating table. Eaton's overestimated Federated's passion for Canada and played hardball on aspects of the talks for too long even as Federated's doubts accumulated. In the end, there were too many unknowns about expansion to a foreign country and too few champions at head office. Federated decided not to proceed. On Friday, August 13, 1999, Eaton's was informed that there would be no deal.

Hap Stephen, the Ernst & Young accountant who had helped Eaton's with the 1997 restructuring and then became Eaton's chief financial officer at $1 million a year, was apparently prepared for any eventuality. Coincident with the announcement by Eaton's that their only potential buyer had walked away from the table, Stephen was appointed chairman of Repap Enterprises Inc., a money-losing papermaker.

The rationale and the timing of the Federated decision were eerily reminiscent of the last-ditch talks in 1975 between Eaton's and JC Penney Co. about the catalogue. One more time Eaton's had gone so far down the road with a U.S. retailing giant, that when the prospective saviour said 'no,' there were no other avenues available. As with the catalogue and so much else about Eaton's in the past, if there was no buyer to bail them out of their self-inflicted mess, they had no choice but to close.

This time, however, the entire empire was involved. As a first step, Eaton's closed the Toronto warehouse to shipments from suppliers, thereby limiting the stores to inventory already in the system. Suppliers were in revolt. Tommy Hilfiger Canada Inc. obtained a Quebec court order allowing the firm to enter the downtown Montreal store and seize some of its high-fashion clothing off the shelves. In Ottawa, a bailiff strode into the Eaton's Rideau Centre store with a court order to obtain $80,000 in cash owed to Jacques Lamont Ltee. and was able to scoop $9,500 from the tills.

With the barbarians at the gates, Eaton's closed its nine Quebec stores to halt further action by suppliers and filed a notice under the *Bankruptcy and Insolvency Act*. As the final act began in earnest, a television commercial made liquidation sound as if it was part of some grand plan. "It's 130 years in the making. It's the sale you've been waiting for," said the audio portion. In the stores, there was a more ominous tone: "All sales final, no refunds or exchanges." Timothy's long-standing promise, "Goods satisfactory or money refunded," was no more.

The value of Eaton's shares had been in free fall from the $15 issue price for a year. The stock market smelled trouble long before management would admit that anything was amiss. In June 1998, when the prospectus giving detailed information about the initial public offering (IPO) was produced by Eaton's and its lead underwriter RBC Dominion Securities Inc., first-year profit was predicted to be $58 million.

In the months that followed, sales and profit forecasts were twice revised downward by the company. When the year-end results were announced in March 1999, there was a $72 million loss — a negative swing of $130 million from the optimistic claim made a mere nine months earlier. Annual sales, projected to be $1.8 billion, were actually $1.6 billion, about the same level as those of the mid-1970s. By comparison, annual sales at Sears had risen from a similar $1.6 billion in the mid-1970s to reach $5 billion in 1999. Sears had also enjoyed two consecutive years of record profits, proof that the full-line department store concept can still work — if properly run. Three months later, Eaton's announced it had lost a further $36 million. In August 1999 when the Toronto Stock Exchange finally suspended trading in Eaton's, the last trade was conducted at forty cents per share.

In the U.S., a class-action suit would long ago have been launched by irate shareholders, but Canadian courts are not quite so user-friendly. "Class-action is available but it's not an easy process. Millions of dollars have been spent chasing Bre-X and so far the court rulings have said they can sue the corporation and the directors and officers — who don't have any money — but not the brokers who do," said Bill Riedl, president of Fairvest Securities Corp, a Toronto-based shareholder rights group. "Because Eaton's did an IPO there could be a lawsuit based on the prospectus document, but shareholders would have to show misrepresentation. It's unlikely DS left themselves vulnerable."

More vulnerable, as always, were the unsecured creditors, as well as the 4,000 full-time and 9,000 part-time employees who were suddenly working for the liquidator, Gordon Brothers of Boston, rather than Eaton's. As soon as the goods were gone, they were told, so were their jobs. Former staffers who had been receiving severance by regular cheques were informed that they'd seen their last payment. Members of staff on sick leave either returned to work immediately or saw their benefits cease. All those years of loyal service to the Royal family counted for nought.

For two weeks, the family remained silent, saying nothing either about themselves or their former loyal employees, until John Craig wrote a letter to the editor of *National Post.* "My family is in mourning, not just because of the loss of a magnificent and noble company, but, more important, because of the impact on its people, both employees and suppliers.

"My wife and I have visited most of the stores across this country every year and sometimes twice a year to meet the employees, and hear of their business concerns. We are on a first-name basis with many of these spirited, loyal and hard-working people and have met a lot of their families. These are the people who built and maintained Eaton's and they are, without question, the unsung heroes. The sadness we find regarding the impact of recent events on these people's families, careers, income and futures is made even worse by the fact that I can't do anything about it."[2]

Fred seemed both surprised and bereft. "I never in my wildest dreams could conceive of this happening. In a perfect world, you keep control of your life. And it's sort of gone out of control," he said in an interview. As for the employees, "I'm am horrified for these people because they've invested their lives, many of them, in the company. I mean, nobody's happy to see something they've supported all their life go down. Look, it's been our *lives*, Whatever way it ended up, we grew up with it . . . It was a special family. It *is* a special family."[3] He was right the first time, it *was* a special family.

———

As the special family fades from view, the family name survives. Sears Canada Inc. announced plans in October to acquire nineteen Eaton's stores. The suburban locations will be converted to Sears outlets, but the deal also included all trademark rights, so Sears says it will continue to fly the Eaton's banner at Toronto Eaton Centre, Winnipeg Polo Park, Calgary Eaton Centre, Vancouver Pacific Centre, and Victoria Eaton Centre. Sears CEO Paul Walters says he intends to rebuild the Eaton's brand using those locations, a web site, and the catalogue.

For Sears, the victory was particularly sweet. Almost fifty years after arriving in Canada, the American retailer had not only vanquished Eaton's, but had also acquired the very stores Federated desired. Keeping a U.S. competitor out of Canada may not have been the main motivation for Sears, but the outcome was the same.

The Eaton family name will also remain on Lady Eaton College at Trent University in Peterborough, Ontario, the Art Gallery of Ontario, Timothy Eaton Memorial Church, and on the Eaton mausoleum.

The only family holding likely to carry on with any profile is the Eaton Foundation. But just as they need not be remembered for their business acumen, nor should the Eatons be revered for their philanthropic deeds. Royal Bank of Canada tops the list of corporate donors at $14 million annually. In 1997 the Eaton Foundation, the main charitable arm of the family, donated only $1.3 million, according to filings with Revenue Canada, the foundation's skimpiest year in the 1990s. In the most generous twelve-month period of the decade, $2.7 million was distributed.

Over the years, however, the Eaton family has received more bang for its buck than most donors. When the Margaret Eaton Wing of the Art Gallery of

Toronto opened in 1935, T. Eaton Co. donated $22,500 to have the name of Timothy's widow memorialized; federal, provincial, and municipal governments contributed a similar sum. William Withrow, gallery director from 1961 to 1991, recalls lining up as a small boy outside the gallery for Saturday painting lessons from Group of Seven artist Arthur Lismer. Neighbours would see him and ask: "What are you doing over at Mr. Eaton's club?"

In 1948 Eaton's donated $15,000 to the gallery to purchase Canadian art. Over the next decade ninety-five works were acquired, including canvases by such artists as A. J. Casson, J. E. H. MacDonald, Goodridge Roberts, Charles Comfort, and Homer Watson. Fred chaired a fundraising campaign for the AGO in the early 1970s. The Eaton Foundation donated $250,000 of the $4.8 million raised. For his efforts and the family's largesse, a gallery was named after Signy in the Canadian wing that was completed in 1977. The next campaign raised $58 million including a $1 million donation from the Eaton Foundation that led to the designation of the Fredrik S. Eaton wing, built in 1991–92, to house international contemporary art and the gallery shop.[4]

Launched by John David in 1958, the Eaton Foundation had assets of $29.6 million in 1997 (the latest year for which figures are available), putting it roughly in the middle of the list of the largest one hundred foundations in Canada. "The reputation comes from a huge long line of doing things, starting with Timothy, but it's not as big a foundation as the reputation might indicate," admits Fred. "I certainly have done my share of charitable things. My brother John has probably done more than any single person that I know."

By contrast, the Ivey family of London, Ontario, has two foundations with assets totalling $75 million, three times as much as the far wealthier Eatons. Size of a foundation is relevant, because at least 4.5 per cent of a foundation's assets must, by law, be given away each year. The Iveys have donated about $40 million to the University of Western Ontario alone.

Until shortly before her death in 1992, Signy's views held sway at the foundation. "She exerted more influence than anybody ever realized. All of the four brothers respected her wishes whatever they were," says Pat Wilson, who ran the foundation from 1988 until he retired in 1997. "The boys would express their positions, she would say something, and they would acquiesce."

Since then, major beneficiaries have tended to be institutions favoured by one of the boys. There was $1 million given to each of Royal Ontario Museum (Nicky Thor is on the board) and Upper Canada College (John Craig was chairman), $250,000 to Headwaters Health Care Centre in Orangeville

(George, who now lives close to the institution, was involved in the campaign), and $200,000 to University of New Brunswick (Fred is chancellor).

Ryerson Polytechnic University in Toronto has also fared well. The foundation regularly gives Ryerson up to $125,000 a year, and in 1994 added a further $100,000 annually to sponsor the Eaton Chair in Retailing. United Way campaigns in Winnipeg, Montreal, and the lower mainland of British Columbia each receive $40,000 to $60,000 annually; Toronto gets up to $200,000, more than the other three combined. The Hospital for Sick Children, Mount Sinai, and Princess Margaret, all in Toronto, have been recent beneficiaries of $50,000 donations. Montreal Children's Hospital got $60,000 in 1996. In 1992 the Eaton Foundation sent Oshawa General a piddling $100 and Montreal's Royal Victoria $50. Each year scores of organizations across the country — from the Tafelmusik Baroque Orchestra to Canadian Guide Dogs for the Blind — are given small amounts ranging from $40 to $1000.

Other lesser-known and less-wealthy donors have been just as generous as the Eatons. For example, the $1 million gift by the Eaton Foundation to the Art Gallery of Ontario was matched in 1994 by Toronto investment firm Gluskin Sheff and Associates, and none of that firm's principals is anything like a billionaire with a multigenerational history in Canadian commerce. For all their wealth, the Eatons have always been nickel-and-dime donors.

Timothy Eaton succeeded in nineteenth-century Canada because he wanted to be somebody. As an immigrant, he was forced to work hard to achieve wealth and standing. The latter-day Eatons already were Canada's Royal family; there was nothing to drive them forward.

As a result, their net worth has plummeted. Cashing out of Desjardins-Laurentian in 1997 and Baton in 1998 yielded a total of approximately $400 million before tax. To which must be added a further $100 million in personal assets and other investments held outside the department stores. In June 1998 the boys sold off approximately half of T. Eaton Co. in a public stock offering, thereby raising $175 million.

Usually when an owner sells a portion of his company, he pockets the funds raised. It's payday. The Eatons chose instead to plough almost half of the money into store renovations, keeping the rest for themselves and leaving the family with 52% of the shares in Eaton's, a holding that's now valueless. In all, the Eaton boys are worth about $450 million, a drop of two-thirds in the family fortune in seven years.

When Roy Thomson died in 1976, his estate was valued at $1 billion. At the time, the Eatons were worth about $500 million. Today, Roy Thomson's son, Ken, oversees assets of $20 billion. If the Eaton boys had done equally well, they would now be worth $10 billion, instead of $450 million. No tag days are required, but an instruction kit might have helped.

Such a diminution of their inherited wealth stands as a damning indictment, but perhaps no other outcome was possible. Novelist Susan Swan summered on Georgian Bay and grew up close to the boys, particularly George and Thor. "I was always fascinated how we brought our values to the landscape," she recalls. "People were returning to the beach every summer to measure themselves against something. There was a community of upper-middle-class people that had cottages on the beach. When you get up the shore near Parry Sound, you needed a lot more money to buy an island, a boat, a boathouse, or an extensive dock that needs to be continuously repaired. People on the beach would see who had a new Evinrude motor. But up in the islands, you were talking yachts and jet boats. The Eatons had big launches.

"They'd already arrived at the place that all the cottagers, and even the islanders, wanted to be. Their birth had placed them into a dilemma. They were put in a dynasty on a continent that believes in being upwardly mobile. When you're at the pinnacle, then what do you do?"

One of the obvious, and often successful, corporate strategies that the boys failed to follow was to hire bright managers who knew retailing. They could also have taken the company public a lot earlier in their sorry regime. Scrutiny by shareholders, analysts, and markets in general helps to create a profit-driven corporate environment. Share ownership by senior management means their commitment to success as well as the ability to attract and keep talent. As it was, senior manager, chauffeur, shop clerk, or fashion buyer — they were all the same. Everyone at Eaton's existed only to do the family's bidding.

In the early 1960s Leo Kolber tried to convince his boss, Charles Bronfman, to allow stock ownership by employees in what was then called Fairview Corporation of Canada Ltd., the real estate arm of CEMP Investments Ltd. Bronfman had no such arrangement at Seagrams; he was unenthusiastic. Bronfman wondered what Eaton's did, so he called Fred. "No bloody way," Fred shouted down the phone. "It's just not done. It's not necessary."

The boys believed that reverence and respect were somehow their due and that the dynasty would automatically flourish without recourse to normal business practices. The judgement of their peers, however, is blistering. "They thought of themselves as being different from others," says family counsellor Allen Lambert. "They thought what applied to others didn't necessarily apply to them."

"The eighties allowed a number of retailers to do well without necessarily operating well," says Peter Saunders, Eaton's chief operating officer from 1995 to 1997. "It wasn't really until we turned into the nineties and we had tough retail years that it became evident that the [1980s] numbers were a function of the economy as opposed to a function of good operations."

"It has been run for a long time by people who don't know anything about merchandising," says Peter Sharpe, executive vice-president of Cadillac Fairview Corp., Eaton's largest landlord. "I don't know if it was loyalty or laziness but they couldn't deal with the staffing. Their hearts just simply were not in it."

"Eaton's had weak management for forty years. They never hired good people; they wouldn't pay," says former TD banker Robin Korthals. "If you stacked up the Eaton boys against the U.S. retail CEOs, it's no contest."

The root cause of the decline was the family's indifference. Says former Eaton's CEO David Kinnear: "John sort of took over but John didn't really have a strong interest to do the job so Fred took over. But then he got a little bored and passed it down to George. Competition got tougher and tougher. We didn't have the right management."

Kinnear claims he made that point so often at Eaton's of Canada board meetings that he was considered a pain in the neck. "The boys had some of their friends on the board and they always had enough votes to carry the day. They were getting by pretty good right through to about '86 when it started to go down the drain. They started to lose share of the market. I couldn't believe how fast that went."

"With all their many other interests you wonder if they gave it the kind of time and personal attention it required," says Bob Butler, who was president in the 1970s. "You must remember that in the midst of all this, all the crises, all the problems, Fred just launched a new yacht. George has built a multimillion-dollar castle. It wasn't what the company needed. It required hard-nosed management."

"Bottom line," says Doug Bassett, a close family friend and an Eaton's of Canada director since 1976, "they didn't have a merchant running the company."

⟶

For decades the Eatons hid behind the high privet hedge of the holy private company, a status that gave them stature while masking the perennial problems from public view. Because their name was not just known, but legendary, onlookers assumed that anyone called Eaton must be both smart and successful.

They were neither.

Whether it was the *Tely*, the catalogue, or Eaton's itself, the mantra was always the same: Don't fix it or finance it — instead, kill it or sell it. For the boys, Eaton's became the ultimate disposable artifact.

"My whole life has been growing and changing and so it doesn't really bother me that I am no longer the chief executive officer of the T. Eaton Co.," says Fred. "It doesn't bother me that I'm no longer the high commissioner, it doesn't bother me that I'm no longer a great shareholder of Baton. I can go on living with all of this change. Life is change and I can live with it. For me, there are still opportunities to do things in the future. Nothing goes on forever."

For all that brave talk about new opportunities, none of the boys is likely to launch a new business; bankruptcy should surely be enough to cure them of any belief they could succeed in another venture. John Craig has been appointed chancellor of Ryerson, so will continue with the type of honorific role that has marked his life. Fred is all but retired and will manage his personal money through his private investment company, White Raven. Thor will continue to race his thoroughbreds. As the brother least involved, he will not miss the stores. George has decided to take up golf and has bought a membership that gives him access to two clubs, Devil's Pulpit and Devil's Paintbrush, both near his Caledon home. Newly mindful of the value of money, he bought an existing membership from someone who wanted to sell. He paid less that way than if he'd gone to the clubs directly and forked out the $45,000 initiation fee.

The attempt to bail out of Eaton's as early as 1996 offers an insight into who the Eaton boys really are. It's as if none of them has an attachment to anything but cold cash. For them there was no need to have an office to go to or a job to do. They feel absolutely no connection between what they create, what they have, and who they are. Signy's art, corporate archives, Lady Eaton's lace, Baton Broadcasting — the empire itself — anything and everything was for sale.

As they tried to peddle their heritage to keep their yachts afloat and their horses fed, the boys could never have imagined that the value of their inheritance would fall to zero. Yet even as the empire headed for bankruptcy, they continued to flit about as if their birthright existed only to fuel their luxurious lifestyle. Give them a boat or a plane, enough gas for the day, some champagne and caviar for a picnic lunch, and the Eaton boys are happy.

As with the sad spectacle of the British Royal family, the comeuppance of the Eatons has been a very public hanging. Canadians pored over every sordid detail, clucked a collective tongue, then went shopping at Wal-Mart.

In fact, the Eatons deserve no more respect than some earl, down on his uppers, who for tuppence a time gives tours of his mouldy mansion in order to maintain the sorry roof in some semblance of repair.

For Canada, it was a time to grieve. Eaton's was the only business with the family name on the door right across the country, one of those rare topics upon which almost everyone could agree.

In the end, however, the root problem was achingly simple. Canadians cared more about Eaton's than did the aristocratic family itself.

They didn't mind the store.

APPENDIX

⸺

Extract from Timothy Eaton's address to the shareholders
at the annual meeting, February 1894[1]

HOW TO IMPROVE THE MANAGEMENT OF YOUR DEPARTMENT

First, "Buy Well," about which we hope to hear from you later. Keep your stock well and constantly assorted. Be attentive and courteous to the humblest customer; have a perfect organization of your staff; fulfill every promise you make to customers; execute every order with promptness and care — mail orders specially.

Be up to the requirements of the times. When you are making out your price lists either for advertising or Bargain Day, do it regularly, truthfully, and thoroughly. Keep no drones about you, none who are not true to the interest of the Company. Earn a reputation for upright dealing by practising it; be prompt in the discharge of every engagement.

Avoid all extravagant expressions in selling, (if the value be good your customer will not have difficulty in discovering it).

Cultivate a cheerful disposition, not only will you feel better yourself, but you will make everyone about all the happier.

We expect the heads of Departments to aim at making their Departments models of their kind, keeping them always well assorted and free from bad stock. If sizes are broken and cannot be replaced or colours bad and won't sell, see that they are put out on Bargain Day at prices that will clean them out. By doing this you will keep your stock clean, save time and money to your Department and the Company.

We are glad to see the good feeling that exists in the house at the present time. We hope it may always continue.

A large house like the one we represent, a large stock, a large capital, and an established reputation, are all good in their way, but they are not everything. Each is an element of power, but only when combined with good management are they agencies by which satisfactory results may be accomplished.

You should have perfect control over your staff, and firmness enough to have all your instructions faithfully carried out.

Manners have so much to do with a man's success in such a position that if lacking it is doubtful to say what would compensate for the loss. This includes assistants as well.

What would the Commanding Officer think of a soldier who came on the ground five minutes or one minute after the regiment had fallen in? Only this, he would simply be confined.

What would be thought of a soldier who would take out his watch on duty to see when the parade would be over? He would expose himself to discipline. It should be so here.

Good service faithfully rendered should characterize every member of the staff from the cash boy to the leader. To get a right idea of the value of time, and the result of combined effort and what diligence will accomplish, watch what is going on at an ant hill. Watch them in the early morning, watch them until your eyes will no longer help you, and the sun has withdrawn its light, and you will see such devotion to work, such good order, such method as can be witnessed in no department of human labour, but which cannot be witnessed without deriving many valuable and important lessons.

No wonder is it that the Wise Man should have said as an antidote to the sloth, "Go to the ant, thou sluggard, consider her ways and be wise, which having no guide, overseer, or ruler, provideth her meat in the summer and gathereth her food in the Harvest."

NOTES

—

For the early days of the store and the family, I am indebted to several books, particularly those by George Nasmith, Flora McCrea Eaton, and Joy Santink. All reference material appears in the bibliography; specific quotations from any source are cited in the Notes. In all other cases, quotes come from author interviews.

INTRODUCTION

1. *Saturday Evening Post,* March 22, 1952.
2. *New York Times* article by H. W. Patterson, January 13, 1960.
3. *Toronto Star* article by John Brehl, February 5, 1977.
4. Cited by William Stephenson, *The Store that Timothy Built* (McClelland and Stewart, Toronto, 1969), p. 66.
5. George Morrissette, *Finding Mom at Eaton's* (Turnstone Press, Winnipeg, 1981), p. 28.

Chapter One / TIMOTHY: THE GOVERNOR

1. George G. Nasmith, *Timothy Eaton* (McClelland & Stewart Ltd., Toronto, 1923), p. 37.
2. Joy Santink, *Timothy Eaton and the Rise of His Department Store* (University of Toronto Press, Toronto, 1990), p. 38.
3. *Evening Tribune,* March 22, 1927.
4. Norah Johnson, *The Irish in Toronto's Old Ward 5* (Community History Project, Toronto, 1992), p. 16.
5. Edith Macdonald, *Golden Jubilee 1869-1919, A Book to Commemorate the Fiftieth Anniversary* (The T. Eaton Co., Ltd., Toronto, 1919), p. 75.
6. Nasmith, p. 68.

7 Michael Bliss, *Northern Enterprise: Five Centuries of Canadian Business* (McClelland & Stewart, Toronto, 1987), p. 289.

8 Ibid., pp. 361-2.

9 Nasmith, p. 150.

10 Mary-Etta Macpherson, *Shopkeepers to a Nation: The Eatons* (McClelland and Stewart, Toronto, 1963), pp. 29-30.

11 Macdonald, p. 53.

12 Macpherson, p. 22.

13 Macpherson, p. 30.

14 Santink, p. 238.

15 Flora McCrea Eaton, *Memory's Wall: The Autobiography of Flora McCrea Eaton* (Clarke, Irwin & Co., Toronto, 1956), p. 76.

16 Macdonald, p. 155.

17 Barry Broadfoot, *The Pioneer Years 1895-1914: Memories of Settlers Who Opened the West* (PaperJacks, Toronto, 1978), pp. 278-80.

18 John M. Bassett, *Timothy Eaton* (Fitzhenry and Whiteside, Don Mills, Ont., 1975), p. 34.

19 Recollections of Mrs. Emily Cowley, July 25, 1962, The Eaton Collection at the Archives of Ontario, Series 151, 162-0-670.

20 *Varsity Graduate*, December 1959. Clark's source was a conversation with Lady Eaton.

21 *Evening Telegram*, March 31, 1922.

22 Macdonald, p. 88.

23 Macpherson, p. 32.

24 Macpherson, p. 39.

25 Ibid., p. 40.

26 Macdonald, p. 84.

27 C. L. Burton, *A Sense of Urgency* (Clarke, Irwin & Co., Toronto, 1952), pp. 196-7.

28 Macpherson, p. 28.

29 Ross Harkness, *J. E. Atkinson of The Star* (University of Toronto Press, Toronto, 1963), p. 52.

30 "The Store that Timothy Built," *Saturday Night*, January 23, 1943, p. 17.

[31] Ibid., p. 29.

[32] From a memo by R.Y. to Edith Macdonald commenting on her draft of the 1919 Golden Jubilee book, The Eaton Collection at the Archives of Ontario, F229, appendix 72, 221-0-1 to 221-0-5, container 5.

[33] Nasmith, p. 253.

[34] Macdonald, p. 83.

[35] Stephenson, p. 50.

[36] Macdonald, p. 222.

[37] A buggy that once belonged to Timothy is displayed in the Western Development Museum in Saskatoon. While curators don't know if the buggy is the fateful vehicle, they do know it was pulled by two dapple-greys and in 1901 was given to Francis Forge, a Yorkshireman and early settler at Windermere who was the original owner of the land on which Ravenscrag was built. His son, James, took the buggy with him that year to Saskatchewan, where he homesteaded. Forge used the buggy until 1945, then donated it to the museum. The museum collection also includes two hundred items sold through the catalogue and a mechanical Christmas-window display made by Winnipeg store employees after the Second World War.

[38] Stephenson, p. 51.

[39] Eaton, p. 39.

[40] Ibid., p. 36.

[41] Ibid., p. 40.

[42] Ibid., p. 47.

[43] Macdonald, p. 131.

[44] Floyd S. Chalmers, *A Gentleman of the Press* (Doubleday Canada, Toronto, 1969), pp. 156-9. This version of events in Chalmers's authoritative biography of Maclean is disputed by some Rolls-Royce historians who argue that Jack did not buy a Rolls-Royce until 1912. While it is true that official records do not list Jack as a buyer in 1906, no buyer is known for at least three vehicles that were shipped to North America at the time. As for the variations in the spellings of Maclean's surname, he also spelled it McLean and MacLean.

[45] Eaton, p. 79.

[46] A Biography of Mrs. T. Eaton, unpublished manuscript, The Eaton Collection at the Archives of Ontario, p. 6.

[47] Ibid., p. 4.

[48] The name was changed to the Margaret Eaton School in 1925, the temple was demolished for road widening, and the school moved to 415 Yonge Street. That building became a CBC studio in 1943 after the school was amalgamated with the faculty of physical and health education at the University of Toronto. Eaton's provided an endowment for scholarships, donated books from the library, and turned over the cash surplus of $10,027. For a more extensive description, see The Margaret Eaton School, 1901-42: Women's Education in Elocution, Drama and Physical Education, 1992 doctoral thesis by John Byl, State University of New York at Buffalo.

[49] Eric Arthur, *Toronto: No Mean City* (University of Toronto Press, Toronto, 1964), p. 230.

[50] Macdonald, p. 93.

[51] William Dendy and William Kilbourn, *Toronto Observed: Its Architecture, Patrons and History* (Oxford University Press, Toronto, 1986), p. 142.

[52] Macdonald, p. 117.

[53] Nasmith, p. 308.

[54] *Toronto Daily Star*, January 31, 1907.

Chapter Two / SIR JOHN: THE MERCHANT PRINCE

[1] Stephenson, p. 62.

[2] Michael Bliss, *A Canadian Millionaire: The Life and Business Times of Sir Joseph Flavelle, Bart., 1858–1939.* (Macmillan of Canada, Toronto, 1978), p. 205.

[3] *Saturday Night*, January 23, 1943, p. 17.

[4] Eaton, p. 103.

[5] Macdonald, p. 109.

[6] Macpherson, p. 58.

[7] *Financial Post*, December 10, 1920.

[8] Cited in the *Toronto Daily Star*, January 2, 1969.

[9] *Toronto World*, February 17, 1912.

[10] "The Rolls-Royce Start in Canada," by John Peirson, *The Flying Lady*, March/April 1989, pp. 3889-90.

[11] *Toronto Star*, February 9, 1977.

[12] Eaton, p. 158.

[13] Stephenson, p. 74.

[14] Ibid.

[15] Eaton, p. 125.

[16] Stephenson, p. 65.

[17] Ibid., pp. 56-61.

[18] Macdonald, p. 276.

[19] Ibid., p. 288.

[20] *World*, December 9, 1919.

[21] *Toronto Daily Star*, December 22, 1919.

[22] *World*, December 22, 1919.

[23] *World*, December 7, 1920.

[24] Ditchett, p. 9.

[25] Ibid., p. 19.

[26] Sir John's comment about his mother being a good sport has often been retold. The *Telegram* carried the comment on March 20, 1933, in an obituary for Margaret. The complete conversation is less well-known. This version appears in A Biography of Mrs. T. Eaton, an unpublished manuscript by Jessie Alexander Roberts in the Eaton Collection at the Archives of Ontario, appendix 72, 221-0-149 to 221-0-180, container no. 5.

[27] Macpherson, p. 70.

[28] Eaton, pp. 140-1.

[29] *Financial Post*, June 23, 1922, p. 12.

[30] *Telegram*, June 9, 1922.

[31] *Montreal Star*, March 31, 1922.

[32] Cited in the *Toronto Daily Star*, January 6, 1969.

[33] Eaton, p. 141.

Chapter Three / R.Y.: THE INTERREGNUM

[1] Macdonald, p. 79.

[2] *Montreal Star*, May 11, 1942.

[3] This description appeared on the occasion of R.Y.'s death in the *Windsor Star*, July 30, 1956.

[4] Macpherson, p. 80.

[5] David Monod, *Store Wars: Shopkeepers and the Culture of Mass Marketing, 1890-1939* (University of Toronto Press, Toronto, 1996), pp. 111-2.

[6] Eaton, p. 144.

[7] Macpherson, p. 82.

[8] Eaton, p. 148.

[9] *Toronto Daily Star*, February 8, 1929.

[10] *Toronto Daily Star*, September 27, 1929.

[11] *Toronto Star*, July 8, 1974.

[12] Stephenson, p. 85.

[13] Macpherson, p. 91.

[14] Ibid., p. 81.

[15] My thanks to Diana and Alan Eaton for supplying this and several other memos cited in this chapter, except where noted, from their eclectic collection of family memorabilia.

[16] Peter C. Newman, *The Canadian Establishment, Volume I* (McClelland and Stewart, Toronto, 1975), p. 103.

[17] *Toronto Daily Star*, February 8, 1929.

[18] *Telegram*, August 16, 1930.

[19] *Star Weekly*, September 5, 1931.

[20] *Montreal Star*, November 19, 1926.

[21] CDS stores were located in Montreal, Ottawa, Hamilton, Brockville, Picton, Napanee, Lindsay, Peterborough, Huntsville, Sudbury, Port Arthur, Sault Ste. Marie, Chatham, Woodstock, Stratford, Hanover, Midland, Pembroke, Brantford, North Bay, and St. Catharines.

[22] Cited in the *Toronto Daily Star*, January 3, 1969.

[23] *Mail and Empire*, September 17, 1929.

[24] Ibid.

[25] *Toronto Daily Star*, September 16, 1929.

[26] *Toronto Daily Star*, September 27, 1929.

[27] Cited by Cynthia Wright, *The Most Prominent Rendezvous of the Feminine Toronto: Eaton's College Street and the Organization of Shopping in Toronto, 1920-1950* (doctoral thesis, University of Toronto, 1993), p. 195.

[28] C. L. Burton, *A Sense of Urgency* (Clarke, Irwin & Co. Ltd., Toronto, 1952), p. 222.

[29] Wright, p. 125.

[30] Macpherson, p. 84.

[31] Cited by Delwyn Higgens, *Art Deco, Marketing and The T. Eaton Co. Department Stores: 1918-30* (Master's thesis, York University, North York, Ont., 1991), p. 41.

[32] Dispatch by Canadian Press from Winnipeg, published by the *Mail*, June 28, 1932.

[33] Raymar has since been razed, but Colonel William's Ballymena remains and was occupied by Ray Lawson, lieutenant-governor of Ontario from 1946 to 1952. The four-thousand-square-foot main house and the coach house with six apartments was listed for sale in mid-1998 at $5.5 million.

[34] *Toronto Daily Star*, March 22, 1933.

[35] Ibid.

[36] *Telegram*, March 20, 1933.

[37] Macpherson, p. 86.

[38] Monod, p. 219.

Chapter Four / LADY EATON: THE DOWAGER QUEEN

[1] *Toronto Daily Star*, October 19, 1927.

[2] Ibid., February 5, 1929.

[3] *Telegram*, August 16, 1930.

[4] *Canadian Comment*, September 1935, p. 18.

[5] *Globe and Mail*, February 22, 1941.

[6] *Toronto Daily Star*, September 27, 1929.

[7] Ibid., January 3, 1933, p. 34.

[8] John Herd Thompson and Allen Seager, *Canada 1922-1939: Decades of Discord* (McClelland and Stewart, Toronto, 1985), p. 259.

[9] *Telegram*, June 12, 1934.

[10] Wright, p. 106.

[11] Fredelle Bruser Maynard, *Raisins and Almonds* (Doubleday Canada, Toronto, 1972), pp. 44-5.

[12] Monod, p. 375.

[13] Wright, p. 209.

[14] Irving Abella, "The Making of a Chief Justice: Bora Laskin, The Early Years," *Law Society of Upper Canada Gazette*, XXV, 3 (Sept./Dec. 1991), p. 424.

[15] Gabrielle Roy, *Enchantment and Sorrow: The Autobiography of Gabrielle Roy*, translated by Patricia Claxton (Lester & Orpen Dennys, Toronto, 1987), p. 5.

[16] Ibid., p. 7.

[17] Ibid., p. 6.

[18] *Toronto Daily Star*, October 28, 1930.

[19] Ibid.

[20] *Liberty,* November 24, 1945, p. 11.

[21] Shirley Ayer, *A Great Church in Action: A History of Timothy Eaton Memorial Church 1909-1977* (Plum Hollow Books, Whitby, Ont., 1978), p. 118.

[22] Austin Seton Thompson, *Spadina 1818-1936: A Story of Old Toronto* (Pagurian Press, Toronto, 1988), p. 213.

[23] The O. D. and Nora Vaughan Collection, City of Toronto archives, box 1, file 12.

[24] *Globe and Mail,* July 20, 1943.

[25] Stephenson, p. 98.

Chapter Five / JOHN DAVID: THE RELUCTANT RULER

[1] *Saturday Night,* January 23, 1943, p. 17.

[2] *Toronto Daily Star,* December 9, 1942.

[3] 1974 interview with *Toronto Star* columnist Bob Pennington, cited in the *Star,* April 26, 1986.

[4] *Financial Post,* December 2, 1950.

[5] *Saturday Night,* January 23, 1943, p. 17.

[6] *Toronto Daily Star,* December 8, 1944.

[7] *Globe and Mail,* January 5, 1945.

[8] *Montreal Star,* September 19, 1946.

[9] *Maclean's,* January 1, 1947, p. 21.

[10] *Coronet,* September 1949.

[11] Frank J. Sulloway, *Born to Rebel: Birth Order, Family Dynamics, and Creative Lives* (Pantheon Books, New York, 1996), p. 352.

[12] Frank Orr, *George Eaton: Five Minutes to Green* (Longmans Canada, Don Mills, Ont., 1970), p. 3.

[13] Conrad Black, *A Life in Progress* (Key Porter Books, Toronto, 1993), p. 19.

[14] James FitzGerald, *Old Boys: The Powerful Legacy of Upper Canada College* (Macfarlane Walter & Ross, Toronto, 1994), p. 28.

[15] Ibid., p. 104.

[16] Ibid., p. 112.

[17] Ibid., p. 113.

[18] Ibid., p. 206.

[19] Eddie Goodman, *Life of the Party* (Key Porter Books, Toronto, 1988), p. 165.

[20] Maggie Siggins, *Bassett* (James Lorimer & Co., Toronto, 1979), pp. 74-5.

[21] Ibid., p. 76.

[22] Ibid., p. 148.

Chapter Six / THE FIRM THAT TIME FORGOT

[1] Eileen Sufrin, *The Eaton Drive: The Campaign to Organize Canada's Largest Department Store 1948 to 1952* (Fitzhenry & Whiteside, Toronto, 1982), p. 57.

[2] James Lorimer, *The Developers* (James Lorimer and Co., Toronto, 1978), p. 186.

[3] Macpherson, p. 111.

[4] Gregory Purchase, *Hard Rock Retailing* (published privately, Toronto, 1996), p. 19.

[5] *Telegram*, May 10, 1948.

[6] *Winnipeg Free Press*, April 2, 1957.

[7] Ibid., May 16, 1957.

[8] *Telegram*, December 4, 1953.

[9] Ibid., November 26, 1959.

[10] *Toronto Daily Star*, October 19, 1927.

[11] *Telegram*, December 4, 1952.

[12] Ibid., December 9, 1969; *Telegram*, January 2, 1969.

[13] Macpherson, p. 115.

[14] *Liberty*, November 24, 1945, p. 15.

[15] *Telegram*, September 29, 1960.

[16] Ian Brown, "The Empire that Timothy Built," *FP Magazine*, May 1978, p. 28.

[17] *Telegram*, August 27, 1962.

[18] *Time*, September 14, 1962.

[19] *Toronto Daily Star*, July 10, 1970.

[20] Eaton, p. 200.

[21] *Globe and Mail*, December 2, 1965.

[22] *Telegram*, July 13, 1970.

[23] Ibid., July 10, 1970.

[24] Ibid.

Chapter Seven / THE BOYS: BORN TO RULE

[1] *Maclean's,* June 1968, p. 63.

[2] *Toronto Star,* February 3, 1977.

[3] Orr, p. 83.

[4] *Montreal Star,* September 20, 1955.

[5] *Toronto Star,* February 3, 1977.

[6] Ibid.

[7] Susan Swan, *The Last of the Golden Girls* (Lester & Orpen Dennys, Toronto, 1989), p. 155.

[8] *Time,* March 7, 1969.

[9] Orr, p. 3.

[10] Ibid., p. 30.

[11] Ibid., p. 33.

[12] Ibid., p. 4.

[13] Ibid., p. 35.

[14] *Time,* December 19, 1969.

[15] *Toronto Star,* undated clip.

Chapter Eight / LOST IN THE SIXTIES

[1] *Time,* May 26, 1958.

[2] *Telegram,* May 16, 1958.

[3] *Maclean's,* June 1968, p. 15.

[4] Company memo cited by Wright, p. 207.

[5] Wright, p. 222.

[6] *Star Weekly,* February 8, 1969, p. 4.

[7] *Maclean's,* June 1968, p. 63.

[8] Ibid.

[9] *Toronto Sun,* January 18, 1977.

[10] *Maclean's,* June 1968, p. 15.

[11] *Toronto Daily Star,* August 30, 1966.

[12] *Maclean's,* June 1968.

[13] Bryan Burrough and John Helyar, *Barbarians at the Gate: The Fall of RJR Nabisco* (Harper & Row, New York, 1990), p. 14.

[14] Alexander R. Aird, Paul Nowack, and James W. Westcott, *Road to the Top: The Chief Executive Officer in Canada* (Doubleday Canada, Toronto, paperback edition, 1989), pp. 55-6.

[15] *Toronto Daily Star,* January 2, 1969.

[16] Stephenson, p. 104.

[17] William Zeckendorf with Edward McCreary, *The Autobiography of William Zeckendorf* (Holt, Reinhart and Winston, New York, 1970), p. 197.

[18] *Telegram,* January 2, 1969.

[19] *Toronto Daily Star,* August 8, 1969.

[20] *Telegram,* January 2, 1969.

[21] *Globe and Mail,* July 21, 1970.

Chapter Nine / BOB BUTLER: THE COMMONER

[1] *Maclean's,* February 1, 1958.

[2] Stephenson, p. 127.

[3] Stephenson, p. 127.

[4] *Executive,* December 1971, p. 42.

[5] *Forbes,* June 15, 1971, p. 37.

[6] Black, p. 78.

[7] Jack Sullivan, *The Grey Cup Story: The Dramatic History of Canada's Most Coveted Award* (Pagurian Press Ltd., Toronto, 1974), p. 198.

[8] *Toronto Star,* October 25, 1975.

[9] Burton, *Memories,* p. 234.

[10] My thanks to Peter C. Newman for supplying me with a copy of John David's will, as well as other material on the Eaton family.

[11] Cited, *Toronto Star,* January 15, 1976.

[12] Cited, *Globe and Mail,* January 16, 1976.

[13] Cited, *Toronto Daily Star,* January 4, 1969.

Chapter Ten / EARL ORSER: THE EXECUTIONER

[1] *Canadian Business,* March 1976, p. 33.

[2] *Toronto Star,* January 15, 1976.

[3] Cited in *Canadian Review,* December 1976, p. 31.

[4] The Eaton Collection, Archives of Ontario, 221-0-1 to 221-0-5, container 6, appendix 72.

[5] Peter C. Newman, *The Canadian Establishment, Volume II: The Acquisitors* (McClelland and Stewart, Toronto, 1981), p. 173.

[6] *Maclean's,* May 31, 1976, p. 26.

[7] Ibid., p. 28.

[8] *Winnipeg Tribune,* August 14, 1976.

[9] *Toronto Star,* February 3, 1977.

[10] Ira Gluskin, Study No. 3, Cadillac Fairview Corp. Ltd., January 1976, p. 97.

[11] Quoted in Leon Whiteson, *The Liveable City* (Oakville, 1982), p. 15.

[12] *Toronto Sun,* February 6, 1977.

[13] *Toronto Star,* January 13, 1977.

[14] *Toronto Star,* November 3, 1984.

[15] *Maclean's,* June 1968, p. 62.

[16] Black, p. 174.

[17] *Toronto Star,* June 25, 1977.

Chapter Eleven / FOUR BOYS, ONE BRAIN

[1] Peter C. Newman, *The Establishment Man: A Portrait of Power* (McClelland and Stewart, Toronto, 1982), p. 138.

[2] *Toronto Star,* November 2, 1976.

[3] *Toronto Star,* June 25, 1977.

[4] Ibid.

[5] *FP Magazine,* May 1978, p. 46.

[6] Diane Francis, *Controlling Interest: Who Owns Canada?* (Macmillan of Canada, Toronto, 1986), p. 80.

[7] Ibid., p. 95.

[8] *Toronto Star,* May 8, 1979.

[9] *Financial Post,* May 28, 1977.

[10] Purchase, p. 53.

[11] *Toronto Star,* February 25, 1982.

[12] *New Liberty,* December 1953, p. 70.

[13] *Financial Post,* August 21, 1982.

[14] *Toronto Star,* August 10, 1982.

[15] Sandra Elizabeth Aylward, *Experiencing Patriarchy: Women, Work and Trade Unionism at Eaton's,* doctoral thesis, McMaster University, Hamilton, Ont., 1991, p. 117.

[16] Ibid., p. 283.

[17] *Ivey Business Quarterly*, Autumn 1997, p. 28.

[18] Curtis Cole, *Portrait of a Partnership: A History of Osler, Hoskin & Harcourt* (McGraw-Hill Ryerson, Toronto, 1995), p. 164.

[19] *Canadian Business*, May 1993, p. 56.

[20] Minutes of proceedings, October 3, 1991, issue no. 9, p. 8.

[21] Ibid., p. 21.

[22] *Financial Post*, November 21, 1991.

[23] *Globe and Mail*, September 12, 1991.

Chapter Twelve / GOING DOWN WITH GEORGE

[1] *Toronto Star*, June 12, 1992.

[2] *Globe and Mail*, February 20, 1993.

[3] The mausoleum contains the remains of Timothy and his wife, Margaret; two of their children, George J. and Kathleen, who died as infants; their son Edward Y., Edward's first and second wives, Tillie and Mabel, and an infant son, Edward C.; Sir John and Lady Eaton; Colonel William F. and his wife, Gertrude Norah; John David and Signy. Other Eatons buried near the mausoleum include Evlyn, as well as cousin R.Y. and his wife, Hazel. The cemetery is also the final resting place of their son Jack and his wife, Phyllis, as well as Nancy, great-great-granddaughter of Timothy, who was murdered in Toronto in 1985.

[4] Affidavit of James F. Kennedy, solicitor for the estate, October 21, 1996.

[5] Last will and testament of Signy Hildur Eaton, November 19, 1990.

[6] Sold, with hammer prices in U.S.$, were *Spitze Akente* by Wassily Kandinsky, for $850,000; *Gray vase and pallet* by Georges Braque, $800,000; *Le Sentier de Bazincourt* by Camille Pisarro, $650,000; *Femme assise en costume rouge sur fond bleu* by Pablo Picasso, $600,000; *Verre, Journal et Feuillage* by Juan Gris, $500,000; *Femmes, oiseau, étoiles* by Joan Miró, $360,000; *Les trois colombes* by Kees van Dongen, $300,000; *Dancing figures* by Lynn Chadwick, $85,000; *Maquette II for R34 memorial* by Lynn Chadwick, $17,000; *Equisse pour un mural* by Fernand Léger, $15,000; *Femme assise* by Émile-Othon Friesz, $2,500.

[7] The Eaton Collection at the Archives of Ontario, G. D. Wotherspoon files, 1967-74, Series 213, Box 1.

[8] *Business Quarterly*, Summer 1997, pp. 34-5.

[9] *Frank*, No. 167, May 12, 1994, p. 4, and No. 204, October 11, 1995, p. 7.

[10] *Toronto Star*, April 27, 1997.

[11] *Globe and Mail*, May 13, 1997.

Chapter Thirteen / SUNSET ON THE EMPIRE

[1] Report on Intercompany Transactions within the Eaton Group of Companies, prepared by KPMG Inc., June 27, 1997, p. 27.

[2] Ibid., p. 52.

[3] Montreal *Gazette*, June 13, 1997, p. F2.

[4] Stores closed were Victoria Tillicum, Kitchener Market Square, Brantford Market Square, Toronto's Yonge Eglinton Centre, Sarnia Bayside Mall, Beloeil Montenach Mall, all in June 1997; Edmonton Heritage in August 1997; Thunder Bay in September 1997; Calgary Sunridge, Edmonton Millwoods, Winnipeg Garden City, Peterborough Square, Guelph Eaton Centre, Gatineau Outaouais, Montreal Cavendish Mall, LaSalle Carrefour Angrignon, Dartmouth Micmac Mall, all in February 1998; Mississauga Sheridan in April 1988; Vernon, B.C., Huntsville, Ont., and Charlottetown, all in May 1998.

Chapter Fourteen / BANKRUPT

[1] *McKinsey Quarterly*, 1997, Number 2, article by Kathryn Bye Burns, Helene Enright, Julie Falstad Hayes, Kathleen McLaughlin, and Christiana Shi, p. 100.

[2] *National Post*, September 1, 1999, p. A19.

[3] *Toronto Star*, September 10, 1999, p. A1.

[4] My thanks to Larry Pfaff for access to material in the AGO archives, including a 1987 Master's thesis by Cynthia A. H. Beach, The Managing of Museums and the Public Performance of Museums During Building Expansion: A Case Study of the Art Gallery of Ontario.

APPENDIX

[1] The Eaton Collection at the Archives of Ontario.

BIBLIOGRAPHY

Aird, Alexander R., Paul Nowack, and James W. Westcott, *Road to the Top: The Chief Executive Officer in Canada*, Doubleday Canada, Toronto, paperback edition, 1989.

Arthur, Eric, *Toronto: No Mean City*, University of Toronto Press, Toronto, 1964.

Ayer, Shirley, *A Great Church in Action: A History of Timothy Eaton Memorial Church 1909-1977*, Plum Hollow Books, Whitby, Ont., 1978.

Aylward, Sandra Elizabeth, *Experiencing Patriarchy: Women, Work and Trade Unionism at Eaton's*, doctoral thesis, McMaster University, Hamilton, Ont., 1991.

Bassett, John M., *Timothy Eaton*, Fitzhenry and Whiteside, Don Mills, Ont., 1975.

Black, Conrad, *A Life in Progress*, Key Porter Books, Toronto, 1993.

Bliss, Michael, *A Canadian Millionaire: The Life and Business Times of Sir Joseph Flavelle, Bart., 1858-1939*, Macmillan of Canada, Toronto, 1978.

———, *Northern Enterprise: Five Centuries of Canadian Business*, McClelland and Stewart, Toronto, 1987.

Broadfoot, Barry, *The Pioneer Years 1895-1914: Memories of Settlers Who Opened the West*, PaperJacks, Toronto, 1978.

Bryant, James, *Department Store Disease*, McClelland and Stewart, Toronto, 1977.

Burrough, Bryan, and John Helyar, *Barbarians at the Gate: The Fall of RJR Nabisco*, Harper & Row, New York, 1990.

Burton, C. L., *A Sense of Urgency*, Clarke, Irwin & Co., Toronto, 1952.

Burton, G. Allan, *A Store of Memories*, McClelland and Stewart, Toronto, 1986.

The Canadian Encyclopedia, Second Edition, Hurtig Publishers, Edmonton, 1988.

Carrier, Roch, *The Hockey Sweater*, translated by Sheila Fischman, Tundra Books, 1984.

Carroll, Jock, *The Death of The Toronto Telegram & Other Newspaper Stories*, Simon and Schuster of Canada, Richmond Hill, Ont., 1971.

Chalmers, Floyd S., *A Gentleman of the Press*, Doubleday Canada, Toronto, 1969.

Cole, Curtis, *Portrait of a Partnership: A History of Osler, Hoskin & Harcourt*, McGraw-Hill Ryerson, Toronto, 1995.

Dendy, William, and William Kilbourn, *Toronto Observed: Its Architecture, Patrons and History*, Oxford University Press, Toronto, 1986.

Ditchett, S. H., *Eaton's of Canada: A Unique Institution of Extraordinary Magnitude*, Federal Printing Co., New York, 1923.

Eaton, Flora McCrea, *Memory's Wall: The Autobiography of Flora McCrea Eaton*, Clarke, Irwin & Co., Toronto, 1956.

Eaton, Nicole, and Hilary Weston, *In a Canadian Garden*, Penguin Books Canada, Markham, Ont., 1989.

Firth, Edith G., *Toronto in Art: 150 Years Through Artists' Eyes*, Fitzhenry & Whiteside, Toronto, 1983.

FitzGerald, James, *Old Boys: The Powerful Legacy of Upper Canada College*, Macfarlane Walter & Ross, Toronto, 1994.

Francis, Diane, *Controlling Interest; Who Owns Canada?*, Macmillan of Canada, Toronto, 1986.

Goldenberg, Susan, *The Thomson Empire*, Methuen, Agincourt, Ont., 1984.

Goodman, Eddie, *Life of the Party*, Key Porter Books, Toronto, 1988.

Harkness, Ross, *J. E. Atkinson of The Star*, University of Toronto Press, 1963.

Higgens, Delwyn, *Art Deco, Marketing and The T. Eaton Co. Department Stores: 1918-30*, Master's thesis, York University, North York, Ont., 1991.

Jackson, Dorothy N. R., *A Brief History of Three Schools*, University of Toronto Press, Toronto, 1953.

Johnson, Norah, *The Irish in Toronto's Old Ward 5*, Community History Project, Toronto, 1992.

Lorimer, James, *The Developers*, James Lorimer and Co., Toronto, 1978.

Macdonald, Edith, *Golden Jubilee 1869-1919, A Book to Commemorate the Fiftieth Anniversary,* The T. Eaton Co., Ltd., Toronto, 1919.

MacKenzie, David, *The Clarkson Gordon Story,* University of Toronto Press, Toronto, 1989.

Macpherson, Mary-Etta, *Shopkeepers to a Nation: The Eatons,* McClelland and Stewart, Toronto, 1963.

Maynard, Fredelle Bruser, *Raisins and Almonds,* Doubleday Canada, Toronto, 1972.

Monod, David, *Store Wars: Shopkeepers and the Culture of Mass Marketing, 1890-1939,* University of Toronto Press, Toronto, 1996.

Morrissette, George, *Finding Mom at Eaton's,* Turnstone Press, Winnipeg, 1981.

Murphy, Rae, and Mark Starowicz, eds., *Corporate Canada: 14 Probes into the Workings of the Branch-Plant Economy,* James Lewis & Samuel, Toronto, 1972.

Nasmith, George G., *Timothy Eaton,* McClelland & Stewart, Toronto, 1923.

Newman, Peter C., *The Canadian Establishment, Volume I,* McClelland and Stewart, Toronto, 1975.

———, *The Canadian Establishment, Volume II, The Acquisitors,* McClelland and Stewart, Toronto, 1981.

———, general editor, *Debrett's Illustrated Guide to the Canadian Establishment,* Methuen Publications, Agincourt, Ont., 1983.

———, *The Establishment Man: A Portrait of Power,* McClelland and Stewart, Toronto, 1982.

———, *Merchant Princes: Company of Adventurers, Volume III,* Penguin Books, Toronto, 1992.

Orr, Frank, *George Eaton: Five Minutes to Green,* Longmans Canada, Don Mills, Ont., 1970.

Purchase, Gregory R., *Hard Rock Retailing,* published privately, Toronto, 1996.

Rayburn, Alan, *Dictionary of Canadian Place Names,* Oxford University Press, Toronto, 1997.

Report of the Royal Commission on Corporate Concentration, Supply and Services Canada, 1978.

Rohmer, Richard, *Golden Phoenix: The Biography of Peter Munk,* Key Porter Books, Toronto, 1997.

Roy, Gabrielle, *Enchantment and Sorrow: The Autobiography of Gabrielle Roy*, translated by Patricia Claxton, Lester & Orpen Dennys, Toronto, 1987.

Santink, Joy L., *Timothy Eaton and the Rise of His Department Store*, University of Toronto Press, Toronto, 1990.

Scoular, William, and Vivian Green, *A Question of Guilt: The Murder of Nancy Eaton*, Stoddart Publishing, Toronto, 1989.

Sexton, Rosemary, *The Glitter Girls: Charity, Vanity, Chronicles of an Era of Excess*, Macmillan Canada, Toronto, 1993.

Siggins, Maggie, *Bassett*, James Lorimer & Co., Toronto, 1979.

Siklos, Richard, *Shades of Black: Conrad Black and the World's Fastest-Growing Press Empire*, Reed Books Canada, Toronto, 1995.

Snider, C.H.J., *Annals of the Royal Canadian Yacht Club 1852-1937*, Rous & Mann, Toronto, 1937.

Stephenson, William, *The Store that Timothy Built*, McClelland and Stewart, Toronto, 1969.

Stevens, G. R., *The Incompleat Canadian: An Approach to Social History*, published privately, Toronto, 1965.

Stott, D. V., *Kawandag: A Story of Changing Muskoka*, published privately, Rosseau, Ont., 1981.

Sufrin, Eileen, *The Eaton Drive: The Campaign to Organize Canada's Largest Department Store 1948 to 1952*, Fitzhenry & Whiteside, Toronto, 1982.

Sullivan, Jack, *The Grey Cup Story: The Dramatic History of Canada's Most Coveted Award*, Pagurian Press, Toronto, 1974.

Sulloway, Frank J., *Born to Rebel: Birth Order, Family Dynamics, and Creative Lives*, Pantheon Books, New York, 1996.

Swan, Susan, *The Last of the Golden Girls*, Lester & Orpen Dennys, Toronto, 1989.

Tedesco, Theresa, *Offside: The Battle for Control of Maple Leaf Gardens*, Viking, Penguin Books Canada, Toronto, 1996.

Thompson, Austin Seton, *Spadina 1818-1936: A Story of Old Toronto*, Pagurian Press, Toronto, 1988.

Thompson, John Herd, and Allen Seager, *Canada 1922-1939: Decades of Discord*, McClelland and Stewart, Toronto, 1985.

Villeneuve, Jacques, with Gerald Donaldson, *Villeneuve: My First Season in Formula 1*, HarperCollins Publishers, Toronto, 1996.

West, Bruce, *Toronto*, Doubleday Canada, Toronto, 1979.

Whiteson, Leon, *The Liveable City*, Oakville, 1982.

Wilton, Carol, editor, *Essays in the History of Canadian Law, Inside the Law: Canadian Law Firms in Historical Perspective*, vol. VII, University of Toronto Press, Toronto, 1996.

Wright, Cynthia Jane, *The Most Prominent Rendezvous of the Feminine Toronto: Eaton's College Street and the Organization of Shopping in Toronto, 1920-1950*, doctoral thesis, University of Toronto, 1993.

Zeckendorf, William, with Edward McCreary, *The Autobiography of William Zeckendorf*, Holt, Reinhart and Winston, New York, 1970.

INDEX